Philosophical Ethical Issues in Legal Studies

Navigating Moral Dilemmas, Promoting Justice, and Shaping a More Equitable, Just, and Sustainable World

Megan Dennis

ISBN: 978-1-77961-914-3
Imprint: The More You Read The Bigger It Gets
Copyright © 2024 Megan Dennis.
All Rights Reserved.

Contents

Introduction to Philosophical and Ethical Issues in Legal Studies

Understanding Legal Studies

Definition and Scope of Legal Studies

Legal studies is an interdisciplinary field that encompasses the study of law and its impact on society. It involves the examination and analysis of legal systems, principles, theories, and practices. Through legal studies, individuals gain a comprehensive understanding of how laws are created, interpreted, and enforced, as well as their effects on individuals, communities, and institutions.

Definition of Legal Studies

Legal studies can be defined as the academic discipline that investigates and evaluates the principles, rules, and procedures that shape the legal system. It involves the systematic study of legal concepts, institutions, and practices in order to understand and interpret the law.

The core focus of legal studies is to examine the principles and theories that underpin the law, as well as the social, political, and economic factors that influence legal decision-making. It also involves critically analyzing the role of law in society and how it interacts with various aspects of human life.

Scope of Legal Studies

The scope of legal studies is broad and encompasses various areas of law, including constitutional law, criminal law, civil law, administrative law, international law, and more. It examines not only the substance of the law but also the processes and institutions through which legal decisions are made and applied.

Legal studies also encompass the study of legal ethics, legal research and writing, legal reasoning and argumentation, legal advocacy, dispute resolution, and the practical skills necessary for legal practice.

In addition to the study of specific areas of law, legal studies also involves exploring the philosophical and ethical foundations of the law. It investigates questions of justice, fairness, morality, and the role of law in promoting and maintaining a just and equitable society.

Moreover, legal studies is not limited to the study of existing laws and legal systems. It also involves examining legal reform, law-making processes, and the potential for improving the legal system to better serve societal needs.

Interdisciplinary Nature of Legal Studies

Legal studies is inherently interdisciplinary, drawing on various fields such as philosophy, political science, sociology, economics, history, and psychology. By integrating these diverse perspectives, legal studies provides a comprehensive understanding of law and its broader societal implications.

For example, the study of legal philosophy helps to uncover the underlying principles and theories that shape the law. Political science provides insights into the power dynamics and political processes that influence legal decision-making. Sociology offers perspectives on how law intersects with social structures, norms, and values. Economics sheds light on the economic consequences and incentives created by legal rules. History provides a context for understanding the evolution of legal systems over time. Psychology contributes to understanding human behavior and decision-making within the legal context.

The interdisciplinary nature of legal studies allows for a more nuanced and holistic understanding of the law and its impact on individuals and society. It enables legal scholars and practitioners to analyze complex legal issues from multiple perspectives, leading to more informed and comprehensive legal solutions.

Contemporary Issues in Legal Studies

Legal studies addresses a wide range of contemporary issues that have profound implications for individuals, communities, and society as a whole. Some of these issues include:

+ **Access to justice:** Examining barriers to accessing legal services and developing strategies to ensure equal access to justice for all individuals, including marginalized and underprivileged communities.

+ **Human rights and social justice:** Analyzing the legal frameworks for protecting human rights and addressing social inequalities, including issues related to racial and gender discrimination, poverty, and environmental justice.

+ **Technology and the law:** Exploring the legal challenges and ethical implications arising from technological advancements such as artificial intelligence, cybersecurity, and data privacy.

+ **Globalization and international law:** Assessing the role of law in governing global interactions, including trade, human rights, and environmental protection, and analyzing the challenges of harmonizing different legal systems and cultural norms.

+ **Legal ethics and professional responsibility:** Investigating the ethical dilemmas faced by legal professionals, such as conflicts of interest, client confidentiality, and the proper balance between advocacy and justice.

+ **Legal reforms and policy advocacy:** Analyzing the need for legal reforms to address emerging societal challenges, promoting policy changes, and advocating for social justice through strategic litigation and law-making processes.

These contemporary issues highlight the dynamic and evolving nature of legal studies, as it seeks to address the complex legal and ethical challenges of our time.

Conclusion

The field of legal studies encompasses a comprehensive and interdisciplinary examination of the law, its principles, and its impact on society. It involves studying legal systems, institutions, and practices, as well as exploring the philosophical, ethical, and societal dimensions of the law.

Through legal studies, individuals gain a deeper understanding of the complexities and nuances of the legal system, and are equipped with the knowledge and skills to critically analyze legal issues, promote justice, and contribute to building a more equitable and sustainable world.

Historical Overview of Legal Studies

In order to fully understand the field of legal studies, it is important to explore its historical roots and development. Throughout history, legal systems have played a crucial role in shaping societies, maintaining order, and resolving conflicts. This section provides a historical overview of the origins and evolution of legal studies, highlighting key developments and influential legal systems.

Ancient Legal Systems

The origins of legal studies can be traced back to ancient civilizations which developed their own legal systems to regulate social behavior and resolve disputes. One of the earliest legal codes is the Code of Hammurabi, established in ancient Babylon around 1754 BCE. This code included a set of laws and punishments, covering a wide range of civil and criminal matters. It emphasized principles of fairness and justice, focusing on the idea of "an eye for an eye" and reflecting the societal norms of the time.

Another significant ancient legal system is the Roman law, which emerged with the establishment of the Roman Republic in 509 BCE. The Twelve Tables, compiled around 450 BCE, formed the basis of Roman civil law and introduced key legal concepts, such as the presumption of innocence and the right to a fair trial. The Roman legal system had a profound influence on subsequent legal developments in Europe and elsewhere.

Development of Common Law

The development of common law in medieval England marked a significant milestone in the evolution of legal studies. Common law originated from the customary practices and decisions of judges, which were based on previous court rulings and traditions. In the 12th century, the English legal system underwent a transformation, where legal decisions were recorded and compiled into authoritative treatises. This codification of legal principles laid the foundation for the common law system, which gradually gained recognition as a unified body of law.

One of the defining features of common law is the doctrine of precedent, which means that earlier court decisions serve as a guide for future cases. This principle contributes to the consistency and predictability of the legal system. Over time, common law developed into a comprehensive legal framework, covering various areas of law, including torts, contracts, property, and criminal law.

Civil Law Systems

While common law developed in England, civil law systems began to emerge in continental Europe. Civil law systems, also known as code law systems, are based on comprehensive legal codes that encompass a wide range of legal rules and principles. The Napoleonic Code, enacted in France in 1804, is one of the most influential civil law codes. It standardized and streamlined French law, providing a model for legal systems in many other countries.

Civil law systems are characterized by a more hierarchical structure, where laws are derived from statutes and regulations created by the legislature. Unlike common law systems, legal decisions in civil law are not binding precedents, but rather serve as persuasive guidance. Civil law systems are prevalent in many countries around the world, including France, Germany, Japan, and most of Latin America.

Modern Legal Studies

The 19th and 20th centuries witnessed further developments in legal studies, driven by societal changes, technological advancements, and the globalization of legal systems. Legal scholars began exploring new fields of study, such as international law, human rights law, and environmental law, reflecting the evolving needs and concerns of society.

One significant development in modern legal studies is the rise of interdisciplinary approaches. Legal scholars started drawing insights from various disciplines, including philosophy, sociology, psychology, and economics, to better understand the role of law in society and address complex legal issues. This interdisciplinary approach has enriched the field of legal studies and contributed to the development of new theories and perspectives.

Furthermore, the rapid advancement of technology has presented unprecedented legal challenges, such as intellectual property rights, cybersecurity, and privacy issues. Legal studies have had to adapt and evolve to keep pace with these emerging areas, requiring legal scholars to explore innovative and dynamic approaches to address these complex legal issues.

Conclusion

The historical overview of legal studies provides a foundation for understanding the evolution of legal systems and the development of legal theories and principles. From ancient legal codes to modern interdisciplinary approaches, legal studies have continuously evolved to meet the changing needs and demands of society. By examining the historical context, we can better appreciate the rich heritage and the ongoing relevance of legal studies in shaping a more equitable, just, and sustainable world.

Exercises

1. Compare and contrast the ancient legal systems of Babylon and Rome. What were the key similarities and differences between these systems?

2. Research and discuss a famous case in common law history. Explain how the doctrine of precedent was applied in that particular case.

3. Choose a country that follows the civil law system. Identify and explain the major components of its legal code. How does the civil law system differ from the common law system?

4. Investigate a recent legal issue related to technology, such as data privacy or intellectual property rights. Analyze the ethical implications of the legal decisions made in that case.

Resources

- Hallaq, W. (2005). *An introduction to Islamic law.* Cambridge University Press.

- Bell, J. J. (2017). *French legal cultures.* In Comparative Law and Anthropology (pp. 86-113). Routledge.

- Kennedy, D. (2010). *The role of law in economic thought: essays on the development of economic institutions.* Cambridge University Press.

- Goldstein, P. S., & Waterman, L. R. (2019). *International law and human rights: cases, materials, and commentary.* West Academic Publishing.

Did You Know?

In ancient Athens, the birthplace of democracy, legal scholars known as sophists emerged. These philosophers and teachers specialized in rhetoric and the art of persuasive speaking, playing a crucial role in legal proceedings. Sophists were sought after by individuals who needed assistance in presenting their cases or arguments effectively in court. Their influence on legal practice and education remains relevant today.

Objectives and Goals of Legal Studies

In the field of legal studies, the objectives and goals are centered around understanding and analyzing the complexities of the law, promoting justice, and contributing to a more equitable, just, and sustainable world. Legal studies encompass a multidisciplinary approach that combines the study of law, philosophy, ethics, sociology, politics, economics, and history. This section will explore the key objectives and goals of legal studies, providing a comprehensive understanding of the field's purpose and significance.

Understanding the Law

One of the primary objectives of legal studies is to develop a deep understanding of the law. This involves examining the legal system and its institutions, including legislation, regulations, court decisions, and legal procedures. Students of legal studies strive to comprehend the framework within which laws operate, the principles that guide legal decision-making, and the intricacies of legal interpretation and application.

Promoting Justice

A fundamental goal of legal studies is to promote justice. Justice, in the legal context, refers to the fair and impartial treatment of individuals and the distribution of benefits and burdens in society. Legal studies aim to explore and assess the various theories of justice, such as egalitarianism, libertarianism, and communitarianism, and their implications for legal systems and practices. By understanding the different conceptions of justice, legal professionals can work towards creating a more just and equitable society.

Analyzing Legal Issues

Legal studies also seek to develop analytical skills necessary to critically evaluate legal issues. This includes examining the social, economic, cultural, and political factors that shape legal norms and practices. Students learn to identify legal challenges and offer innovative solutions that address these issues. Through rigorous analysis, legal studies contribute to the development of effective legal policies and mechanisms that can resolve societal problems and foster positive change.

Understanding Legal Ethics

Ethics is an inherent part of legal studies, and another objective is to cultivate a strong ethical foundation among legal professionals. Students explore the ethical considerations in legal practice, such as the duty to maintain confidentiality, conflicts of interest, and the responsibility to act in the best interests of clients. By examining real-world ethical dilemmas, legal studies help individuals develop ethical decision-making skills and understand the broader implications of their actions on the legal system and society.

Advancing Sustainable Development

In recent years, there has been a growing recognition of the importance of the legal system in promoting sustainable development. Legal studies aim to explore the intersection of law, policy, and sustainable development. This includes analyzing environmental regulations, promoting responsible business practices, and addressing social justice issues. By integrating sustainable development principles into legal studies, future legal professionals can contribute to the creation of a more environmentally and socially conscious society.

Addressing Contemporary Legal Challenges

Legal studies respond to the evolving nature of the law by addressing contemporary legal challenges. This includes exploring emerging areas of law, such as technology and intellectual property, human rights, criminal justice reform, and business ethics. Students are encouraged to engage with current legal debates and propose innovative solutions to address these challenges. By keeping abreast of contemporary legal issues, legal studies equip individuals with the knowledge and skills necessary to navigate the complexities of the modern legal landscape.

Encouraging Interdisciplinary Collaboration

Legal studies recognize that the law intersects with various disciplines. Therefore, an important objective is to foster interdisciplinary collaboration. By engaging with scholars and professionals from diverse fields, legal studies promote a holistic understanding of legal issues. This multidisciplinary approach allows for innovative thinking, enables a broader perspective on legal problems, and encourages the development of comprehensive solutions that consider social, economic, and political dimensions.

Conclusion

The objectives and goals of legal studies encompass understanding the law, promoting justice, analyzing legal issues, understanding legal ethics, advancing sustainable development, addressing contemporary legal challenges, and encouraging interdisciplinary collaboration. By achieving these objectives, legal studies contribute to the cultivation of knowledgeable and ethically conscious legal professionals who can navigate the complexities of the legal system and actively work towards a more equitable and just society.

Key Concepts in Legal Studies

In this section, we will explore some of the key concepts in legal studies that provide the foundation for understanding the field. These concepts help us navigate the complex, dynamic, and ever-evolving landscape of law and legal systems. By grasping these fundamental ideas, we can better appreciate the challenges and opportunities in legal studies and make informed decisions in the pursuit of justice and fairness.

Legal System

The legal system is a central concept in legal studies. It refers to the set of institutions, procedures, and rules that govern and regulate a society. The legal system encompasses various branches of law, such as constitutional law, criminal law, civil law, and administrative law. It also includes the courts, legislative bodies, and executive agencies responsible for interpreting and enforcing the law.

The legal system serves several functions, including resolving disputes, maintaining order, protecting individual rights, and promoting social justice. It provides a framework for individuals and organizations to interact, negotiate, and seek legal remedies in case of harm or wrongdoing. By understanding the legal system, students can appreciate its strengths and weaknesses and explore avenues for reform and improvement.

Rule of Law

The rule of law is a principle that emphasizes the supremacy of law in a just society. It means that everyone, including individuals, organizations, and government officials, is subject to and accountable to the law. The rule of law ensures that laws are applied consistently, impartially, and without favoritism or discrimination. It also guarantees fundamental rights and freedoms, such as due process, equality before the law, and access to justice.

The rule of law acts as a safeguard against arbitrary exercise of power and prevents the abuse of authority. It fosters public trust, confidence, and predictability in the legal system. By upholding the rule of law, societies can establish a stable, fair, and orderly environment where individuals and businesses can thrive.

Legal Rights

Legal rights are entitlements or privileges recognized and protected by the law. They define the boundaries of permissible conduct and provide individuals with claims, powers, or immunities against others. Legal rights can be classified into different categories, such as civil rights, human rights, constitutional rights, and property rights.

Civil rights encompass a broad range of individual liberties, including freedom of speech, religion, and assembly. Human rights are universal entitlements that protect individuals' inherent dignity and respect for their basic needs and fundamental freedoms. Constitutional rights are guaranteed by a country's constitution and often include protection against government intrusion and discrimination. Property rights refer to the legal ownership, use, and control of property, both tangible and intangible.

Understanding legal rights is crucial for legal studies because they form the foundation for legal claims, obligations, and remedies. They play a central role in legal decision-making and can often be the subject of legal disputes and controversies.

Legal Responsibility

Legal responsibility refers to the obligation to answer for one's actions or omissions under the law. It involves being held accountable for the consequences of one's behavior and complying with legal duties and obligations. Legal responsibility can be both individual and collective, depending on the context and circumstances.

Individual legal responsibility holds individuals liable for their own wrongful acts or failures, imposing legal consequences such as fines, penalties, or imprisonment. It is based on the principle of individual autonomy and personal accountability. Collective legal responsibility, on the other hand, holds groups, organizations, or governments accountable for their actions or policies that cause harm or violate legal norms.

Legal responsibility is a key concept in legal studies as it helps determine liability, determine legal remedies, and allocate legal obligations. It also plays a crucial role in promoting justice, fairness, and social order.

Legal Interpretation and Application

Legal interpretation and application refer to the process of understanding and giving effect to the law. It involves analyzing legal texts, such as statutes, regulations, and court decisions, to determine their meaning and intended scope of application. Legal interpretation aims to ascertain the legislative intent or purpose behind the law and adapt it to specific factual situations.

Legal interpretation can be a complex and contentious process, as different interpreters may arrive at different conclusions. Various theories and approaches to legal interpretation exist, including textualism, originalism, purposivism, and pragmatism. These approaches guide judges, lawyers, and legal scholars in determining the intent behind laws and how they should be applied in particular cases.

Legal interpretation and application are critical in legal studies as they shape the development and evolution of the law. They ensure consistency, predictability, and fairness in legal decision-making, and provide guidance for legal practitioners and policymakers.

Ethics and Justice

Ethics and justice are fundamental concepts that intersect with legal studies. Ethics is concerned with moral principles and values that guide human behavior and decision-making. Justice, on the other hand, refers to the fair and equitable distribution of rights, resources, and opportunities in society.

Legal studies explore the ethical dimensions of legal practice, including the professional responsibilities of lawyers, the ethical implications of legal rules, and the ethical dilemmas that arise in legal decision-making. It also examines the role of the law in promoting justice and addressing societal inequities.

Understanding ethics and justice in the context of legal studies is crucial for developing a comprehensive understanding of the law's role in society and exploring ways to create a more equitable and just legal system.

Contemporary Issues

Legal studies cannot be detached from the contemporary issues and challenges that societies face. It is vital to recognize and engage with the evolving legal landscape, which is shaped by factors such as technological advancements, globalization, environmental concerns, human rights violations, and social inequality.

Some contemporary issues in legal studies include the impact of emerging technologies on legal practice, the role of law in addressing climate change, the protection of human rights in the context of national security, the regulation of artificial intelligence, and the intersection of law and social justice movements.

Students of legal studies should be aware of these contemporary issues and consider their implications for the law and legal systems. This knowledge equips them to analyze and critically evaluate legal developments and engage in debates on how to address the challenges of the modern world.

Conclusion

In this section, we have explored key concepts that form the foundation of legal studies. These concepts, including the legal system, rule of law, legal rights, legal responsibility, legal interpretation and application, ethics, justice, and contemporary issues, provide a framework for understanding and analyzing the law's complexities.

By mastering these concepts, students will be better equipped to navigate the ethical dilemmas, moral challenges, and societal issues that arise in legal practice. Through critical thinking, analysis, and engagement with legal concepts, students can contribute to shaping a more equitable, just, and sustainable world.

Interdisciplinary Nature of Legal Studies

The field of legal studies is inherently interdisciplinary, drawing from various academic disciplines and integrating their theories and perspectives to provide a comprehensive understanding of law and its implications. In this section, we will explore the interdisciplinary nature of legal studies, discussing the key disciplines that contribute to the field and the ways in which they intersect with each other.

Key Disciplines in Legal Studies

Legal studies encompass a wide range of disciplines, each providing a unique lens through which law is understood and analyzed. Some of the key disciplines that contribute to legal studies include:

- **Philosophy**: Philosophy examines fundamental questions about the nature of law, ethics, and justice. It explores theories of morality, the relationship between law and morality, and the foundations of legal systems. Philosophical theories, such as natural law theory and legal positivism, provide important frameworks for understanding the ethical and moral dimensions of law.

+ **Ethics:** Ethics focuses on moral principles and their application to human behavior. In the context of legal studies, ethics helps us evaluate the ethical implications of legal rules and decisions. It provides a framework for understanding and analyzing ethical dilemmas faced by legal professionals and explores the ethical values that should guide legal practice.

+ **Political Science:** Political science investigates the distribution of power, the functioning of political systems, and the influence of politics on legal institutions and decision-making. It examines the role of law in shaping and maintaining political order, as well as the impact of political ideologies on legal systems.

+ **Sociology:** Sociology studies social interaction, social structures, and social institutions. In legal studies, sociology helps us understand how law is constructed, enforced, and experienced in society. It explores the relationship between law and society, the social factors that influence legal decision-making, and the impact of law on different social groups.

+ **Psychology:** Psychology provides insights into the cognitive and emotional processes that shape legal decision-making, behavior, and perceptions. It helps us understand how individuals make moral judgments, respond to legal norms, and interact with the legal system. Psychological research is particularly relevant in areas such as eyewitness testimony, jury decision-making, and legal advocacy.

+ **Economics:** Economics examines the production, distribution, and consumption of goods and services. In legal studies, economics helps us understand the economic implications of legal rules and policies. It explores topics such as law and economics, the role of incentives in shaping legal behavior, and the impact of legal regulations on economic outcomes.

+ **History:** History provides important insights into the development of legal systems, legal doctrines, and legal institutions over time. It helps us understand the context in which legal rules and practices emerge, as well as the historical forces that have shaped the evolution of the law.

+ **Criminology:** Criminology focuses on the causes of crime, the behavior of criminals, and the functioning of the criminal justice system. It helps us understand the social, economic, and psychological factors that contribute to criminal behavior, as well as the effectiveness of different legal interventions in reducing crime.

+ **Environmental Studies:** Environmental studies explore the impact of legal regulations on the environment and the sustainability of natural resources. It examines the intersection of law and environmental policy, as well as the legal mechanisms for promoting environmental protection and sustainability.

+ **Gender Studies:** Gender studies investigate the ways in which law constructs and regulates gender, as well as the impact of legal rules on gender equality. It explores the intersections of law, gender, and identity, and examines the legal challenges faced by marginalized gender groups.

Interdisciplinary Approaches in Legal Studies

The interdisciplinary nature of legal studies allows for the exploration of complex legal issues from different perspectives. It recognizes that law is not a standalone discipline but is deeply interconnected with other areas of knowledge. Interdisciplinary approaches in legal studies offer several benefits:

+ **Holistic Understanding:** By drawing on multiple disciplines, interdisciplinary approaches provide a holistic understanding of law and its implications. They consider a wide range of factors, including ethical, social, economic, and historical, which contribute to a comprehensive analysis of legal issues.

+ **Critical Analysis:** Interdisciplinary approaches encourage critical thinking by challenging traditional legal assumptions and paradigms. They help identify biases and limitations in legal doctrines and explore alternative perspectives that may lead to more just and equitable outcomes.

+ **Practical Application:** The integration of different disciplines allows legal studies to have practical applications in the real world. By considering the social, economic, and psychological effects of legal rules and policies, interdisciplinary approaches contribute to the development of effective legal solutions.

Example: Interdisciplinary Approach to Criminal Justice Reform

To illustrate the practical application of interdisciplinary approaches, let's consider the issue of criminal justice reform. An interdisciplinary approach would involve drawing on knowledge from sociology, psychology, criminology, and political science to address the complex problems inherent in the criminal justice system.

For instance, sociology can contribute by analyzing the social factors that contribute to criminal behavior and how they intersect with race, class, and gender. Psychology can help us understand the cognitive and emotional processes that shape criminal behavior and influence decision-making within the criminal justice system. Criminology can provide insights into the effectiveness of different interventions, such as restorative justice or rehabilitation programs. Political science can shed light on the role of politics in shaping criminal justice policies and the influence of public opinion on law enforcement practices.

By integrating these perspectives, an interdisciplinary approach to criminal justice reform can offer a more comprehensive understanding of the root causes of crime, the systemic issues within the criminal justice system, and the potential solutions that address both individual rehabilitation and broader social justice concerns.

Resources for Further Exploration

Legal studies being an interdisciplinary field, there are numerous resources available for further exploration. Some recommended readings include:

+ *The Philosophy of Law: A Very Short Introduction* by Raymond Wacks

+ *Law and Society* by Matthew Lippman

+ *Introduction to Criminology: Theories, Methods, and Criminal Behavior* by Frank E. Hagan

+ *Legal Ethics* by Kent Kauffman.

These resources delve into the key concepts and theories of legal studies, providing a solid foundation for interdisciplinary exploration.

Conclusion

The interdisciplinary nature of legal studies enriches our understanding of law, ethics, and justice. By drawing knowledge from various disciplines, legal studies offer a comprehensive analysis of legal issues and explore practical solutions to complex problems. Understanding the interdisciplinary nature of legal studies allows us to navigate moral dilemmas, promote justice, and shape a more equitable, just, and sustainable world.

In the next section, we will explore the relevance of philosophy and ethics in legal studies, examining the major philosophical and ethical theories that inform legal practice and decision-making.

Contemporary Issues in Legal Studies

In the field of Legal Studies, there are numerous contemporary issues that shape the discourse and practice of law. These issues are constantly evolving and reflect the ever-changing social, political, and technological landscape. In this section, we will explore some of the key contemporary issues that legal professionals and scholars grapple with today. By gaining a deeper understanding of these issues, we can more effectively address the challenges of a rapidly changing legal environment.

Technology and the Law

One of the most significant contemporary issues in Legal Studies is the intersection of technology and the law. Rapid advancements in technology have revolutionized the way legal professionals operate, presenting both opportunities and challenges. One such challenge is the ethical implications of technological advancements, particularly in the areas of privacy and data protection. For example, the proliferation of social media and the collection of vast amounts of personal data raise questions about individual privacy rights and the extent to which legal frameworks can effectively safeguard them.

Another technology-related issue in Legal Studies is the use of artificial intelligence (AI) and automation in legal practice. AI-powered tools are increasingly being used for tasks such as legal research, document review, and contract analysis. While these technologies enhance efficiency and accuracy, they also raise concerns about the potential displacement of certain legal jobs and the need to redefine professional responsibilities.

Furthermore, the rise of cybercrime and the need for effective cybersecurity measures have become pressing legal issues in the digital age. Legal professionals must navigate the complexities of cyber law to protect individuals and organizations from online threats. Additionally, issues regarding intellectual property rights and technology licensing agreements have emerged as areas of contention in the technological landscape.

Access to Justice

Access to justice is another pressing contemporary issue in the field of Legal Studies. Despite the principle of equal protection under the law, marginalized and disadvantaged populations often face obstacles in accessing legal services. Factors such as financial constraints, lack of awareness, geographical barriers, and systemic inequalities contribute to this issue.

Efforts are being made to address these challenges through various means, including the provision of legal aid services and the use of technology to enhance access to justice. For instance, online dispute resolution platforms and virtual legal clinics have emerged as innovative solutions to bridge the gap between legal services and individuals who might otherwise struggle to access them.

However, addressing the issue of access to justice requires systemic changes, including legal education reforms, the expansion of pro bono services, and the promotion of legal empowerment initiatives. These efforts aim to ensure that everyone, regardless of their socio-economic background, can effectively navigate the legal system and exercise their rights.

Environmental Law and Sustainability

In an era of increased environmental awareness, environmental law and sustainability have become critical contemporary issues. Environmental law encompasses legal frameworks and regulations aimed at protecting natural resources, preserving biodiversity, and mitigating the harmful impact of human activities on the environment. With the threat of climate change and ecological degradation, legal professionals play a vital role in shaping policies and advocating for sustainable practices.

Challenges in environmental law include balancing economic development with environmental protection, enforcing regulations, and addressing transnational environmental issues. Legal professionals must navigate complex international agreements, such as the Paris Agreement, and work towards the implementation of sustainable development goals.

Additionally, environmental justice is an important aspect of contemporary legal studies. Historically marginalized communities often bear a disproportionate burden of environmental harm. Legal professionals work to address these injustices by advocating for equitable distribution of environmental resources and ensuring that marginalized communities have a meaningful voice in environmental decision-making processes.

Legal Ethics and Professional Responsibility

The ethical dimensions of legal practice and professional responsibility remain relevant and evolving contemporary issues in Legal Studies. Legal professionals are expected to adhere to high standards of ethical conduct, uphold the rule of law, and prioritize the interests of their clients. However, ethical dilemmas arise in various contexts, challenging legal professionals to navigate complex moral landscapes.

Conflicts of interest, confidentiality concerns, and the duty to report misconduct are recurring ethical challenges faced by practitioners. For example, legal professionals must balance their obligation to represent clients faithfully with the duty to disclose relevant information to the court. The increasing globalization of legal practice also raises ethical questions related to cultural competency, diversity, and the duty to act in the best interests of justice on a global scale.

The advent of technology has also brought ethical implications for legal professionals. Issues such as the unauthorized practice of law, the use of AI tools in decision-making, and the responsibility to maintain technological competence are becoming more prominent in legal ethics discussions. The legal community must adapt to these technological changes while upholding ethical principles and ensuring professionalism.

Addressing these contemporary issues requires ongoing dialogue, research, and collaboration across legal disciplines. Legal professionals and scholars must remain vigilant to the changing landscape of the legal profession and the broader societal context to effectively navigate the challenges and opportunities that lie ahead.

Conclusion

In this section, we have explored some of the significant contemporary issues in Legal Studies. The intersection of technology and the law, access to justice, environmental law and sustainability, and legal ethics and professional responsibility are just a few examples of the multifaceted challenges legal professionals face in today's world.

By understanding these issues and their implications, legal professionals can better advocate for justice, navigate ethical dilemmas, and contribute to the development of a more equitable and sustainable society. As Legal Studies continue to evolve, it is essential to stay informed, engaged, and proactive in addressing the contemporary issues that shape the future of the legal profession. Together, we can build a legal system that fosters social justice, promotes ethical conduct, and responds to the complex needs of our times.

Future Directions in Legal Studies

The field of legal studies is constantly evolving, driven by societal changes, technological advancements, and emerging ethical considerations. As we look to the future, several key areas are likely to shape the direction of legal studies and influence the practice of law. In this section, we explore these future directions and their potential impact on the field.

Technology and Legal Practice

The integration of technology in legal practice has already begun, and its influence is only expected to grow in the coming years. Advancements in artificial intelligence, machine learning, and automation have the potential to transform the way legal professionals work. These technologies can streamline legal research, document analysis, and contract drafting, freeing up time for lawyers to focus on more complex and strategic tasks.

However, the increased reliance on technology also raises ethical considerations. For example, issues of data privacy and protection become crucial as law firms handle vast amounts of sensitive client information. Furthermore, the use of algorithms and AI systems in decision-making processes may introduce biases or undermine the fair application of the law. Legal professionals of the future must be well-versed in both the benefits and ethical challenges associated with technological integration.

Access to Justice

Access to justice has long been a concern within the legal system, as marginalized communities often face barriers in obtaining legal representation and navigating the complexities of the law. In the future, addressing this issue will become even more critical.

The advancement of technology presents opportunities to bridge the justice gap. Online dispute resolution platforms, virtual hearings, and chatbots for legal advice are just a few examples of how technology can enhance access to justice. These innovations can provide affordable and efficient legal solutions to individuals who may otherwise be excluded from the legal process.

However, it is important to recognize that technology alone cannot solve the access to justice problem. Adequate funding and support for legal aid services, community legal clinics, and pro bono initiatives are also crucial. Future legal professionals should be advocates for improving access to justice through innovative approaches and policy changes.

International and Comparative Law

The interconnectedness of our globalized world necessitates an understanding of international and comparative law. As economies become increasingly intertwined and cross-border issues arise, legal professionals with knowledge and expertise in international law will be in high demand.

Future legal studies programs should incorporate courses that delve into the complexities of international legal systems, treaties, and conventions. Students should be equipped with the skills to navigate diverse legal cultures and address complex transnational legal issues.

Additionally, addressing global challenges such as climate change, terrorism, and human rights violations requires collaborative efforts among nations. The role of international law in fostering cooperation and resolving disputes will become even more significant in the future. Legal professionals with a strong understanding of international law will be crucial in shaping a more just and sustainable world.

Ethics and Professional Responsibility

Ethical considerations have always been at the core of legal studies. As the legal profession evolves, legal professionals will face new ethical challenges and dilemmas. The future of legal studies should place a strong emphasis on ethics and professional responsibility, equipping students with the skills to navigate complex moral issues.

For example, emerging technologies like AI raise questions about the ethical use of algorithms in decision-making processes. Legal professionals must understand the implications of their actions on the privacy, autonomy, and rights of individuals. Additionally, addressing issues of diversity, inclusion, and social justice within the legal profession will require a commitment to ethical conduct.

Incorporating ethics into the curriculum and promoting ongoing ethical education for legal professionals will ensure that future lawyers are equipped to make informed, morally responsible decisions in their practice.

Interdisciplinary Collaboration

The nature of legal studies inherently requires interdisciplinary collaboration. The complex legal issues of the future will demand a deep understanding of not only the law but also fields such as technology, economics, psychology, and environmental science.

Future legal professionals will need to work closely with experts from various disciplines to effectively address modern challenges. Collaborative approaches that integrate diverse perspectives and knowledge will foster innovation and enhance the development of sustainable legal solutions.

Legal studies programs should embrace interdisciplinary education, encouraging students to explore subjects outside of traditional legal coursework. This will equip them with a well-rounded skill set and a broader understanding of the complex societal issues they will encounter in their careers.

Conclusion

The future of legal studies is dynamic and multifaceted, driven by rapid technological advancements, changing societal values, and global interconnectedness. Legal professionals of the future must adapt to these changes and proactively engage with emerging ethical considerations.

Embracing technology, improving access to justice, understanding international and comparative law, fostering ethical conduct, and promoting interdisciplinary collaboration are key areas that will shape the future of legal studies. By equipping students with the skills and knowledge to navigate these areas, legal studies can play a vital role in promoting justice and shaping a more equitable and sustainable world.

Conclusion

In conclusion, this chapter has introduced you to the fascinating world of philosophical and ethical issues in legal studies. We have explored the definition and scope of legal studies, delved into the historical overview of the field, and examined its objectives, goals, and key concepts. We have also emphasized the interdisciplinary nature of legal studies and discussed various contemporary issues and future directions.

Furthermore, we have provided an introduction to philosophy and ethics, highlighting their definitions and the relationship between the two disciplines. We have explored major philosophical and ethical theories and their relevance in legal studies. Throughout this discussion, we have underscored the importance of ethical considerations in legal practice, research, and decision-making.

Ethical decision-making in legal studies is a crucial aspect that aspiring legal professionals must understand. We have presented various ethical decision-making frameworks and discussed the ethical principles and values that guide legal studies. Moreover, we have examined the ethical dilemmas that legal practitioners often encounter and the factors that influence their decision-making process.

Professional codes of conduct and ethics play an essential role in regulating the behavior of legal professionals. We have explored the significance of these codes and discussed their implications in legal education. By understanding and adhering to these codes, legal professionals can maintain ethical integrity and ensure that justice is promoted in legal practice.

Moving on to the moral foundations of law and justice, we have examined concepts of morality and justice and their relationship. We have discussed the ethical foundations of legal systems and their implications in decision-making and the interpretation and application of laws. Additionally, we have explored various theories of law, including natural law theory, legal positivism, legal realism, critical legal studies, and feminist legal theory.

Legal rights and responsibilities are integral components of legal studies. We have delved into the definition and classification of rights, the theories of legal rights, and the ethical implications of rights and responsibilities. Furthermore, we have explored constitutional rights and liberties and the balance between individual rights and collective responsibilities. By understanding these concepts, legal professionals can uphold the ethical enforcement of rights and contribute to a more just society.

Ethics in the legal profession is a topic of great importance. We have discussed the role and responsibilities of legal professionals and the ethical obligations they must uphold. We have emphasized the significance of professional codes of conduct and legal ethics and examined the ethical challenges that legal professionals often face. By implementing strategies to maintain ethical integrity, legal professionals can ensure the delivery of justice and promote the public interest.

Confidentiality and attorney-client privilege are critical ethical considerations in legal practice. We have highlighted the importance of maintaining confidentiality and the limitations of attorney-client privilege. Additionally, we have discussed the ethical challenges and dilemmas that legal professionals may encounter in balancing confidentiality with other ethical obligations. By navigating these challenges responsibly, legal professionals can maintain trust and uphold ethical standards.

Conflict of interest is another ethical issue that legal professionals must address. We have defined conflict of interest and explored its types, avoidance, and management. Moreover, we have discussed the ethical implications of conflicts of interest and the challenges in identifying and addressing them. By promoting transparency and accountability, legal professionals can effectively manage conflicts of interest and ensure ethical conduct.

Social justice and human rights are integral to legal studies. We have examined theories of social justice and their implications in promoting equality and addressing discrimination. Furthermore, we have explored the historical evolution of human rights and the international and domestic frameworks for their protection. By understanding the challenges and controversies surrounding human rights, legal professionals can contribute to a more just society.

Ethical issues in criminal justice have significant implications for the legal system. We have discussed the principles of criminal justice ethics and the ethical dilemmas in law enforcement, criminal prosecution, and the correctional system. Through an understanding of these issues, legal professionals can work towards achieving social and criminal justice, as well as rehabilitation.

Capital punishment represents a significant ethical controversy in the criminal justice system. We have explored the arguments for and against capital punishment and the ethical implications of this practice. Additionally, we have discussed alternatives to capital punishment and international perspectives on this issue. By engaging in the debate and considering policy reforms, legal professionals can contribute to discussions on human rights and social justice.

Policing presents unique ethical challenges. We have explored the ethical dilemmas associated with police use of force, bias, accountability, and community engagement. By addressing these challenges, legal professionals can work towards ensuring ethical decision-making in law enforcement and maintaining public trust.

Ethical issues in business and commerce are also essential to legal studies. We have discussed the concept of business ethics, corporate governance, and corporate social responsibility. Moreover, we have explored the ethical considerations in intellectual property rights and the challenges of globalization in promoting ethical business practices. By upholding ethical decision-making, legal professionals can contribute to a sustainable and just business environment.

Lastly, we have emphasized the role of law in social change and reform. We have discussed how law can be a tool for social change, from legal activism and impact litigation to policy advocacy. Additionally, we have explored the relationship between law, policy, and sustainable development and the ethical implications of technological advancements. By understanding these dynamics, legal professionals can work towards a more equitable, just, and sustainable world.

In conclusion, this chapter has provided a comprehensive overview of philosophical and ethical issues in legal studies. By understanding the foundations, principles, and challenges of these issues, legal professionals can navigate moral dilemmas, promote justice, and contribute to shaping a more equitable and sustainable world.

Introduction to Philosophy and Ethics

Definitions of Philosophy and Ethics

In order to understand the role of philosophy and ethics in legal studies, we must first establish clear definitions of these terms. Philosophy is a broad field that seeks to answer fundamental questions about existence, knowledge, ethics, and more. It explores the nature of reality, the limits of human understanding, and the principles that shape human behavior and society.

Ethics, on the other hand, is a branch of philosophy that focuses specifically on moral principles and values. It deals with questions of right and wrong, good and evil, and the responsibilities and obligations that individuals and societies have towards one another.

While philosophy as a whole encompasses a wide range of disciplines and areas of inquiry, ethics is concerned specifically with the exploration and analysis of moral principles, theories, and behaviors. It seeks to examine how individuals make decisions, what informs their moral judgments, and how societies establish ethical frameworks and standards.

In the context of legal studies, philosophy and ethics play a crucial role in shaping legal systems, guiding legal decision-making, and ensuring the just and fair implementation of laws. They provide the foundation for evaluating the moral implications and consequences of legal principles, rules, and actions.

By examining ethical theories and philosophies, legal scholars and practitioners gain a deeper understanding of the fundamental values and principles that underpin legal systems. This knowledge allows them to critically analyze and evaluate legal structures, laws, and legal practices to ensure they promote justice, fairness, and the common good.

Ethical considerations in legal practice involve examining the professional responsibilities and obligations of legal practitioners. This includes issues such as client confidentiality, conflict of interest, and honesty in legal representation. Legal professionals must navigate these ethical dilemmas and make sound moral judgments to uphold their ethical obligations to clients, the legal system, and society as a whole.

Ethical thinking and decision-making are essential skills for legal professionals. They must be able to critically analyze complex legal issues, weigh the ethical implications of various courses of action, and make informed decisions that align with their ethical responsibilities. This requires a deep understanding of ethical theories, principles, and frameworks, as well as a strong sense of personal and professional integrity.

Legal research also entails ethical considerations. Researchers have a responsibility to ensure the accuracy, reliability, and fairness of their findings and conclusions. They must adhere to ethical guidelines and standards when conducting research, including obtaining informed consent and protecting the privacy and confidentiality of participants.

In conclusion, philosophy and ethics are indispensable components of legal studies. They provide the intellectual foundation for understanding legal principles, guide ethical decision-making in legal practice, and help shape a more equitable, just, and sustainable world. By integrating philosophical and ethical perspectives into legal education and practice, we can promote a more socially responsible and ethically conscious legal profession.

Relationship between Philosophy and Ethics

In order to fully understand the field of legal studies, it is important to examine the relationship between philosophy and ethics. Philosophy and ethics are two closely related disciplines that provide the foundation for ethical decision making and moral reasoning in legal practice. In this section, we will explore the interconnections between philosophy and ethics and their significance in the context of legal studies.

Definitions of Philosophy and Ethics

To begin, let us define philosophy and ethics. Philosophy is a branch of knowledge that seeks to address fundamental questions about the nature of reality, knowledge, values, and existence. It engages in critical analysis and rational inquiry to explore abstract concepts and fundamental principles.

On the other hand, ethics is the study of moral principles, values, and conduct. It deals with questions of right and wrong, good and bad, and what actions are morally permissible or impermissible. Ethics provides a framework for evaluating human behavior and making moral judgments. It seeks to understand and define concepts such as justice, fairness, and equality.

Relationship between Philosophy and Ethics

Philosophy and ethics are closely intertwined and often inform and shape each other. Philosophy provides the underlying theoretical framework and methodologies that guide ethical inquiry. It explores concepts such as metaphysics, epistemology, and ontology, which have a direct impact on ethical theories and principles. In turn, ethics applies philosophical theories to guide moral decision making and action.

There are several ways in which philosophy and ethics are interconnected:

+ **Ethical Foundations in Philosophy**: Ethics draws on philosophical theories to establish moral foundations. For example, ethical theories such as consequentialism, deontological ethics, and virtue ethics are grounded in philosophical ideas about the nature of good, the role of reason, and the nature of moral agency.

+ **Metaethics**: Metaethics is a branch of philosophy that examines the nature of ethical statements and moral concepts. It explores questions such as whether moral truths exist, the status of moral values, and the nature of moral judgments. Metaethics provides a philosophical framework for understanding the basis of ethical claims and moral reasoning.

+ **Normative Ethics**: Normative ethics is concerned with establishing moral standards and principles that guide ethical behavior. It is heavily influenced by philosophical theories, such as utilitarianism, which advocates maximizing overall happiness, and Kantian ethics, which emphasizes the importance of duty and moral obligations.

+ **Applied Ethics**: Applied ethics applies ethical theories and principles to real-world situations and specific contexts. It addresses ethical issues in areas such as bioethics, environmental ethics, business ethics, and of course, legal ethics. Philosophy provides the conceptual tools and frameworks for analyzing and resolving moral dilemmas in these domains.

+ **Ethics and Reasoning**: Philosophy equips individuals with critical thinking skills, logical reasoning, and argumentation techniques, which are vital for ethical reasoning. Ethical judgments require careful analysis, evaluation of evidence, and consideration of alternative viewpoints. Philosophy develops these skills and helps individuals to engage in ethical decision making.

Implications for Legal Studies

The relationship between philosophy and ethics has significant implications for legal studies. Understanding the philosophical foundations of ethics enables legal professionals to develop a deeper understanding of the ethical dimensions of legal practice. It equips them with the tools to critically evaluate ethical dilemmas and make informed moral judgments.

Ethics in legal studies provides a framework for analyzing and resolving complex moral dilemmas that arise in legal practice. Legal professionals are often confronted with conflicts of interest, difficult ethical choices, and competing values. By drawing on philosophical theories and ethical principles, they can navigate these challenges and promote justice and fairness.

Furthermore, incorporating philosophy and ethics into legal education encourages the development of ethical thinking and decision-making skills among future legal professionals. It promotes a culture of ethical conduct, integrity, and professionalism in the legal profession.

Ethical Considerations in Legal Practice

Ethical considerations play a crucial role in legal practice, where legal professionals are entrusted with upholding justice and ensuring the protection of individual rights. Some key ethical considerations in legal practice include:

- **Confidentiality:** Legal professionals have a duty to maintain client confidentiality and protect sensitive information. Confidentiality is essential for preserving trust and ensuring open communication between lawyers and their clients.

- **Conflict of Interest:** Legal professionals must avoid conflicts of interest that could compromise their professional judgment or unduly influence their representation of clients. They have a duty to act in the best interests of their clients and avoid any conflicts that may compromise their loyalty and fiduciary duty.

- **Honesty and Candor:** Legal professionals should be honest, truthful, and candid in their dealings with clients, colleagues, and the court. They have an ethical obligation to provide accurate information, disclose relevant facts, and avoid misleading or deceptive practices.

- **Access to Justice:** Legal professionals have a responsibility to ensure access to justice for all individuals, irrespective of their socioeconomic status, race, gender, or other factors. They should strive to provide equal representation and fair treatment to all clients, promoting the principles of justice and fairness.

Ethical Thinking and Decision Making

Ethical thinking and decision making are essential skills for legal professionals. They rely on philosophical theories and ethical frameworks to navigate complex moral dilemmas. Here are some key elements of ethical thinking and decision making in legal studies:

- **Identifying Ethical Dilemmas:** Legal professionals must be able to recognize ethical dilemmas and conflicts that may arise in legal practice. This requires an understanding of ethical principles, values, and professional responsibilities.

- **Considering Consequences and Impacts:** When faced with an ethical dilemma, legal professionals should consider the potential consequences and impacts of their actions. They should evaluate the potential benefits and harms that may result from different courses of action.

- **Analyzing and Evaluating Ethical Theories:** Legal professionals should be familiar with major ethical theories and principles and be able to apply them to analyze and evaluate ethical dilemmas. This involves understanding the strengths and weaknesses of different theories and considering their relevance to specific situations.

- **Balancing Competing Interests:** Ethical decision making often involves balancing competing interests and values. Legal professionals should consider the rights and interests of all stakeholders involved and strive to achieve a fair and just resolution.

- **Consultation and Collaboration:** When facing complex ethical dilemmas, legal professionals can seek advice and guidance from colleagues, mentors, and professional bodies. Collaboration and consultation can provide valuable perspectives and help legal professionals make well-informed ethical decisions.

Conclusion

The relationship between philosophy and ethics is integral to legal studies. Philosophy provides the theoretical underpinnings and methodologies for ethical inquiry, while ethics applies these theories to guide moral decision making in legal practice. By understanding this relationship, legal professionals can navigate ethical challenges, promote justice, and uphold fundamental ethical principles. Developing ethical thinking and decision-making skills is essential for maintaining integrity and professionalism in the legal profession.

Major Philosophical and Ethical Theories

In the study of legal studies, it is essential to have a strong foundation in the major philosophical and ethical theories that underpin the field. These theories provide us with frameworks for understanding the fundamental principles of law, justice, and moral reasoning. In this section, we will explore some of the key theories that have shaped legal philosophy and ethics.

Natural Law Theory

Natural law theory holds that there is a higher moral law that supersedes human-made laws. According to this theory, laws derived from natural law are considered just and moral, while laws that contradict natural law are considered unjust and immoral. Natural law theorists argue that individuals have certain inherent rights and that laws should protect and promote these rights.

One of the most influential figures in natural law theory is St. Thomas Aquinas, who believed that natural law is derived from God's eternal law. Aquinas argued that human laws must be in harmony with divine laws to be considered legitimate. Natural law theory emphasizes the idea that there are objective moral principles that are discoverable through reason.

Legal Positivism

Legal positivism, on the other hand, holds that the validity of laws is determined solely by their source. According to legal positivists, laws are the product of social institutions and are not inherently moral or immoral. The key proponent of legal positivism is Jeremy Bentham, who argued that laws should be based on utility and the greatest happiness of the greatest number of people.

Legal positivism separates law from morality and ethics, suggesting that the law should be understood in purely descriptive terms. This theory focuses on the formal aspects of law, such as the rules and procedures that govern legal systems, rather than the moral content of laws.

Utilitarianism

Utilitarianism is an ethical theory that is closely related to legal positivism. Utilitarianism holds that the right action is the one that maximizes overall happiness or utility. According to this theory, laws and legal decisions should be based on the principle of maximizing the overall happiness of society.

Utilitarianism was popularized by philosophers such as Jeremy Bentham and John Stuart Mill. Bentham developed the principle of the greatest happiness, which states that actions are morally right if they produce the greatest amount of happiness for the greatest number of people. Mill, on the other hand, refined utilitarianism by emphasizing the importance of individual rights and the need to protect the rights of minorities.

Deontological Ethics

Deontological ethics, also known as duty ethics, focuses on the inherent moral duties and obligations that individuals have. Deontologists argue that certain actions are inherently right or wrong, regardless of their consequences. This theory places emphasis on the intentions behind actions and the adherence to moral principles.

Immanuel Kant is a prominent figure in deontological ethics. He argued that morality should be based on universal principles that can be derived through rationality. Kant's categorical imperative is a key principle in deontological ethics, stating that individuals should act according to rules that they would want everyone to follow.

Virtue Ethics

Virtue ethics looks at the character and virtues of individuals instead of focusing on actions or consequences. This theory emphasizes the cultivation of moral virtues and qualities such as honesty, courage, and compassion. Virtue ethicists believe that by developing virtuous traits, individuals will naturally act in morally right ways.

Aristotle is one of the most influential proponents of virtue ethics. He argued that living a virtuous life is the key to human flourishing and achieving eudaimonia, or the good life. According to virtue ethics, the ultimate aim of moral action is to cultivate virtuous character traits.

Feminist Ethics

Feminist ethics aims to challenge traditional ethical theories and promote gender equality and justice. This theory recognizes the gender biases that exist in traditional ethical frameworks and seeks to address them. Feminist ethics emphasizes the importance of including women's experiences and perspectives in moral decision-making.

Feminist ethicists critique the androcentrism and patriarchal biases in traditional ethical theories, highlighting the need for a more inclusive and diverse understanding of ethics. They argue that ethics should address issues such as gender-based violence, reproductive rights, and social injustices faced by women.

Ethics of Care

The ethics of care is a relational ethical theory that prioritizes the importance of relationships, empathy, and compassion. This theory emphasizes the moral responsibility to care for others, especially vulnerable individuals and marginalized groups. The ethics of care challenges the traditional emphasis on individualism and rights-based ethics.

Carol Gilligan is a key figure in the development of the ethics of care. She argued that traditional ethical theories, such as deontology and utilitarianism, neglect the values of care and compassion, which are traditionally associated with femininity. The ethics of care emphasizes the need to recognize and address power imbalances and to prioritize the well-being of others.

Conclusion

The major philosophical and ethical theories discussed in this section provide different perspectives on the nature of law, justice, and moral reasoning. Natural law theory emphasizes the existence of objective moral principles, while legal positivism separates law from morality. Utilitarianism focuses on the maximization of overall happiness, while deontological ethics emphasizes moral duties and obligations. Virtue ethics looks at moral character traits, while feminist ethics and the ethics of care highlight the importance of gender equality and compassionate relationships.

By understanding these theories, legal scholars and professionals can navigate the complex moral dilemmas and ethical issues that arise in legal studies. These theories serve as foundations for critical analysis, decision-making, and shaping a more equitable, just, and sustainable world.

Resources

1. Austin, J. (1995). How to do Things with Words. Oxford University Press.

2. Gardner, J. (2012). Legal Positivism: 5 Questions. Automatic Press / VIP.

3. Gilligan, C. (1982). In a Different Voice: Psychological Theory and Women's Development. Harvard University Press.

4. Kant, I. (1994). Grounding for the Metaphysics of Morals. Hackett Publishing Company.

5. MacIntyre, A. (2007). After Virtue: A Study in Moral Theory. University of Notre Dame Press.

6. Nussbaum, M. C. (2011). Creating Capabilities: The Human Development Approach. Harvard University Press.

Exercises

1. Discuss a contemporary legal issue from the perspective of natural law theory, legal positivism, and utilitarianism. What are the implications of each theory for understanding and resolving the issue?

2. Consider a moral dilemma such as the trolley problem (a thought experiment in ethics). Analyze the dilemma from the perspectives of deontological ethics and virtue ethics. What are the key considerations and possible solutions offered by each theory?

3. Explore a real-world case where feminist ethics and the ethics of care provide valuable insights and critiques. Discuss how these theories challenge traditional ethical frameworks and contribute to a more inclusive understanding of morality and justice.

Relevance of Philosophy and Ethics in Legal Studies

Philosophy and ethics play a crucial role in legal studies by providing essential frameworks and principles for understanding and addressing the complex moral dilemmas that arise in the field of law. In this section, we will explore the relevance of philosophy and ethics in legal studies, focusing on how these disciplines inform legal theory and practice, enhance the understanding of legal concepts, and contribute to the pursuit of justice.

Philosophy and its Connection to Legal Studies

Philosophy, derived from the Greek word "philosophia" meaning "love of wisdom," is a discipline that examines fundamental questions about knowledge, reality, existence, ethics, and the nature of human experience. In the context of legal studies, philosophy provides a conceptual framework for understanding the nature and purpose of law, as well as the ethical considerations that shape legal decision-making.

Ethics and its Importance in Legal Studies

Ethics, derived from the Greek word "ethos" meaning "character," is the branch of philosophy that deals with moral principles and values. In the realm of legal studies, ethics plays a vital role in guiding the behavior and decision-making of legal professionals, as well as in analyzing the ethical implications of legal principles, rules, and practices.

Understanding Legal Concepts through Philosophy

Philosophical inquiry deepens our understanding of legal concepts by challenging assumptions, clarifying ambiguities, and providing a broader perspective on the foundations of law. For example, the study of philosophy helps us explore questions such as the nature of justice, the relationship between law and morality, and the limits of legal authority. By critically examining these concepts, legal scholars and practitioners can develop more nuanced and comprehensive approaches to resolving legal issues.

Ethics in Legal Decision-Making

Ethics provides a framework for ethical decision-making in legal practice. Legal professionals often encounter complex ethical dilemmas when balancing competing interests, ensuring the fairness of legal processes, and upholding the principles of justice. By incorporating ethical theories and principles into their decision-making processes, legal practitioners can navigate these dilemmas more effectively and promote ethical conduct in the field.

Ethics in Legal Research

Legal research often involves investigating complex legal issues, analyzing legal precedents, and formulating legal arguments. Ethical considerations are essential in ensuring the integrity of legal research. Legal researchers must adhere to ethical standards such as accuracy, honesty, objectivity, and respect for intellectual property rights. By incorporating ethical practices into their research methodologies, legal researchers contribute to the advancement of knowledge and the quality of legal scholarship.

Promoting Justice Through Ethics

Justice is a fundamental goal of legal systems, and ethics provides the foundation for realizing this goal. Ethical principles, such as fairness, equality, and respect for human rights, shape the development and application of laws, ensuring equitable outcomes and protecting the rights and interests of individuals and communities. By incorporating ethical considerations into legal practice, legal professionals contribute to the promotion of justice and the resolution of social inequalities.

Ethical Challenges in Legal Practice

Legal professionals often face ethical challenges that test their moral character and professional integrity. These challenges can include conflicts of interest, maintaining client confidentiality, exercising discretion, and navigating the complexities of legal advocacy. By understanding and addressing these ethical challenges, legal practitioners can uphold ethical standards, build public trust, and ensure the legitimacy of the legal system.

Ethics Education in Legal Studies

Ethics education is a crucial component of legal studies curriculum. By incorporating ethics education, legal programs equip future legal professionals with the knowledge and skills necessary to navigate ethical dilemmas, promote ethical conduct, and uphold the principles of justice. Ethics education also nurtures ethical reasoning and moral sensitivity, enabling legal professionals to make ethically informed decisions in their practice.

Conclusion

Philosophy and ethics are indispensable in legal studies, providing the conceptual frameworks, analytical tools, and ethical principles necessary for understanding and addressing the complexities of law. By integrating philosophy and ethics into legal theory and practice, legal professionals can navigate moral dilemmas, promote justice, and contribute to a more equitable, just, and sustainable world.

Ethical Considerations in Legal Practice

Ethics plays a crucial role in legal practice, as legal professionals are entrusted with upholding justice and ensuring the fairness of the legal system. This section will explore the ethical considerations that lawyers and other legal practitioners need to navigate in their day-to-day work. We will delve into the ethical principles that guide legal practice, explore the challenges and dilemmas that arise, and discuss strategies for maintaining ethical integrity.

Principles of Legal Ethics

Legal ethics encompasses a set of principles that govern the behavior and conduct of legal professionals. These principles aim to ensure fairness, integrity, and professionalism in the legal system. While different jurisdictions may have varying codes of conduct, there are some overarching ethical principles that are widely recognized and accepted.

- **Confidentiality**: Lawyers have a duty to protect the confidentiality of client information. This duty helps foster trust between lawyers and clients and ensures that clients can provide full and honest disclosure to their legal representatives.

- **Conflict of Interest**: Legal professionals must avoid situations where their personal interests or affiliations may compromise their professional judgment or the representation of their clients. They must disclose any conflicts of interest and take appropriate steps to address them.

- **Competence**: Lawyers must possess the knowledge, skills, and expertise necessary to provide competent legal representation to their clients. They should continually update their legal knowledge and, if necessary, seek assistance or collaboration to ensure the best possible outcomes for their clients.

- **Zealous Advocacy**: Lawyers have a duty to represent their clients zealously within the bounds of the law. However, this duty does not give them license to engage in unethical or illegal conduct. They must act ethically and with integrity while advocating for their clients' interests.

- **Honesty and Candor**: Legal professionals must be honest and candid in their communications with clients, other lawyers, the court, and all other stakeholders involved in the legal process. This includes providing accurate and complete information, refraining from making false statements, and diligently correcting any errors or misrepresentations.

These principles provide a foundational framework for ethical conduct in legal practice. However, applying these principles in real-world scenarios can sometimes pose challenges and dilemmas.

Challenges and Dilemmas

Legal practice often presents complex and ethically challenging situations that require careful consideration and decision-making. Here are some common challenges and dilemmas that legal professionals may encounter:

1. **Conflicts of Interest:** Legal practitioners may face conflicts of interest when their obligations to one client conflict with the interests of another client, a third party, or even their own personal interests. Resolving such conflicts requires careful analysis, disclosure, and, if necessary, withdrawal from representation.

2. **Candor and Honesty:** Lawyers have a duty to be honest and forthright in their communications. However, they may face situations where withholding information or revealing it could have serious consequences. Balancing the duty of candor with other ethical considerations can be challenging.

3. **Client Communication and Consent:** Effective communication with clients is essential for providing competent legal representation. Lawyers must ensure that their clients fully understand the nature of the legal matter, the risks involved, and the available options. Obtaining informed consent from clients can sometimes be challenging when complex legal concepts are involved.

4. **Tensions between Zealous Advocacy and Objectivity:** While lawyers have an obligation to advocate for their clients' interests, they must also maintain objectivity and respect for the legal system. Balancing the duty of zealous advocacy with the duty of candor and fairness can be ethically demanding.

5. **Access to Justice:** Legal professionals face challenges in ensuring access to justice for marginalized communities, low-income individuals, and other disadvantaged groups. The ethical obligation to provide pro bono services and promote equal access to legal services can be challenging to fulfill.

Addressing these challenges and dilemmas requires a thoughtful and comprehensive approach to ethical decision-making.

Ethical Decision-Making Frameworks

Ethical decision-making frameworks provide a systematic approach for analyzing ethical dilemmas and determining the most ethically justifiable course of action. While different frameworks exist, most involve a similar step-by-step process:

1. **Identify the ethical dilemma:** Clearly identify the specific ethical issue or conflict at hand. Determine the stakeholders involved and understand the potential consequences of different courses of action.

2. **Gather relevant information:** Collect all necessary information related to the ethical dilemma. Seek input from colleagues, refer to professional codes of conduct, review legal precedents, and consult applicable ethical guidelines.

3. **Identify applicable ethical principles:** Assess the ethical principles that are relevant to the dilemma. Consider how each principle applies to the specific context and evaluate their relative importance and potential conflicts.

4. **Generate alternative solutions:** Brainstorm and evaluate different possible courses of action that could address the ethical dilemma. Consider the potential risks, benefits, and consequences associated with each option.

5. **Evaluate each alternative:** Assess the strengths and weaknesses of each proposed solution in light of the ethical principles and the specific circumstances. Consider how each alternative aligns with the broader goals of justice, fairness, and professional integrity.

6. **Make a decision:** Select the most justifiable course of action based on the analysis and evaluation of the alternative solutions. Ensure that the chosen decision upholds ethical principles and aligns with professional obligations.

7. **Implement the decision:** Put the chosen course of action into practice while considering the potential impact on all stakeholders involved. Communicate the decision to relevant parties and take any necessary steps to mitigate potential harms.

8. **Reflect and learn:** After implementing the decision, reflect on the outcome and the overall ethical decision-making process. Learn from the experience to improve future decision-making and ethical judgment.

By following a structured ethical decision-making framework, legal professionals can navigate complex ethical dilemmas with greater clarity and consistency.

Strategies for Maintaining Ethical Integrity

Maintaining ethical integrity throughout a legal career requires ongoing self-reflection, commitment to professional development, and adherence to ethical principles. Here are some strategies that can help legal professionals uphold ethical standards:

- **Continuing Education**: Stay updated on changes in laws, regulations, and ethical guidelines through professional development activities, seminars, and workshops. Engage in lifelong learning to enhance legal knowledge and ethical understanding.

- **Supervision and Consultation**: Seek guidance and supervision from experienced legal professionals in navigating complex ethical issues. Consult peers, mentors, or professional bodies when faced with challenging dilemmas.

- **Ethics Codes and Guidelines**: Familiarize yourself with the ethical codes and guidelines relevant to your jurisdiction and area of practice. Regularly review and refer to these resources to ensure adherence to professional standards.

- **Ethics Committees and Consultation Services**: Take advantage of ethics committees or consultation services offered by professional associations. These resources provide guidance and assistance in addressing ethical concerns and dilemmas.

- **Self-Reflection and Ethical Journals**: Engage in regular self-reflection to develop a deeper understanding of your own values, biases, and ethical decision-making processes. Consider keeping an ethical journal to record and reflect on your ethical challenges and decisions.

- **Mentorship and Role Models**: Seek mentorship from experienced legal professionals known for their ethical conduct. Emulate the behavior and ethical practices of respected role models in the legal profession.

By employing these strategies, legal professionals can actively promote and maintain ethical integrity in their professional practice.

Conclusion

Ethical considerations are integral to legal practice, ensuring fairness, integrity, and justice within the legal system. Lawyers and other legal professionals must navigate complex challenges and dilemmas while upholding the principles of confidentiality, conflict of interest, competence, zealous advocacy, honesty, and candor. By employing ethical decision-making frameworks and strategies for maintaining ethical integrity, legal professionals can effectively confront ethical dilemmas and fulfill their ethical obligations. Upholding ethical standards is crucial for promoting justice and fostering public trust in the legal profession.

Ethical Thinking and Decision Making

In the field of legal studies, ethical thinking and decision making play a critical role in guiding the actions and choices of legal professionals. Ethical considerations are essential in ensuring justice, fairness, and the protection of individual rights within the legal system. This section will explore the principles and frameworks that underpin ethical decision making in legal studies and provide practical guidance for navigating ethical dilemmas in the field.

Foundations of Ethical Thinking

Ethical thinking is rooted in philosophical and ethical theories that provide a framework for understanding and evaluating moral dilemmas. These theories help legal professionals examine ethical issues and make informed decisions. Here are some key philosophical and ethical theories relevant to ethical thinking in legal studies:

1. **Deontological Ethics:** This theory, proposed by Immanuel Kant, emphasizes the importance of moral duties and obligations. According to deontological ethics, certain actions are inherently right or wrong, regardless of their consequences. Legal professionals can use deontological ethics to assess the ethical implications of their actions based on universally applicable moral principles.

2. **Consequentialist Ethics:** Consequentialism, associated with utilitarianism, focuses on the outcomes or consequences of actions. According to this theory, the rightness or wrongness of an action is determined by its overall impact on maximizing happiness or well-being. Legal professionals can use consequentialist ethics to evaluate the ethical consequences of their decisions and choose actions that promote the greatest overall good.

3. **Virtue Ethics:** Virtue ethics emphasizes the development of moral character traits or virtues. Legal professionals can cultivate virtues such as honesty, integrity, and fairness to guide their ethical thinking and decision making. Virtue ethics encourages individuals to act in ways that embody these virtues, contributing to a just and ethical legal system.

4. **Principlism:** Principlism is an ethical theory that involves identifying and applying ethical principles to specific situations. Legal professionals can use a principled approach to ethical decision making by considering fundamental

principles such as autonomy, beneficence, non-maleficence, and justice. These principles serve as benchmarks for evaluating the moral dimensions of legal dilemmas.

Ethical Decision Making Frameworks

Ethical decision making in legal studies often involves complex situations where multiple ethical principles or values may come into conflict. To navigate these dilemmas, legal professionals can rely on various ethical decision making frameworks. Here are a few commonly used frameworks:

1. **The Four-Component Model:** This model, proposed by James Rest, consists of four components: (a) moral sensitivity, (b) moral judgment, (c) moral motivation, and (d) moral character. Legal professionals can use this model to systematically analyze ethical dilemmas by considering the various factors that impact their ethical decision making.

2. **The Oath Model:** The Oath Model, developed by Sissela Bok, emphasizes the importance of ethical principles and promises made by legal professionals. The model guides ethical decision making by focusing on factors such as honesty, confidentiality, and avoiding conflicts of interest. Legal professionals can take an oath or make a commitment to uphold these ethical principles in their practice.

3. **The Professional Ethical Decision Making Model:** This model, based on the work of Michael Davis, provides a step-by-step approach to ethical decision making in professional settings. It involves assessing the facts, identifying ethical issues, considering different options, evaluating the consequences, and making a decision that aligns with professional and ethical standards.

These frameworks offer structured approaches to analyzing ethical dilemmas and making ethical decisions. However, it is crucial to recognize that each situation is unique, and no single model can perfectly dictate the right course of action. Legal professionals must also consider the specific legal context, professional codes of conduct, and individual judgment when making ethical decisions.

Balancing Competing Ethical Principles

In legal studies, ethical decision making often requires balancing competing ethical principles. Legal professionals may encounter situations where multiple ethical principles or values are at stake, and it can be challenging to navigate these tensions. Here are some strategies for balancing conflicting ethical principles:

1. **Principle-based Reasoning:** Legal professionals can analyze the ethical dimensions of a situation by applying different ethical principles and considering

their relative importance. By weighting the relevance and significance of each principle, they can determine which should take precedence in the decision-making process.

2. **Case-by-Case Analysis:** Resolving ethical dilemmas may involve a careful examination of the specific circumstances and context. Legal professionals should consider the unique factors of each case, including the interests of all stakeholders involved, when weighing conflicting ethical principles.

3. **Consultation and Collaboration:** Seeking input from colleagues, supervisors, or ethics committees can provide valuable perspectives and help legal professionals evaluate the ethical dimensions of a situation. Collaboration can facilitate a more comprehensive understanding of the issue and support the development of a balanced ethical decision.

Navigating competing ethical principles requires careful thought and ethical reasoning. Legal professionals must weigh the potential consequences of their decisions while considering the primacy of human rights, fairness, and justice in the pursuit of ethical outcomes.

Promoting Ethical Thinking and Decision Making

To promote ethical thinking and decision making in legal studies, it is essential for legal professionals and educational institutions to prioritize ethics education. Here are some strategies to foster ethical thinking and decision making:

1. **Ethics Education:** Law schools and legal organizations should incorporate ethics courses and workshops into their curricula. These educational programs can provide legal professionals with the necessary knowledge and tools to navigate ethical dilemmas.

2. **Reflective Practice:** Legal professionals should engage in self-reflection and continuous evaluation of their ethical decision making. Regularly reviewing and critiquing one's ethical choices can contribute to personal growth and the development of ethical competence.

3. **Professional Mentoring:** Encouraging experienced legal professionals to mentor younger colleagues can provide guidance and support in ethical decision making. Mentors can share their experiences and provide insight into ethical challenges, helping shape the ethical thinking of the next generation of legal professionals.

4. **Ethics Committees and Hotlines:** Establishing ethics committees within legal organizations and offering confidential hotlines can provide a safe space for legal professionals to seek advice and report ethical concerns. These mechanisms promote a culture of transparency, accountability, and ethical engagement.

By implementing these strategies, the legal profession can cultivate a stronger ethical foundation, ensuring that legal professionals have the necessary skills and mindset to navigate the complex ethical landscape of legal studies.

Conclusion

Ethical thinking and decision making are essential components of legal studies. By understanding the foundations of ethical thinking, legal professionals can approach ethical dilemmas with depth and clarity. The use of ethical decision making frameworks and strategies for balancing competing ethical principles can guide legal professionals toward making just and informed decisions. Promoting ethical thinking and decision making in legal education and practice is crucial for creating a more equitable, just, and sustainable legal system.

Ethics in Legal Research

Ethics plays a crucial role in legal research, as it guides researchers in conducting their work with integrity, honesty, and fairness. Legal research involves the exploration of legal principles, statutes, and case law to provide a foundation for legal arguments and decision-making. In this section, we will delve into the ethical considerations that researchers must take into account when conducting legal research.

The Importance of Ethical Research

Ethical research ensures that legal scholars and practitioners produce reliable and trustworthy work that upholds the principles of justice and fairness. Conducting research with ethical considerations in mind is essential for maintaining the credibility of the legal field and promoting the pursuit of truth. Ethical research also helps to protect the rights and well-being of participants who may be involved in empirical legal research studies.

Informed Consent

One of the key ethical considerations in legal research involving human participants is obtaining informed consent. Researchers must ensure that participants have a clear understanding of the purpose, risks, and benefits of their involvement in the research study. Informed consent involves providing participants with all the necessary information to make an informed decision about their participation, and it is crucial to respect their autonomy and right to self-determination.

Confidentiality and Anonymity

Respecting the privacy and confidentiality of research participants is another ethical obligation in legal research. Researchers must take appropriate measures to protect the identity and personal information of participants, especially when handling sensitive or confidential data. Anonymizing data by removing identifying information is a common practice to safeguard participant confidentiality while still allowing for meaningful analysis.

Avoiding Bias

Maintaining objectivity and avoiding bias are fundamental ethical principles in legal research. Researchers must strive to ensure that their personal beliefs, values, or prior assumptions do not influence their research findings. By employing rigorous methodologies, researchers can minimize the risk of bias and enhance the credibility and validity of their research outcomes.

Responsible Use of Sources

Integrity in legal research demands the responsible use of sources. Researchers must accurately attribute the ideas, theories, and findings of others by citing their sources appropriately. Plagiarism, the act of presenting someone else's work as one's own, is a grave ethical violation and undermines the integrity of the research process. Proper referencing and citation practices are essential to acknowledge the contributions of previous scholars and to give credit where it is due.

Ethics in Data Collection and Analysis

Ethics also come into play during the data collection and analysis phases of legal research. Researchers must ensure that their methods for collecting data are ethical and respectful of participants' rights and privacy. They should obtain data through lawful means and conduct their analysis in a transparent and unbiased manner. Additionally, researchers must consider the potential social, cultural, and legal implications of their findings and use their data responsibly and ethically.

Transparency and Openness

Promoting transparency and openness is a crucial ethical principle in legal research. Researchers should strive to make their research process, methods, and findings accessible and understandable to the broader community. Transparent reporting allows for peer review, replication, and the advancement of knowledge. Openness in research also fosters collaboration and ensures accountability.

Ethics in Interdisciplinary Research

Legal research often intersects with other disciplines, such as sociology, psychology, and economics. Researchers engaged in interdisciplinary research must be aware of the ethical principles and methodologies specific to each field. Collaborative efforts across disciplines should respect the ethical norms of all involved disciplines and ensure that ethical guidelines from each field are appropriately integrated into the research process.

Ethics Committees and Institutional Review Boards

In many research institutions, ethics committees or institutional review boards (IRBs) exist to oversee and ensure the ethical conduct of research involving human participants. Researchers are often required to seek approval from these committees before commencing their research. Ethics committees and IRBs evaluate research proposals, assess the potential risks and benefits to participants, and ensure that the research conforms to ethical guidelines and legal requirements.

Concluding Thoughts

Ethics in legal research are essential for maintaining the integrity, credibility, and fairness of the legal field. Researchers must uphold ethical principles throughout the research process, from obtaining informed consent to responsibly using sources and ensuring transparency. By conducting research ethically, legal scholars and practitioners contribute to building a more just and equitable legal system.

Conclusion

In this chapter, we have explored the importance of philosophy and ethics in the field of legal studies. We began by defining legal studies and understanding its historical development. We also discussed the interdisciplinary nature of legal studies and explored several contemporary issues and future directions in the field.

Next, we delved into the concepts of philosophy and ethics. We defined these terms and examined their relationship to legal studies. We discussed major philosophical and ethical theories and their relevance in understanding legal practices and decision-making. Furthermore, we explored how ethical considerations play a crucial role in legal research and practice, emphasizing the need for ethical thinking and decision-making in the field.

Ethical decision-making frameworks were introduced as tools to navigate moral dilemmas in legal studies. We explored the ethical principles and values that guide legal professionals in their decision-making process. Additionally, we discussed various factors that may influence ethical decision-making and the importance of balancing competing ethical principles. Examining professional codes of conduct and ethics within the legal profession, we highlighted the significance of ethical issues in legal education.

Moving forward, we discussed the moral foundations of law and justice. We explored different theories of justice and the relationship between morality and justice. We also examined the ethical foundations of legal systems and the ethical implications of legal principles, rules, and interpretations. Furthermore, we discussed the theories of law, including natural law theory, legal positivism, legal realism, critical legal studies, feminist legal theory, and their impact on legal interpretation and social change.

In the realm of legal rights and responsibilities, we explored the definition and classification of rights. We discussed theories of legal rights and examined the ethical dimension of constitutional rights and individual rights versus collective responsibilities. Additionally, we considered the ethical enforcement of rights and the correlation between legal ethics and human rights.

We then shifted our focus to the ethical issues in the legal profession. We explored the role and responsibilities of legal professionals, emphasizing the importance of professionalism and ethics. We also discussed the ethical obligations in legal practice and the significance of professional codes of conduct. Ethical challenges in the legal profession were examined, along with strategies for maintaining ethical integrity in legal practice. Furthermore, we discussed the ethical considerations related to confidentiality and attorney-client privilege, along with the challenges and dilemmas associated with maintaining confidentiality.

Conflict of interest was another important topic we covered. We defined conflict of interest and discussed its avoidance and management. Additionally, we explored the ethical implications of conflicts of interest and strategies for promoting transparency and accountability in conflict of interest situations.

In the realm of social justice and human rights, we examined theories of social justice and their ethical implications. We discussed the historical evolution of human rights and explored international and domestic legal frameworks for their protection. Moreover, we addressed social justice issues in legal studies, such as poverty, inequality, gender equality, racial and ethnic justice, LGBTQ+ rights, and environmental justice.

The ethical issues in the criminal justice system were explored, focusing on law enforcement, criminal prosecution, and the correctional system. We discussed principles of criminal justice ethics, ethical dilemmas, challenges, and the correlation between criminal justice and social justice. Capital punishment and its ethical controversies were examined, along with alternatives, international perspectives, and policy recommendations.

Policing and ethical challenges were also discussed, including police use of force, bias, accountability, and community policing. We emphasized the importance of ethical decision-making in law enforcement and the connection between policing and social justice.

Moving into the realm of business and commerce, we addressed ethics in the business environment. We explored corporate governance, corporate social responsibility, ethical considerations in marketing and advertising, and the decision-making process in business ethics. Intellectual property rights and ethical dilemmas were also discussed, including the balance between copyright protection and access to knowledge.

Finally, we examined the ethical challenges posed by globalization. We considered ethical considerations in international business, human rights in global supply chains, corruption and bribery, and environmental sustainability. We emphasized the role of ethical leadership in addressing these challenges and the correlation between globalization, social justice, and human rights.

In conclusion, this chapter has shed light on the philosophical and ethical issues in legal studies. We have explored the moral foundations of law and justice, the ethical challenges in the legal profession, the importance of social justice and human rights, the ethical issues in criminal justice, and the ethical challenges in business and commerce. By understanding and addressing these issues, legal professionals can contribute to the construction of a more equitable, just, and sustainable world. As future legal practitioners, it is crucial to navigate moral dilemmas, promote justice, and shape a better tomorrow.

Ethical Decision Making in Legal Studies

Ethical Decision Making Frameworks

Ethical decision making is a central aspect of legal studies, as it determines the values and principles that guide the actions and choices of legal professionals. In this section, we will explore various ethical decision making frameworks that can assist in navigating complex moral dilemmas encountered in the legal field.

Utilitarianism

Utilitarianism is an ethical theory that suggests that the right course of action is the one that maximizes overall happiness or utility for the greatest number of people. According to utilitarianism, an ethical decision is deemed "good" if it produces more positive consequences than negative ones. This framework focuses on the outcome of a decision rather than the inherent rights or wrongs of the action itself.

To apply utilitarianism in ethical decision making, one must consider the potential consequences of different courses of action and identify which option would yield the greatest overall happiness. However, it is important to be cautious of the dangers of sacrificing the rights and well-being of minority groups or individuals for the sake of the majority. Utilitarianism also requires the ability to accurately predict and measure the potential consequences of actions, which can be challenging in practice.

Deontology

Contrary to utilitarianism, deontology is an ethical theory that emphasizes the inherent rightness or wrongness of actions, regardless of their consequences. Deontologists believe that certain actions are intrinsically moral or immoral based on universal principles or duties. Immanuel Kant, one of the most notable proponents of deontological ethics, argued that morality is grounded in rationality and that individuals have a duty to adhere to universal moral principles.

When employing a deontological framework in ethical decision making, legal professionals focus on the moral principles involved and the ethical duties they have. For example, if a lawyer is faced with a situation where they know a client is guilty but is still obligated to defend them, a deontological approach would prioritize the duty to provide zealous representation, despite the potential negative consequences.

Virtue Ethics

Virtue ethics is an ethical framework that centers around the development of virtuous character traits. According to this theory, ethical decision making is rooted in the cultivation of qualities such as honesty, fairness, justice, compassion, and integrity. Virtue ethics looks beyond individual actions and focuses on developing a morally admirable character.

In the context of legal studies, the application of virtue ethics involves considering the underlying character traits and virtues that guide legal professionals in their decision making. Legal professionals should strive to develop and embody virtues that promote justice, fairness, and the greater good of society.

Rights-Based Approaches

Rights-based approaches to ethical decision making are centered on the belief that individuals possess fundamental rights that should be protected. These rights may be inherent, granted by law, or derived from societal moral standards. Ethical decisions are evaluated based on their compatibility with protecting and respecting these rights.

There are different types of rights-based approaches, including the consequentialist rights theory, which balances individual rights against the overall consequences, and the non-consequentialist rights theory, which assigns absolute value to certain rights and prohibits their violation under any circumstances.

In legal studies, rights-based approaches are typically applied when considering the rights and liberties delineated in constitutions and legal frameworks. Legal professionals need to carefully consider the balancing of individual rights against the common good and the potential limitations or restrictions that may be imposed for the benefit of society.

The Prima Facie Duty Theory

The prima facie duty theory, developed by philosopher W.D. Ross, suggests that ethical decision making involves considering multiple prima facie duties, which are moral obligations that hold unless overridden by a more pressing duty. These duties include duties of fidelity, reparation, gratitude, justice, beneficence, self-improvement, and non-maleficence.

To apply this framework in legal studies, one must carefully consider competing prima facie duties and determine which holds more weight in a particular context. This approach acknowledges that ethical decision making involves complex trade-offs and the evaluation of different moral obligations.

Ethical Decision Making Process

While these ethical decision making frameworks provide guidance, it is important to have a structured process for ethical decision making. The following steps can help legal professionals navigate moral dilemmas:

1. Identify the ethical issue: Clearly define the problem and identify the values and principles at stake.

2. Gather relevant information: Collect all the facts and relevant data related to the issue at hand.

3. Identify alternative courses of action: Generate a range of possible actions that can be taken to address the issue.

4. Evaluate the alternatives: Apply the selected ethical frameworks to assess the potential consequences, moral duties, virtues, or rights related to each alternative.

5. Make a decision: Select the course of action that best aligns with the ethical frameworks applied.

6. Implement the decision: Put the chosen course of action into practice.

7. Reflect and learn: Evaluate the outcome and consequences of the decision, and use it as a learning experience for future ethical decision making.

It is important to note that ethical decision making is not always clear-cut, and conflicts between different frameworks may arise. Legal professionals should engage in ongoing reflection and dialogue to continuously refine their ethical decision making skills and approach.

Conclusion

Ethical decision making is a critical aspect of legal studies, guiding legal professionals in navigating complex moral dilemmas. Different ethical decision making frameworks, such as utilitarianism, deontology, virtue ethics, rights-based approaches, and the prima facie duty theory, provide valuable insights into the complexities of ethical decision making. By following a structured ethical decision making process, legal professionals can ensure that their actions uphold the values and principles necessary for a just and equitable legal system.

Ethical Principles and Values in Legal Studies

Ethics plays a crucial role in legal studies as it provides a framework for understanding the moral principles and values that guide the practice of law. In this section, we will explore the ethical principles and values that are particularly relevant and influential in the field of legal studies. We will examine how these principles and values shape the conduct of legal professionals, influence decision-making in legal practice, and contribute to the promotion of justice and fairness in society.

Ethical Principles

Ethical principles are fundamental guidelines that govern the behavior and actions of individuals in a particular field. In legal studies, several ethical principles have been identified as essential to uphold the integrity and ethical standards of the profession. Let's explore some of these principles:

1. **Justice:** The principle of justice emphasizes treating every individual fairly and impartially, regardless of their social status, background, or personal characteristics. It entails promoting equal access to legal resources, fair treatment in legal proceedings, and equitable distribution of legal remedies. Legal professionals are ethically obligated to work towards the attainment of justice and ensure that their actions contribute to a just and fair legal system.

2. **Integrity:** Integrity is a core ethical principle that underlies the legal profession. It involves adhering to high moral and ethical standards, demonstrating honesty, and upholding the principles of truthfulness and sincerity. Legal professionals are expected to act with integrity in all aspects of their practice, maintaining their credibility and trustworthiness.

3. **Confidentiality:** Confidentiality is a critical ethical principle in legal studies, particularly in the attorney-client relationship. Legal professionals have a duty to maintain the confidentiality of information shared by their clients, safeguarding their rights to privacy and ensuring that privileged information is not disclosed without informed consent. Upholding confidentiality instills trust and confidence in the legal system and promotes effective legal representation.

4. **Impartiality:** Impartiality is the principle of being unbiased and neutral in decision-making. Legal professionals are required to base their actions and decisions solely on legal merits, without any personal bias or prejudice. Impartiality ensures equal treatment and fair outcomes and upholds the principles of justice and fairness in the legal system.

5. **Competence:** Competence is an essential ethical principle for legal professionals. It involves possessing the necessary knowledge, skills, and expertise to provide effective legal services to clients. Legal professionals have a responsibility to stay updated with relevant legal developments, engage in continuous professional development, and provide competent representation and advice to clients.

These ethical principles form the foundation of ethical conduct in legal studies and guide the behavior and actions of legal professionals. By adhering to these principles, legal professionals contribute to the promotion of justice, fairness, and ethical practice within the legal system.

Ethical Values

In addition to ethical principles, ethical values play a significant role in shaping the ethical landscape of legal studies. Ethical values are broad ideals or concepts that guide moral decision-making and behavior. Let's explore some of the key ethical values in legal studies:

1. **Respect for Autonomy:** Respect for autonomy is an important ethical value in legal studies. It emphasizes the right of individuals to make informed choices and decisions regarding their own lives. Legal professionals should respect and uphold the autonomy of their clients, ensuring that they have the necessary information and support to make decisions that align with their values and interests.

2. **Dignity:** Dignity is a fundamental ethical value that recognizes and respects the inherent worth and value of every individual. Legal professionals have an ethical obligation to treat clients, colleagues, and all individuals involved in the legal process with dignity and respect, regardless of their circumstances or positions.

3. **Fairness:** Fairness is a core ethical value that aligns with the principles of justice and equality. Legal professionals should strive to ensure that legal processes and outcomes are fair and equitable, promoting equal treatment, and avoiding any form of discrimination or bias.

4. **Social Responsibility:** Social responsibility is an ethical value that recognizes the obligation of legal professionals to contribute to the well-being of society. It involves using legal knowledge and skills to address social issues, promote access to justice, and advocate for positive social change. By embracing social responsibility, legal professionals can contribute to the achievement of a more equitable and just society.

5. **Accountability:** Accountability is an ethical value that emphasizes the responsibility of legal professionals for their actions and decisions. Legal professionals should be accountable for the consequences of their actions and ensure that they comply with relevant laws, regulations, and ethical standards. Accountability promotes transparency, integrity, and trust in the legal system.

These ethical values serve as guiding principles for legal professionals, shaping their ethical decision-making, and encouraging ethical behavior. By embracing these values, legal professionals contribute to the ethical practice of law and strengthen the overall integrity of the legal system.

Case Study: Balancing Ethical Principles in Legal Practice

To better understand how ethical principles and values operate in legal studies, let's consider a hypothetical case study.

Imagine that an attorney represents a client who has been accused of a serious crime. The attorney believes in the client's innocence based on the available evidence, but also recognizes that the client's acquittal could potentially jeopardize public safety. In this case, the attorney faces a dilemma in balancing the ethical principles of justice and impartiality.

The principle of justice requires the attorney to provide their client with a vigorous defense and work towards achieving a just outcome. However, the principle of impartiality demands that the attorney consider the broader implications of their client's actions on societal well-being.

To navigate this ethical dilemma, the attorney must carefully consider the ethical principles and values at play. They must respect their client's autonomy and provide competent representation while also considering the potential impact on public safety. This may involve engaging in ethical decision-making frameworks, consulting colleagues or legal ethics experts, and critically examining the available legal and moral arguments.

By evaluating the ethical principles and values from multiple perspectives, the attorney can strive to make an ethically informed decision that upholds the integrity of the legal system and serves the interest of justice.

Additional Resources

For further reading and exploration of ethical principles and values in legal studies, consider the following resources:

- *Legal Ethics: A Comparative Perspective* by Richard L. Abel and Philip S.C. Lewis

- *Ethics in Practice: Lawyers' Roles, Responsibilities, and Regulation* by Deborah L. Rhode

- *Ethics in Law: Lawyers' Responsibility and Accountability in Australia* by John F. Kearney and Lucinda M. A. Beames

These resources provide valuable insights into the nuances of ethical principles and values in legal studies, offering practical guidance and ethical frameworks for legal professionals.

Conclusion

Ethical principles and values play a central role in legal studies, shaping the behavior and actions of legal professionals, guiding decision-making processes, and promoting justice and fairness in society. By upholding ethical principles such as justice, integrity, confidentiality, impartiality, and competence, legal professionals contribute to the ethical practice of law. Ethical values such as respect for autonomy, dignity, fairness, social responsibility, and accountability further guide their conduct and moral decision-making. By understanding and embracing these ethical principles and values, legal professionals can navigate complex moral dilemmas, promote ethical engagement, and contribute to a more equitable and just legal system.

Ethical Dilemmas in Legal Practice

In the field of legal practice, professionals often encounter ethical dilemmas that require careful consideration and decision-making. These dilemmas arise when there is a conflict between different ethical principles, values, or obligations, making it challenging to determine the right course of action. This section explores some common ethical dilemmas faced by legal practitioners and provides frameworks for resolving these dilemmas in an ethical manner.

Conflicts of Interest

One significant ethical dilemma that often arises in legal practice is conflicts of interest. A conflict of interest occurs when a lawyer's personal or professional interests interfere with their ability to provide unbiased and loyal representation to a client. For example, if a lawyer represents both the defendant and the plaintiff in a case, it can create a conflict of interest and compromise the lawyer's duty of loyalty to each client.

Resolving conflicts of interest requires careful analysis and adherence to professional codes of conduct. Legal professionals must identify potential conflicts at the outset and disclose them to the affected clients. In some cases, the lawyer may need to withdraw from representing one or both parties to avoid a conflict of interest. By maintaining transparency and acting in the best interests of their clients, legal practitioners can navigate this ethical dilemma effectively.

Duty of Confidentiality

The duty of confidentiality is a fundamental ethical obligation for legal professionals. It requires lawyers to protect the information shared by their clients and refrain from disclosing it without the client's consent. However, this obligation can create ethical dilemmas when it conflicts with other legal or ethical duties.

For instance, a lawyer may learn information from a client that suggests they pose a threat to themselves or others. In such cases, the duty of confidentiality conflicts with the lawyer's ethical obligation to protect the safety and well-being of individuals. Resolving this dilemma involves striking a balance between maintaining confidentiality and fulfilling the broader duty to prevent harm.

Legal practitioners must carefully consider the exceptions to the duty of confidentiality outlined in legal and ethical guidelines. For example, they may be required to disclose certain information to prevent imminent harm or comply with legal obligations, such as reporting child abuse. By navigating these complexities, lawyers can uphold their duty of confidentiality while addressing potential ethical issues.

Ethical Responsibilities in Negotiations

Ethical dilemmas often arise during negotiations when legal professionals must balance advocating for their clients' interests while adhering to ethical principles. Negotiations involve strategic decision-making that may require lawyers to push the boundaries of ethical conduct.

One common dilemma is the tension between truth-telling and the duty to advocate zealously. Lawyers may face ethical dilemmas when deciding how much information to disclose or whether to provide accurate but potentially damaging information about the opposing party. Engaging in deceptive practices during negotiations can undermine the integrity of the legal profession and erode public trust.

To address this dilemma, legal professionals can adopt principled negotiation approaches that focus on mutual gains and fairness. This involves being honest and transparent while seeking to create collaborative solutions. By prioritizing ethical conduct during negotiations, lawyers can maintain their professional integrity while still zealously representing their clients.

Ethics in Social Media Use

The rise of social media has introduced new ethical dilemmas for legal practitioners. Lawyers must navigate the use of social media platforms professionally while upholding their ethical duties.

One ethical concern is the attorney-client privilege and the potential risks associated with communicating about legal matters through social media. Lawyers must educate their clients about the risks of discussing legal cases or sharing sensitive information on social media platforms, which can compromise confidential communications.

Moreover, legal professionals should be cautious about their own social media presence. Inappropriate or unprofessional behavior on social media platforms can damage their professional reputation and create conflicts of interest.

To address these dilemmas, legal practitioners should establish clear social media policies for themselves and their clients. By exercising caution and using social media platforms responsibly, lawyers can avoid ethical pitfalls and protect their clients' interests.

Conclusion

Ethical dilemmas are an inherent part of legal practice, requiring legal professionals to navigate complex situations where competing ethical principles or obligations exist. By recognizing and understanding these dilemmas, adhering to professional codes of conduct, and engaging in thoughtful decision-making, legal practitioners can uphold their ethical responsibilities and promote justice in their profession. When faced with ethical dilemmas, legal professionals should seek guidance from legal ethics committees, professional organizations, or mentors to ensure they make informed choices that uphold the values and principles of the legal profession.

Factors Influencing Ethical Decision Making

Ethical decision making in legal studies is a complex and multifaceted process. It involves considering a variety of factors that can influence the ethical choices made by legal professionals. These factors can include personal values, professional obligations, societal norms, legal principles, and the specific context in which the decision is being made. In this section, we will explore some of the key factors that can influence ethical decision making in legal studies.

Personal Values

Personal values play a significant role in ethical decision making. Legal professionals bring their own set of values and beliefs to their practice, which can guide their decision-making process. These values may include honesty, integrity, fairness, and respect for others. However, personal values can also vary among individuals, and conflicts between personal values and professional obligations can arise. For example, a lawyer may personally oppose a particular law or legal action due to their moral convictions. In such cases, legal professionals must navigate the tension between their personal values and their professional responsibilities.

Professional Obligations

Legal professionals have specific professional obligations that influence their ethical decision making. These obligations are outlined in professional codes of conduct and ethics, which provide guidance on how legal professionals should conduct themselves in their practice. For example, lawyers are obligated to maintain client confidentiality, act in the best interests of their clients, and provide competent and diligent representation. These obligations can sometimes come into conflict with other ethical considerations, requiring legal professionals to carefully balance their responsibilities.

Societal Norms and Expectations

Societal norms and expectations can also impact ethical decision making in legal studies. The legal profession is deeply interconnected with society, and legal professionals often face pressure to align their actions and decisions with societal expectations. For instance, changing societal attitudes towards issues like gender equality, racial justice, and environmental sustainability can influence legal professionals to advocate for social change through their work. However, societal norms and expectations are not static and can vary across different cultures and contexts. Legal professionals need to critically evaluate these norms and ensure that they uphold the principles of justice and fairness.

Legal Principles and Rules

Legal principles and rules establish the framework within which ethical decision making takes place. Legal professionals must consider legal precedents, statutes, regulations, and case law when making ethical decisions. These legal principles and rules help guide the interpretation and application of the law in specific cases. However, legal principles and rules can be subject to interpretation and may not always provide clear-cut answers to ethical dilemmas. Legal professionals must carefully analyze the relevant legal framework and consider the potential ethical implications of their decisions.

Context and Consequences

The context in which an ethical decision is made and its potential consequences are crucial factors that influence decision making in legal studies. Legal professionals must consider the specific circumstances surrounding a case, such as the nature of the legal issue, the parties involved, and the potential impact of their decision. They need to weigh the potential benefits and harms that may result from their actions. Additionally, legal professionals should consider the long-term consequences of their decisions and how they align with the principles of justice and fairness.

Ethical Reasoning and Reflection

Ethical decision making in legal studies requires ethical reasoning and reflection. Legal professionals need to engage in thoughtful analysis and consider the ethical implications of their choices. They may use ethical frameworks and models to guide their thinking, such as consequentialism, deontology, virtue ethics, or the ethics of care. Ethical reasoning involves considering the potential ethical problems, evaluating the available options, and selecting the course of action that aligns with ethical principles and values.

Influence of Stakeholders

Stakeholders play a significant role in ethical decision making in legal studies. Stakeholders may include clients, colleagues, judges, regulatory bodies, the public, and the media. These stakeholders can have different interests, priorities, and perspectives that can influence the decision-making process. For example, legal professionals may face pressure from clients to act in their best interests, even if it conflicts with ethical considerations. Understanding and managing these stakeholder influences is crucial for ethical decision making.

Challenges and Ethical Dilemmas

Ethical decision making in legal studies often involves facing challenging ethical dilemmas. These are situations where there are multiple competing ethical considerations and no clear or easy solution. Legal professionals must navigate these dilemmas by carefully considering the relevant factors and exploring potential solutions. Ethical decision-making frameworks, such as the four principles approach or the ethics decision tree, can offer guidance in resolving these dilemmas.

Navigating ethical decision making in legal studies requires a careful and thoughtful approach. Legal professionals must consider personal values, professional obligations, societal norms, legal principles, the context, consequences, ethical reasoning, stakeholder influences, and the presence of ethical dilemmas. By reflecting on these factors and engaging in critical ethical analysis, legal professionals can make informed and ethical decisions that promote justice and uphold the principles of a fair and just legal system.

Case Study: Balancing Client Confidentiality and Public Safety

Consider the case of a defense attorney who represents a client charged with a serious crime. The attorney learns that their client plans to harm an individual who is not involved in the case. The attorney is faced with a dilemma: maintain client confidentiality as required by professional obligations or disclose the information to prevent harm to an innocent person.

In this case, the attorney must navigate the tension between their duty of confidentiality to their client and their obligation to protect public safety. They should consider the legal and ethical principles surrounding confidentiality and the potential consequences of their decision. While maintaining client confidentiality is essential to the attorney-client relationship, it does not absolve the attorney from the duty to prevent harm to others. The attorney may need to assess the level of threat posed by their client's intentions and consider potential alternatives, such as seeking the client's consent to disclose the information or consulting with legal and ethical experts for guidance.

This case exemplifies the intricate decision-making process legal professionals face when ethical obligations come into conflict. It underscores the importance of carefully weighing the relevant factors and exercising ethical reasoning in making ethically informed decisions.

Key Takeaways

+ Ethical decision making in legal studies is influenced by personal values, professional obligations, societal norms, legal principles, context, consequences, ethical reasoning, stakeholder influences, and the presence of ethical dilemmas.

+ Legal professionals must navigate the tension between personal values and professional obligations, ensuring they uphold the principles of justice and fairness.

+ Societal norms and expectations shape ethical decision making and can drive legal professionals to advocate for social change.

+ Legal principles and rules provide a framework for ethical decision making, but their interpretation and application may require careful analysis.

- The context in which a decision is made and its potential consequences should be considered, including the long-term impact on justice and fairness.

- Ethical reasoning and reflection, guided by ethical frameworks, help legal professionals analyze ethical problems and select the most ethically sound course of action.

- Stakeholder influences, such as clients, colleagues, and the public, can shape ethical decision making and should be managed ethically.

- Ethical dilemmas are common in legal studies, and legal professionals must navigate these challenges using ethical decision-making frameworks and models.

Further Reading

- Arin N. Reeves, *The Next IQ: The Next Level of Intelligence for 21st Century Leaders* (2012).

- Deborah L. Rhode, *The Trouble with Lawyers* (2015).

- David Luban et al., *Legal Ethics: Law Stories* (2010).

- Lisa G. Lerman and Philip G. Schrag, *Ethical Problems in the Practice of Law* (2017).

- Z. Bankowski, *Ethics in Law: Lawyers' Responsibility and Accountability in Australia* (2016).

- Stephen Kohn, *The Whistleblower's Handbook: A Step-by-Step Guide to Doing What's Right and Protecting Yourself* (2017).

Exercises

1. Identify a recent legal case that involved a conflict between personal values and professional obligations. Discuss how the legal professional navigated this conflict and the ethical considerations at stake.

2. Choose a legal principle, such as fairness or justice, and discuss how it can influence ethical decision making in legal studies. Provide examples of how this principle might be applied in practice.

3. Research a legal profession's code of ethics or conduct, and identify key ethical obligations outlined in the code. Discuss the significance of these obligations in guiding ethical decision making.

4. Consider a specific legal issue or case. Analyze how different societal norms and expectations might influence ethical decision making in relation to that issue or case.

5. Imagine you are a legal professional faced with an ethical dilemma. Apply an ethical decision-making framework, such as consequentialism or deontology, to analyze the dilemma and propose a course of action.

Balancing Competing Ethical Principles

In legal studies, professionals often face complex ethical dilemmas where they must balance competing ethical principles. These dilemmas arise when different ethical values or principles come into conflict, making it challenging to determine the appropriate course of action. Balancing these competing ethical principles requires careful consideration and analysis.

Understanding Competing Ethical Principles

Competing ethical principles can emerge from various sources, including different philosophical theories, legal rules, professional codes of conduct, and societal values. These principles may include concepts such as justice, autonomy, beneficence, non-maleficence, honesty, fairness, and equality. For example, consider a situation where a lawyer represents a client charged with a serious crime. The lawyer's duty to advocate zealously for the client's interests (a principle of legal representation) may conflict with the lawyer's duty to ensure justice and fairness (a principle of legal ethics).

Identifying and Analyzing Ethical Dilemmas

To balance competing ethical principles effectively, legal professionals must first identify and analyze the ethical dilemmas they face. This involves evaluating the conflicting principles, understanding their underlying values, and considering the consequences of each possible action. For instance, in the previous example of a lawyer representing a client charged with a serious crime, the attorney must consider the potential harm caused by advocating for a client they believe to be guilty, while also ensuring the client's legal rights are upheld.

Ethical Decision-Making Frameworks

To navigate the complexities of balancing competing ethical principles, legal professionals can employ ethical decision-making frameworks. These frameworks provide a structured approach to analyze ethical dilemmas, weigh different considerations, and make ethically sound decisions. One widely used framework is the "principlism approach," which involves identifying the relevant ethical principles, evaluating their weight and importance in the given context, and considering the potential consequences of each course of action.

Case Study: Balancing Confidentiality with Public Safety

A common scenario that highlights the challenges of balancing ethical principles is the duty of confidentiality in the legal profession. Lawyers have a professional responsibility to maintain client confidentiality, but there are instances where it may conflict with public safety. For example, if a client discloses an intention to commit a serious crime that could harm others, the lawyer faces a dilemma between upholding their duty of confidentiality and preventing harm to potential victims.

In such cases, legal professionals need to consider the principle of confidentiality, the principle of preventing harm, and the legal and ethical obligations involved. This requires a careful analysis of the potential consequences of maintaining confidentiality versus breaching it to protect public safety. Legal professionals may have to consult their professional codes of conduct, seek guidance from colleagues, or even involve relevant authorities to address such complex situations.

Tips for Balancing Competing Ethical Principles

Balancing competing ethical principles is a nuanced and challenging task. Here are some tips to help legal professionals navigate these dilemmas effectively:

1. Understand the relevant ethical principles and their underlying values. 2. Consider the context and specific circumstances of the dilemma. 3. Analyze the potential consequences of each course of action. 4. Consult professional codes of conduct and legal rules relevant to the situation. 5. Seek guidance from experienced colleagues or ethics committees. 6. Reflect on personal values and ethical beliefs to aid decision-making. 7. Consider the long-term implications and ethical implications of the decision. 8. Regularly engage in ethics training and stay updated on current ethical debates and controversies.

Conclusion

Balancing competing ethical principles is an essential skill for legal professionals. By applying ethical decision-making frameworks, analyzing the context of ethical dilemmas, and considering the consequences of different actions, legal professionals can navigate these dilemmas and make morally justifiable choices. It is important to recognize that ethical dilemmas are complex and require thoughtful reflection, continuous learning, and a commitment to ethical practice to ensure justice and fairness in the legal profession.

Professional Codes of Conduct and Ethics in Legal Studies

In the field of legal studies, professionals are guided by a set of ethical principles and codes of conduct that help navigate the complex landscape of the legal profession. These codes of conduct provide a framework for legal professionals to uphold moral and ethical standards in their practice, promoting fairness, justice, and professional integrity. This section will explore the importance of professional codes of conduct and ethics in legal studies, discuss their application in different legal contexts, and highlight some of the key ethical challenges faced by legal professionals.

The Importance of Professional Codes of Conduct

Professional codes of conduct serve as a compass for legal professionals, guiding their behavior and ensuring the delivery of justice in an ethical and accountable manner. These codes provide a framework for legal practice based on principles such as integrity, confidentiality, competence, and fairness. Adhering to these codes helps maintain the trust and confidence of clients, the public, and the legal profession itself.

Application of Professional Codes of Conduct

Professional codes of conduct apply to various aspects of legal practice, including client representation, advocacy, conflict resolution, and professional relationships. Let's explore some key areas where ethical considerations come into play:

1. **Client Representation:** Legal professionals have a duty to act in the best interests of their clients while maintaining professional integrity. This requires maintaining client confidentiality, avoiding conflicts of interest, and providing competent and zealous representation.

2. **Advocacy:** Legal professionals have a responsibility to act as advocates for their clients, presenting their cases diligently and ethically. This involves adhering to rules of professional conduct during courtroom proceedings, maintaining honesty in presenting facts and evidence, and respecting the dignity and rights of all parties involved.

3. **Conflict Resolution:** Legal professionals often find themselves in situations where conflicts of interest may arise. Ethical codes provide guidance on how to identify, address, and mitigate conflicts of interest, ensuring that the interests of clients are not compromised.

4. **Professional Relationships:** Codes of conduct also govern professional relationships, emphasizing respectful and professional interactions among legal professionals, clients, colleagues, and the judiciary. These codes aim to prevent harassment, discrimination, and unethical behavior within the legal profession.

Ethical Challenges in Legal Practice

Legal professionals face various ethical challenges in their day-to-day practice. It is important to recognize and address these challenges to uphold professional integrity and promote justice. Some common ethical challenges include:

1. **Confidentiality:** Maintaining client confidentiality is a cornerstone of the attorney-client relationship. However, legal professionals may face dilemmas when balancing confidentiality with other ethical obligations, such as preventing harm to others or complying with legal requirements. Resolving these conflicts requires careful ethical reasoning and adherence to professional codes of conduct.

2. **Conflicts of Interest:** Identifying and managing conflicts of interest can be challenging, especially in complex legal matters involving multiple parties. Legal professionals must navigate these conflicts ethically to ensure impartiality and avoid compromising the interests of their clients.

3. **Client Relations:** Building and maintaining effective client relationships may sometimes involve difficult decisions and delicate ethical considerations. Legal professionals must navigate issues such as client autonomy, informed consent, and the duty to provide honest and realistic advice.

4. **Ethics in Courtroom Advocacy:** Balancing zealous advocacy with ethical obligations in the courtroom can present challenges for legal professionals. Ethical issues may arise when presenting evidence, questioning witnesses, or making arguments. Legal professionals must uphold their duty to the court while representing their clients' interests.

5. **Professional Responsibility:** Legal professionals have a responsibility to maintain their professional competence and to ensure their actions align with legal and ethical standards. Staying informed about changes in the law, engaging in continuing education, and seeking advice from colleagues or ethics committees are essential for meeting these responsibilities.

Resources for Ethical Guidance

To assist legal professionals in navigating ethical challenges, there are several resources available:

1. **Professional Associations:** Legal professionals often belong to professional associations that provide guidance on ethical conduct. These associations may have their own codes of conduct and ethics committees to address specific ethical issues.

2. **Bar Associations:** Bar associations regulate the legal profession and often provide guidance on ethical conduct specific to the jurisdiction. They may offer ethics hotlines or committees to address ethical inquiries or complaints.

3. **Legal Ethics Opinions:** Ethics opinions issued by professional associations, bar associations, or ethics committees offer guidance on specific ethical issues. Legal professionals can consult these opinions to better understand the application of ethical principles in practice.

4. **Continuing Legal Education (CLE):** Lifelong learning through CLE programs is essential for legal professionals to stay updated on changes in the law and ethical best practices. These programs often address ethical issues and provide guidance on navigating ethical challenges.

Promoting Ethical Conduct

Promoting ethical conduct in legal studies requires a collective effort from legal professionals, educators, and regulatory bodies. Some strategies to promote ethical conduct include:

1. **Education and Training:** Including ethics education as a core component of legal studies programs is crucial for instilling ethical values and promoting critical thinking about ethical dilemmas. Educators should integrate case studies, discussions, and simulations into their curriculum to enhance ethical decision-making skills.

2. **Strong Codes of Conduct:** Professional associations, bar associations, and regulatory bodies should regularly review and update their codes of conduct to reflect evolving ethical challenges in the legal profession. These codes should provide clear guidance on ethical standards, address emerging ethical issues, and support professional development.

3. **Mentoring and Supervision:** Establishing mentoring programs and promoting effective supervision in legal practice settings can help guide new legal professionals in ethical decision making. Experienced practitioners can provide valuable insights and support in navigating ethical challenges.

4. **Ethics Committees:** Professional associations and regulatory bodies should establish ethics committees to address ethical concerns, provide guidance, and address complaints regarding ethical misconduct. These committees play a crucial role in upholding ethical standards and ensuring accountability within the legal profession.

5. **Ongoing Professional Development:** Legal professionals should engage in ongoing professional development, including participation in CLE programs, to enhance their ethical knowledge and skills. By staying informed about changes in the law and emerging ethical issues, legal professionals can make well-informed ethical decisions.

Conclusion

Professional codes of conduct and ethics serve as a moral compass for legal professionals, guiding their behavior and promoting ethical practices in legal studies. Adhering to these codes is essential for maintaining the integrity of the legal profession and upholding the principles of justice. By understanding the application of ethical principles in different legal contexts and being aware of the challenges they may face, legal professionals can navigate moral dilemmas and ensure the promotion of justice in their practice.

Ethical Issues in Legal Education

Ethical issues in legal education encompass a range of complex and important considerations that arise in the process of educating future legal professionals. Legal education plays a crucial role in shaping the moral compass and ethical conduct of lawyers, judges, and other legal practitioners. This section explores some of the key ethical issues that arise in the context of legal education and offers insights into addressing these challenges.

Importance of Ethical Education in Legal Training

Ethical education is an essential component of legal training as it helps develop the moral character and professional behavior of future legal practitioners. It provides students with a foundation for understanding the ethical dimensions of the legal profession and equips them with the necessary tools to navigate ethical challenges they may encounter throughout their careers.

One of the primary goals of legal education is to cultivate a deep understanding of legal principles and doctrines. However, legal education must also emphasize the importance of ethical standards and personal integrity, as these qualities are fundamental to promoting justice and upholding the rule of law. Ethical education within legal training helps instill a sense of ethical responsibility, critical thinking, and professionalism in students.

Ethical Challenges in Legal Education

Ethical challenges arise in legal education in various ways, necessitating careful consideration and effective strategies for their resolution. Some of the key ethical issues include:

1. Ensuring Academic Integrity   Maintaining academic integrity is crucial in legal education. Any form of cheating, plagiarism, or academic dishonesty undermines the integrity of the educational process. Law schools must establish clear policies and procedures to promote academic integrity, conduct regular assessments, and enforce academic honesty rules.

2. Balancing Competing Interests   Legal education often involves reconciling competing interests, such as in the selection of course materials or curriculum design. Educators must navigate these complexities ethically by considering the diverse perspectives and needs of students while maintaining the integrity of the curriculum and legal principles.

3. Promoting Diversity and Inclusion   Promoting diversity and inclusion is an ethical imperative in legal education. Law schools must strive to create an inclusive and equitable learning environment that respects the dignity and worth of all individuals, irrespective of their race, gender, ethnicity, or background. Educators need to be mindful of implicit biases and incorporate diverse perspectives into the curriculum and classroom discussions.

4. Addressing Power Dynamics   Power dynamics within legal education can create ethical challenges. Educators must be cognizant of their power and influence over students and exercise that authority responsibly. They should promote a respectful learning environment where students are encouraged to question and engage critically with the subject matter, while still maintaining appropriate boundaries.

5. Providing Practical Skills Training   Legal education should not only focus on theoretical knowledge but also provide practical skills training. Ethically, educators have a responsibility to equip students with the competencies required for effective legal practice. This includes teaching professional ethics, legal writing, negotiation skills, oral advocacy, and client counseling, among others.

Strategies for Addressing Ethical Issues in Legal Education

To address ethical issues in legal education, several strategies can be employed:

1. Incorporating Ethics Across the Curriculum   Ethical considerations should be integrated throughout the entire legal curriculum. Rather than treating ethics as a standalone subject, it should be woven into various courses, ensuring that students develop a deep understanding of ethical dilemmas across different areas of law.

2. Engaging Ethical Role Models   Law schools should invite legal professionals with high ethical standards to interact with students and serve as role models. These guest speakers can provide practical insights into ethical decision-making and share their experiences and challenges in upholding ethical principles in their practice.

3. Encouraging Reflective Practice   Reflection is a powerful tool for ethical development. Law schools should encourage students to engage in reflective practice, which involves thoughtful consideration of the ethical implications of legal theories and their application. Through guided reflection exercises, students can enhance their ethical awareness and decision-making skills.

4. Fostering Peer Discussions Promoting open and respectful dialogue among students fosters critical thinking and enhances ethical literacy. Law schools should encourage group discussions, seminars, and moot court sessions, creating spaces for students to reflect on and debate ethical issues, helping them develop ethical reasoning and communication skills.

5. Emphasizing Professional Development Legal education should not solely focus on academic knowledge but also prioritize professional development. This includes instilling ethical values, promoting professionalism, and educating students on the importance of ethical conduct in their future legal careers. Workshops, mentorship programs, and internships can help students develop the skills and ethical mindset necessary for legal practice.

Case Study: Addressing Bias in Legal Education

One concrete example of an ethical issue faced in legal education is addressing bias. Bias can manifest in various forms, including racial bias, gender bias, and unconscious bias. To address this issue, law schools can take proactive steps:

Recognizing and Acknowledging Bias Law schools should acknowledge the presence of bias and the need to address it within the educational environment. This can be done through public statements, workshops, or seminars that highlight the importance of addressing biases in legal education.

Developing Inclusive Curricula Faculty members should critically evaluate the existing curriculum for any biases and ensure that course materials and examples reflect diversity and inclusivity. Introducing case studies and scenarios that highlight different perspectives and experiences can help students develop a better understanding of bias and its implications.

Training Faculty and Staff Law schools should provide training and workshops to faculty and staff on recognizing and addressing bias. This includes bringing in experts to facilitate discussions on unconscious bias, systemic bias, and promoting inclusive teaching practices. Faculty members should be equipped with tools to create an inclusive and respectful learning environment.

Promoting a Diverse Learning Community Law schools should actively recruit faculty, staff, and students from diverse backgrounds to create a vibrant learning community. This diversity enhances the richness of perspectives and fosters a more open and inclusive dialogue on ethical issues.

Encouraging Dialogue and Reflection Law schools should create opportunities for open dialogue and reflection on bias and its impact. This can be done through student-led initiatives, guest lectures, or moderated panel discussions. It is important to provide a safe space for students to express their concerns, challenge biases, and engage in conversations that promote mutual respect and understanding.

By addressing bias in legal education, law schools can cultivate a more inclusive and equitable learning environment, preparing students to become ethical legal professionals who are sensitive to the diverse needs of their clients and communities.

Conclusion

Ethical issues in legal education require careful attention and proactive strategies to ensure the ethical development of future legal professionals. By incorporating ethics throughout the curriculum, engaging ethical role models, fostering reflective practice, encouraging peer discussions, and emphasizing professional development, law schools can equip students with the knowledge and skills necessary to navigate ethical challenges in their legal careers. Addressing specific ethical issues, such as bias, is imperative to create a more inclusive and just legal education system. Legal educators have a vital role in shaping the ethical landscape of the legal profession and promoting a more equitable and sustainable world through ethical legal education.

Conclusion

In this section, we have explored the ethical issues in legal studies. We have discussed various frameworks for ethical decision making, the importance of ethical principles and values, and the role of professional codes of conduct and ethics in legal practice. We have also examined the moral foundations of law and justice, including the concepts of morality, justice, and the relationship between them.

Furthermore, we have delved into the theories of law, such as natural law theory, legal positivism, legal realism, critical legal studies, and feminist legal theory. We have analyzed the ethical implications of legal principles and rules, as well as the complexities surrounding legal interpretation and application. Additionally, we have examined the concept of legal rights and responsibilities, exploring various theories and their implications.

The section also addressed ethical issues in the legal profession. We discussed the role and responsibilities of legal professionals, the ethical obligations in legal practice, and the challenges faced by legal professionals in maintaining ethical integrity. We explored topics such as confidentiality and attorney-client privilege, conflict of interest, and professional codes of conduct.

Moreover, we explored the intersection of social justice and human rights in legal studies. We examined theories of social justice and their implications, as well as the historical evolution and implementation of human rights. We also discussed social justice issues in legal studies, including poverty, inequality, gender equality, racial and ethnic justice, LGBTQ+ rights, environmental justice, and access to justice.

The section then moved on to ethical issues in criminal justice, specifically focusing on the ethics of the criminal justice system, capital punishment, and policing. We analyzed the principles of criminal justice ethics, the role and responsibilities of criminal justice professionals, and the various ethical dilemmas faced by law enforcement, prosecutors, and corrections officials.

Additionally, we explored the ethical challenges in business and commerce, including business ethics, corporate social responsibility, intellectual property rights, and the ethical implications of globalization. We also examined the role of law in social change and reform, discussing how law can be used as a tool for social change, as well as its impact on sustainable development and technological advancements.

In conclusion, the study of philosophical and ethical issues in legal studies is crucial in navigating moral dilemmas, promoting justice, and shaping a more equitable, just, and sustainable world. By understanding the interdisciplinary nature of legal studies, the relationship between philosophy and ethics, and the ethical frameworks and principles that guide legal practice, we can ensure that the legal profession upholds its responsibilities to society and promotes fairness, equality, and social justice. It is through critical analysis, thoughtful decision making, and adherence to ethical standards that legal professionals can contribute to a more just and equitable society.

Moral Foundations of Law and Justice

Concepts of Morality and Justice

Definition and Nature of Morality

Morality is a fundamental concept in philosophical and ethical discussions, serving as a guide for human behavior and decision-making. It refers to principles or standards of right and wrong, good and bad, that govern individuals and societies. In the context of legal studies, an understanding of morality is crucial in analyzing, critiquing, and shaping laws and legal systems.

Morality as a Human Construct

Morality is a human construct, shaped by cultural, social, and individual factors. It is a product of human reasoning, emotions, values, and experiences. While some argue for universal moral principles, it is widely acknowledged that moral beliefs and practices vary across cultures and historical periods.

Subjectivity vs. Objectivity of Morality

The nature of morality has long been a subject of debate. Some argue that morality is subjective, meaning it is based on individual beliefs or cultural norms. Others contend that morality has objective elements, rooted in universal principles or ethical theories.

Subjective morality sees moral judgments as a matter of personal preference or cultural relativism. It suggests that what is considered morally right or wrong can differ from person to person or culture to culture. However, this perspective raises challenges when faced with conflicting moral perspectives, as it may lead to a moral relativism that undermines widely accepted principles of justice.

Contrarily, proponents of objective morality argue that certain moral principles are inherent in human nature or derived from rationality. These principles are grounded in ethical theories such as utilitarianism, deontology, virtue ethics, or natural law theory. The objective stance allows for moral judgments that apply universally, providing a framework for assessing the morality of laws and legal systems.

Ethics vs. Morality: Understanding the Difference

While morality and ethics are often used interchangeably, they have distinct meanings. Morality refers to the principles and values that guide individuals' actions, whereas ethics refers to the study of moral principles, theories, and systems. Ethics seeks to understand and evaluate moral conduct, making it an essential component of legal studies.

Legal professionals must engage in ethical reasoning and decision-making, applying moral principles and considering the consequences of their actions. Ethical conduct is vital in maintaining public trust and upholding the integrity of the legal profession.

Moral Relativism vs. Moral Absolutism

Two contrasting approaches to morality are moral relativism and moral absolutism. Moral relativism posits that moral judgments are relative to individuals, cultures, or societies. It maintains that no moral principle is universally applicable, and judgments are shaped by cultural and historical contexts.

Moral absolutism, on the other hand, holds that certain moral principles are universally valid and binding, regardless of cultural differences or individual perspectives. This perspective asserts the existence of objective moral truths that should guide human behavior, even if they conflict with personal or cultural beliefs.

The debate between moral relativism and moral absolutism influences discussions on legal rights, social justice, and ethical decision-making. Striking a balance between cultural diversity and the pursuit of universal moral principles is a challenge that legal studies address.

Ethical Theories and Morality

Ethical theories provide frameworks for understanding and evaluating moral issues, including those encountered in legal studies. Some prominent ethical theories include:

- Utilitarianism: This theory evaluates actions based on their contribution to maximizing overall happiness or utility.

- Deontology: Deontological theories focus on the inherent rightness or wrongness of actions, based on duties and moral rules.

- Virtue ethics: Virtue ethics emphasizes the development of virtuous character traits and moral excellence.

- Natural law theory: Natural law theory posits that ethical principles are inherent in nature and can be discerned through human reason.

These theories offer different perspectives on how to determine what is morally right or wrong in a given situation. Legal professionals can draw on these theories to navigate ethical challenges and make morally informed decisions.

Ethical Dilemmas and Moral Decision Making

Legal studies often involve complex ethical dilemmas that require moral decision-making. Ethical dilemmas arise when there are conflicting moral principles or duties, making it challenging to determine the morally correct course of action.

Moral decision-making involves a process of ethical reasoning, whereby individuals evaluate the consequences, duties, and principles involved in a particular situation. Factors such as cultural norms, personal values, legal obligations, and pragmatic considerations may influence the decision-making process.

Resolving ethical dilemmas requires balancing competing moral principles and considering the potential consequences of different actions. This process is rarely easy, as moral choices often involve inherent trade-offs and conflicts.

Real-world Example: The Trolley Problem

The trolley problem is a classic ethical dilemma that demonstrates the challenges of moral decision-making. Imagine a trolley hurtling down a track towards five workers. You have the option to redirect the trolley to a different track, where only one worker will be harmed.

This scenario presents a conflict between the moral principles of minimizing harm (saving five lives) and not directly causing harm to others. Different ethical theories offer various perspectives on the morally correct course of action in this situation.

For instance, a utilitarian might argue that redirecting the trolley maximizes overall happiness by saving more lives. On the other hand, a deontologist may argue that intentionally causing harm to the single worker violates the moral rule against harming others.

The trolley problem highlights the complexities of moral decision-making and the role of ethical theories in analyzing real-world ethical dilemmas.

Conclusion

Understanding the definition and nature of morality is crucial for examining ethical issues in legal studies. Morality plays a vital role in shaping laws, legal systems, and the conduct of legal professionals. It is essential to consider differing perspectives on subjectivity vs. objectivity, moral relativism vs. moral absolutism, and how ethical theories inform moral decision-making. By exploring these concepts, legal studies can contribute to the development of a more just and ethical society.

Theories of Justice

In the study of legal studies, understanding the concepts of justice is crucial. Justice is a fundamental principle that guides the functioning of legal systems and the decision-making processes within those systems. Various theories have been proposed to explain the nature and principles of justice. In this section, we will explore some of the major theories of justice and their relevance in legal studies.

Distributive Justice

Distributive justice is concerned with the fair distribution of goods and resources in society. It seeks to answer the question of how society should allocate its resources, such as wealth, income, opportunities, and rights, in a just manner. There are several theories of distributive justice, each offering a different perspective on how resources should be distributed.

1. **Egalitarianism:** This theory emphasizes the equal distribution of resources among individuals. It argues that everyone should have an equal share of society's resources, regardless of their individual characteristics or contributions. Egalitarianism promotes equality and minimizes social inequalities.

2. **Utilitarianism:** Utilitarianism focuses on maximizing overall social welfare or happiness. According to this theory, resources should be distributed in a way that maximizes the overall well-being of society. It places importance on the greatest good for the greatest number of people, advocating for the allocation of resources based on their utility.

3. **Rawlsian Justice** (Theory of Justice as Fairness): Proposed by the philosopher John Rawls, this theory emphasizes fairness in resource distribution. It argues that resources should be distributed in a way that benefits the least advantaged members of society. Rawls proposes the concept of the "veil of ignorance," where individuals make decisions about resource distribution without knowing their own position in society. This ensures impartiality and fairness in the distribution process.

Retributive Justice

Retributive justice focuses on punishment and the moral responsibility of individuals who have committed wrongdoing. It aims to determine the appropriate punishment for individuals who have violated the law and seeks to find a balance between punishment and societal retribution.

1. **Retributivism:** Retributivism argues that individuals should be punished in proportion to the harm they have caused. It emphasizes the importance of individual responsibility and accountability for one's actions. The severity of punishment is based on the severity of the crime committed.

2. **Restorative Justice:** Restorative justice focuses on repairing the harm caused by criminal behavior and restoring the relationships between the victim, offender, and the community. It emphasizes healing and rehabilitation rather than punishment. Restorative justice approaches seek to involve all parties affected by the crime in the resolution process, promoting dialogue and understanding.

Procedural Justice

Procedural justice is concerned with the fairness and transparency of the decision-making process in legal systems. It focuses on the procedures and mechanisms used to resolve disputes and make decisions, rather than the outcomes themselves. This ensures that individuals are treated fairly and have equal access to justice.

1. **Rule of Law:** The principle of the rule of law forms the foundation of procedural justice. It emphasizes that laws should be applied uniformly and consistently, and that individuals should be treated equally before the law. The rule of law ensures that legal processes are predictable and transparent, enhancing public trust in the legal system.

2. **Procedural Due Process:** Procedural due process guarantees that individuals involved in legal proceedings are provided with fair and impartial processes. It ensures that individuals have the right to be heard, present evidence, and challenge decisions made against them. Procedural due process safeguards against arbitrary or unfair treatment in legal proceedings.

Social Justice

Social justice is concerned with the fair and equitable distribution of benefits and burdens in society. It addresses systemic inequalities and aims to create a more just and inclusive society.

1. **Economic Justice:** Economic justice focuses on addressing economic inequalities and ensuring that individuals have access to basic needs and opportunities. It seeks to reduce poverty, promote social welfare, and create a more equitable economic system.

2. **Gender Justice:** Gender justice aims to eliminate discrimination and promote equality between genders. It seeks to ensure equal opportunities, rights, and protections for all individuals, regardless of their gender identity or expression.

3. **Racial and Ethnic Justice:** Racial and ethnic justice focuses on eliminating racism and discrimination based on race or ethnicity. It aims to create a society where individuals are treated fairly and equally, regardless of their racial or ethnic background.

4. **LGBTQ+ Justice:** LGBTQ+ justice advocates for the fair and equal treatment of individuals who identify as lesbian, gay, bisexual, transgender, or queer/questioning. It seeks to eliminate discrimination and promote equal rights and protections for LGBTQ+ individuals.

In legal studies, these theories of justice provide a framework for understanding and analyzing legal systems, laws, and ethical considerations. They inform debates on social policy, human rights, and the role of law in promoting justice and equality. It is important for legal professionals to be aware of these theories and their implications in order to navigate moral dilemmas and shape a more just and equitable world.

Key Concepts

+ Distributive justice focuses on the fair distribution of resources in society, with theories such as egalitarianism, utilitarianism, and Rawlsian justice offering different perspectives on how resources should be allocated.

+ Retributive justice concerns punishment and determining appropriate consequences for individuals who have committed wrongdoing, with retributivism and restorative justice offering contrasting approaches.

+ Procedural justice emphasizes fairness and transparency in the decision-making process, ensuring that individuals are treated fairly and have equal access to justice through principles such as the rule of law and procedural due process.

+ Social justice addresses systemic inequalities and seeks to create a more just and inclusive society, addressing issues such as economic justice, gender justice, racial and ethnic justice, and LGBTQ+ justice.

Ethical Considerations

Understanding and applying theories of justice in legal studies raise ethical considerations. Legal professionals must balance the competing interests of fairness, equality, and social welfare while respecting individual rights and upholding the rule of law. Ethical decision-making frameworks and professional codes of conduct guide legal professionals in navigating these complex ethical dilemmas.

For example, legal professionals must consider the potential biases and limitations of different theories of justice and determine the most appropriate approach in a given context. They must also be aware of the potential implications of their actions on marginalized communities and work towards promoting social justice and equal opportunities within the legal system.

Ethics also play a crucial role in conducting legal research. Legal researchers must adhere to ethical guidelines and norms, ensuring the accuracy and integrity of their research methods and findings.

Key Takeaways

+ Theories of justice provide a framework for understanding the principles and values that underpin legal systems and decision-making processes.

+ Distributive justice focuses on the fair distribution of resources, while retributive justice concerns punishment and accountability for wrongdoing.

+ Procedural justice ensures fairness and transparency in legal processes, and social justice addresses systemic inequalities in society.

+ Ethical considerations play a crucial role in applying theories of justice in legal studies, guiding legal professionals in making ethical decisions and promoting social justice.

Unconventional Insight: Consider the case of affirmative action in college admissions. This policy aims to address historical inequalities in educational opportunities by providing preferential treatment to individuals from marginalized groups. The debate surrounding affirmative action involves different theories of justice. Supporters argue that it promotes distributive justice by rectifying past disadvantages, while opponents argue that it violates principles of fairness and meritocracy. This complex issue challenges us to critically analyze and apply theories of justice in real-world contexts.

Relationship between Morality and Justice

In order to understand the relationship between morality and justice, it is crucial to first define these two terms and explore their individual meanings. Morality refers to a set of principles or values that guide human behavior and determine what is right or wrong. It encompasses concepts such as fairness, honesty, compassion, and respect for the well-being of others. Justice, on the other hand, refers to the fair treatment of individuals and the distribution of resources and opportunities in a society.

Morality and justice are closely interconnected, as the principles of morality often form the foundation for the development and implementation of just laws and legal systems. Justice is ultimately achieved when moral ideals are translated into fair and equitable outcomes for all members of society. However, the relationship between morality and justice can be complex and nuanced, giving rise to ethical dilemmas and challenges.

One major aspect of the relationship between morality and justice is the question of whose moral principles should guide the determination of what is just. Different individuals and communities may have varying moral beliefs and values, leading to divergent interpretations of justice. For example, some may argue that justice requires the equal distribution of resources, while others may prioritize individual liberties and the free market.

There are several major philosophical theories that explore the relationship between morality and justice. These theories provide different perspectives on how moral principles should influence the exercise of justice. Utilitarianism, for instance, posits that justice should be based on the greatest overall happiness or well-being for the greatest number of people. This theory emphasizes the consequentialist aspect of justice, where the moral value of an action is determined by its outcomes.

In contrast, deontological ethics emphasizes the intrinsic value of moral principles and argues that justice should be based on adherence to certain duties or rights. Proponents of deontological ethics believe that justice is derived from universal principles that should be applied universally, regardless of the consequences.

Another important theory that explores the relationship between morality and justice is virtue ethics. This theory focuses on the development of virtuous character traits and argues that justice is achieved when individuals cultivate and embody these virtues. Virtue ethics emphasizes the importance of personal morality and integrity in the pursuit of justice.

Ethical dilemmas often arise when the principles of morality and justice appear to conflict with one another. For example, a moral obligation to protect individual rights and liberties may conflict with the need for social equality and the distribution of resources. Resolving such dilemmas requires careful consideration and a balancing of competing moral principles.

In legal studies, the relationship between morality and justice is crucial in shaping legal decision-making and the development of just legal systems. Legal principles and rules are often derived from moral values and principles, reflecting societal norms and expectations. However, the application of justice in a legal context also requires considerations of fairness, impartiality, and the protection of individual rights.

The relationship between morality and justice is not always clear-cut, as different moral perspectives and interpretations can lead to differing conceptions of justice. It is important for legal professionals and scholars to critically examine the moral foundations of legal systems and to actively engage in ethical decision-making. This includes considering the ethical implications of legal principles, rules, and practices, and finding ways to promote fair and equitable outcomes for all members of society.

In conclusion, the relationship between morality and justice is complex and multifaceted. Morality provides the foundation for the development and implementation of just laws and legal systems, but different moral perspectives can lead to divergent interpretations of justice. Resolving ethical dilemmas and promoting justice requires careful consideration of competing moral principles and a commitment to fairness, impartiality, and the protection of individual rights. Legal professionals and scholars have a crucial role to play in navigating these moral dilemmas and shaping a more equitable and just world.

Ethical Foundations of Legal Systems

In order to understand the ethical foundations of legal systems, we must first examine the relationship between ethics and the law. Ethics refers to the moral principles and values that guide human behavior, while the law consists of rules and regulations enforced by a governing authority. While ethics and the law are closely related, they are distinct concepts. Ethics provides the moral framework upon which the law is built, and the law reflects society's ethical values and norms.

Importance of Ethics in Legal Systems

Ethics plays a crucial role in shaping and maintaining legal systems. It ensures fairness, justice, and accountability in the administration of law. Without a strong ethical foundation, legal systems can become corrupt, unjust, and ineffective. Ethical principles provide the basis for determining what is right and wrong, and guide legal professionals in their decision-making and actions.

Ethical Principles in Legal Systems

There are several key ethical principles that guide legal systems:

1. **Justice:** This principle emphasizes fairness and equality. It requires that individuals be treated impartially and without discrimination. Legal systems aim to ensure that individuals receive just outcomes and that societal resources are allocated equitably.

2. **Rule of Law:** The rule of law is a fundamental principle in legal systems. It asserts that all individuals, including those in positions of power, are subject to the law and must abide by it. This principle promotes the idea of equal protection under the law and the enforcement of laws in a consistent and predictable manner.

3. **Integrity:** Integrity refers to the honesty, transparency, and ethical behavior expected of legal professionals. It involves adhering to professional standards of conduct, maintaining confidentiality, and avoiding conflicts of

interest. Integrity is crucial for the effective functioning of legal systems and for building public trust and confidence.

4. **Respect for Human Rights**: Legal systems are based on the recognition and protection of human rights. Human rights include civil, political, economic, social, and cultural rights that all individuals possess by virtue of being human. Legal systems strive to uphold and safeguard these rights, ensuring that individuals are treated with dignity and respect.

Ethical Dilemmas in Legal Systems

Legal systems often present ethical dilemmas that require careful consideration and decision-making. These dilemmas can arise when there is a conflict between ethical principles or when there is a tension between legal requirements and personal values. Some common ethical dilemmas in legal systems include:

+ Balancing the right to privacy with the need for public safety in criminal investigations.

+ Balancing the duty of loyalty to clients with the duty of candor to the court in legal advocacy.

+ Balancing the duty to maintain attorney-client confidentiality with the duty to disclose information in the best interests of the client.

+ Balancing the duty to zealous advocacy with the duty to maintain professional integrity and ethics.

These dilemmas require legal professionals to carefully consider the consequences of their actions and make ethically sound decisions that promote justice and uphold the integrity of the legal system.

Examples and Case Studies

To better understand the ethical foundations of legal systems, let's consider a few examples:

1. **The right to privacy in criminal investigations**: In the digital age, law enforcement agencies have increasingly relied on technology to gather evidence. However, this raises ethical questions about the extent to which individuals' privacy should be invaded in the name of public safety. Striking

a balance between ensuring public safety and protecting individuals' privacy rights is a complex ethical dilemma faced by legal systems worldwide.

2. **Conflicts of interest in legal practice:** Legal professionals often encounter conflicts of interest, where their personal interests or relationships may compromise their ability to represent clients effectively and ethically. Resolving these conflicts requires careful navigation of ethical responsibilities and professional obligations, ensuring that legal professionals prioritize the best interests of their clients while maintaining their integrity.

3. **Human rights and asylum law:** Legal systems play a critical role in upholding human rights, particularly in the context of asylum law. Ethical considerations come into play when legal professionals decide whether to grant or deny asylum to individuals fleeing persecution and violence. Striving to balance the protection of human rights with national security concerns is a complex ethical challenge faced by legal systems around the world.

Resources and Recommendations

For those interested in further exploring the ethical foundations of legal systems, here are some recommended resources:

+ *Ethics in Practice: Lawyers' Roles, Responsibilities, and Regulation* by Deborah L. Rhode - This book provides an in-depth analysis of ethics in the legal profession, discussing the challenges and dilemmas lawyers face in their practice and offering practical solutions.

+ *Law, Justice, and Society: A Sociolegal Introduction* by Anthony Walsh and Craig Hemmens - This comprehensive textbook explores the intersection of law, ethics, and society, providing a solid understanding of the ethical foundations of legal systems.

+ *The Stanford Encyclopedia of Philosophy* - This online resource offers a wealth of articles on various topics in philosophy and ethics, including ethics in legal systems. It provides a comprehensive overview of the key concepts, theories, and debates in the field.

Conclusion

In conclusion, the ethical foundations of legal systems are essential for promoting justice, upholding the rule of law, and protecting human rights. Ethical principles guide legal professionals in their decision-making and provide a moral framework for the administration of law. However, legal systems also face ethical dilemmas that require careful consideration and balancing of competing interests. By understanding and appreciating the ethical foundations of legal systems, we can work towards a more equitable, just, and sustainable world.

Ethical Standards in Legal Decision Making

In the field of legal studies, ethical decision making plays a crucial role in maintaining the integrity and fairness of the legal system. Legal professionals are often faced with complex moral dilemmas that require careful consideration and a commitment to ethical standards. In this section, we will explore the ethical standards that guide legal decision making and discuss their significance in promoting justice and professional conduct.

Understanding Ethical Standards

Ethical standards serve as a framework for evaluating the rightness or wrongness of actions within a particular profession. In the legal field, ethical standards provide guidance for legal professionals in their decision making and actions. These standards help ensure that legal practitioners uphold the principles of justice, fairness, and integrity in their work.

Ethical standards in legal decision making are based on various sources, including professional codes of conduct, legal norms, and moral philosophy. These standards reflect the values and principles that should guide legal practitioners in their interactions with clients, colleagues, and the legal system as a whole.

A key ethical standard in legal decision making is the duty of competence. Legal professionals are expected to possess the necessary knowledge, skills, and expertise to provide effective legal representation and advice to their clients. This includes staying updated on legal developments, conducting thorough research, and ensuring that their actions are in line with the law.

Another fundamental ethical standard is the duty of loyalty. Legal professionals have a duty to prioritize the interests of their clients and act in their best interests. This duty requires maintaining client confidentiality, avoiding conflicts of interest, and providing undivided loyalty and dedication to clients.

Additionally, legal decision making is guided by the principles of integrity and honesty. Legal professionals are expected to act with honesty, truthfulness, and transparency in their interactions with clients, colleagues, and the court. They should refrain from engaging in fraudulent, deceptive, or misleading practices that undermine the integrity of the legal system.

Ethical Considerations and Balancing Conflicting Interests

Legal decision making often involves balancing conflicting interests and ethical considerations. Legal professionals may face situations where the interests of their clients clash with their own personal values, the interests of the opposing party, or broader societal considerations.

In such cases, legal practitioners are expected to navigate these ethical dilemmas by considering the consequences of their actions, the rights and interests of all parties involved, and the principles of justice and fairness. They must strive to make decisions that are guided by ethical standards and promote the overall public good.

For example, in criminal defense cases, attorneys may have to represent clients they believe to be guilty. Balancing the duty of loyalty to the client with the duty to the legal system and society can present significant ethical challenges. Legal professionals must carefully consider how to best uphold their ethical responsibilities while ensuring the fair administration of justice.

To assist with ethical decision making, legal professionals can use ethical decision making frameworks, such as the "principle-based" approach or the "consequence-based" approach. These frameworks provide a structured way of considering the ethical implications of different courses of action and help ensure that legal professionals make well-informed and ethically sound decisions.

Professional Codes of Conduct and Ethics

Professional codes of conduct and ethics further contribute to the establishment of ethical standards in legal decision making. These codes, developed by legal associations and governing bodies, outline the ethical obligations and responsibilities of legal professionals.

For instance, the American Bar Association (ABA) has developed the Model Rules of Professional Conduct, which serve as a foundation for legal ethics in the United States. Similarly, other countries and jurisdictions have their own professional codes of conduct that guide legal professionals in their decision making and behavior.

Professional codes of conduct provide guidance on various ethical issues, including conflict of interest, attorney-client privilege, and candor toward the tribunal. Compliance with these codes is expected of all legal practitioners and failure to adhere to them can result in disciplinary action.

Promoting Ethical Standards in Legal Education

The development and promotion of ethical standards in legal decision making begins in legal education. Law schools play a crucial role in imparting ethical principles and cultivating ethical decision-making skills in future legal professionals.

Law students are provided with opportunities to explore and reflect upon ethical issues through case studies, debates, and legal clinics. They engage in discussions around ethical dilemmas and are encouraged to develop a strong ethical foundation that will guide their decision making throughout their legal careers.

Legal education also emphasizes the importance of professional responsibility and ethical conduct. Students learn about the ethical obligations and standards that they will be expected to uphold once they enter the legal profession.

Conclusion

Ethical standards in legal decision making are essential for maintaining the integrity and fairness of the legal system. Legal professionals are guided by ethical principles and codes of conduct that help them navigate complex moral dilemmas and balance conflicting interests. Upholding these ethical standards is crucial for promoting justice, ensuring the welfare of clients, and preserving the public's trust in the legal profession. By instilling ethics in legal education and continuously evaluating and reinforcing ethical standards, the legal community can contribute to a more equitable and just society.

Ethical Implications of Legal Principles and Rules

In the field of legal studies, the ethical implications of legal principles and rules play a crucial role in shaping the legal system and guiding legal professionals in their practice. Legal principles and rules provide the foundation for the functioning of the legal system and dictate the rights, obligations, and responsibilities of individuals and organizations. However, the application of these principles and rules can raise ethical concerns and dilemmas that must be carefully considered and addressed.

Balancing Competing Ethical Principles

Legal principles and rules are not always straightforward and may sometimes conflict with each other. For instance, the principle of justice may conflict with the principle of autonomy in certain cases. In such situations, legal professionals must navigate the competing ethical principles and make decisions that strike a balance between them.

Consider a hypothetical case where a lawyer represents a client accused of a serious crime. The lawyer has a professional duty to provide zealous representation and protect the client's interests. However, the lawyer also has an ethical responsibility to uphold justice and ensure a fair trial. Balancing these competing ethical principles can be a complex task for the lawyer.

To address this dilemma, legal professionals may employ various ethical decision-making frameworks, such as the utilitarian approach, the deontological approach, or the virtue ethics approach. These frameworks provide guidance on how to prioritize and reconcile conflicting ethical principles.

Ethics in Legal Interpretation and Application

Legal principles and rules are open to interpretation and application, which can lead to ethical implications. The way legal professionals interpret and apply the law can significantly impact the rights and interests of individuals and communities. Therefore, legal professionals must exercise ethical judgment in their interpretation and application of the law.

One ethical concern in legal interpretation is the potential for bias. Judges and legal professionals must guard against personal biases and ensure that their interpretations are unbiased and objective. The principle of impartiality is a key ethical consideration in legal interpretation.

Additionally, legal professionals must consider the consequences of their interpretations and how they align with broader ethical principles. For example, if a legal professional's interpretation of a statute leads to a result that infringes on individual rights or perpetuates systemic inequality, it raises ethical concerns. Legal professionals should strive to interpret and apply the law in a manner that promotes justice, fairness, and the public good.

Professional Codes of Conduct and Ethics

Legal professionals are guided by professional codes of conduct and ethics, which outline the standards and expectations for their behavior in legal practice. These codes address various ethical issues that arise in legal studies and provide guidance on how to handle them.

Codes of conduct typically include obligations such as maintaining client confidentiality, avoiding conflicts of interest, and promoting access to justice. Legal professionals must adhere to these ethical obligations to maintain their professional integrity and ensure the proper functioning of the legal system.

In cases where ethical dilemmas arise, legal professionals can turn to these codes of conduct for guidance. For example, if a lawyer uncovers evidence that could exonerate their client but is protected by attorney-client privilege, the lawyer must carefully balance their duty of confidentiality with their duty to pursue justice. Professional codes of conduct provide a framework for resolving such dilemmas and making ethical decisions.

Ethical Issues in Legal Education

The ethical implications of legal principles and rules extend beyond legal practice and into legal education. Legal educators have a responsibility to instill ethical values and principles in their students, preparing them to navigate the complex ethical landscape of the legal profession.

Legal education should go beyond teaching the technical aspects of the law and encompass critical thinking skills, ethical reasoning, and moral development. Students should be encouraged to analyze and evaluate the ethical implications of legal principles and rules, as well as consider the social and moral consequences of legal decisions.

Moreover, legal education should address the evolving ethical challenges posed by advancements in technology, globalization, and social justice. Students must be equipped with the knowledge and skills to address these issues in their future legal careers.

Conclusion

The ethical implications of legal principles and rules are integral to the field of legal studies. Legal professionals must navigate the competing ethical principles, exercise ethical judgment in legal interpretation and application, adhere to professional codes of conduct, and continuously reflect on the ethical dimensions of their practice. Furthermore, legal education plays a vital role in preparing students to understand and address the ethical challenges they will encounter in their future careers. By considering and addressing the ethical implications of legal principles and rules, legal professionals contribute to the promotion of justice and the creation of a more equitable and sustainable world.

Ethical Issues in Legal Interpretation and Application

In the field of legal studies, the interpretation and application of laws play a crucial role in ensuring justice and fairness. However, these processes are not without ethical challenges. Legal interpretation involves the analysis and understanding of legal texts, while legal application involves the implementation of laws in specific cases. Both of these processes can give rise to ethical dilemmas that require careful consideration.

Background

Legal interpretation refers to the process of understanding the meaning and intent of legal texts, such as statutes, regulations, and court decisions. This process involves examining the language, historical context, legislative intent, and judicial precedent to determine how the law should be understood and applied in a given situation.

Legal application, on the other hand, involves the practical implementation of legal rules and principles to resolve disputes or establish rights and obligations. This process requires judges, lawyers, and other legal professionals to apply relevant laws and legal principles to the facts of a particular case.

Ethical Issues in Legal Interpretation

1. **Textualism vs. Contextualism:** One of the key ethical issues in legal interpretation is the debate between textualism and contextualism. Textualism emphasizes a strict interpretation of the text, focusing on the plain meaning of the words used. Contextualism, on the other hand, takes into account the broader context, including legislative intent and public policy considerations. The ethical dilemma arises when there is ambiguity in the text, and different interpretive approaches can lead to differing outcomes.

    Example: In a case involving a statute prohibiting the possession of firearms in public places, textualism may strictly prohibit any possession, while contextualism may consider exceptions for self-defense in certain situations. The ethical question is whether the court should prioritize the text or consider the broader context in interpreting the statute.

2. **Originalism vs. Living Constitution:** Another ethical issue in legal interpretation is the clash between originalism and the concept of a living constitution. Originalism argues that the Constitution should be interpreted based

on the original understanding of the framers. In contrast, the living constitution theory contends that the Constitution should be viewed as a living document, capable of adapting to new social and cultural realities. The ethical question here is how to balance the intent of the framers with the need for a Constitution that can address evolving societal issues.

Example: In a case involving a question of privacy, originalists may argue that the framers did not explicitly mention a right to privacy in the Constitution, while proponents of the living constitution may argue that the concept of privacy is implied in other constitutional provisions. The ethical dilemma is to determine which interpretive approach best promotes justice and upholds constitutional values.

Ethical Issues in Legal Application

1. **Discretion and Bias**: Legal application requires judges, prosecutors, and other decision-makers to exercise discretion in their decision-making. However, this discretion can be susceptible to bias, leading to unfair outcomes. Ethical considerations arise when personal beliefs, prejudices, or external influences impact the application of the law.

Example: A judge's personal beliefs or biases may influence their decision in a case involving controversial social issues, such as abortion or LGBTQ+ rights. The ethical challenge is to ensure that legal decisions are based on valid legal principles rather than personal biases.

2. **Justice and Equity**: The pursuit of justice and equity is a fundamental ethical concern in legal application. The challenge lies in determining how to balance the individual circumstances of a case with the need for consistent and equitable treatment under the law.

Example: Sentencing disparities in criminal cases, where individuals from marginalized communities are disproportionately affected, raise ethical questions about the fairness and equity of the legal system. Addressing these disparities requires careful consideration of both individual circumstances and broader societal factors.

Addressing Ethical Issues

To address ethical issues in legal interpretation and application, several approaches can be adopted:

1.   **Transparency and Accountability**: Promoting transparency and accountability in legal decision-making can help mitigate ethical challenges. This

can be achieved through clear and well-reasoned judgments, publicly available legal reasoning, and ensuring that decision-makers are held accountable for their actions.

2. **Ethics Education:** Providing ethics education to legal professionals can enhance their awareness of ethical issues and improve their ability to navigate ethical dilemmas. By developing a strong ethical framework, legal professionals can make more informed decisions and uphold justice.

3. **Guidelines and Codes of Conduct:** Establishing clear guidelines and codes of conduct can provide ethical guidance to legal professionals. These guidelines can outline principles and standards for legal interpretation and application, emphasizing fairness, impartiality, and the avoidance of conflicts of interest.

4. **Diverse Legal Perspectives:** Promoting diversity and inclusivity within the legal profession can help address biases and provide alternative perspectives in legal interpretation and application. A diverse legal community is more likely to consider a wide range of ethical issues and potential solutions.

Conclusion

Ethical issues in legal interpretation and application are inevitable due to the complexity and subjectivity of the legal process. Resolving these ethical dilemmas requires a commitment to transparency, accountability, ethics education, and diverse perspectives. By addressing these challenges, legal professionals can strive for a more equitable and just application of the law in a rapidly changing world.

Conclusion

In this section, we have explored the moral foundations of law and justice. We began by delving into the concepts of morality and justice, understanding their definitions and exploring the theories that underpin our understanding of these concepts. We examined the relationship between morality and justice and the ethical foundations of legal systems.

We discussed the importance of ethical standards in legal decision making, and the ethical implications of legal principles and rules. We recognized that legal interpretation and application can present ethical challenges and explored the role of ethics in guiding these processes. By understanding the ethical considerations in legal practice, we develop a deeper appreciation for the role of morality in shaping the law.

We then turned our attention to theories of law, examining natural law theory, legal positivism, legal realism, critical legal studies, and feminist legal theory. Each of these theories offers unique perspectives on the nature and purpose of law, and understanding them is crucial in comprehending the complexities of legal studies.

Furthermore, we explored the concept of legal rights and responsibilities, discussing the definition and classification of rights, as well as the theories that underpin their existence. We examined the ethical implications of rights and responsibilities and the role of ethics in legal enforcement. This discussion reminds us that the law is not simply a set of rules, but a reflection of our moral and ethical obligations to one another.

In this section, we also explored the ethical issues that arise within the legal profession. We considered professionalism and ethics, understanding the role and responsibilities of legal professionals and the ethical obligations that come with practicing law. We examined the importance of confidentiality and attorney-client privilege, recognizing the challenges that exist in maintaining confidentiality while upholding other ethical obligations. Additionally, we discussed the ethical considerations surrounding conflicts of interest and the importance of transparency and accountability in addressing them.

Moving beyond the realm of legal practice, we delved into the broader concepts of social justice and human rights. We explored theories of social justice, understanding their different perspectives on equality and fairness. We recognized the historical evolution of human rights and the international and domestic instruments that have been established to protect them. Moreover, we discussed the social justice issues that are prevalent in legal studies, such as poverty, inequality, racial and ethnic justice, and environmental justice.

Lastly, we examined the ethical issues in criminal justice, focusing on the principles of criminal justice ethics and the ethical dilemmas faced by law enforcement, prosecutors, and correctional systems. We also explored the ethical controversies surrounding capital punishment, discussing different perspectives and alternatives. By addressing the ethical challenges in policing, we highlighted the importance of accountability, transparency, and community engagement.

In conclusion, this section has provided a comprehensive understanding of the moral foundations of law and justice. By examining philosophical and ethical theories, as well as ethical considerations in legal practice and societal contexts, we have developed a deeper appreciation for the role of ethics in guiding legal decision making. Understanding the ethical issues within the legal profession and the criminal justice system allows us to critically analyze and address them in a manner that promotes justice and fairness. By recognizing the importance of social justice and human rights, we are better equipped to address the inequalities and injustices that persist in our society. Ultimately, by navigating moral dilemmas and promoting ethical practices, we contribute to shaping a more equitable, just, and sustainable world.

Theories of Law

Natural Law Theory

In the study of legal philosophy, one prominent theory is the Natural Law Theory. This theory posits that there are certain universal moral principles that are inherent in nature and can be discovered through reason. The principles derived from natural law are believed to provide a foundation for creating just laws and governing society.

Background

The concept of natural law dates back to ancient Greek and Roman philosophy, where thinkers like Aristotle and Cicero explored the idea of an inherent moral order in the universe. However, the theory gained prominence during the Middle Ages when scholars like Thomas Aquinas integrated natural law into Christian theology.

According to natural law theorists, morality is not subjective or culturally relative but is grounded in objective principles that can be discerned through reason. These principles are believed to be universal and immutable, applicable to all individuals and societies regardless of time and place.

Principles of Natural Law

Natural law theory is based on several fundamental principles. These principles serve as a guide for ethical behavior and the creation of just laws:

1. **Human Nature:** Natural law theorists argue that human beings have an inherent nature that is characterized by certain essential qualities. These qualities include rationality, sociality, and the pursuit of well-being. Human beings are believed to have a purpose or telos, which is the fulfillment of their inherent nature.

2. **Morality and Reason:** Natural law is based on the idea that moral principles can be discovered through reason. Rationality is seen as the basis for understanding the fundamental truths about human nature and the natural order of things. By using reason, individuals can discern the moral principles that govern their actions.

3. **Objective Morality:** Natural law theorists believe in the existence of objective moral principles that are grounded in the nature of reality. These principles are not dependent on individual preferences or cultural norms but are universally applicable. They are discovered through reason and are inherent in the nature of things.

4. **Hierarchy of Laws:** According to natural law theory, there is a hierarchy of laws. The highest level is the natural law, which is considered to be the fundamental moral principles derived from human nature. Human-made laws are considered valid only to the extent that they align with the principles of natural law. If a law contradicts natural law, it is considered unjust and can be disregarded.

5. **Justice:** Justice is a central concept in natural law theory. It is understood as the virtue of giving each person what is due to them based on their inherent value and dignity. Just laws are those that promote the common good and respect the inherent rights and dignity of individuals.

Application of Natural Law Theory

Natural law theory has been applied in various areas of legal studies and ethics. Here are a few examples:

+ **Legal Interpretation:** Natural law principles can guide judges in interpreting laws. Judges may consider the moral principles derived from natural law when interpreting ambiguous statutes or resolving conflicts between different legal principles.

+ **Bioethics:** Natural law theory has been utilized in the field of bioethics to assess the morality of medical interventions, such as euthanasia, abortion, and genetic engineering. The principles of human dignity and the inherent value of human life are central to these discussions.

+ **Human Rights:** Natural law theory has influenced the development and understanding of human rights. The idea that all individuals have inherent rights based on their human nature aligns with the principles of natural law. Human rights are seen as universal and inalienable, applying to all individuals regardless of cultural or legal considerations.

+ **Environmental Ethics:** Some natural law theorists argue for the inclusion of environmental ethics within the framework of natural law. They argue that respect for the inherent value of the natural world should guide human behavior and the protection of the environment.

Critiques and Limitations

While natural law theory has its proponents, it is not without its critics. Here are some common critiques and limitations associated with this theory:

+ **Reliance on Reason:** Critics argue that natural law theory places excessive reliance on reason and may lead to a rigid and inflexible understanding of morality. They argue that there are multiple sources of moral knowledge, including emotions, empathy, and cultural values, which should be taken into account.

+ **Pluralism and Diversity:** Critics argue that natural law theory does not adequately account for the diversity of moral beliefs and cultural practices. They contend that moral principles derived from natural law may not be universally applicable or applicable in all cultural contexts.

+ **Conflicting Interpretations:** Natural law theory can lead to conflicting interpretations and disagreements. Different individuals or communities may have divergent interpretations of what constitutes natural law and its principles, leading to moral relativism and disputes over moral truths.

+ **Dynamic Nature of Morality:** Critics argue that natural law theory does not sufficiently account for the evolving nature of morality. They contend that moral principles may change over time as societies and understanding of human nature evolve.

Real-World Example

A real-world example that illustrates the application of natural law theory is the debate over same-sex marriage. Natural law theorists who oppose same-sex marriage argue that marriage, by its very nature, is based on the complementary union of a man and a woman. They contend that this understanding of marriage is rooted in natural law principles derived from human nature.

On the other hand, proponents of same-sex marriage argue that natural law principles, such as the inherent dignity and equality of all individuals, support the recognition of same-sex relationships. They argue that restricting marriage to opposite-sex couples is a violation of these principles.

This example highlights how natural law theory can be invoked on both sides of a legal and ethical debate, demonstrating its significance and relevance in contemporary issues.

Further Reading

For a deeper understanding of natural law theory and its applications, consider exploring the following resources:

1. Finnis, J. (2011). Natural law and natural rights. Oxford University Press.

2. Murphy, M. C. (2001). Natural law in jurisprudence and politics. Cambridge University Press.

3. George, R. P., & Wolfe, C. (Eds.). (2011). Natural law and public reason. Georgetown University Press.

Conclusion

Natural law theory offers an approach to understanding morality and law that is grounded in universal principles derived from human nature and reason. While subject to criticism and debate, this theory provides a framework for ethical decision-making and the creation of just laws. Understanding natural law theory is essential for students of legal studies and anyone interested in exploring the philosophical and ethical underpinnings of the law.

Legal Positivism

Legal positivism is a school of thought within the philosophy of law that emphasizes the role of social rules and conventions in defining and determining the legitimacy of legal systems. It posits that law is a human creation and is separate from morality or natural law. According to legal positivism, the validity of a law depends solely on its sources, such as legislation, precedent, or custom, rather than on its moral content or conformity to higher principles.

Origins and Key Principles

Legal positivism traces its roots back to the 19th-century works of legal scholars such as John Austin, Jeremy Bentham, and H.L.A. Hart. These thinkers laid the foundation for legal positivism by presenting a distinction between what the law is (its existence and validity) and what the law ought to be (any moral or ethical considerations).

The key principles of legal positivism arise from this distinction. Firstly, legal positivists argue that there is no necessary connection between law and morality. They reject the idea that laws must necessarily be just or morally right to be considered valid. Instead, they focus on the observable facts of legal systems, such as legislation and judicial decisions.

Secondly, legal positivism insists on a separation between legal and moral judgments. Legal positivists argue that judges should base their decisions solely on the law as it is, rather than introducing personal or moral considerations. This separation is seen as necessary for a stable legal system that can be applied objectively and consistently.

Finally, legal positivism emphasizes the importance of the rule of recognition. The rule of recognition is a social rule or convention that gives authority to certain sources of law and establishes criteria for identifying valid legal rules. It is the ultimate criterion for determining whether a rule is legally valid within a particular legal system.

Critiques of Legal Positivism

Legal positivism has faced criticism from various perspectives. One of the main critiques is that it fails to account for the moral dimension of law. Critics argue that there are moral principles that serve as an inherent part of the legal system, and that legal positivism cannot fully capture the normative aspect of law.

Another criticism is that legal positivism's emphasis on the rule of recognition can lead to arbitrary and unjust laws being considered valid. If a law meets the formal criteria established by the rule of recognition, legal positivism would consider it valid, even if it violates fundamental principles of justice or human rights.

Additionally, legal positivism's separation of law and morality has been challenged on the grounds that law necessarily reflects and enforces moral values. Critics argue that the law cannot be divorced from the society in which it exists, and that moral considerations must be taken into account when evaluating legal systems.

Application of Legal Positivism

Legal positivism has found practical application in various legal systems around the world. It provides a framework for understanding and analyzing the sources, validity, and interpretation of laws.

In a legal positivist system, judges are expected to interpret laws based on their primary sources, such as legislation and precedent, without introducing personal moral judgments. This approach aims to ensure consistency and predictability in legal decision-making.

Legal positivism also helps to promote legal certainty by providing a clear set of criteria for determining the validity of laws. It allows for the identification and analysis of legal rules and principles within a given legal system.

However, legal positivism's limitations should be acknowledged. While it provides a useful framework for understanding legal systems, it does not inherently address issues of justice or morality. Legal positivism alone may not adequately address the complex ethical questions that arise in legal practice.

Emerging Issues and Debates

Legal positivism continues to be the subject of ongoing debates and discussions within the field of jurisprudence. Scholars and philosophers raise critical questions about the relationship between law and morality, the role of judges in interpreting and applying the law, and the impact of legal systems on society.

One emerging issue is the tension between legal positivism and the recognition of human rights. Critics argue that legal positivism, with its emphasis on the rule of recognition and positive law, may fail to protect fundamental human rights in situations where positive laws are unjust or violate human rights norms. This debate highlights the need to balance legal positivism with moral and ethical considerations, particularly in issues of social justice.

Another area of debate concerns the application of legal positivism in multicultural societies. As legal systems interact with diverse cultural norms and values, questions arise about the compatibility of legal positivism with the recognition and accommodation of different cultural perspectives within the law.

In conclusion, legal positivism provides an important framework for understanding the sources and validity of laws. It emphasizes the role of social rules and conventions in defining legal systems, and the separation of law from morality. While it has faced criticism for neglecting moral considerations and potential arbitrariness in legal systems, legal positivism offers valuable insights into the nature and interpretation of law. Society continues to grapple with the balance between legal positivism and moral principles in promoting a just and equitable legal order.

Legal Realism

Legal realism is a school of thought in legal theory that emerged in the early 20th century. It challenges the traditional view that law is a fixed set of rules and principles that can be applied objectively. Instead, legal realists argue that law is shaped by social, economic, and political factors and that legal decisions are influenced by the personal beliefs and values of judges.

Overview of Legal Realism

Legal realism rejects the idea that law exists in a vacuum, separate from the social and political context in which it operates. According to legal realists, the law is not a static, pre-determined set of rules, but rather a dynamic and evolving system that reflects the changing needs and values of society.

Legal realists view legal decisions as the product of judicial discretion, influenced by a variety of factors such as personal beliefs, social norms, and political pressures. They argue that judges are not neutral arbiters of the law, but rather active participants in the legal process, shaping and interpreting the law in accordance with their own perspectives.

Key Figures in Legal Realism

Several key figures contributed to the development and popularity of legal realism:

- Oliver Wendell Holmes Jr.: Holmes, a U.S. Supreme Court Justice, is often considered one of the pioneers of legal realism. He emphasized the importance of looking at the actual effects of legal decisions, rather than relying solely on abstract legal principles.

- Jerome Frank: Frank, a legal scholar and judge, further developed the ideas of legal realism. He argued that judges' personal experiences and values play a significant role in decision-making and that the law should be understood as a reflection of societal norms and interests.

- Karl Llewellyn: Llewellyn, another prominent legal realist, focused on the language and interpretation of legal texts. He believed that legal language is inherently ambiguous and that judges' interpretations are influenced by their own backgrounds and experiences.

Critiques and Responses

Legal realism has faced criticism from various quarters. One common critique is that it undermines the rule of law by suggesting that legal decisions are arbitrary and subjective. Critics argue that legal realism opens the door to judicial activism and undermines the predictability and stability of the legal system.

In response, legal realists highlight the importance of recognizing the role of human judgment in the legal process. They argue that acknowledging the subjectivity of legal decision-making allows for a more nuanced understanding of the law and promotes the development of just and equitable outcomes.

Contemporary Relevance of Legal Realism

Legal realism continues to be relevant in contemporary legal theory. It reminds us that law is a social institution deeply embedded within a particular context and subject to various influences. The insights of legal realism have informed subsequent legal theories, such as critical legal studies and feminist legal theory.

Legal realism also has practical implications for legal practice. It encourages lawyers, judges, and policymakers to consider the social consequences of legal decisions and to critically examine the underlying values and biases that may shape legal outcomes. By recognizing the subjectivity and contextuality of law, legal professionals can work towards a more just and equitable legal system.

Case Study: Brown v. Board of Education

A notable example where legal realism played a significant role is the landmark U.S. Supreme Court case of Brown v. Board of Education (1954). In this case, the Court ruled that racial segregation in public schools violated the Fourteenth Amendment's equal protection clause.

The decision in Brown was influenced by legal realist thinking. The Court recognized that segregation had a detrimental impact on the education and psychological development of Black children, and they considered the social and psychological evidence that supported the claim of "separate but equal" being inherently unequal.

The Brown decision reflected the legal realist perspective that legal reasoning should consider the broader social implications of racial segregation and challenge the prevailing legal doctrine. The case marked a significant step towards desegregation and the fight for civil rights in the United States.

Further Reading

To delve deeper into legal realism, the following texts are highly recommended:

+ *The Common Law* by Oliver Wendell Holmes Jr.

+ *Law and the Modern Mind* by Jerome Frank

+ *The Bramble Bush* by Karl Llewellyn

+ *Legal Realism and American Law* edited by William W. Fisher III and Morton J. Horwitz

These texts provide valuable insights into the historical development and philosophical underpinnings of legal realism, as well as its ongoing relevance in contemporary legal discourse.

Summary

Legal realism challenges the traditional view of law by emphasizing the role of social, economic, and political factors in shaping legal decisions. It recognizes the subjectivity and contextuality of law and highlights the importance of considering the social consequences of legal outcomes. Legal realism has influenced legal theory and practice and continues to provide valuable insights into the nature of law and its relationship with society.

Critical Legal Studies

The field of Critical Legal Studies (CLS) emerged in the 1970s as a critical response to traditional legal theories and practices. It challenges the conventional idea that law is neutral and objective, and instead focuses on the social and political power dynamics that influence legal systems. CLS scholars argue that legal rules and doctrines are shaped by dominant ideologies and reflect the interests of powerful groups in society.

Overview and Key Principles

At its core, Critical Legal Studies aims to expose and critique the underlying assumptions and values embedded in legal systems. CLS scholars believe that law is not an autonomous discipline, but rather a tool that is used to maintain existing power structures and perpetuate inequality. They argue that law is inherently political and that legal decisions are influenced by social, economic, and cultural factors.

One key principle of Critical Legal Studies is the rejection of "formalism," which is the idea that legal decisions can be made solely based on logical reasoning and legal rules. CLS scholars argue that legal reasoning is not objective, and that judges and lawyers bring their own biases and interests into legal decision-making. They also critique legal formalism for ignoring the social context in which legal disputes arise.

Another important principle of CLS is its focus on the relationship between law and social change. CLS scholars believe that law is not a neutral force, but rather a mechanism that can be used to shape social norms and facilitate social transformation. They advocate for the use of law as a tool for challenging oppressive structures and promoting social justice.

Critiques of CLS

While Critical Legal Studies has made significant contributions to legal theory, it has also faced some criticism. One common critique is that CLS scholars often focus on abstract theoretical debates and fail to provide practical solutions to legal problems. Critics argue that CLS is too focused on deconstructing existing legal theories and does not offer concrete alternatives or strategies for legal reform.

Another criticism of CLS is its tendency to downplay the role of legal principles and rules. Critics argue that while CLS scholars highlight the political nature of law, they often neglect the importance of legal norms in ensuring stability and predictability in society. They argue that legal rules and doctrines play a crucial role in governing behavior and resolving disputes, and that CLS should not disregard their significance.

Contemporary Applications

Despite its critiques, CLS has had a lasting impact on legal scholarship and has influenced various areas of legal practice. One area where CLS has been particularly influential is in the field of legal interpretation. CLS scholars argue that legal texts are open to multiple interpretations and that judges often shape the meaning of laws based on their own biases and values. This critique has led to a greater emphasis on understanding the social and political context in which legal texts are interpreted.

CLS has also influenced the study of human rights law. CLS scholars argue that human rights discourse can sometimes serve as a tool of Western imperialism and reinforce global power imbalances. They advocate for a critical approach to human rights law that examines the underlying power dynamics and challenges the dominant narratives.

In addition, CLS has been instrumental in critiquing traditional legal concepts such as property rights and contract law. CLS scholars argue that these legal concepts are rooted in a capitalist ideology that prioritizes individual rights over collective well-being. They propose alternative frameworks that take into account social and economic inequalities.

Case Study: Critical Race Theory

One prominent offshoot of Critical Legal Studies is Critical Race Theory (CRT), which applies CLS principles to the study of race and racism in the law. CRT emerged in the 1980s and seeks to uncover the ways in which law reinforces and perpetuates racial inequalities.

One example of the application of CRT is the critique of colorblindness in the legal system. CRT scholars argue that claims of colorblindness, or the idea that race should not be a factor in legal decision-making, often mask and perpetuate systemic racism. They argue that acknowledging and addressing race explicitly is necessary to address racial inequalities.

Another key concept in CRT is the idea of "intersectionality," which recognizes that race intersects with other identities such as gender, class, and sexuality, and that multiple forms of discrimination can compound and intersect. This perspective challenges the notion that race can be analyzed in isolation from other social factors.

Conclusion

Critical Legal Studies has played a significant role in challenging traditional legal theories and exposing the political nature of law. By examining the power dynamics and social context of legal systems, CLS offers a critical perspective that encourages a more nuanced understanding of how law operates in society. While facing criticism, CLS continues to shape legal scholarship and inspire interdisciplinary approaches to the study of law.

Feminist Legal Theory

Feminist legal theory is a branch of legal studies that examines the law through a gendered lens, with a focus on how the law affects women and other marginalized groups. It seeks to challenge and transform the dominant legal framework by uncovering and critiquing gender biases and advocating for gender equality within the legal system. In this section, we will explore the principles and key concepts of feminist legal theory, its critiques of traditional legal theories, and its impact on contemporary legal discourse.

Principles of Feminist Legal Theory

Feminist legal theory is grounded in several key principles that guide its analysis and critique of the law. These principles include:

1. Gender equality: Feminist legal theory advocates for the equal treatment of women and men under the law. It seeks to challenge the discriminatory laws and practices that perpetuate gender disparities and promote gender justice and equality.

2. Intersectionality: Feminist legal theory recognizes that gender oppression intersects with other forms of oppression based on race, class, sexuality, disability, and other social categories. It emphasizes the need to consider these intersecting identities when examining legal issues and developing legal solutions.

3. Social context: Feminist legal theory acknowledges that the law does not operate in a vacuum but is shaped by broader social, political, and cultural contexts. It examines how power dynamics and social inequalities influence legal norms, practices, and outcomes.

4. Voice and representation: Feminist legal theory highlights the importance of including diverse perspectives and voices in legal decision-making processes. It seeks to challenge the male-dominated legal profession and promote equal representation of women and marginalized groups in lawmaking bodies and judicial positions.

Critiques of Traditional Legal Theories

Feminist legal theory offers a critique of traditional legal theories, such as legal positivism, natural law theory, and legal realism, for their failure to address gender biases and inequalities. It points out several limitations of these theories:

1. Androcentrism: Traditional legal theories often adopt a male-centric perspective, assuming that the male experience is universal and disregarding women's unique experiences and concerns. Feminist legal theory aims to challenge this androcentric bias by centering women's experiences and perspectives in legal analysis.

2. Gender-blindness: Traditional legal theories tend to overlook the ways in which gender constructs and norms shape legal concepts and institutions. Feminist legal theory highlights the need to examine the gendered dimensions of legal issues and to develop gender-sensitive legal frameworks.

3. Exclusion of women's voices: Traditional legal theories have historically marginalized women's voices and excluded women from positions of power in the

legal system. Feminist legal theory advocates for amplifying women's voices and experiences, recognizing them as valuable contributions to legal scholarship and practice.

Themes in Feminist Legal Theory

Feminist legal theory explores a wide range of themes that are relevant to understanding the impact of gender on legal systems. Some of the key themes include:

1. Sexual and reproductive rights: Feminist legal theory addresses issues such as reproductive freedom, contraception, abortion, and access to healthcare. It aims to challenge laws and policies that restrict women's autonomy over their bodies and reproductive choices.

2. Violence against women: Feminist legal theory examines various forms of violence against women, including domestic violence, sexual assault, and trafficking. It seeks to develop legal strategies to protect and empower survivors, holding perpetrators accountable and dismantling systems that perpetuate gender-based violence.

3. Workplace discrimination: Feminist legal theory analyzes laws governing employment and the workplace to identify and challenge gender-based discrimination, such as pay disparities, sexual harassment, and occupational segregation. It seeks to promote equal opportunities and fair treatment for women in the workplace.

4. Family law and feminist parenting: Feminist legal theory critically examines laws related to marriage, divorce, child custody, and parenting. It seeks to challenge traditional gender roles and biases within the family law system, aiming for more equitable outcomes that prioritize the best interests of all family members.

Case Study: Intersectional Feminism and the Law

To illustrate the practical application of feminist legal theory, let's examine a case study on intersectional feminism and the law. Intersectionality recognizes that individuals may experience multiple forms of oppression and discrimination simultaneously, and that these intersecting identities must be considered when addressing legal issues.

In a custody dispute between a divorced couple, a court may traditionally favor granting custody to the mother, assuming that she is the primary caregiver and has a natural affinity for nurturing. However, an intersectional feminist analysis would recognize that this assumption perpetuates gender stereotypes and neglects other factors, such as race, class, and ability, which may also influence parenting abilities.

In this case, an intersectional feminist approach would consider the unique circumstances of the individuals involved, taking into account their race, socioeconomic background, and any disabilities or challenges they face. It would challenge the presumption of "mother knows best" and aim for a custody decision that promotes the best interests of the child while ensuring equal consideration of both parents' abilities.

Resources and Further Reading

To delve deeper into feminist legal theory, consider exploring the following resources:

1. "Feminist Legal Theory: An Anti-Essentialist Reader" edited by Nancy E. Dowd and Michelle S. Jacobs 2. "Feminist Legal Theory: A Primer" by Nancy Levit 3. "Feminist Jurisprudence: Cases and Materials" by Cynthia Bowman, Elizabeth M. Schneider, and Ann C. McGinley 4. "Intersectionality and the Law: Theory, Policy, and Practice" edited by Adrien Katherine Wing 5. "Feminist Legal Theory: Foundations" edited by D. Kelly Weisberg

These resources provide comprehensive insights into the principles, theories, and applications of feminist legal theory, offering a robust foundation for understanding and engaging with gender justice in the legal field.

Exercises

1. Choose a legal issue that affects women disproportionately, such as domestic violence or pay equity. Analyze the issue from a feminist legal theory perspective, identifying the underlying gender biases and proposing potential legal solutions to address the issue.

2. Conduct research on a landmark court case that advanced women's rights. Explain the legal arguments made, the outcome of the case, and the implications it had for feminist legal theory and gender equality.

3. Critically examine a recent law or policy related to reproductive rights. Assess its impact on women's autonomy and reproductive healthcare access, highlighting any gender biases or inequalities that may arise.

4. Explore the principles of intersectional feminism and its relevance to the legal system. Identify a specific legal issue that intersects with other forms of oppression, such as race or class, and discuss how an intersectional feminist analysis could inform a more nuanced and equitable legal response.

5. Engage in a debate or discussion regarding the inclusion of diverse voices and perspectives in the legal profession. Consider the benefits and challenges of promoting equal representation and diversity within the legal field, discussing potential strategies for overcoming barriers to inclusion.

Remember, feminist legal theory is an evolving field that constantly grapples with new challenges and perspectives. As you engage with these exercises and further explore the topic, you contribute to the ongoing discourse on gender justice and shape a more equitable legal system for all.

Legal Interpretation and Theory

Legal interpretation is a fundamental aspect of the legal system, as it determines the meaning and application of laws. It plays a crucial role in shaping legal decisions, resolving disputes, and ensuring the fair and just operation of the legal system. In this section, we will explore the theories and principles of legal interpretation and their significance in legal studies.

The Role of Legal Interpretation

Legal interpretation is the process of deriving meaning from legal texts, such as statutes, constitutions, and judicial opinions. It involves analyzing the language, structure, and context of these texts to determine their intended interpretation and application. The role of legal interpretation is to bridge the gap between the text of the law and its real-world implications.

The importance of legal interpretation lies in its ability to ensure the effectiveness and legitimacy of laws. Without proper interpretation, laws may be ambiguous, contradictory, or insufficiently clear, leading to confusion and inconsistency in their application. Legal interpretation provides a framework for understanding the intent and purpose of laws, allowing for consistent and fair decision-making.

Theories of Legal Interpretation

Legal interpretation is a complex and nuanced process that has sparked various theories and approaches. While there is no single correct method of interpretation, different theories highlight different factors to consider when interpreting the law. Here are some prominent theories of legal interpretation:

1. **Textualism:** This theory emphasizes the literal text of the law as the sole determinant of its meaning. Textualists argue that judges should adhere

strictly to the plain language of the law and refrain from considering external sources or intentions.

2. **Originalism:** Originalism posits that the meaning of the law should be determined by its original intent or understanding at the time of its enactment. Originalists often rely on historical context, legislative history, and the intentions of the law's framers to interpret its meaning.

3. **Living Constitution:** The living constitution theory holds that the interpretation of the law should adapt and evolve with changing social, cultural, and technological circumstances. Proponents of this theory argue that judges should consider the underlying principles and purposes of the law rather than adhering rigidly to its original meaning.

4. **Purposivism:** Purposivism focuses on the underlying purposes and goals of the law. It suggests that judges should interpret the law in a manner that promotes its intended objectives, even if it requires departing from the literal text or original intent.

5. **Pragmatism:** Pragmatism prioritizes practical considerations and the consequences of legal interpretation. It advocates for interpreting the law in a way that produces the best outcome or promotes societal welfare, taking into account the potential impact on individuals and communities.

It is important to note that these theories are not mutually exclusive, and judges may employ different theories depending on the context and nature of the legal issue at hand. The choice of theory can significantly impact the outcome and implications of legal interpretation.

Tools and Methods of Legal Interpretation

Legal interpretation involves the application of various tools and methods to analyze and understand the law. These tools provide a framework for systematic and reasoned interpretation. Here are some commonly used tools of legal interpretation:

1. **Plain Meaning Rule:** This rule suggests that if the language of the law is clear and unambiguous, it should be given its plain and ordinary meaning. This approach is often associated with textualism.

2. **Statutory Construction:** Statutory construction involves analyzing the language, structure, and context of a statute to determine its proper interpretation. This includes considering the legislative intent, the statute's purpose, and any relevant legislative history.

3. **Presumptions:** Presumptions are legal assumptions that guide the interpretation of ambiguous or unclear laws. For example, the presumption of constitutionality presumes that legislative acts are constitutional unless proven otherwise. Presumptions help resolve uncertainties and guide judges in their interpretation.

4. **Canons of Construction:** Canons of construction are general principles or rules that assist in interpreting statutory language. They are derived from legal tradition, precedents, and common sense. Canons of construction guide judges in resolving ambiguities or conflicts in the law.

5. **Legislative History:** Legislative history includes documents and records, such as committee reports, hearings, and debates, that provide insights into the intent and purpose of a statute. Examining legislative history can aid in understanding the legislative intent and context of the law.

Legal interpretation is not a mechanical or formulaic exercise. It requires the application of legal reasoning, critical thinking, and a deep understanding of legal principles and precedents. Judges must balance the text, history, purpose, and consequences of the law to arrive at a reasoned interpretation.

Controversies and Challenges in Legal Interpretation

Legal interpretation is not without controversies and challenges. Interpreting complex and multifaceted laws can be subjective and contentious. Here are some common controversies and challenges in legal interpretation:

1. **Ambiguity and Vagueness:** Laws may contain ambiguous or vague language, which makes interpretation difficult. Different interpretations can lead to conflicting outcomes and undermine the predictability and consistency of the legal system.

2. **Judicial Activism vs. Restraint:** Debates arise regarding the appropriate role of judges in interpreting the law. Some argue for judicial activism, where judges actively shape the law to promote justice and social change.

Others advocate for judicial restraint, where judges limit their role to strictly interpreting the law as written.

3. **External Influences:** External factors, such as political ideology, public opinion, and social pressures, can influence legal interpretation. It raises concerns about the impartiality and objectivity of judges and the potential for biased decision-making.

4. **Inconsistent Precedents:** Precedents, or prior court decisions, play a crucial role in legal interpretation. However, inconsistencies in precedents or conflicting interpretations can create confusion and uncertainty. Courts must grapple with reconciling conflicting precedents or overturning them.

5. **Evolution of Society:** As society evolves, new legal issues and challenges emerge. Legal interpretation must adapt to these changes, leading to debates about how traditional legal principles and precedents apply or need to be reinterpreted in a contemporary context.

Resolving these controversies and challenges requires thoughtful analysis, open dialogue, and a commitment to the principles of justice and fairness.

Examples and Exercises

To better understand legal interpretation, let's consider an example:

Suppose a state statute prohibits the "sale of alcohol to minors." How would different theories of legal interpretation approach the interpretation of this provision?

- A textualist would focus solely on the plain meaning of the words "sale of alcohol to minors" and interpret the provision as prohibiting the act of selling alcohol to individuals below the legal drinking age.

- An originalist would examine the historical context and the intent of the lawmakers at the time of enacting the statute. They might consider the legal drinking age during that period and interpret the provision accordingly.

- A proponent of the living constitution theory would consider the underlying purpose of the provision and its societal implications. They might analyze the current legal drinking age and interpret the provision in light of contemporary social norms and values.

By examining this example from multiple theoretical perspectives, we can see how legal interpretation can lead to different outcomes and implications.

To further enhance your understanding, here are some exercises:

1.   Analyze a recent court case and identify the specific theory of legal interpretation employed by the court.   Discuss the reasoning behind the interpretation and its implications.

2. Consider a controversial legal issue, such as the interpretation of the Second Amendment of the United States Constitution. Explore different theories of legal interpretation and their application to this issue.   Assess the strengths and weaknesses of each approach.

3.   Research a landmark case where conflicting precedents were reconciled. Analyze the court's reasoning and its impact on legal interpretation.

4. Engage in a group discussion or a debate on the role of judges in interpreting the law. Discuss the advantages and disadvantages of judicial activism and judicial restraint.

Remember, legal interpretation is a dynamic and evolving field. Continuously engaging with real-world examples, current legal debates, and relevant case law will sharpen your understanding of legal interpretation and its practical implications.

Additional Resources

1. *Reading Law: The Interpretation of Legal Texts* by Antonin Scalia and Bryan A. Garner - This book provides an in-depth analysis of textualism and its application in legal interpretation.

2. *Interpreting Precedents: A Comparative Study* by Brian Simpson - This comparative study offers insights into the challenges and controversies surrounding precedent-based legal interpretation.

3. Legal research databases, such as Westlaw and LexisNexis, provide access to court decisions, legal commentary, and academic journals, enabling further exploration of legal interpretation and theory.

4. Academic journals, such as the *Harvard Law Review* and the *Yale Law Journal*, publish scholarly articles on legal interpretation and its theoretical underpinnings.

Remember to consult relevant legal authorities, such as statutes, case law, and legal treatises, to ensure accurate interpretation and analysis of legal issues.

Law and Social Change

Law plays a crucial role in shaping and influencing society. It has the power to bring about social change, transform norms, and address systemic issues of injustice. This section explores the relationship between law and social change, examining how legal mechanisms are used to promote a more equitable and just society.

Understanding Social Change

Social change refers to the process of altering societal structures, behaviors, and values. It involves the transformation of social norms, institutions, and power dynamics to address prevalent social issues. Social change can be driven by various factors, including political movements, technological advancements, cultural shifts, and legal reforms.

The Role of Law in Social Change

Law acts as a crucial tool for social change by providing a framework to address social problems and promote justice. It sets the boundaries for acceptable behavior in society and establishes the rights and obligations of individuals. Through legislation, courts, and regulatory agencies, the law has the power to shape social behavior and drive social change.

Legal Strategies for Social Change

Legal strategies for social change encompass a range of approaches to challenge and transform unjust social systems. Some of the key legal strategies employed are:

1. **Impact Litigation:** Impact litigation involves strategic lawsuits filed to challenge existing laws or practices. By targeting specific cases with broad implications, impact litigation can set legal precedents and bring about systemic change.

2. **Legislative Advocacy:** Advocacy for legislative reforms plays a significant role in driving social change. Activists and organizations engage in lobbying, drafting bills, and mobilizing public support to sway lawmakers and enact progressive policies.

3. **Constitutional Challenges:** Challenging laws or government actions on constitutional grounds can be a powerful way to bring about social change. By asserting violations of constitutional rights, individuals and groups can prompt courts to strike down discriminatory laws or practices.

4. **Public Interest Litigation:** Public interest litigation involves legal action initiated for the betterment of society as a whole. It empowers marginalized individuals or groups to seek legal remedies for social justice causes, such as environmental protection, healthcare access, or educational equity.

5. **Policy Advocacy:** Advocacy for policy changes aims to influence public opinion, shape legislative agendas, and promote progressive policies. Through research, public education campaigns, and grassroots organizing, advocates can generate momentum for social change at the policy level.

6. **Community Organizing:** Community organizing involves mobilizing communities to address social issues collectively. It focuses on empowering marginalized communities and fostering grassroots movements to demand change.

7. **International Human Rights Advocacy:** Advocacy at the international level, through engagement with human rights organizations and international treaties, can put pressure on governments to uphold human rights standards and affect social change.

Case Study: The Civil Rights Movement

The Civil Rights Movement in the United States serves as a powerful example of how law can drive social change. The movement fought for racial equality and an end to racial segregation and discrimination.

Impact litigation played a crucial role in challenging segregation laws. The landmark case *Brown v. Board of Education* (1954) led to the Supreme Court declaring racial segregation in public schools unconstitutional, setting the stage for desegregation efforts.

Legislative advocacy also played a vital role, culminating in the passage of the Civil Rights Act of 1964 and the Voting Rights Act of 1965. These laws outlawed racial segregation, discrimination, and barriers to voting rights, leading to significant social change.

The Civil Rights Movement also utilized public interest litigation and constitutional challenges. For instance, the case of *Loving v. Virginia* (1967) challenged laws banning interracial marriage, resulting in the Supreme Court striking down such laws as unconstitutional.

Community organizing and grassroots activism were integral to the movement's success. Through nonviolent protests, sit-ins, and marches, activists brought attention to the injustices faced by African Americans, generated public support, and pressured lawmakers to enact change.

Challenges and Limitations

While law can be a powerful force for social change, it also faces challenges and limitations. Some of these include:

1. **Resistance to Change:** Powerful interests may resist legal reforms that threaten their privilege and power. This resistance can manifest through opposition in courts, lobbying efforts, or even non-compliance with legal rulings.

2. **Slow Pace of Legal Processes:** Legal processes can be time-consuming, leading to delays and impeding swift social change. Litigation, for example, can take years to reach a verdict, slowing down the impact of legal strategies.

3. **Limited Access to the Legal System:** Marginalized individuals and communities often face barriers to accessing the legal system, including financial constraints, lack of legal representation, and systemic biases. This limited access limits their ability to drive social change through legal mechanisms.

4. **Interplay of Law and Power:** The law itself can be used as a tool of oppression and inequality, reflecting and perpetuating existing power structures. Challenging deeply entrenched systems of injustice requires addressing institutional biases and power imbalances.

5. **Co-optation of Reforms:** Sometimes, legal reforms may be co-opted or watered down to appease powerful interests. This can dilute the potential for meaningful social change and hinder progress.

Conclusion

Law plays a significant role in driving social change by providing a framework to challenge oppression, address inequalities, and promote justice. Through legal strategies such as impact litigation, legislative advocacy, and constitutional challenges, individuals and communities can bring about meaningful and lasting social change. However, challenges and limitations must be acknowledged, and efforts should be made to overcome systemic barriers to ensure the law's potential for social transformation is realized. Striving for a more just and equitable society requires ongoing engagement with the law and collective action to challenge unjust norms and systems.

Conclusion

In this chapter, we have explored various theories of law and their implications for legal studies. We have discussed the concepts of natural law theory, legal positivism, legal realism, critical legal studies, feminist legal theory, and their impact on legal interpretation and social change.

Natural law theory suggests that there are inherent moral principles that should guide the creation and application of laws. It emphasizes the importance of justice and the natural rights of individuals. On the other hand, legal positivism argues that the validity of law is determined by its source, such as legislation or legal precedent, rather than its moral content. Legal realists, however, criticize legal positivism for ignoring the social and political context in which laws are created. They emphasize the need for judges to consider the consequences and social impact of their decisions.

Critical legal studies provide a framework for analyzing the power dynamics embedded within legal systems and institutions. It highlights the role of law in perpetuating social inequality and seeks to challenge and transform oppressive legal structures. Feminist legal theory, on the other hand, emphasizes the importance of gender equality in legal analysis and advocates for the inclusion of women's experiences and perspectives in legal decision-making.

Legal interpretation is a complex process that involves not only applying the law to specific cases but also considering its ethical implications. Ethical considerations play a vital role in legal interpretation and application, as they guide judges in determining the just and fair outcome. Moreover, ethical principles inform the development of legal systems and shape the values and norms upon which laws are based.

Understanding the theories of law enables legal professionals to critically analyze the legal system and its impact on society. It also helps us to question and challenge the existing legal framework and advocate for change to promote justice and fairness.

As we move forward, it is crucial to recognize the ethical dimensions of legal studies and the importance of ethical decision-making. Legal professionals have an obligation to uphold and promote ethical conduct in their practice, including maintaining confidentiality, avoiding conflicts of interest, and prioritizing public interest.

The field of legal studies is constantly evolving and responding to contemporary ethical challenges. It is essential for legal practitioners and scholars to stay abreast of new ethical issues, such as advancements in technology, globalized business practices, and environmental concerns. By addressing these challenges with ethical awareness and critical thinking, we can strive towards a more equitable, just, and sustainable world.

In the next chapter, we will explore the ethical issues in the legal profession. We will examine the role and responsibilities of legal professionals, the challenges they face in maintaining ethical integrity, and strategies for upholding ethical standards in legal practice.

Legal Rights and Responsibilities

Definition and Classification of Rights

In the study of legal studies, it is crucial to understand the concept of rights as they form the very foundation of our legal system. Rights can be defined as legally recognized entitlements or privileges that individuals possess and can exercise. They serve as a framework for determining what individuals are permitted to do or possess, and what others are obligated to respect or provide.

Rights can be classified in various ways, depending on their nature, source, or the level of protection they enjoy. Let us examine some of the key classifications of rights:

Natural Rights and Legal Rights

One way to classify rights is by distinguishing between natural rights and legal rights. Natural rights are considered inherent to human beings, grounded in our nature or existence as rational and moral beings. These rights are often seen as universal, inalienable, and unalienable, meaning they cannot be taken away or transferred. Examples of natural rights include the right to life, liberty, and property.

On the other hand, legal rights are rights that are created, recognized, and enforced by the legal system. They are rights that individuals possess as a result of legal provisions, such as statutes, constitutions, or international treaties. Legal rights can vary across jurisdictions and may differ in their scope and protection. For example, the right to a fair trial is a legal right that is guaranteed in many legal systems.

Civil Rights and Political Rights

Civil rights and political rights are two important categories of rights often recognized in legal systems. Civil rights are concerned with individual freedoms, liberties, and protections from government interference. These rights ensure that individuals have the freedom to act and are protected from unlawful discrimination. Examples of civil rights include the right to freedom of speech, religion, and privacy.

Political rights, on the other hand, are rights that relate to participation in political processes and the governance of a society. These rights enable individuals to have a say in choosing their leaders, running for office, and participating in political activities. Examples of political rights include the right to vote, the right to political association, and the right to engage in peaceful assembly.

Positive Rights and Negative Rights

Rights can also be classified as positive rights or negative rights. Positive rights are rights that place a positive obligation on others to provide certain goods or services to individuals. These rights require action to be taken to fulfill them. For instance, the right to education is a positive right as it places an obligation on the government to provide access to education.

In contrast, negative rights are rights that impose a duty of non-interference on others. Negative rights require others to refrain from interfering with the exercise of these rights. Examples of negative rights include the right to freedom of expression and the right to personal property. Negative rights are often considered to be more closely aligned with the concept of negative liberty, which emphasizes the absence of constraints or interference.

Individual Rights and Collective Rights

Another way to classify rights is by distinguishing between individual rights and collective rights. Individual rights are rights that are possessed by individual persons and are exercised by them as individuals. These rights are typically focused on protecting individual interests and freedoms.

On the other hand, collective rights are rights that are held by a group of individuals who share a common characteristic, such as race, ethnicity, religion, or indigenous status. These rights are typically concerned with protecting the rights and interests of the group as a whole. Examples of collective rights include the right to self-determination of indigenous peoples and the right to cultural preservation.

Fundamental Rights and Derivative Rights

In many legal systems, certain rights are considered fundamental rights, which are deemed to be of paramount importance and enjoy a higher level of protection. These rights are often enshrined in constitutions or international human rights instruments. Examples of fundamental rights include the right to life, freedom from torture, and equality before the law.

Derivative rights, on the other hand, are rights that are derived from or dependent on fundamental rights. These rights are often derived from interpreting or applying fundamental rights in specific contexts. For example, the right to privacy is a derivative right that is derived from a broader interpretation of the right to personal liberty.

Conclusion

The definition and classification of rights are essential concepts in legal studies. Understanding the nature and scope of rights allows us to navigate the complexities of our legal system and better comprehend the principles and values that underpin it. By examining different classifications of rights, such as natural rights versus legal rights, civil rights versus political rights, positive rights versus negative rights, individual rights versus collective rights, and fundamental rights versus derivative rights, we can gain a comprehensive understanding of the diverse rights that individuals possess and the legal framework that protects and enforces these rights.

Remember, the classification of rights is not static and can evolve over time. Changes in society, advancements in technology, and shifts in political and cultural landscapes may lead to the recognition of new rights or the reinterpretation of existing ones. Stay engaged with current legal debates and developments to grasp the ever-evolving nature of rights and their significance in shaping a more equitable, just, and sustainable world.

Theories of Legal Rights

In the field of legal studies, understanding the concept of legal rights is essential. Legal rights define the entitlements that individuals have within a legal system. These rights not only shape the relationship between individuals and the state but also serve as the foundation for a just and equitable society. This section will explore various theories of legal rights, providing a comprehensive understanding of their nature, classification, and significance.

Nature of Legal Rights

Legal rights can be defined as legally recognized claims or entitlements that individuals possess. These rights are generally enforceable and protected by the legal system. They establish a framework within which people can exercise their freedoms and pursue their interests. Legal rights often arise from legal rules, laws, or constitutional provisions.

Several theories have been proposed to explain the nature of legal rights. These theories can be broadly categorized into two main perspectives: natural rights theory and positivist theory.

Natural Rights Theory　　Natural rights theory posits that legal rights are inherent to all individuals by virtue of their humanity. According to this perspective, legal rights are not created by the state but are rather discovered or recognized by it. Natural rights theorists argue that there are fundamental principles of justice and morality that exist independently of human-made laws.

One influential proponent of natural rights theory is John Locke. Locke argued that individuals possess natural rights to life, liberty, and property, and that the primary function of government is to protect these rights. The notion of natural rights serves as the basis for many legal systems around the world.

Positivist Theory　　In contrast to natural rights theory, positivist theory suggests that legal rights are created and defined by the state. According to this perspective, legal rights have no inherent or universal significance. They are solely derived from the laws and regulations enacted by the governing authority.

Legal positivists emphasize the importance of a clear legal framework in society. They argue that legal rights should be understood in the context of the legal system in which they are granted. The positivist perspective provides a foundation for understanding the role of legislation, court decisions, and other legal sources in defining and protecting legal rights.

Classification of Legal Rights

Legal rights can be classified in various ways, depending on their nature, scope, and source. Understanding the different categories of legal rights is crucial for analyzing legal issues and resolving disputes.

Individual Rights　　Individual rights refer to the rights held by individuals as separate entities. These rights protect individual autonomy, privacy, and personal liberties. Examples of individual rights include the right to freedom of speech, the right to due process, and the right to own property.

Individual rights are fundamental to democratic societies, as they safeguard the dignity and freedom of individuals. These rights are often protected by constitutional or human rights legislation and can be enforced through legal mechanisms, such as judicial review.

Collective Rights   Collective rights, also known as group or community rights, pertain to the rights held by communities or groups of individuals. These rights recognize the importance of collective identity, cultural heritage, and social cohesion. Examples of collective rights include the right to self-determination, the right to cultural preservation, and the right to collective bargaining.

Collective rights reflect the recognition that individuals are not merely isolated entities but are interconnected with and influenced by their social environment. These rights are particularly relevant in contexts of cultural diversity and indigenous populations, where the protection of collective rights is essential for maintaining social harmony.

Legal Rights vs. Moral Rights   Another important classification of legal rights is the distinction between legal rights and moral rights. Legal rights are granted and protected by the legal system, while moral rights are based on ethical or moral principles. Although there is often an overlap between legal and moral rights, not all moral rights are legally recognized, and not all legal rights are morally justified.

This distinction highlights the evolving nature of legal systems and the complex relationship between law and ethics. Legal theorists grapple with the challenge of reconciling conflicting moral values and societal norms when determining the scope and content of legal rights.

Theories of Legal Rights

Several theories have been developed to explain the foundation and justification of legal rights. These theories provide different perspectives on the nature, source, and limits of legal rights.

Interest Theory   The interest theory of legal rights posits that legal rights are based on the protection of individual or societal interests. According to this theory, legal rights are defined to safeguard core interests and promote social welfare. The interests that are considered essential may vary depending on cultural, social, and political contexts.

The interest theory provides a pragmatic approach to understanding legal rights. It emphasizes the importance of balancing and prioritizing different interests within a legal framework. For example, in the context of environmental law, legal rights may be granted to individuals or groups to protect their interests in clean air and water, even if these rights may restrict the interests of others.

Dignity Theory   The dignity theory of legal rights asserts that legal rights are grounded in human dignity. According to this theory, individuals possess inherent dignity by virtue of their humanity, and legal rights are necessary to respect and protect this dignity.

This theory has its roots in moral philosophy, particularly in the works of Immanuel Kant. Kant argued that individuals should be treated as ends in themselves, rather than means to an end. Legal rights, in this view, serve as a means to uphold human dignity and ensure equal treatment and respect for all individuals.

Capabilities Approach   The capabilities approach, developed by economist Amartya Sen and philosopher Martha Nussbaum, provides a different framework for understanding legal rights.   This approach emphasizes the importance of enabling individuals to have the capabilities to lead flourishing and fulfilled lives.

According to the capabilities approach, legal rights should not only focus on protecting basic interests but also on promoting the capabilities necessary for individuals to live meaningful lives. These capabilities include access to education, healthcare, and opportunities for self-determination and self-development.

Significance of Legal Rights

Legal rights play a crucial role in shaping a just and equitable society. They provide a framework for individuals to exercise their freedoms and pursue their interests, while also recognizing the importance of collective identity and social cohesion. Legal rights establish the boundaries of permissible actions, ensure equal treatment under the law, and provide remedies for violations.

Understanding and defending legal rights is crucial for individuals, legal professionals, and policymakers. It requires a nuanced analysis of legal principles, ethical considerations, and social contexts.

Conclusion

Theories of legal rights provide a foundation for understanding the nature, classification, and significance of legal rights in a legal system. The perspective one adopts regarding the nature of legal rights influences how laws are interpreted and applied.

The classification of legal rights helps to categorize and analyze different types of rights, such as individual rights and collective rights. Moreover, the distinction between legal rights and moral rights highlights the complex relationship between law and ethics.

Lastly, theories of legal rights, such as the interest theory, dignity theory, and capabilities approach, provide different perspectives on the foundation and justification of legal rights. These theories contribute to the ongoing discussion about the principles and values that underpin legal systems.

By examining the theories of legal rights, legal professionals, scholars, and students can gain a deeper understanding of the complexities and nuances involved in the field of legal studies.

Constitutional Rights and Liberties

Constitutional rights and liberties refer to the fundamental freedoms and protections granted to individuals under the Constitution of a country. These rights serve as a safeguard against government intrusion and ensure that citizens can enjoy certain inherent and inalienable rights. In this section, we will explore the concept of constitutional rights and liberties, their significance, the constitutional basis for these rights, and the challenges and controversies surrounding their implementation.

Understanding Constitutional Rights and Liberties

Constitutional rights and liberties encompass a wide range of civil, political, and social rights that are protected by the constitution. These rights are considered fundamental and are typically accorded a high level of legal protection. They provide individuals with the necessary freedom and autonomy to live their lives without unwarranted interference from the government or other entities.

Constitutional rights can include freedom of speech, freedom of religion, freedom of the press, the right to privacy, the right to a fair trial, the right to bear arms, and many others. These rights are essential for fostering a democratic society, ensuring equal treatment under the law, and upholding the principles of justice and fairness.

Constitutional Basis for Rights and Liberties

The constitutional basis for rights and liberties varies across different countries and legal systems. In some countries, these rights are explicitly enumerated in a bill of rights or a separate constitutional provision. For example, the United States

Constitution includes the Bill of Rights, which guarantees various individual rights and liberties.

In other countries, rights and liberties may be protected through constitutional principles, such as the right to human dignity, equality, or due process. These principles provide a broader framework for interpreting and protecting individual rights, allowing for flexibility in adapting to societal changes and evolving needs.

Challenges and Controversies

The implementation of constitutional rights and liberties is not without challenges and controversies. One of the key challenges is striking a balance between individual rights and the common good. While constitutional rights aim to protect individual freedoms, they must also consider the broader societal interests and the need for public order and safety.

Another major challenge is the interpretation and application of constitutional rights in specific situations. Courts often face difficult questions regarding the scope and limits of certain rights, especially when rights conflict or when there is a clash between individual rights and other societal interests. For example, the right to freedom of speech may need to be balanced against the right to a fair trial or protection against hate speech.

Controversies also arise when determining the boundaries of constitutional rights. As society evolves and new challenges emerge, courts and lawmakers must grapple with the application of constitutional rights to novel circumstances. Issues such as technological advancements, privacy concerns, and the balancing of competing rights often present complex legal and ethical dilemmas.

Additionally, there can be disparities in the realization of constitutional rights and liberties among different groups within society. Marginalized communities, minorities, and vulnerable individuals may face systemic barriers that hinder their full enjoyment of these rights. Addressing these disparities and promoting equal access to and protection of constitutional rights is an ongoing challenge.

Example: Freedom of Speech and Hate Speech

Freedom of speech is a fundamental constitutional right that allows individuals to express their thoughts, opinions, and beliefs without censorship or government interference. However, the line between protected speech and impermissible speech, such as hate speech, can be contentious.

Hate speech refers to speech, gestures, or other forms of expression that offends, threatens, or insults individuals or groups based on attributes such as race, religion, ethnic origin, sexual orientation, or gender identity. Balancing the right to freedom of speech with the need to protect individuals from harm poses a challenge for legal systems worldwide.

Courts and lawmakers must carefully delineate the boundaries of hate speech regulation to prevent the infringement of free expression rights while also safeguarding individuals from discrimination and harm. Striking the right balance requires a nuanced understanding of the cultural, social, and historical contexts in which hate speech occurs.

For example, in the United States, the First Amendment protects a broad interpretation of freedom of speech, including hate speech, unless it incites imminent violence. In contrast, many European countries have enacted legislation that criminalizes hate speech, even if it does not explicitly incite violence.

Resolving the tension between protecting individuals from harmful speech and upholding free expression requires ongoing debate and consideration of the specific societal context. It highlights the complex nature of constitutional rights and the need for continual reassessment of their boundaries in the face of evolving challenges.

Resources and Further Reading

- Amar, A. R. (2007). America's Constitution: A Biography. Random House. - Chemerinsky, E. (2019). Constitutional law: Principles and policies. Wolters Kluwer. - Sunstein, C. R. (2017). Free Speech: Ten Principles for a Connected World. Yale University Press. - Waldron, J. (2012). The harm in hate speech. Harvard University Press.

Exercises

1. Consider a case where freedom of speech conflicts with another constitutional right. Discuss the factors that courts should consider when balancing these conflicting rights.

2. Research a country that has recently faced a controversy related to constitutional rights and liberties. Analyze the arguments presented by both sides and discuss the potential implications for the protection of individual rights.

3. Explore a landmark court case that addressed the interpretation and application of a specific constitutional right. Explain the significance of the case and its impact on the legal landscape.

4. Investigate the constitutional rights in your own country's constitution or bill of rights. Identify any gaps or areas that could benefit from further clarification or protection.

5.   Interview a legal expert or practitioner on the challenges they have encountered when dealing with constitutional rights and liberties. Discuss their perspectives on the importance of upholding these rights and the complexities involved in their implementation.

Remember to consult relevant legal sources and academic materials to deepen your understanding of constitutional rights and liberties.

Individual Rights vs. Collective Responsibilities

In legal studies, the tension between individual rights and collective responsibilities is a recurring ethical dilemma. It raises questions about how to balance the rights of individuals with the needs and well-being of the broader society. This section will explore the philosophical underpinnings of individual rights and collective responsibilities, the challenges in reconciling them, and potential strategies for finding a delicate balance.

Concept of Individual Rights

Individual rights refer to the entitlements and freedoms that individuals possess by virtue of being human beings. These rights are often considered fundamental and inherent, and they are protected by various legal frameworks and human rights instruments. Examples of individual rights include the right to life, liberty, property, privacy, and freedom of expression.

Concept of Collective Responsibilities

Collective responsibilities, on the other hand, emphasize the obligations and duties that individuals have towards the larger society or community. They recognize that individual actions can have a significant impact on the well-being of others and the broader social fabric. Collective responsibilities may include participating in community service, respecting and promoting social justice, and contributing to the betterment of society.

The Balancing Act

Finding the right balance between individual rights and collective responsibilities can pose significant challenges. On one hand, excessive emphasis on individual rights can lead to a disregard for the common good and result in social inequality and injustice. On the other hand, an overemphasis on collective responsibilities can infringe upon individual freedoms and limit personal autonomy.

To address this tension, legal systems often rely on legal principles, moral reasoning, and democratic decision-making processes. Principles such as proportionality, subsidiarity, and the rule of law can guide the interpretation and application of individual rights and collective responsibilities.

Case Study: Balancing Individual Privacy and Public Safety

An illustrative example of the interplay between individual rights and collective responsibilities is the debate surrounding privacy rights and public safety measures. In the context of combating terrorism or crime, there is an inherent tension between an individual's right to privacy and the collective responsibility to maintain public safety.

For instance, the use of surveillance technologies, such as CCTV cameras or digital surveillance tools, can potentially infringe on individual privacy rights. However, proponents argue that these measures are necessary for ensuring public safety and preventing potential threats. Striking a balance requires careful consideration of the specific circumstances, the effectiveness of the measures in achieving their stated objectives, and the potential impact on individual rights.

Theoretical Perspectives

Various theories and ethical frameworks offer insights into the balance between individual rights and collective responsibilities. Utilitarianism, for example, argues that actions should be judged based on their overall utility and the greatest happiness for the greatest number of people. From a utilitarian perspective, individual rights may be restricted if doing so serves the greater collective good.

Conversely, deontological ethics, as championed by philosophers like Immanuel Kant, emphasizes the intrinsic value of individual rights and holds that they should not be violated, regardless of the potential social benefits.

Promoting Dialogue and Deliberation

Given the complexity of balancing individual rights and collective responsibilities, fostering open dialogue and deliberation is crucial. Engaging in informed discussions, considering diverse perspectives, and respecting the principles of fairness and justice can lead to more nuanced and thoughtful decision-making.

Educational institutions, legal professionals, and civil society organizations play a vital role in promoting such dialogue and raising awareness about the ethical dimensions of this tension. Through the teaching of ethics in legal education, public awareness campaigns, and advocacy efforts, individuals can develop a deeper understanding of the ethical considerations involved and work towards a more equitable and just society.

Conclusion

The tension between individual rights and collective responsibilities is a pervasive issue in legal studies. Balancing the two can be challenging, as it requires considering the impact on both individuals and society as a whole. By engaging in thoughtful discussions, exploring different theoretical perspectives, and promoting ethical decision-making, we can navigate this dilemma and strive towards a harmonious coexistence of individual rights and collective responsibilities.

Legal Enforcement of Rights

In this section, we will explore the concept of legal enforcement of rights, which plays a crucial role in ensuring the protection and promotion of individual and collective rights within a legal system. The legal enforcement of rights refers to the mechanism through which rights are upheld, defended, and guaranteed by legal authorities, such as courts or administrative bodies. This involves the application of laws, regulations, and legal procedures to address violations of rights and provide remedies for those affected.

Principles of Legal Enforcement

Legal enforcement of rights is guided by several key principles that are fundamental to the functioning of a just legal system. These principles include:

1. **Access to Justice:** The principle of access to justice ensures that all individuals have the right to seek legal remedies and have their cases heard by a competent and impartial judicial or administrative body.

2. **Equality before the Law:** The principle of equality before the law guarantees that all individuals, regardless of their social status, wealth, or power, are subject to the same legal rules and are entitled to equal protection of their rights.

3. **Rule of Law:** The principle of the rule of law signifies that the legal system operates based on clear, predictable, and transparent laws and procedures. It requires that laws be applied consistently and impartially to ensure fairness and prevent arbitrary actions by those in power.

4. **Procedural Fairness:** Legal enforcement of rights requires adherence to principles of procedural fairness, including the right to a fair and public hearing, the right to be heard, the right to legal representation, and the right to present evidence and challenge opposing arguments.

5. **Enforceability:** For legal enforcement to be effective, it is crucial that the rights being enforced are clear, specific, and enforceable. This requires the existence of legislation, regulations, or judicial precedents that recognize and protect these rights.

These principles provide a foundation for the legal enforcement of rights, ensuring the preservation of a just and equitable society.

Mechanisms of Legal Enforcement

There are several mechanisms through which legal enforcement of rights takes place. These mechanisms may vary depending on the nature of the rights being enforced and the legal system in which they operate. Some common mechanisms include:

1. **Legal Proceedings:** Legal enforcement often involves the initiation of legal proceedings, such as filing a lawsuit or complaint, to seek a remedy for a violation of rights. This may include civil litigation for damages, administrative proceedings for regulatory enforcement, or criminal prosecution for the violation of criminal laws.

2. **Judicial Review:** Judicial review is a mechanism through which courts evaluate the constitutionality and legality of laws, regulations, or government actions. It allows individuals or groups to challenge laws or actions they believe violate their rights and seek remedies through the court system.

3. **Injunctive Relief:** In cases where immediate action is required to prevent further harm or protect rights, injunctive relief may be sought. This involves requesting a court to issue an injunction, which is a court order that prohibits or compels certain actions.

4. **Alternative Dispute Resolution:** In addition to formal court proceedings, alternative dispute resolution methods, such as mediation or arbitration, can be used to resolve disputes and enforce rights. These methods provide a less formal and more collaborative approach to resolving conflicts outside of the traditional court system.

5. **Remedies and Damages:** Legal enforcement of rights aims to provide remedies for individuals whose rights have been violated. Remedies may include compensation for damages, restitution, specific performance, or other forms of relief as deemed appropriate by the court or administrative body.

By utilizing these mechanisms, legal systems work to ensure that individuals can enforce their rights and seek redress for any violations they may have experienced.

Challenges in Legal Enforcement

While legal enforcement of rights is essential for the protection of individuals and the promotion of justice, it is not without its challenges. Some common challenges include:

1. **Access to Justice:** Limited access to legal resources, high costs of legal representation, and complex legal procedures can create barriers for individuals seeking to enforce their rights. This can result in unequal access to justice, particularly for marginalized and disadvantaged communities.

2. **Delays in Legal Proceedings:** Lengthy court processes and backlogs can significantly delay the resolution of cases and impede timely access to justice. This can undermine the effectiveness of the legal enforcement of rights, as justice delayed is often justice denied.

3. **Lack of Awareness:** Many individuals may not be aware of their rights or how to enforce them. This lack of awareness can prevent people from taking appropriate legal action when their rights are violated, perpetuating the violation and weakening the overall legal enforcement framework.

4. **Enforcement Gaps:** In some cases, the laws may exist to protect rights, but their enforcement may be weak or inconsistent. This can occur due to limited resources, corruption, or lack of political will. These enforcement gaps can undermine the effectiveness of the legal system in upholding rights.

Addressing these challenges requires a multi-faceted approach, including legal reforms, increased access to legal aid, public education on rights, and the promotion of transparency and accountability within the legal system.

Case Example: Enforcing Environmental Rights

One pertinent example of legal enforcement of rights is the enforcement of environmental rights. As societies become more aware of the importance of protecting the environment, laws and regulations have been developed to safeguard the right to a clean and healthy environment.

In many countries, constitutional provisions, statutes, and international agreements recognize the right to a clean environment. However, enforcing these rights can be challenging due to various factors. For instance, in cases where industries are causing environmental harm, affected communities may face obstacles in accessing justice due to limited financial resources or a lack of awareness of their rights and legal remedies.

To address these challenges, legal strategies have been developed to enforce environmental rights. Public interest litigation, for example, allows individuals or organizations to take legal action on behalf of the general public or affected communities. This approach can help overcome the barriers faced by individuals and promote the public's environmental interests.

In some cases, non-governmental organizations (NGOs) play a vital role in enforcing environmental rights. They may engage in advocacy, research, and litigation to seek legal remedies for environmental harm. Through strategic litigation, NGOs can raise awareness, hold polluters accountable, and contribute to the development of environmental jurisprudence.

Furthermore, alternative dispute resolution mechanisms, such as mediation or negotiation, can also be employed to resolve environmental disputes without resorting to lengthy and costly legal proceedings. These processes facilitate stakeholder involvement and cooperation, leading to more sustainable solutions that consider the interests of all parties involved.

Overall, the enforcement of environmental rights demonstrates the critical role of legal mechanisms in protecting the environment and ensuring future generations' well-being. By employing innovative legal strategies and fostering public participation, the legal enforcement of environmental rights can contribute to sustainable development and social justice.

Conclusion

The legal enforcement of rights is an integral part of ensuring justice and upholding individual and collective rights within a legal system. Guided by principles of access to justice, equality, the rule of law, procedural fairness, and enforceability, the legal enforcement of rights aims to protect individuals from rights violations and provide remedies for those affected.

Mechanisms such as legal proceedings, judicial review, injunctive relief, alternative dispute resolution, and remedies and damages play a crucial role in enforcing rights. However, challenges such as limited access to justice, delays in legal proceedings, lack of awareness, and enforcement gaps can hinder the effectiveness of legal enforcement.

Addressing these challenges requires a comprehensive and multi-faceted approach, including legal reforms, increased access to justice, public education, and the promotion of transparency and accountability within the legal system. Through the enforcement of rights, legal systems can contribute to a more equitable, just, and sustainable world.

Ethics of Rights and Responsibilities

In this section, we explore the ethical considerations related to rights and responsibilities within the legal framework. We examine the moral foundation of rights, the ethical implications of legal rights and enforcement, and the ethical responsibilities associated with exercising these rights.

Moral Foundation of Rights

Rights are moral and legal entitlements that individuals possess, which empower them to act or be protected in a certain manner. The moral foundation of rights is based on the idea that all individuals have inherent dignity and worth, and as such, deserve certain basic rights and freedoms. These rights are often seen as universal and inalienable.

Several theories explain the moral foundation of rights. One prominent theory is natural rights theory, which asserts that rights are inherent to human nature and exist independently of any legal or social structures. According to natural rights theory, individuals possess rights simply by virtue of being human, and these rights cannot be justifiably violated.

Another theory is the social contract theory, which posits that individuals enter into a social contract, either implicitly or explicitly, to form a society and government. In this contract, individuals give up certain freedoms in exchange for protection and the guarantee of basic rights. This theory emphasizes the reciprocal nature of rights and responsibilities within a society.

Ethical Implications of Legal Rights

Legal rights are a subset of moral rights that are recognized and enforceable by law. While legal rights provide individuals with protections and freedoms, they also come with ethical implications.

One ethical implication is the balance between individual rights and the collective responsibilities of society. While individuals have the right to freedom of speech, for example, this right is not absolute and may be limited to protect the rights and well-being of others. Ethical considerations arise when determining the extent to which individual rights can be curtailed for the common good.

Another ethical consideration is the potential for rights to be used in an exploitative or discriminatory manner. Legal rights can be weaponized to promote discrimination or perpetuate social inequalities. For example, the right to private property can be used to reinforce wealth disparities and exclude marginalized groups from accessing resources. Ethical reasoning must be applied to ensure that legal rights are not being misused to the detriment of others.

Ethical Responsibilities

With rights come responsibilities. Individuals who are endowed with certain rights also have ethical responsibilities to ensure the fair and just exercise of those rights. These responsibilities include but are not limited to:

1. Respect for the rights of others: Individuals must respect the rights of others and avoid actions that infringe upon or violate their rights. This requires recognizing the equal worth and dignity of all individuals and treating them with fairness and respect.

2. Exercising rights responsibly: Individuals have a responsibility to exercise their rights in a manner that does not cause harm to others or undermine the rights of others. For example, freedom of speech should not be used to spread hate speech or incite violence.

3. Promoting justice and equality: Individuals who possess certain rights have a moral responsibility to advocate for justice and equality. This may involve standing up against injustices, advocating for policy changes, or supporting marginalized communities in their quest for equal rights and opportunities.

4. Balancing individual and collective interests: Individuals must strike a balance between their individual rights and the collective interests of society. This requires considering the impact of one's actions on others and making choices that promote the overall well-being of society.

5. Upholding the rule of law: Individuals have an ethical responsibility to abide by the laws of their society, provided those laws are just and equitable. Respecting the rule of law ensures a fair and orderly society where the rights of all individuals are protected.

Case Study: Balancing Rights and Responsibilities

Consider the case of a newspaper publishing company that is facing a dilemma regarding the publication of controversial content. The company has the legal right to publish the content under freedom of the press, but it also has a responsibility to consider the potential harm that the content may cause to individuals or communities.

In this case, the company must navigate the ethical tension between protecting the right to freedom of expression and avoiding harm or discrimination. It needs to consider whether the potential benefits of publishing the content outweigh the potential harm that may result. Ethical reasoning and a careful assessment of the impact on individuals or communities involved can guide the decision-making process.

Resources for Further Exploration

1. "Ethics in the Practice of Law: A Guide to the Model Rules of Professional Conduct" by Richard Zitrin and Carol M. Langford. 2. "Ethics in Law: Lawyers' Responsibility and Accountability in Australia" by Prue Vines. 3. "Human Rights: A Very Short Introduction" by Andrew Clapham. 4. The Stanford Encyclopedia of Philosophy: Entry on "Rights" by Leif Wenar. 5. The United Nations Universal Declaration of Human Rights.

Key Takeaways

- Rights are moral and legal entitlements that individuals possess based on their inherent dignity and worth. - Legal rights have ethical implications, including the balance between individual rights and collective responsibilities and the potential for rights to be used in discriminatory ways. - Individuals with rights have ethical responsibilities, such as respecting the rights of others, exercising rights responsibly, promoting justice and equality, and upholding the rule of law. - Balancing rights and responsibilities requires thoughtful ethical reasoning and consideration of the potential impact on others. - Resources such as books, articles, and international documents can provide further insights into the ethical dimensions of rights and responsibilities.

Legal Ethics and Human Rights

Legal ethics and human rights are two essential and interconnected aspects of the legal profession. Lawyers have a moral and ethical responsibility to uphold and promote human rights through their practice. In this section, we will explore the intersection of legal ethics and human rights, examining the ethical considerations lawyers face when representing clients and advocating for justice.

The Importance of Legal Ethics in Protecting Human Rights

Legal ethics provide a framework for ensuring that lawyers act with integrity, professionalism, and respect for the rule of law. When it comes to human rights, lawyers play a crucial role in advocating for and protecting the rights of individuals and communities. It is through ethical practice that lawyers can effectively contribute to the development and enforcement of human rights laws.

Confidentiality and Attorney-Client Privilege: Ethical Challenges

One of the core ethical obligations of lawyers is maintaining client confidentiality and preserving attorney-client privilege. This duty ensures that clients can trust their lawyers to keep their information confidential and provide them with a safe and secure environment to discuss their legal issues.

However, preserving confidentiality can pose ethical challenges in cases where lawyers become aware of potential human rights violations. For example, if a lawyer learns that their client is engaging in illegal activities that infringe upon the rights of others, they face a conflict between their duty to their client and their duty to uphold the principles of justice and human rights.

In such situations, lawyers must carefully navigate their ethical responsibilities and consider whether disclosure of information to the appropriate authorities is necessary to prevent further harm or protect the rights of others. This dilemma requires lawyers to balance their loyalty to their client with their broader obligations to society and uphold the principles of justice and human rights.

Balancing Zealous Advocacy with Ethical Considerations

As advocates for their clients, lawyers have a duty to provide zealous representation and advance their clients' interests to the best of their abilities. However, this duty must be balanced with ethical considerations, particularly when representing clients whose actions may violate human rights.

Lawyers must navigate ethical dilemmas when their client's interests collide with the principles of justice and human rights. In such situations, lawyers may need to engage in a thoughtful and nuanced approach, seeking alternative legal remedies, engaging in negotiations, or advising clients on the ethical implications of their actions. It is essential for lawyers to uphold their ethical responsibilities while still providing the best possible representation for their clients.

Ethics in Public Interest Litigation

Public interest litigation is a powerful tool for promoting human rights and challenging unjust laws and practices. Lawyers engaged in public interest litigation often represent marginalized communities, seeking justice and social change on their behalf.

In this context, lawyers face unique ethical considerations. They must carefully choose cases and causes that align with their values and principles of human rights. Public interest lawyers must also exercise caution when dealing with potential conflicts of interest and maintain transparency and accountability in their representation.

Moreover, public interest lawyers must navigate the delicate balance between advocating for the rights of their clients and working towards broader systemic change. Ethics play a crucial role in ensuring that lawyers engage in responsible and effective advocacy that drives social justice without sacrificing the interests and rights of individual clients.

Resources for Legal Ethics and Human Rights

To deepen your understanding of legal ethics and human rights, here are some resources that you can explore:

1. *The ABA Model Rules of Professional Conduct* - This publication provides a comprehensive set of ethical rules and guidelines for lawyers in the United States. It covers various aspects of legal ethics, including client confidentiality, conflicts of interest, and advocacy for justice and fairness.

2. *United Nations Human Rights Treaties and Declarations* - These international legal instruments outline the fundamental human rights and provide a framework for ensuring their protection and promotion. Reading these treaties will provide valuable insights into the principles and values underlying human rights.

3. *Ethics in the Practice of Law* by Lisa G. Lerman and Philip G. Schrag - This book explores the ethical dilemmas and challenges faced by lawyers in their

professional practice. It discusses real-world cases and provides practical guidance on ethical decision-making.

4. Legal ethics and human rights organizations - Many organizations focus on the intersection of legal ethics and human rights. Exploring the work and publications of organizations such as the International Bar Association's Human Rights Institute or the American Civil Liberties Union can provide valuable insights into contemporary issues and debates in this field.

Conclusion

Legal ethics and human rights are inextricably linked, and lawyers have a crucial role to play in promoting and protecting human rights through their ethical practice. By balancing the duty of zealous advocacy with broader concerns for justice and fairness, lawyers can contribute to shaping a more equitable and just society. It is essential for aspiring legal professionals to develop a deep understanding of legal ethics and human rights to navigate the complex ethical challenges they will face in their careers.

Conclusion

In this section, we have explored the ethical issues in legal studies, focusing on the moral foundations of law and justice. We began by discussing the concepts of morality and justice, and their relationship to each other. We examined various theories of justice, including egalitarianism, libertarianism, communitarianism, and feminist theories. These theories provide different perspectives on what is considered fair and just in society.

We also delved into the theories of law, such as natural law theory, legal positivism, legal realism, critical legal studies, and feminist legal theory. These theories shed light on the nature and purpose of law, and the ethical implications of legal principles and rules. We explored the tension between individual rights and collective responsibilities, and the ethical considerations involved in the enforcement of legal rights.

Furthermore, we examined the ethical issues that arise in the legal profession. We discussed the role and responsibilities of legal professionals, and the ethical obligations they have in their practice. We explored the importance of confidentiality and attorney-client privilege, and the challenges in maintaining confidentiality while fulfilling other ethical duties. We also delved into the concept of conflict of interest and the ethical implications it poses in legal practice.

Next, we considered the concept of social justice and human rights. We explored theories of social justice, such as egalitarianism, libertarianism, communitarianism, and feminist theories, and their implications for promoting equality and fairness in society. We examined the historical evolution of human rights and international instruments that protect them.   We discussed the challenges and controversies surrounding human rights protection, and the intersection between human rights and social justice.

We then turned our attention to the ethical issues in criminal justice. We discussed the principles of criminal justice ethics and the role and responsibilities of criminal justice professionals.   We examined ethical dilemmas in law enforcement, criminal prosecution, and the correctional system. We also explored the ethical controversies surrounding capital punishment and the ethical challenges faced by the police force.

Moving on, we explored the ethical issues in business and commerce. We discussed the concept of business ethics and the ethical considerations in corporate governance, corporate social responsibility, marketing and advertising, and decision making in business. We also examined the ethical dilemmas associated with intellectual property rights and the challenges of balancing copyright protection with access to knowledge. We considered the ethical implications of globalization in the business environment, including human rights in global supply chains, corruption, and environmental sustainability.

Finally, we examined the role of law in social change and reform. We discussed law as a tool for social change, legal activism, and the impact of litigation on promoting social justice. We explored the role of law in promoting sustainable development and addressing environmental regulation. We examined the ethical implications of technological advancements in the legal field, including privacy and data protection, artificial intelligence, and cybersecurity.

In conclusion, navigating the philosophical and ethical issues in legal studies is essential for promoting justice and shaping a more equitable, just, and sustainable world. By understanding the moral foundations of law and justice, recognizing the ethical challenges in legal practice, and addressing social justice and human rights issues, we can create a legal system that upholds the principles of fairness, equality, and integrity. The legal profession plays a crucial role in ensuring ethical conduct and advocating for social change. As future legal professionals, it is our responsibility to navigate moral dilemmas, promote justice, and contribute to a more equitable and just society.

Key Terms:

+ Morality

+ Justice

+ Egalitarianism

+ Libertarianism

+ Communitarianism

+ Feminist theories of justice

+ Natural law theory

+ Legal positivism

+ Legal realism

+ Critical legal studies

+ Feminist legal theory

+ Conflict of interest

+ Social justice

+ Human rights

+ Criminal justice ethics

+ Capital punishment

+ Business ethics

+ Intellectual property rights

+ Globalization

+ Law and social change

+ Sustainable development

+ Technology and ethics

Resources:

+ *Ethics in the Legal Profession: Navigating the Gray Area*, by Deborah L. Rhoads

+ *Theories of Justice: A Treatise on Social Justice*, by Brian Barry

+ *Legal Ethics: A Comparative Study*, by Terrence Cain

- *Human Rights: Concepts, Issues, and Debates,* edited by Paul Allott and Roma K. Hanks

- *Global Business Ethics: Responsible Decision Making in an International Context,* by Ronald Francis

- *Law and Social Change,* edited by W. A. Parent and Ruth R. McVey

- *Sustainable Development Law: Principles, Practices, and Prospects,* by Marie-Claire Cordonier Segger and Ashfaq Khalfan

- *Technology and Ethics: A European Quest for Responsible Engineering,* edited by Teun Lucassen and Pieter E. Vermaas

Exercises

1. Discuss the ethical implications of the natural law theory in legal decision making. Provide examples to illustrate your points.

2. Choose a contemporary social justice issue (e.g., income inequality, racial discrimination, climate change) and analyze the ethical challenges it presents in the field of law. Explain how legal professionals can contribute to addressing these challenges.

3. Consider the role of ethics in the criminal justice system. Discuss the potential conflicts between upholding ethical principles and achieving social justice. How can these conflicts be resolved?

4. Explore the ethical considerations in intellectual property rights protection in the digital age. Discuss the challenges of balancing the rights of creators with the need for access to knowledge and information.

Ethical Issues in Legal Profession

Professionalism and Ethics

Role and Responsibilities of Legal Professionals

In the field of legal studies, legal professionals play a crucial role in upholding the principles of justice and maintaining the integrity of the legal system. They are entrusted with various responsibilities that require a high level of ethical conduct and adherence to professional standards. In this section, we will explore the role and responsibilities of legal professionals, discussing their obligations, the challenges they face, and strategies for maintaining ethical integrity in legal practice.

Obligations of Legal Professionals

Legal professionals, including lawyers, judges, and other legal practitioners, have a set of obligations that guide their professional behavior. These obligations are derived from ethical principles and professional codes of conduct. It is essential for legal professionals to recognize and uphold these obligations in order to fulfill their role within the legal system effectively.

1. **Duty to the Legal System:** Legal professionals have a duty to uphold the integrity of the legal system. This includes respecting and obeying the law, maintaining the principles of justice, and promoting fairness and equality. They should strive to ensure that the legal process is accessible, efficient, and impartial.

2. **Duty to Clients:** Legal professionals have a primary duty to their clients. They must provide competent and diligent representation, acting in their clients' best interests within the bounds of the law. This duty includes maintaining

confidentiality, protecting attorney-client privilege, and providing accurate and honest advice.

3. Duty to the Court: Legal professionals have a duty to the court and the administration of justice. They must act honestly and with integrity in their dealings with the court, presenting arguments and evidence accurately and avoiding any conduct that may undermine the fairness of the judicial process.

4. Duty to Opposing Parties and Counsel: Legal professionals have an ethical duty to treat opposing parties and counsel with respect and candor. They should avoid engaging in unethical tactics or behavior that could harm the reputation or rights of others involved in the legal process.

5. Duty to the Public: Legal professionals have a broader duty to the public. They should promote public trust and confidence in the legal system and the rule of law. They should strive to enhance access to justice, advocate for the disadvantaged, and participate in pro bono activities.

Challenges and Ethical Dilemmas

Legal professionals often face various challenges in their role, which can give rise to ethical dilemmas. These challenges may arise from conflicts between their obligations, uncertainties in the law, competing interests, or external pressures. It is crucial for legal professionals to navigate these challenges while maintaining ethical integrity.

1. Conflicts of Interest: Legal professionals may encounter conflicts of interest, where their personal, financial, or professional interests interfere with their duty to their clients, the court, or the public. Identifying and addressing conflicts of interest is essential to maintain trust and avoid compromising the integrity of the legal profession.

2. Ethical Dilemmas in Advocacy: Legal professionals often face ethical dilemmas in their advocacy role. Balancing their duty to provide zealous representation for their clients with their obligation to ensure fairness and integrity in the legal process can be challenging. They must make ethical decisions when confronted with sensitive issues, such as presenting evidence, cross-examining witnesses, or challenging the credibility of opposing parties.

3. Maintaining Confidentiality: Legal professionals are entrusted with confidential information by their clients. Maintaining confidentiality and attorney-client privilege is crucial, but it can present challenges, particularly when there are competing obligations, such as preventing harm or complying with the law. Legal professionals must navigate these situations while preserving the trust and confidence of their clients.

4. Ethical Implications of Technology: The use of technology in legal practice presents ethical challenges for legal professionals. Issues such as cybersecurity, privacy rights, and the use of artificial intelligence raise complex ethical considerations. Legal professionals must adapt to technological advancements while ensuring the protection of client information and upholding ethical standards.

Strategies for Maintaining Ethical Integrity

Maintaining ethical integrity is vital for legal professionals to uphold the principles of justice and promote the public's trust and confidence in the legal system. There are several strategies that can help legal professionals navigate ethical challenges and ensure ethical conduct in their practice.

1. Continuing Education and Professional Development: Legal professionals should actively engage in continuing education programs and professional development activities. Staying informed about changes in the law, ethical guidelines, and best practices is essential for maintaining ethical competence and professional growth.

2. Building a Support Network: Creating a support network of peers, mentors, and professional organizations can provide valuable guidance and assistance when facing ethical dilemmas. Engaging with colleagues and participating in ethical discussions can help legal professionals gain different perspectives and make more informed ethical decisions.

3. Ethical Decision-Making Frameworks: Legal professionals can utilize ethical decision-making frameworks to guide their choices in challenging situations. These frameworks provide a structured approach for analyzing ethical issues, considering various perspectives, and identifying the most ethically justifiable course of action.

4. Regular Ethical Reflection: Engaging in regular ethical reflection allows legal professionals to assess their behavior and decisions in light of their ethical obligations. Reflecting on past experiences, evaluating the ethical implications of their actions, and seeking feedback can help legal professionals continuously improve their ethical practice.

5. Seeking Ethical Guidance: When faced with complex ethical dilemmas, legal professionals should seek ethical guidance from supervisors, ethics committees, or legal professional organizations. Consulting with experts in legal ethics can help navigate challenging situations and ensure compliance with ethical obligations.

Conclusion

The role and responsibilities of legal professionals are critical in maintaining the integrity of the legal system and promoting justice. Upholding ethical conduct, fulfilling obligations to clients, courts, and the public, and navigating ethical challenges are essential aspects of the legal profession. By employing ethical decision-making frameworks, continuous learning, and seeking guidance when needed, legal professionals can maintain their ethical integrity and contribute to a more equitable and just society.

Ethical Obligations in Legal Practice

In the field of legal practice, professionals are bound by ethical obligations that guide their conduct and ensure the integrity and fairness of the legal system. These obligations are designed to maintain high ethical standards throughout the legal profession and promote trust and confidence in the justice system. In this section, we will explore the fundamental ethical obligations that legal practitioners must uphold in their practice.

Duty to the Court

One of the primary ethical obligations of legal practitioners is their duty to the court. This duty requires lawyers to act with honesty, fairness, and integrity in their interactions with the court. Lawyers are officers of the court and have a responsibility to assist in the administration of justice.

Example: Consider a criminal defense attorney who represents a client accused of a serious crime. The attorney's duty to the court requires them to present their client's case honestly and not to make false or misleading statements to the court. They must also respect the rules of evidence and refrain from engaging in any conduct that undermines the integrity of the legal process.

Duty to the Client

Legal practitioners have a primary duty to act in the best interests of their clients. This duty requires lawyers to provide competent and diligent representation, maintain client confidentiality, and avoid conflicts of interest. Lawyers must also keep their clients informed about the progress of their case and provide them with accurate and honest advice.

Example: Imagine a scenario where a lawyer is representing a client in a civil lawsuit. The lawyer's duty to the client requires them to provide competent representation by thoroughly researching the relevant legal issues and presenting the strongest possible arguments on behalf of their client. The lawyer must also maintain client confidentiality and avoid sharing any privileged information without the client's consent.

Duty of Professionalism

Legal practitioners have a duty to conduct themselves in a professional manner both inside and outside the courtroom. This duty includes treating opposing parties, witnesses, and other professionals with respect and courtesy. Lawyers should also avoid engaging in conduct that may bring the legal profession into disrepute.

Example: Suppose a lawyer is involved in a contentious courtroom trial. The lawyer's duty of professionalism requires them to refrain from making personal attacks on opposing counsel or witnesses. Instead, they should focus on presenting their arguments based on the merits of the case, maintaining a respectful and dignified demeanor throughout the proceedings.

Duty of Confidentiality

Confidentiality is a crucial ethical obligation in the legal profession. Lawyers are required to protect the confidentiality of client information and not disclose it without the client's informed consent. This duty helps promote trust between lawyers and their clients and ensures that clients feel comfortable sharing sensitive information with their legal representatives.

Example: Consider an immigration lawyer who is providing legal advice to a client seeking asylum. The lawyer has a duty of confidentiality and must not disclose any information related to the client's immigration status or personal circumstances to third parties without the client's permission. This duty extends even after the lawyer-client relationship has ended.

Duty of Competence

Legal practitioners have an ethical obligation to provide competent representation to their clients. This duty requires lawyers to possess the necessary knowledge, skill, and resources to handle the legal matters entrusted to them. Lawyers should also stay updated on legal developments and engage in ongoing professional development to enhance their competence.

Example: Suppose a lawyer is handling a complex merger and acquisition transaction. The lawyer has a duty of competence and must have a thorough understanding of corporate laws, transactional procedures, and contract drafting to ensure the best interests of their client are protected. They may also engage in collaborative efforts with other lawyers or experts to facilitate legal research and analysis.

Conflict of Interest

Legal practitioners have a duty to avoid conflicts of interest that may compromise their ability to provide unbiased and diligent representation. A conflict of interest arises when a lawyer's professional interests or loyalty to other clients conflicts with their duty to act in the best interests of their current client. Lawyers must identify and address potential conflicts of interest promptly to maintain their ethical obligations.

Example: Imagine a law firm that represents both spouses in a divorce proceeding. However, as the process progresses, it becomes evident that the interests of one spouse may be adverse to the interests of the other. The duty to avoid conflicts of interest requires the law firm to withdraw from representing both clients, as it would be impossible to provide unbiased advice and representation to each party.

Conclusion

Ethical obligations form the foundation of legal practice and are essential for maintaining the integrity, fairness, and trustworthiness of the legal system. From the duty to the court and the duty to the client to the obligations of professionalism, confidentiality, competence, and avoiding conflicts of interest, legal practitioners must adhere to these ethical principles in their day-to-day practice. By upholding these obligations, legal professionals contribute to the promotion of justice and the preservation of the rule of law in society.

Professional Codes of Conduct and Legal Ethics

Professional codes of conduct and legal ethics serve as guiding principles for legal professionals to ensure ethical behavior in their practice. These codes outline the responsibilities, duties, and ethical obligations that lawyers and other legal practitioners must adhere to in order to maintain the integrity of the legal profession. This section will explore the importance of professional codes of conduct and legal ethics, the key principles they encompass, and the ethical challenges faced by legal professionals.

Importance of Professional Codes of Conduct

Professional codes of conduct play a vital role in promoting ethical behavior and maintaining public trust in the legal profession. They provide a framework for lawyers and other legal professionals to uphold high standards of professionalism, integrity, and ethical conduct. These codes serve as a reference point for professionals, ensuring that their actions align with ethical standards and that their clients receive competent, diligent, and confidential representation.

By adhering to professional codes of conduct, legal professionals commit to upholding fundamental ethical principles, such as honesty, integrity, confidentiality, independence, and loyalty. These principles are essential for establishing and maintaining trust between lawyers and their clients, as well as promoting justice and fairness in the legal system. Professional codes of conduct also help to regulate the behavior of legal practitioners and maintain the reputation and credibility of the legal profession as a whole.

Key Principles of Legal Ethics

Professional codes of conduct and legal ethics are based on a set of key principles that guide the ethical behavior of legal professionals. These principles include:

1. **Confidentiality**: Lawyers have a duty to preserve the confidentiality of their clients' information, ensuring that it is not disclosed without proper authorization. This principle is crucial for establishing trust and effective attorney-client relationships.

2. **Conflicts of Interest**: Legal professionals must avoid conflicts of interest that could compromise their loyalty, independence, or professional judgment. They should not represent clients whose interests conflict with those of other clients or themselves.

3. **Competence and Diligence**: Lawyers have a duty to provide competent and diligent representation to their clients. They must possess the necessary knowledge, skills, and experience to handle their clients' legal matters effectively.

4. **Integrity and Honesty**: Legal professionals are expected to act with integrity, honesty, and fairness in their dealings with clients, colleagues, courts, and the public. They should not engage in dishonesty or misrepresentation.

5. **Candor and Fairness:** Lawyers have a duty to be candid and truthful in their interactions with the court, opposing counsel, and other parties involved in legal proceedings. They should also strive to promote fairness and justice in the legal system.

6. **Professional Independence:** Legal professionals must maintain their professional independence and exercise their professional judgment free from external influences that could compromise their integrity.

7. **Pro Bono and Public Service:** Lawyers have a responsibility to provide pro bono legal services to individuals or organizations in need and to contribute to the improvement of the legal system and access to justice.

These principles collectively form the foundation of legal ethics and shape the behavior and responsibilities of legal professionals.

Ethical Challenges Faced by Legal Professionals

Legal professionals frequently encounter various ethical challenges in their practice. Some of the common ethical dilemmas faced by lawyers include:

1. **Conflicts of Interest:** Lawyers often face situations where their personal or financial interests may conflict with their duty to provide loyal and unbiased representation to their clients. Identifying and resolving conflicts of interest is essential to maintain ethical integrity.

2. **Client Communication and Consent:** Lawyers must effectively communicate with their clients, ensuring they have a clear understanding of the legal process, potential outcomes, and available options. Obtaining informed consent from clients is crucial to make well-informed decisions.

3. **Candor with the Court:** Lawyers have an obligation to be truthful and candid with the court. However, they may face challenges in balancing the duty of candor with the duty to vigorously advocate for their clients' interests.

4. **Multidimensional Roles:** Legal professionals often have multiple roles and responsibilities, such as representing clients, acting as advisors, and serving the interests of justice. Balancing these roles ethically can be complex and challenging.

5. **Professional Independence:** Legal professionals may face pressure from clients, employers, or external factors that can compromise their professional independence. Maintaining independence and avoiding conflicts of interest is essential for ethical practice.

6. **Client Confidentiality:** Lawyers must safeguard client confidentiality, but they may face situations where disclosure is required by law or necessary to prevent harm. Balancing the duty of confidentiality with other ethical obligations can be difficult.

To address these challenges, legal professionals must maintain a comprehensive understanding of professional codes of conduct and legal ethics, and apply ethical decision-making frameworks to navigate complex situations. Continuing education, professional development, and ethical reflection are essential for legal practitioners to effectively address ethical challenges and ensure ethical conduct.

Examples and Case Studies

Consider the following case study to illustrate the ethical challenges faced by legal professionals:

Case Study: Conflict of Interest Julia is a lawyer specializing in environmental law. She recently represented an environmental organization in a lawsuit against a manufacturing company accused of polluting a nearby river. Julia's brother-in-law works as an executive in the manufacturing company. Although Julia believes in the validity of the environmental organization's case, she is conflicted about representing them due to her personal relationship with her brother-in-law.

In this scenario, Julia faces a conflict of interest. Her personal relationship with her brother-in-law may compromise her loyalty, independence, and judgment in representing the environmental organization. She must carefully analyze the situation and consider recusing herself from the case to maintain the integrity of the legal profession and avoid ethical violations.

Resources and Further Reading

To delve deeper into professional codes of conduct and legal ethics, the following resources and references are recommended:

- American Bar Association, Model Rules of Professional Conduct

- International Bar Association, IBA International Principles on Conduct for the Legal Profession

+ Legal Ethics: A Handbook for Zimbabwean Lawyers by Gabriel Machinga

+ Legal Ethics in a Nutshell by Ronald Rotunda and John Dzienkowski

+ Ethical Problems in the Practice of Law: Model Rules, State Variations, and Practice Questions by Lisa G. Lerman and Philip G. Schrag

These resources provide valuable insights into the principles, rules, and practical application of professional codes of conduct and legal ethics.

Conclusion

Professional codes of conduct and legal ethics form the ethical backbone of the legal profession.   By adhering to these codes, legal professionals uphold fundamental principles such as confidentiality, conflicts of interest, competence, integrity, and fairness.   Ethical challenges faced by legal professionals, such as conflicts of interest and maintaining professional independence, require careful consideration   and   adherence   to   ethical   decision-making   frameworks. Understanding and applying professional codes of conduct and legal ethics is crucial for legal professionals to maintain public trust, preserve the integrity of the legal profession, and promote justice and fairness in the legal system.

Ethical Challenges in Legal Profession

In the field of legal profession, practitioners encounter numerous ethical challenges that they must navigate with integrity and responsibility. These challenges arise from the complexities of legal practice, the competing interests of clients and society, and the need to maintain professional ethics and standards. This section will explore some of the key ethical challenges faced by legal professionals and provide guidance on how to address them.

Conflicts of Interest

One of the most significant ethical challenges in the legal profession is conflicts of interest. A conflict of interest occurs when a lawyer's personal or professional interests conflict with the interests of a client, potentially compromising the lawyer's professional judgment and loyalty to the client. Conflicts can arise in various situations, such as representing multiple clients with conflicting interests or when personal relationships with clients create bias.

To address conflicts of interest, legal professionals must exercise diligence in identifying   and   disclosing   any   potential   conflicts   at   the   outset   of   a   client engagement. This includes conducting thorough conflict checks and maintaining effective conflict screening systems. Should a conflict be identified, lawyers must take appropriate actions, such as obtaining informed consent from affected parties or, in some cases, declining representation.

For example, consider a scenario where a lawyer previously represented a company in a legal matter and is now approached to represent an individual suing that same company. In this situation, the lawyer must carefully assess whether their prior representation creates a conflict of interest that may impact their ability to advocate effectively for the new client. Transparency and open communication with all parties involved are crucial in managing conflicts of interest.

Maintaining Confidentiality

Another critical ethical challenge in the legal profession is maintaining confidentiality. Lawyers have a duty to protect the confidentiality of client information, which includes both the content of communications and any other information related to the representation. Ensuring confidentiality is crucial to fostering trust between lawyers and clients, promoting candid communication, and upholding the attorney-client privilege.

However, maintaining confidentiality can become challenging when legal professionals are faced with situations where disclosure may be necessary or required by law. For instance, lawyers may be obligated to disclose client confidences to prevent ongoing criminal activity or to comply with court orders. Striking a balance between the duty of confidentiality and other legal and ethical obligations is a constant ethical challenge.

Legal professionals must be well-versed in the rules of professional conduct regarding confidentiality and stay updated on any changes or developments in the law. They should also establish robust systems and safeguards to protect client information, such as securing electronic files, limiting access to confidential information, and using encryption technologies.

Furthermore, legal professionals must be prepared to navigate the gray areas of confidentiality dilemmas. This involves carefully assessing the potential risks and benefits of disclosure, engaging in ethical reasoning, and seeking guidance from professional organizations or legal ethics committees when necessary.

Professional Independence and Integrity

Maintaining professional independence and integrity is an ongoing ethical challenge for legal professionals. Lawyers must be able to exercise their professional judgment without undue influence or pressure from clients, other lawyers, or external parties. Upholding the rule of law and the administration of justice requires lawyers to act honestly, diligently, and in accordance with ethical rules and principles.

In practice, legal professionals may face ethical dilemmas that test their professional independence and integrity. For example, a lawyer may be asked to provide legal advice or conduct legal research that aligns with the client's desired outcome but may not be ethically or legally sound. Resisting such pressures and adhering to professional standards can be challenging, particularly in situations where client expectations conflict with the lawyer's duty to act in the best interests of justice.

To address this challenge, legal professionals should develop a strong moral compass and a commitment to professional ethics. They should be knowledgeable about the rules of professional conduct and be proactive in seeking guidance when faced with ethical dilemmas. Continuing legal education programs and engagement with professional associations can help lawyers stay updated on ethical issues and build a supportive network of peers.

Cultural Competence and Diversity

In an increasingly diverse and interconnected world, cultural competence is an emerging ethical challenge for legal professionals. Cultural competence refers to the ability to understand and navigate the cultural, linguistic, and social norms of clients from different backgrounds. It requires lawyers to respect and appreciate the diversity of their clients, as well as the communities they serve.

Failing to demonstrate cultural competence can lead to misunderstandings, inadequate representation, and limited access to justice for marginalized communities. Legal professionals must actively work towards developing cultural competence by educating themselves about different cultural practices, beliefs, and values. This includes recognizing and challenging their own biases and assumptions.

Moreover, legal professionals should strive to create an inclusive and equitable legal environment that embraces diversity. This may involve promoting diverse legal representation, challenging discriminatory practices, and advocating for equal access to justice. By doing so, legal professionals can uphold the principles of fairness, justice, and equal treatment under the law.

Technology and Ethical Challenges

With the increasing reliance on technology in the legal profession, ethical challenges related to technology have become more pronounced. Legal professionals must navigate the ethical implications of using technology in their practice, such as confidentiality concerns, data protection, and potential biases in artificial intelligence systems.

For instance, when using electronic communication tools or cloud storage, lawyers must ensure that client information remains secure and confidential. They must also be cautious about the potential risks of data breaches or unauthorized access to sensitive information.

Additionally, the use of artificial intelligence and machine learning algorithms in legal research and decision-making poses ethical challenges. These technologies may inadvertently perpetuate biases or discriminatory practices, requiring legal professionals to critically assess their use and mitigate any potential risks.

To address these challenges, legal professionals should stay informed about the latest technological advancements and their ethical implications. They should adopt best practices for technology use, such as implementing robust cybersecurity measures, conducting privacy impact assessments, and being transparent with clients about the use of technology in their legal matters.

Conclusion

Ethical challenges are pervasive in the legal profession, requiring legal professionals to navigate complex situations with integrity, professionalism, and a commitment to justice. By understanding and addressing these challenges, lawyers can uphold the ethical standards of their profession and promote trust, fairness, and access to justice for their clients and society as a whole.

Strategies for Maintaining Ethical Integrity in Legal Practice

Maintaining ethical integrity is of utmost importance in the field of legal practice. It ensures that legal professionals uphold the highest standards of conduct and ethical behavior while serving their clients and the justice system. In this section, we will explore various strategies that can be employed to promote and maintain ethical integrity in legal practice.

1. **Ethical Leadership**: Ethical integrity starts with the leadership within the legal profession. Law firms and legal organizations should establish a strong ethical culture and provide guidance and support to their employees. Ethical leaders lead by example, demonstrating integrity and ethical behavior in their own actions. They

emphasize the importance of ethical decision-making and create a safe environment where ethical concerns can be raised and addressed.

2.   **Ethics Training and Education:** Continuous education and training programs are essential to equip legal professionals with the necessary knowledge and skills to navigate ethical challenges. Law schools, legal organizations, and professional associations should incorporate ethics courses and workshops into their curriculum. These programs should cover ethical principles, codes of conduct, and case studies to enhance ethical reasoning and decision-making abilities.

3. **Clear Ethical Guidelines and Policies:** Establishing clear ethical guidelines and policies provides a framework for legal professionals to adhere to. These guidelines should cover areas such as conflicts of interest, client confidentiality, honesty, and professional courtesy. It is important to ensure that these guidelines are readily accessible, well-communicated, and regularly updated to reflect changes in legal and ethical standards.

4.   **Client Communication and Informed Consent:** Open and honest communication with clients is crucial for maintaining ethical integrity. Legal professionals should effectively communicate legal advice, potential outcomes, risks, and costs to their clients. Informed consent should be obtained from clients before undertaking any legal action. This ensures that clients are aware of the implications and consequences of their decisions, fostering trust and transparency.

5. **Conflict Resolution Mechanisms:** Establishing effective conflict resolution mechanisms within law firms and legal organizations promotes ethical integrity. These mechanisms can provide a safe and confidential space for legal professionals to discuss ethical dilemmas, seek guidance, and resolve conflicts. Encouraging open dialogue and valuing diverse perspectives can lead to better decision-making and ethical outcomes.

6. **Supervision and Accountability:** Implementing robust supervision and accountability mechanisms within legal practice reinforces ethical integrity. Supervisors should actively oversee the work of junior legal professionals, providing guidance, monitoring ethical compliance, and addressing any ethical concerns. Regular performance evaluations and feedback sessions can help maintain accountability and ensure adherence to ethical standards.

7. **Whistleblower Protection:** Encouraging and protecting whistleblowers is essential in maintaining ethical integrity. Legal professionals should feel empowered to report unethical behavior without fear of retaliation. Law firms and legal organizations should have policies in place to protect whistleblowers and investigate allegations of misconduct promptly and impartially.

8. **Ethical Use of Technology:** Technological advancements have transformed the legal landscape, but they also come with ethical challenges. Legal professionals

should understand and adhere to ethical standards related to data privacy, confidentiality, and cybersecurity. They should use technology responsibly and ensure that client information is securely protected.

9. **Continuing Professional Development**: Engaging in ongoing professional development is crucial for legal professionals to stay updated on changes in laws, regulations, and ethical standards. Participating in seminars, conferences, and webinars allows legal professionals to enhance their knowledge, skills, and ethical awareness.

10. **Ethics Committees and Consultation Services**: Establishing ethics committees or consultation services within law firms and legal organizations can provide a valuable resource for legal professionals. These committees can offer guidance, advice, and support in navigating complex ethical matters. They can also provide a forum for discussing ethical dilemmas and fostering a culture of ethical reflection.

It is important to note that all legal professionals have a personal responsibility to uphold ethical standards. By embracing these strategies and adhering to ethical principles, legal professionals can contribute to a more just and ethical legal system, fostering trust and confidence in the profession.

Case Study: Conflict of Interest

Consider the following scenario: A lawyer is approached by two potential clients who are involved in a legal dispute. Client A is a long-standing client of the lawyer's firm, while Client B is a new client. The lawyer believes that representing both clients would create a conflict of interest as their interests are directly opposed to each other.

To maintain ethical integrity in this situation, the lawyer should:

+ Disclose the conflict of interest to both clients and explain the potential risks and implications.

+ Advise both clients to seek independent legal counsel to protect their interests fully.

+ Withdraw from representing either client if the conflict of interest cannot be effectively managed.

+ Prioritize the duty of loyalty and confidentiality to each client, ensuring their information is not shared with the other party.

+ Document the steps taken to address the conflict of interest to demonstrate compliance with ethical standards.

By handling the conflict of interest ethically, the lawyer upholds the principles of integrity, loyalty, and confidentiality, building trust with both clients and maintaining ethical integrity in legal practice.

Key Takeaways

+ Ethical integrity in legal practice is essential for upholding professional standards and promoting public trust in the legal system.

+ Strategies such as ethical leadership, education and training, clear ethical guidelines, client communication, conflict resolution, supervision and accountability, whistleblower protection, ethical use of technology, continuing professional development, and ethics committees can all contribute to maintaining ethical integrity in legal practice.

+ Legal professionals have a personal responsibility to adhere to ethical principles, make sound ethical decisions, and continuously reflect on their ethical obligations.

Further Reading

+ Law Society of England and Wales: "Ethical Principles for Attorneys" - Available at: http://www.sra.org.uk/students/Handbook/code/content.page

+ American Bar Association: "Model Rules of Professional Conduct" - Available at: http://www.americanbar.org/groups/professional_responsibility/publications/model_rules_of_professional_conduct.html

+ Legal Ethics: A Handbook for Zimbabwean Lawyers by Sternford Moyo

Discussion Questions

1. How can ethical leadership contribute to maintaining ethical integrity within law firms and legal organizations?

2. Discuss the importance of open communication and informed consent in maintaining ethical integrity in legal practice.

3. What steps can legal professionals take to ensure the ethical use of technology in their practice?

Ethics in Legal Advocacy

Legal advocacy plays a pivotal role in the legal profession, as it involves representing clients and advocating for their rights and interests in a court of law. However, ethical considerations are crucial in ensuring that legal practitioners uphold the principles of justice, fairness, and integrity throughout the process of legal advocacy. This section will explore the ethical issues that arise in legal advocacy, the responsibilities of legal advocates, and guidelines for maintaining ethical integrity in this crucial aspect of legal practice.

Understanding Legal Advocacy

Legal advocacy refers to the act of representing clients in legal proceedings, such as litigation, arbitration, or mediation. It involves presenting arguments, producing evidence, and persuasively advocating for the client's position or desired outcome. Legal advocates, including lawyers and attorneys, have a duty to zealously represent their clients within the bounds of the law and legal ethics.

Ethical Responsibilities of Legal Advocates

Legal advocates have several ethical responsibilities that guide their conduct during legal advocacy. These responsibilities include:

1. **Duty of loyalty:** Legal advocates must prioritize the best interests of their clients and act in their clients' best interests without any conflict of interest.

2. **Duty of competence:** Legal advocates must possess the necessary legal knowledge, skills, and expertise to effectively represent their clients. They should continuously update their legal knowledge and stay informed about changes in the law.

3. **Duty of diligence:** Legal advocates must be diligent in representing their clients, which includes promptness, preparation, and thoroughness in handling legal matters.

4. **Duty of candor:** Legal advocates must be truthful and honest in their interactions with the court, opposing counsel, and the client. They should not knowingly present false evidence or make false statements.

5. **Duty of confidentiality:** Legal advocates must maintain client confidentiality and protect the attorney-client privilege. They should not

disclose any confidential information obtained from the client unless authorized or legally required to do so.

6. **Duty of fairness:** Legal advocates should strive to ensure a fair and impartial administration of justice. They should not engage in unethical tactics, such as hiding evidence or misleading the court.

By fulfilling these ethical responsibilities, legal advocates contribute to the effective functioning of the legal system and enhance the public's trust in the profession.

Ethical Issues in Legal Advocacy

Legal advocacy can give rise to various ethical issues, including:

1. **Truthfulness and accuracy:** Legal advocates must ensure that the information presented to the court is truthful and accurate. They should not misrepresent facts or present false evidence.

2. **Candor with the court:** Legal advocates have a duty of candor towards the court and should disclose any legal authority or precedent that is directly adverse to their client's position. They should not omit or misrepresent legal authorities that are binding or persuasive.

3. **Respectful and professional conduct:** Legal advocates should maintain a respectful and professional demeanor towards the court, opposing counsel, and all parties involved in the legal proceedings. They should avoid disrespectful or inflammatory language or conduct that undermines the integrity of the court.

4. **Avoidance of conflicts of interest:** Legal advocates must be vigilant in identifying and disclosing any conflicts of interest that may impair their representation of the client. They should avoid situations where personal, financial, or other interests could compromise their loyalty to the client.

5. **Zealous advocacy within ethical boundaries:** Legal advocates are expected to zealously represent their clients' interests. However, this must be done within the boundaries of the law and legal ethics. They should not engage in unethical or frivolous arguments or tactics that could harm the administration of justice.

Addressing these ethical issues is crucial to maintaining the integrity of legal advocacy and upholding the principles of justice and fairness.

Guidelines for Ethical Legal Advocacy

To ensure ethical legal advocacy, legal practitioners can follow these guidelines:

1. **Know and abide by professional codes of conduct:** Familiarize yourself with the rules and ethical guidelines set forth by professional organizations and regulatory bodies governing the legal profession. Adhere to these rules in all aspects of legal advocacy.

2. **Continuing education and skills development:** Stay updated with changes in the law and enhance your legal knowledge and skills through continued education and professional development programs. This will enable you to better serve your clients and uphold ethical standards in legal advocacy.

3. **Maintain open communication with clients:** Establish open and transparent communication with your clients. Keep them informed about the progress of their case, any developments, and the available legal options. Ensure that they understand the ethical boundaries within which legal advocacy must operate.

4. **Conduct thorough research and preparation:** Conduct comprehensive research and preparation to effectively represent your clients. This includes analyzing relevant laws, regulations, and precedents to build a strong legal argument.

5. **Respect courtroom etiquette and decorum:** Adhere to the rules and protocols of the courtroom. Maintain a respectful and professional demeanor in all interactions during legal proceedings.

6. **Avoid conflicts of interest:** Be diligent in identifying and avoiding conflicts of interest that may compromise your ability to provide unbiased and effective representation. Prioritize the best interests of your clients while maintaining integrity and impartiality.

7. **Strive for ethical settlement negotiations:** Explore settlement options that align with your client's interests while considering the ethical implications. Engage in fair and ethical negotiation practices that promote justice and equitable outcomes.

By adhering to these guidelines, legal advocates can maintain ethical integrity and promote justice in their legal advocacy efforts.

Case Study: Ethical Challenges in Legal Advocacy

Let's consider a case study to explore the ethical challenges that can arise in legal advocacy. Imagine a criminal defense attorney representing a client accused of a serious crime. The attorney strongly believes in the client's innocence based on the evidence available.

However, during the trial, the attorney discovers a key piece of evidence that might prove the client's guilt. The attorney faces a dilemma: Should they present this evidence to the court, risking their client's conviction, or withhold it to maintain their client's chances of acquittal?

In this scenario, the attorney must navigate ethical considerations, such as the duty of candor towards the court and the duty of loyalty to the client. They must weigh the ethical responsibility of presenting all relevant evidence against their obligation to zealously advocate for the client's interests.

A potential resolution to this ethical dilemma could involve discussing the situation with the client, explaining the discovery of the evidence, and seeking their input. Depending on the client's wishes and the attorney's professional assessment, a decision can be made on the best course of action that upholds ethical responsibilities while ensuring effective representation.

This case study illustrates the complex ethical challenges that legal advocates may face, underscoring the need for thoughtful decision-making and adherence to ethical principles.

Additional Resources

To further explore the topic of ethics in legal advocacy, refer to the following resources:

1. American Bar Association (ABA) Model Rules of Professional Conduct: This document outlines the ethical guidelines for lawyers in the United States and provides valuable insights into the principles of legal ethics.

2. Legal Ethics: A Handbook for Zimbabwean Lawyers by James Mutizwa: This book provides a comprehensive overview of legal ethics, including chapters specifically addressing ethical issues in legal advocacy.

3. Ethics and Professional Responsibility for Paralegals by Therese A. Cannon: This resource explores the ethical responsibilities of paralegals in the legal profession, including their role in legal advocacy.

4. The Oxford Handbook of Legal Ethics edited by David Luban and Thomas L. Shaffer: This comprehensive handbook offers a multidisciplinary perspective on legal ethics, encompassing various aspects of legal practice.

By engaging with these resources, legal practitioners can deepen their understanding of ethical considerations in legal advocacy and enhance their ability to navigate complex ethical challenges.

Conclusion

Ethics play a vital role in legal advocacy, providing a framework for upholding justice, fairness, and integrity in legal practice. Legal advocates must navigate a range of ethical responsibilities, ensuring loyalty to their clients, respect for the court, and adherence to professional standards. By addressing ethical issues, following guidelines, and seeking continual professional development, legal advocates can contribute to a more just and ethical legal system.

Legal Ethics and Public Interest

In legal practice, ethical considerations play a crucial role in ensuring the protection of the public interest. Legal professionals have an ethical obligation to serve the public with integrity, honesty, and fairness. This section explores the intersection of legal ethics and the public interest, examining the ethical responsibilities of lawyers in promoting justice and serving the common good.

Understanding Legal Ethics

Legal ethics refers to the professional standards and rules of conduct that govern the behavior of lawyers. These ethics guide lawyers in their relationships with clients, courts, and the general public. The legal profession recognizes the importance of upholding ethical values to maintain public trust and confidence in the legal system.

The Public Interest and Legal Practice

The public interest encompasses the collective well-being and welfare of society as a whole. In legal practice, lawyers have a duty to act in the best interests of their clients while also considering the broader public interest. This duty requires lawyers to balance the needs of their individual clients with the principles of justice, fairness, and the common good.

Ethical Obligations in Serving the Public Interest

Lawyers have several ethical obligations that are directly linked to serving the public interest:

+ **Conflict of Interest:** Lawyers have a duty to avoid conflicts of interest that could compromise their ability to act in the best interests of their clients or the public. They must disclose any potential conflicts and take appropriate steps to mitigate them.

+ **Pro Bono Service:** Lawyers have a professional responsibility to provide pro bono legal services to those who cannot afford legal representation. By offering their skills and expertise, lawyers contribute to equal access to justice and the public interest.

+ **Candor and Honesty:** Lawyers must be honest and candid in their communication with clients, the court, and other parties. This includes providing accurate information, counseling clients about the legal process, and advocating within the bounds of the law.

+ **Confidentiality:** Lawyers have a duty to maintain the confidentiality of client information, which is essential for maintaining client trust and promoting the public interest. However, this duty is not absolute and may be limited in certain circumstances, such as preventing harm to others.

Promoting Justice and the Common Good

As legal professionals, lawyers have a unique role in promoting justice and the common good. They can contribute to the public interest by:

+ **Advocacy for Marginalized Groups:** Lawyers can champion the rights of marginalized groups and advocate for their equal treatment under the law. This includes challenging discriminatory practices and promoting social justice.

+ **Promoting Access to Justice:** Lawyers play a critical role in ensuring that all individuals have meaningful access to legal representation and the justice system. This includes providing legal assistance to underserved communities and advocating for reforms to improve access to justice.

+ **Promoting Transparency and Accountability:** Lawyers have a duty to promote transparency and accountability in legal proceedings. They can help uncover and address misconduct or corruption, ensuring that the legal system operates fairly and in the public interest.

+ **Law Reform and Policy Advocacy:** Lawyers can contribute to the public interest by engaging in law reform efforts and policy advocacy. By identifying areas of legal reform and advocating for change, lawyers can influence the development of laws and policies that promote justice and the common good.

Potential Challenges and Ethical Considerations

While the pursuit of the public interest is a central tenet of legal ethics, lawyers may face challenges and ethical considerations in fulfilling this duty:

+ **Balancing Competing Interests:** Lawyers may need to navigate competing interests and obligations, such as those between individual clients and the broader public interest. This requires careful consideration and judgment to ensure ethical decision-making.

+ **Difficult Client Situations:** Lawyers may encounter clients or cases that present ethical challenges, such as clients with questionable motives or cases that involve controversial issues. It is essential for lawyers to navigate these situations while upholding their ethical obligations.

+ **Conflicts between Personal and Professional Interests:** Lawyers must manage potential conflicts between their personal interests and their professional obligations. It is crucial for lawyers to maintain objectivity, independence, and integrity in their decision-making and actions.

Conclusion

Legal ethics and the public interest are intertwined in legal practice. Lawyers have an ethical duty to promote justice, fairness, and the common good in their work. By serving the public interest, lawyers contribute to a more equitable and just society. Upholding ethical principles not only ensures the integrity of the legal profession but also fosters public trust in the legal system.

Conclusion

In this section, we have explored the ethical issues that arise in the legal profession. We have examined the role and responsibilities of legal professionals, the importance of confidentiality and attorney-client privilege, and the challenges posed by conflicts of interest. These issues are essential for maintaining ethical integrity in legal practice and upholding the principles of justice.

One of the key aspects of professionalism in the legal field is understanding and adhering to the ethical obligations that come with the profession. Legal professionals have a duty to act in the best interests of their clients, while also promoting justice and fairness. By following professional codes of conduct and legal ethics, they can navigate ethical challenges and maintain their ethical integrity.

Confidentiality and attorney-client privilege are essential for building trust between lawyers and their clients. Clients must feel comfortable sharing sensitive information with their attorneys to receive proper legal representation. However, maintaining confidentiality can sometimes clash with other ethical obligations, such as the duty to report potential harm or prevent illegal activities. Legal professionals must carefully navigate these ethical dilemmas and strike a balance that upholds both the client's rights and the interests of justice.

Conflict of interest is another ethical issue that often arises in the legal profession. Lawyers must avoid situations where their personal interests or relationships may compromise their professional judgment. Identifying and addressing conflicts of interest is crucial to maintaining professionalism and ensuring that legal decisions are made based on the merits of the case rather than personal biases or interests. Transparency and accountability, coupled with strong ethical standards, are vital in preventing conflicts of interest from undermining the integrity of the legal profession.

In conclusion, ethical issues in the legal profession are complex and multifaceted. Legal professionals must navigate ethical dilemmas with knowledge, skill, and integrity. By adhering to professional codes of conduct, maintaining client confidences, addressing conflicts of interest, and upholding the principles of justice, legal professionals can promote ethical practices and contribute to a more just and equitable society.

Further Reading:

+ Legal Ethics: A Comparative Perspective by Megan Richardson

+ Lawyers' Ethics and Professional Regulation by W. Bradley Wendel

+ The Oxford Handbook of Legal Ethics by Professor Leslie C. Levin and Professor Steven Lubet

+ The Lawyer's Guide to Professional Responsibility by Martyn Frost

Exercises:

1. Research and analyze a recent case where conflicts of interest impacted the outcome of a legal proceeding. Discuss how the conflict of interest could have been avoided or managed ethically.

2. Imagine you are a legal professional representing a client who has disclosed confidential information that may be harmful to a third party. How would you balance your duty of confidentiality with your obligation to prevent harm? Discuss the ethical considerations involved and propose a course of action.

3. Conduct research on a high-profile legal case where ethical issues concerning attorney-client privilege were raised. Analyze the implications of the case on the preservation of attorney-client privilege and discuss any changes or improvements that could be made to protect this privilege in the future.

Confidentiality and Attorney-Client Privilege

Importance of Confidentiality in Legal Practice

Confidentiality is a fundamental principle in the legal profession and plays a crucial role in maintaining the trust and integrity of the legal system. It is the duty of every legal practitioner to ensure that client information remains confidential and is not disclosed to any third party without the client's consent. This section will discuss the importance of confidentiality in legal practice, the reasons behind its significance, and the potential consequences of breaching this duty.

Preserving Client Trust

Confidentiality is the cornerstone of the lawyer-client relationship. When individuals seek legal assistance, they often divulge sensitive and personal information to their lawyers. This information could range from financial records and personal history to intimate details of their personal lives. Without the assurance of confidentiality, clients may be hesitant to disclose all relevant facts, which can hinder the effective representation and jeopardize the outcome of their case.

Maintaining client trust is essential not only for individual lawyers but also for the legal profession as a whole. Lawyers have a duty to act in their clients' best interests and protect their rights. By honoring the principle of confidentiality, lawyers demonstrate their commitment to building a strong attorney-client relationship based on trust, honesty, and open communication.

Protecting Privacy and Reputation

Confidentiality in legal practice is not only about protecting the information shared by clients but also about safeguarding their privacy and reputation. Lawyers must ensure that client information is not misused or disclosed in a way that could harm their clients' personal or professional lives.

In many legal matters, clients may share confidential information that, if disclosed, could have serious consequences. For example, a client facing criminal charges may reveal details that could implicate them in the commission of a crime. By safeguarding this information, lawyers protect their clients from potential harm, including public humiliation, damage to their reputation, or even physical threats.

Encouraging Open Communication

One of the advantages of confidentiality is that it encourages open and honest communication between lawyers and clients. Clients need to feel comfortable sharing all relevant information, even if it may be embarrassing or incriminating. By maintaining client confidentiality, lawyers create a safe and supportive environment for clients to share their concerns, anxieties, and fears, enabling lawyers to provide the best possible advice and representation.

When clients know that their conversations with their lawyers are confidential, they are more likely to be forthcoming and transparent. This ensures that lawyers have access to all the necessary details to formulate a strong legal strategy and make informed decisions on behalf of their clients. Without confidentiality, clients may be reluctant to share critical information and, ultimately, compromise the effectiveness of legal representation.

Ethical and Legal Obligations

Confidentiality is not just a professional courtesy; it is also an ethical and legal obligation for lawyers. Legal practitioners are bound by professional codes of conduct and rules that mandate the protection of client confidentiality. Breaching this duty can result in severe disciplinary consequences, including professional sanctions, loss of reputation, and even the revocation of the license to practice law.

Moreover, there are legal protections in place to safeguard client information. In many jurisdictions, attorney-client privilege is recognized by law, which means that communications between lawyers and clients are protected from disclosure in court proceedings or by governmental entities. This privilege allows clients to be completely open with their lawyers without fear that their conversations will be used against them in legal proceedings.

Consequences of Breaching Confidentiality

The consequences of breaching client confidentiality can be significant and far-reaching. Not only can it damage the lawyer-client relationship, but it can also have legal, professional, and reputational ramifications.

From a legal perspective, breaching client confidentiality may lead to civil liability, wherein the client can sue the lawyer for damages resulting from the unauthorized disclosure of information. Additionally, disciplinary actions by professional regulatory bodies can be taken against lawyers who violate their ethical obligations, which may include fines, suspension, or disbarment.

Professionally, lawyers who breach confidentiality may find it challenging to rebuild their reputation and regain the trust of clients and colleagues. Legal practitioners rely on their integrity and ethical conduct to establish themselves as trustworthy professionals within the legal community. Breaching confidentiality erodes this foundation and can irreversibly damage their standing.

Case Study: Breach of Confidentiality

To illustrate the importance of maintaining client confidentiality, let's consider a real-life case study.

In 2014, a prominent law firm suffered a massive data breach, resulting in the unauthorized disclosure of confidential client information. The breach compromised sensitive data, including financial records, personal contact information, and details of ongoing legal matters. The firm faced significant legal and reputational consequences as a result, including lawsuits from affected clients and a loss of trust from the legal community.

This case study highlights the potential devastating effects of a breach of confidentiality. It serves as a reminder that lawyers must take appropriate measures to protect client information and ensure the security of their digital systems to prevent such breaches from occurring.

Conclusion

Confidentiality is essential in legal practice as it promotes trust, protects privacy and reputation, encourages open communication, and fulfills ethical and legal obligations. By honoring the duty of confidentiality, lawyers foster strong attorney-client relationships, enable effective legal representation, and uphold the integrity of the legal profession. Understanding the importance of confidentiality is crucial for all legal practitioners and should be an integral part of legal education and professional development.

Attorney-Client Privilege and Its Limitations

Attorney-client privilege is a fundamental principle in the legal profession that ensures open and honest communication between attorneys and their clients. This privilege, also known as lawyer-client confidentiality, protects the confidentiality of information shared between an attorney and a client during the course of their professional relationship. It is a cornerstone of the legal system as it allows clients to feel safe and secure in seeking legal advice and representation.

Understanding Attorney-Client Privilege

Attorney-client privilege refers to the legal protection that prevents attorneys from disclosing information provided by their clients without their clients' consent. This protection extends to all forms of communication, including oral, written, and electronic. The privilege covers not only the attorney but also their staff, such as paralegals and legal assistants, as long as they are providing legal services under the direction of the attorney.

The purpose of attorney-client privilege is to encourage clients to be fully open and transparent with their attorneys, enabling the attorneys to provide competent and effective legal advice. It fosters a relationship of trust and confidence between clients and their legal representatives, which is crucial for the successful resolution of legal matters.

Elements of Attorney-Client Privilege

For attorney-client privilege to apply, certain elements must be present:

1. **Confidential communication:** The communication must be confidential, meaning that it is intended to be kept private and not disclosed to third parties. This confidentiality requirement ensures that clients feel comfortable disclosing sensitive and private information to their attorneys.

2. **Communication with an attorney:** The communication must be made with an attorney who is providing legal advice or representation. This includes discussions, meetings, and any written or electronic correspondence between the client and their attorney.

3. **For legal advice or representation:** The communication must be made for the purpose of seeking legal advice or representation. This requirement ensures that the privilege only applies to communications directly related to the legal matter at hand.

4. **Client identity established:** The attorney-client relationship must be established, meaning that the individual communicating with the attorney must be seeking legal advice or representation. This requirement prevents non-clients from invoking attorney-client privilege.

Limitations of Attorney-Client Privilege

Although attorney-client privilege is a crucial protection, it is not absolute and can be subject to certain limitations. Understanding these limitations is essential for both attorneys and clients to ensure they do not inadvertently waive or breach the privilege.

1. **Waiver:** Clients have the power to waive attorney-client privilege and voluntarily disclose privileged information to third parties. Once the privilege is waived, the information may no longer be protected, and the attorney may be required to disclose it if legally compelled to do so.

2. **Crime-fraud exception:** Attorney-client privilege does not apply if the communication is for the purpose of committing a crime or fraud. The privilege cannot be used as a shield to protect illegal activities, and if an attorney becomes aware of a client's intent to commit a crime or fraud, they may have a duty to disclose that information.

3. **Joint clients:** When two or more clients share the same attorney and communicate together, the privilege generally extends to their joint communications. However, if there is a dispute between the joint clients, the privilege may be waived, and the attorney may have to disclose the communication to resolve the dispute.

4. **Business advice vs. legal advice:** If an attorney provides business or non-legal advice to a client, that advice may not be protected by

attorney-client privilege. Only communications made in the context of providing legal advice or representation are covered by the privilege.

5. **Future crime or harm:** If a client reveals their intention to commit a future crime or cause harm to others, the attorney may have a duty to take action to prevent that harm. This duty may override the attorney-client privilege in certain circumstances.

Examples of Attorney-Client Privilege and Limitations

To illustrate the application of attorney-client privilege and its limitations, let's consider a hypothetical scenario:

Sarah consults an attorney, Emily, regarding a potential lawsuit against her employer for wrongful termination. During their meeting, Sarah provides detailed information about her employment history, conversations with her supervisor, and evidence she has collected to support her claim. Sarah expects that everything she shares with Emily will remain confidential.

In this scenario, the attorney-client privilege protects the confidentiality of Sarah's communication with Emily. Emily cannot disclose any of the information Sarah provided without her consent. This enables Sarah to be open and honest with Emily, allowing her to provide the best possible legal advice and representation.

However, there are limitations to attorney-client privilege that Sarah and Emily should be aware of. For example, if Sarah later decides to discuss her case with her spouse and reveals confidential information, the privilege may be waived, and Emily may no longer be bound by the duty of confidentiality.

Additionally, if Sarah reveals that she plans to forge evidence to strengthen her case, the crime-fraud exception may apply. Emily may have a duty to disclose this information to prevent Sarah from engaging in illegal activities.

It is important for both clients and attorneys to understand the nuances of attorney-client privilege and its limitations to ensure the protection of confidential information while adhering to legal and ethical standards.

Resources for Further Learning

For further exploration of attorney-client privilege and its limitations, the following resources are recommended:

+ American Bar Association (ABA) Model Rules of Professional Conduct: This comprehensive guide provides ethical rules and standards for attorneys, including those related to attorney-client privilege and confidentiality.

+ Legal Ethics: Rules, Statutes, and Comparisons by Richard Zitrin and Carol M. Langford: This book offers a detailed examination of ethical rules and principles in the legal profession, covering attorney-client privilege and other important topics.

+ ABA Section of Litigation, Young Advocates Committee: This committee provides resources and educational materials on various aspects of litigation, including attorney-client privilege and its limitations.

+ Law school courses on legal ethics and professional responsibility: Many law schools offer specialized courses that explore the ethical considerations and challenges faced by attorneys, including topics related to attorney-client privilege.

+ Local and state bar associations: Bar associations often organize seminars, workshops, and conferences on legal ethics and professional responsibility, providing opportunities for attorneys to stay updated on the latest developments in the field.

Conclusion

Attorney-client privilege is a crucial protection that promotes open and candid communication between clients and their attorneys. It allows clients to feel comfortable seeking legal advice and representation, knowing that their confidential information will be safeguarded. However, it is important to understand the limitations of attorney-client privilege to ensure compliance with ethical and legal standards. By respecting and preserving the attorney-client privilege, we uphold the integrity of the legal profession and maintain trust between attorneys and their clients.

Balancing Confidentiality with Other Ethical Obligations

One of the key ethical dilemmas that legal professionals often encounter is the challenge of balancing the duty of confidentiality with other ethical obligations. Confidentiality is a fundamental principle in the legal profession, which ensures that clients can trust their attorneys with sensitive and private information. However, this duty of confidentiality must be carefully balanced with other ethical considerations, such as the duty to disclose information to prevent harm or uphold the integrity of the legal system.

The Duty of Confidentiality

Confidentiality is a cornerstone of the attorney-client relationship and is essential for maintaining trust between lawyers and their clients. It ensures that clients can freely share information with their attorneys, knowing that it will be kept confidential. The duty of confidentiality extends not only to information disclosed by the client but also to information learned during the course of representation.

Confidentiality is not only an ethical obligation but is also protected by legal rules and professional codes of conduct. In many jurisdictions, attorneys have a legal duty to maintain client confidentiality, and any unauthorized disclosure of client information can result in disciplinary action or legal consequences.

Ethical Obligations and Conflicts

While the duty of confidentiality is paramount, there are situations where other ethical obligations may conflict with maintaining confidentiality. Legal professionals must navigate these conflicts carefully and make informed decisions that uphold the principles of justice and fairness.

One example of a conflict is when a client confesses to a past crime that may put others at risk. In such cases, the attorney may face an ethical dilemma between respecting the client's confidentiality and the duty to prevent harm to potential victims. The attorney must carefully consider the potential harm and evaluate whether there is a legal or ethical obligation to disclose this information to the appropriate authorities.

Similarly, attorneys may face conflicts when they become aware of their client's ongoing illegal activities. While the duty of confidentiality protects the client's information, attorneys also have a general duty to uphold the law and promote the administration of justice. In such situations, legal professionals must carefully weigh the competing ethical considerations and make a judgment regarding the disclosure of relevant information.

Balancing Confidentiality with Other Ethical Obligations

To effectively balance the duty of confidentiality with other ethical obligations, legal professionals can consider the following guidelines:

1. Understanding the Scope of Confidentiality: Attorneys should clearly communicate to their clients the limits of confidentiality and any exceptions that

may apply. This helps clients understand that there are situations where the attorney may need to disclose certain information.

2. Informed Consent: Legal professionals can seek their clients' informed consent regarding the potential disclosure of confidential information in certain situations. This empowers clients to make informed decisions and actively participate in the balancing process.

3. Assessing the Level of Potential Harm: When facing a conflict between confidentiality and preventing harm, legal professionals should carefully assess the level of potential harm. This assessment can involve evaluating the immediacy and severity of the harm, considering alternative courses of action, and involving appropriate authorities if necessary.

4. Seeking Legal Advice: In complex situations, attorneys can seek guidance from legal ethics committees, Bar association ethics hotlines, or their colleagues. Consulting with trusted experts can help attorneys navigate challenging ethical dilemmas and make well-informed decisions.

5. Documenting Decision-Making: When attorneys face conflicts between confidentiality and other ethical obligations, it is essential to document the reasoning behind their decisions. This documentation can help demonstrate that the attorney carefully considered the ethical implications and acted in accordance with professional standards.

While it is vital to balance confidentiality with other ethical obligations, legal professionals must also be mindful of potential risks and challenges. Violating client confidentiality can have severe consequences not only for the attorney but also for the legal system as a whole. Attorneys should therefore approach balancing confidentiality with other ethical obligations with utmost care and consideration.

Case Study: Duty of Confidentiality vs. Preventing Harm

Consider the following case study: A civil litigation attorney represents an individual who confessed to her involvement in an environmental crime that caused significant harm to the community. The attorney is torn between honoring her duty of confidentiality and the ethical obligation to prevent harm to the affected community.

In this situation, the attorney can follow the ethical guidelines mentioned earlier. She can communicate the limits of confidentiality to her client and explain the potential consequences of the confessed crime. The attorney can seek her client's informed consent to disclose the information to the appropriate authorities or work with the client to explore alternative ways to address the harm caused.

By carefully considering the potential harm, consulting with legal ethics experts if necessary, and documenting the decision-making process, the attorney can navigate the ethical dilemma and find a balance between her duty of confidentiality and preventing harm to the community.

Conclusion

Balancing confidentiality with other ethical obligations is a complex and challenging task for legal professionals. The duty of confidentiality is essential for maintaining client trust, but it must be weighed against the duty to prevent harm and uphold the integrity of the legal system. By following ethical guidelines, seeking informed consent, assessing potential harm, seeking legal advice, and documenting decision-making, attorneys can navigate these ethical dilemmas effectively. In doing so, they can maintain the trust of their clients while ensuring that justice and fairness prevail in the legal profession.

Challenges and Dilemmas in Maintaining Confidentiality

Confidentiality is a fundamental principle in legal practice, ensuring that clients can trust their attorneys to protect their sensitive information. However, maintaining confidentiality can present challenges and dilemmas for legal professionals. In this section, we will explore some of these challenges and dilemmas, along with strategies to address them.

Challenge 1: Balancing Confidentiality with Other Ethical Obligations

Legal professionals often face a delicate balance between maintaining client confidentiality and fulfilling their other ethical obligations. For example, attorneys have a duty to act in the best interest of their clients, but they also have a responsibility to report certain illegal activities or protect the public interest. This can create ethical dilemmas when information that should ideally be kept confidential may have wider implications.

To navigate this challenge, legal professionals must carefully consider the legal and ethical obligations at play. They should thoroughly assess the potential consequences of breaching confidentiality and seek guidance from professional codes of conduct, legal experts, or ethics committees. Open communication with clients is crucial during these situations, allowing attorneys to explain the legal and ethical limits of confidentiality and explore alternative solutions.

Challenge 2: Challenges and Dilemmas in Maintaining Confidentiality in the Digital Age

Advancements in technology have introduced new challenges in maintaining client confidentiality. Electronic communications, cloud storage, and data sharing platforms have made information more vulnerable to unauthorized access, interception, or hacking. Legal professionals must employ robust cybersecurity measures to safeguard confidential client information.

Additionally, legal professionals may face dilemmas concerning the privacy of electronic communications. For example, the use of personal devices for work-related communications can blur the line between personal and professional data, potentially compromising client confidentiality. Professionals must implement secure communication channels, educate clients about the risks involved, and establish clear protocols for electronic communications to address these challenges.

Challenge 3: Emerging Issues in Confidentiality and Attorney-Client Privilege

Confidentiality and attorney-client privilege traditionally protected communications between attorneys and their clients from disclosure in legal proceedings. However, recent legal developments have raised new questions and challenges regarding the extent and scope of these protections.

For instance, in some jurisdictions, courts have ruled that certain communications shared through third-party providers, such as email or cloud storage, may not enjoy the same level of protection as traditional one-on-one communications. Legal professionals must stay informed about the evolving legal landscape and proactively address potential challenges to client confidentiality.

To navigate emerging issues, legal professionals should review jurisdiction-specific laws and rules regarding attorney-client privilege. They should also maintain open lines of communication with clients to ensure they are aware of any potential risks to their confidentiality and work collaboratively to develop effective strategies to protect sensitive information.

Dilemma: Whistleblowing and Confidentiality

Legal professionals may face a moral dilemma when they become aware of their client's involvement in illegal or unethical activities. While attorneys have a duty to maintain client confidentiality, they may also have an ethical obligation to report such activities in the interests of justice or public safety.

To address this dilemma, legal professionals should consult the ethical rules and guidelines of their jurisdiction, professional codes of conduct, and legal experts. They may also consider the potential harm caused by the illegal or unethical activities in question and weigh it against their duty of confidentiality. It may be appropriate to seek legal advice, involve ethics committees, or even withdraw from representing the client in extreme cases.

Example: Confidentiality in Corporate Settings

Imagine a scenario where an attorney is representing a corporation that has been accused of engaging in fraudulent activities. The attorney is aware of internal documents that could prove the corporation's guilt, but disclosing these documents would breach client confidentiality.

In this situation, the attorney faces the challenge of balancing their obligation to maintain client confidentiality with their duty to uphold the law and protect the public interest. To address this dilemma, the attorney may consult with legal experts, ethics committees, or other trusted advisors. They could also explore alternative solutions, such as encouraging the corporation to self-disclose the information or engaging in negotiations that protect both client confidentiality and the interests of justice.

Conclusion

Maintaining confidentiality is a core principle of legal practice, but it is not without its challenges and dilemmas. Legal professionals must carefully navigate the complex landscape of ethical obligations, new technologies, and evolving legal interpretations to protect client confidentiality effectively. By staying informed, seeking guidance, and engaging in open communication with clients, legal professionals can address these challenges and uphold the trust placed in them.

Emerging Issues in Confidentiality and Attorney-Client Privilege

Confidentiality and attorney-client privilege are fundamental principles in the legal profession that protect the client's trust and ensure effective legal representation. However, with the rapid advancement of technology, globalization, and changes in legal practice, there are emerging issues that pose challenges to maintaining confidentiality and attorney-client privilege. In this section, we will explore some of these emerging issues and discuss their implications for the legal profession.

Digital Communication and Information Security

One of the most significant emerging issues in confidentiality and attorney-client privilege is the use of digital communication and information security. With the widespread use of email, instant messaging, and cloud storage, lawyers and clients often communicate and exchange confidential information electronically. However, these digital platforms are prone to cybersecurity threats, such as hacking and unauthorized access, which can compromise the confidentiality of attorney-client communications.

To address this issue, lawyers must adopt robust cybersecurity measures to protect client information. This includes using secure email providers, implementing encryption technologies, and regularly updating software to mitigate vulnerabilities. Additionally, lawyers must educate their clients about the risks associated with digital communication and advise them on best practices for securing their information.

Social Media and Online Presence

Another emerging issue in confidentiality and attorney-client privilege is the use of social media and online presence. Lawyers and their clients are increasingly utilizing social media platforms to share information, connect with others, and promote their professional profiles. However, the use of social media can inadvertently lead to the disclosure of confidential information or compromise attorney-client privilege.

Lawyers must be cautious when using social media and ensure that they do not inadvertently reveal confidential information or establish client relationships online. Additionally, lawyers should educate their clients about the risks of sharing sensitive information on social media and advise them on privacy settings and responsible online behavior.

Cloud Computing and Data Storage

Cloud computing has revolutionized the way information is stored and accessed. Many law firms and legal professionals now use cloud-based platforms to store and manage their documents and client files. However, this shift to cloud computing raises concerns about the security and privacy of client information.

Lawyers need to carefully select cloud service providers that prioritize data security and have robust encryption and access control measures in place. They should also ensure that their cloud service contracts comply with legal and ethical obligations regarding confidentiality and attorney-client privilege. Regular audits and risk assessments should be conducted to ensure ongoing compliance with data protection regulations.

Cross-Border Communication and Jurisdictional Challenges

In an increasingly globalized world, lawyers often need to communicate and collaborate with clients and legal professionals from different jurisdictions. However, this can create challenges in maintaining confidentiality and protecting attorney-client privilege.

Different countries have different laws and regulations governing privacy and information sharing. Lawyers must navigate these jurisdictional challenges and ensure that they comply with the applicable legal and ethical obligations. They should seek advice from local counsel or experts in the jurisdiction to ensure that confidentiality is maintained when communicating and sharing information across borders.

Emerging Technologies and Artificial Intelligence

The emergence of new technologies, such as artificial intelligence (AI), presents both opportunities and challenges in maintaining confidentiality and attorney-client privilege. AI technology is increasingly being used in legal research, document review, and prediction of legal outcomes. While AI can enhance efficiency and accuracy in legal practice, it also raises concerns about the privacy and security of client information.

Lawyers must navigate the ethical and legal implications of using AI and ensure that client confidentiality is not compromised. They should conduct due diligence when selecting AI tools and ensure that these technologies comply with legal and ethical standards regarding confidentiality and attorney-client privilege. Additionally, lawyers should stay updated on the evolving legal landscape surrounding AI to ensure that they are aware of any changes that may impact client confidentiality.

Case Study: Confidentiality in a Remote Working Environment

The COVID-19 pandemic has accelerated the adoption of remote working in the legal profession. Many lawyers and law firms have had to quickly transition to virtual workplaces, raising concerns about maintaining confidentiality and attorney-client privilege outside of the traditional office setting.

Consider the case of a lawyer who is working remotely and uses their personal computer to communicate with clients and access confidential information. The lawyer must ensure that their home network is secure, that their personal computer has the necessary security measures in place, and that they are mindful of their physical environment to prevent unauthorized access to confidential information.

To address these concerns, lawyers should establish policies and procedures for remote working that emphasize data security and confidentiality. This may include using virtual private networks (VPNs) for secure communication, implementing multi-factor authentication, and conducting regular training on cybersecurity best practices.

Conclusion

Emerging issues in confidentiality and attorney-client privilege present both challenges and opportunities for the legal profession. As technology continues to evolve and legal practices adapt, it is essential for lawyers to stay informed, proactive, and vigilant in maintaining client confidentiality and upholding the principles of attorney-client privilege. By adopting robust cybersecurity measures, staying updated on relevant laws and regulations, and educating clients on responsible digital behavior, lawyers can navigate these emerging issues and ensure that confidentiality and attorney-client privilege are preserved in a rapidly changing legal landscape.

Ethics in Legal Counseling

Ethics play a crucial role in the practice of law, especially when it comes to counseling clients. When providing legal advice and guidance, attorneys must adhere to ethical standards to ensure the trust and confidence of their clients. In this section, we will explore the ethical considerations that arise in the context of legal counseling, examining the duties and responsibilities of attorneys and the challenges they may encounter.

Duty of Competence

One of the fundamental ethical obligations of attorneys is the duty of competence. Attorneys have a responsibility to provide competent representation to their clients, which includes possessing the necessary knowledge, skill, and diligence to handle a particular legal matter effectively. However, attorneys may face ethical challenges when dealing with complex or unfamiliar areas of law.

To fulfill their duty of competence, attorneys must stay updated on the latest legal developments, engage in continuing education, and seek assistance or consultation when needed. This may involve collaborating with other attorneys or experts who possess the requisite expertise. By recognizing their limitations and seeking assistance, attorneys can ensure that they provide competent advice to their clients.

Client Confidentiality

Client confidentiality is a cornerstone of the attorney-client relationship, and attorneys have an ethical duty to protect the confidential information disclosed by their clients. The duty of confidentiality extends to all information relating to the representation, regardless of its source or the nature of the information.

Attorneys must take reasonable steps to safeguard client confidences and protect against unauthorized access or disclosure. This duty continues even after the attorney-client relationship ends. Confidentiality is crucial for fostering trust between attorneys and clients and encouraging clients to share all necessary information openly.

However, attorneys may encounter ethical dilemmas when balancing the duty of confidentiality with other competing obligations. For example, if an attorney becomes aware of a client's intention to commit a crime, they may face a moral dilemma about whether to maintain confidentiality or report the client's illegal plans to law enforcement.

Avoiding Conflicts of Interest

Attorneys have an ethical duty to avoid conflicts of interest that could compromise their ability to provide independent and unbiased advice to their clients. Conflicts of interest can arise in various situations, such as representing clients with adverse interests or having personal or financial relationships that may affect the attorney's judgment.

To fulfill their duty to avoid conflicts of interest, attorneys must conduct a thorough conflict check before taking on a new client or accepting a new matter from an existing client. This involves identifying any potential conflicts and obtaining informed consent from the affected clients after disclosing the conflict.

However, attorneys may face challenges in identifying and addressing conflicts of interest, especially in complex legal matters involving multiple parties or entities. In such cases, attorneys must exercise careful judgment and seek guidance from their state bar association or legal ethics committees to ensure they comply with ethical obligations.

Maintaining Professionalism and Integrity

Professionalism and integrity are core values in legal counseling. Attorneys must maintain a high level of professionalism in their interactions with clients, colleagues, and the public. This includes being honest, respectful, and diligent in their representation.

Attorneys should provide candid advice to their clients and avoid misleading or deceptive practices. They should also refrain from engaging in behavior that could undermine the administration of justice or damage the legal profession's reputation.

However, attorneys may face ethical challenges in maintaining professionalism and integrity, particularly in adversarial situations. It can be tempting to engage in aggressive or unethical tactics to gain an advantage in litigation. Nevertheless, attorneys must prioritize their ethical obligations and uphold the dignity of the legal profession.

Addressing Cultural and Diversity Issues

In the increasingly diverse and multicultural society we live in, attorneys must be mindful of cultural and diversity issues in legal counseling. Clients from different backgrounds may have unique needs or expectations, and attorneys must navigate these differences sensitively and ethically.

Attorneys should strive to understand their clients' cultural perspectives and provide legal advice that respects their values and beliefs. This may require cultural competence training and ongoing self-education to ensure attorneys can effectively represent clients from diverse backgrounds.

Additionally, attorneys should be aware of potential biases or prejudices that could affect their representation. It is essential to approach legal counseling without discriminatory assumptions or stereotypes and to treat all clients with fairness and respect.

Conclusion

Ethics in legal counseling encompass various responsibilities and considerations. Attorneys must be competent, maintain client confidentiality, avoid conflicts of interest, uphold professionalism and integrity, and address cultural and diversity issues. By adhering to these ethical principles, attorneys can provide effective and ethical legal counseling, ensuring the best possible representation for their clients. Remember, in legal counseling, ethics is not just a professional requirement but also a moral imperative that contributes to a more just and equitable society.

Legal Ethics and Privilege

In the field of legal studies, ethics play a vital role in determining the behavior and conduct of professionals in the legal profession. Legal ethics encompass a set of principles and rules that guide lawyers and other legal professionals in their practice. One crucial aspect of legal ethics is the concept of privilege, which concerns the protection of confidential information shared between an attorney and their client.

Understanding Attorney-Client Privilege

Attorney-client privilege is a fundamental legal principle that protects the confidentiality of communications between a lawyer and their client. It ensures that clients can fully and openly disclose information to their attorneys without fear of it being disclosed to others. This privilege encourages clients to provide all the relevant facts to their lawyers, enabling them to provide the best legal representation possible.

The attorney-client privilege exists to promote trust and confidence between attorneys and their clients. It recognizes that effective legal representation depends on open and honest communication. By fostering a safe and confidential space, clients can share sensitive information with their lawyers, including personal facts, strategies, and potential legal violations, without fear of adverse consequences.

Scope and Limitations of Privilege

While attorney-client privilege is a cornerstone of legal ethics, it is not an absolute right and has certain limitations. It is essential for legal professionals and clients to be aware of these limitations to avoid any misunderstandings or breaches of confidentiality.

Firstly, the privilege only applies to confidential communications made between an attorney and their client in the context of seeking legal advice or representation. Information shared with third parties or in the presence of others who are not necessary for the legal representation may not be protected by privilege.

Secondly, the privilege belongs to the client, not the attorney. The client has the authority to waive the privilege and disclose the information if they choose to do so. Attorneys must respect their client's decision and act in their best interests.

Thirdly, privilege may be waived if the client voluntarily discloses the information to a third party. If this occurs, the privilege may no longer shield the communication from disclosure.

Finally, privilege does not apply to communications made with the intent to commit a crime or to further an ongoing illegal activity. The privilege cannot be used to protect clients who seek legal advice to perpetrate fraudulent, illegal, or harmful actions.

Ethical Considerations in Maintaining Privilege

Legal professionals have a moral and ethical obligation to maintain and protect the confidentiality of their client's information. Lawyers must adhere to strict ethical guidelines to ensure that privileged communications remain confidential to the fullest extent possible.

It is crucial for attorneys to understand the scope and limitations of the privilege. They must advise clients about the nature and extent of the protection provided by attorney-client privilege. Attorneys should explain the potential risks and exceptions to privilege and inform clients about any situations where the privilege may not apply. This transparency helps clients make informed decisions about sharing information.

Attorneys should also take necessary precautions to maintain confidentiality. This includes using secure communication channels, limiting access to privileged information within their law firm, and avoiding any unnecessary disclosures of client information. Additionally, lawyers must be vigilant to prevent inadvertent disclosures, such as discussing client matters in public or leaving sensitive documents unattended.

In cases where multiple clients are involved, such as in joint representation, attorneys must clearly establish the scope of the privilege and ensure that all clients are aware of any potential conflicts of interest. Lawyers should obtain informed consent from all clients involved to address any potential issues that may arise during the representation.

Challenges and Dilemmas in Maintaining Privilege

Maintaining attorney-client privilege can pose challenges and ethical dilemmas. Legal professionals must navigate these complexities carefully to uphold their ethical obligations.

One common challenge is balancing privilege with the duty of zealous advocacy. Attorneys are obligated to vigorously represent and defend their clients' interests. However, they must do so within the boundaries of the law and without engaging in unethical behavior. This includes refraining from using privileged information to manipulate or deceive others.

Another challenge is maintaining privilege in the digital age.   With the widespread use of electronic communications, preserving the confidentiality of client information has become more complex. Attorneys need to be aware of the potential vulnerabilities of digital platforms and take appropriate steps to safeguard privileged communications from unauthorized access.

Conflicts of interest can also create dilemmas in maintaining privilege. When representing multiple clients with potentially conflicting interests, attorneys must navigate carefully to avoid compromising privileged communications. They may need to implement screening procedures or, in some cases, withdraw from representing one or more clients to protect privileged information and prevent conflicts of interest.

Case Study: Privilege in Corporate Law

One example where attorney-client privilege plays a crucial role is in corporate law. In the corporate setting, attorneys often provide legal advice and guidance to corporations, their executives, and employees. The attorney-client privilege allows these individuals to confidentially discuss legal matters, potential risks, and compliance issues without fear of their communications being used against them in legal proceedings.

However, maintaining privilege in the corporate context can be challenging. Corporate counsel often find themselves in situations where they have dual roles, representing both the company and its employees. This duality can complicate privilege issues, especially when conflicts of interest arise or when there is potential misconduct within the organization.

To navigate these challenges, corporate attorneys must clearly define their roles and establish the scope of privilege with all relevant parties.   They should communicate the limitations of privilege to employees, ensuring they understand when it applies and when it may be waived. Corporate counsel must also remain independent and act in the best interests of their clients while maintaining their ethical obligations.

Conclusion

Attorney-client privilege is a critical ethical principle in legal practice. It fosters open communication, trust, and effective representation between attorneys and their clients. Legal professionals must understand the scope and limitations of privilege, maintain confidentiality with utmost care, and navigate the challenges and dilemmas that may arise. By upholding the principles of privilege, legal practitioners contribute to a more just and equitable legal system.

Conclusion

In this chapter, we have explored the ethical issues in the legal profession. We began by discussing the role and responsibilities of legal professionals and the importance of professionalism and ethics in legal practice. We examined the ethical obligations that lawyers have towards their clients, the court, and society. We also delved into the professional codes of conduct that govern legal practice and the ethical challenges that lawyers face on a daily basis.

Confidentiality and attorney-client privilege emerged as crucial ethical considerations in legal practice. We discussed the significance of maintaining confidentiality in lawyer-client relationships and the ethical dilemmas that can arise when balancing confidentiality with other ethical obligations. We examined some of the challenges faced by lawyers in maintaining confidentiality, especially in the age of digital communication and social media. While confidentiality is essential for fostering trust and open communication between lawyers and clients, it must be balanced with the duty to uphold the administration of justice.

Conflict of interest was another significant ethical issue that we analyzed. We explored the different types of conflicts of interest that lawyers may encounter and the ethical implications that arise from such conflicts. We discussed strategies for avoiding and managing conflicts of interest and highlighted the importance of promoting transparency and accountability in this regard. Ethical decision making in legal negotiation and mediation was also examined in the context of potential conflicts of interest.

Furthermore, we acknowledged the broader social justice and human rights concerns within the legal profession. We emphasized the need for lawyers to engage in public interest work and to advocate for marginalized communities. We explored the ethical considerations inherent in legal advocacy, including the responsibility to promote access to justice and uphold constitutional rights and liberties. We also touched upon the ethical challenges faced by lawyers in balancing their professional obligations with considerations of the public interest.

Overall, the ethical issues in the legal profession are complex and multifaceted. Legal professionals must constantly navigate moral dilemmas and make decisions that are both legally and ethically sound. Upholding ethical standards is crucial not only for maintaining the integrity of the legal profession, but also for promoting justice and social change in society. As future legal practitioners, it is essential to be mindful of these ethical issues and to strive for ethical excellence in our professional endeavors.

To further reflect on the ethical issues in the legal profession, consider the following exercises:

1. Case Study: Analyze a scenario in which a lawyer faces a conflict of interest. Identify the potential ethical implications and propose strategies for addressing the conflict.

2. Reflective Writing: Share your thoughts and reflections on the importance of maintaining confidentiality in legal practice. Discuss any ethical dilemmas you anticipate encountering in this regard and propose strategies for maintaining confidentiality while upholding other ethical obligations.

3. Research Project: Investigate a recent legal case that involved ethical issues. Analyze the ethical considerations that arose in the case, the decisions made by the legal professionals involved, and the impact of those decisions on justice and society.

Resources for further exploration:

- American Bar Association, Model Rules of Professional Conduct: This resource provides a comprehensive framework for legal ethics and can serve as a guide for ethical decision making in the legal profession.

- Legal Ethics: The Lawyer's Deskbook on Professional Responsibility: This book offers practical guidance on navigating ethical issues in legal practice, including the areas of confidentiality, conflicts of interest, and professional responsibility.

- The Center for Professional Responsibility: This organization provides resources, publications, and continuing education opportunities for legal professionals to improve their understanding of ethical issues in the legal profession.

Remember, ethical decision making is a continuous process, and it requires constant reflection, self-awareness, and a commitment to upholding the principles of justice and the public interest. As legal practitioners, we have the power to shape a more equitable, just, and sustainable world.

Conflict of Interest

Definition and Types of Conflict of Interest

In the field of legal studies, conflicts of interest are a common ethical concern that can arise in various professional settings. A conflict of interest occurs when a person or organization is in a position where their personal or financial interests may potentially influence their impartiality, objectivity, or judgment in carrying out their professional responsibilities. Resolving conflicts of interest is crucial to maintaining the integrity of legal practice and ensuring fairness and justice.

Definition of Conflict of Interest

A conflict of interest can be defined as a situation in which a person or entity has competing obligations, loyalties, or interests that could compromise their ability to act in the best interests of another party. The conflict may arise when a person's personal interests, such as financial gain, personal relationships, or other affiliations, are in conflict with their professional duties and responsibilities.

Conflict of interest can manifest in various ways, ranging from minor to significant ethical concerns. It is essential for legal professionals to identify and address conflicts of interest promptly to avoid compromising their professional ethics and the integrity of the legal system.

Types of Conflict of Interest

Conflicts of interest in legal practice can occur in different contexts and take on various forms. Some common types of conflicts of interest include:

1. **Financial Conflicts of Interest:** This type of conflict arises when a lawyer or legal professional has a financial interest that could potentially interfere with their objectivity or impartiality. For example, if a lawyer is representing a client in a lawsuit and also has a personal financial interest in the outcome of the case, it creates a conflict that must be resolved.

2. **Personal Relationship Conflicts of Interest:** When a legal professional has a personal or familial relationship with a party involved in a case, it can create a conflict of interest. For instance, if a lawyer is representing a family member or close friend, their personal relationship may compromise their ability to provide unbiased legal advice or representation.

3. **Advocacy Conflicts of Interest:** Advocacy conflicts of interest occur when a lawyer's loyalty to one client conflicts with their duty to act in the best interests of another client. For example, if a lawyer represents two clients with conflicting interests in the same legal matter, such as in a business transaction or divorce case, it presents a conflict that needs to be addressed.

4. **Organizational Conflicts of Interest:** In some cases, conflicts of interest can arise within organizations or institutions. For example, if a law firm represents clients who have competing interests, there is a potential conflict that needs to be managed appropriately. Similarly, conflicts of interest may arise in government

agencies or other organizations that have overlapping responsibilities or conflicting objectives.

5. **Confidentiality Conflicts of Interest**: Legal professionals have a duty to maintain client confidentiality and protect their client's information. However, conflicts of interest can arise when a lawyer's duty of confidentiality conflicts with their responsibility to disclose information or prevent harm. Resolving these conflicts requires a careful balance between maintaining confidentiality and fulfilling other ethical obligations.

Resolving Conflicts of Interest

Resolving conflicts of interest in legal practice requires careful consideration and adherence to ethical guidelines. Legal professionals have a responsibility to avoid conflicts of interest whenever possible and to address them promptly when they arise. Here are some steps that can be taken to effectively resolve conflicts of interest:

1. **Identify and Disclose**: The first step is to identify and acknowledge the existence of a potential conflict of interest. Legal professionals should have a system in place to regularly assess their professional responsibilities and relationships for potential conflicts. Once identified, the conflict should be disclosed to all relevant parties affected by the conflict.

2. **Evaluate and Assess**: After identifying a conflict, it is important to evaluate the nature and severity of the conflict. This involves considering the potential impact on the affected parties, the ethical implications, and any legal obligations that may be applicable. An objective assessment of the conflict is crucial in determining how best to proceed.

3. **Mitigate or Eliminate**: Whenever possible, legal professionals should take steps to mitigate or eliminate conflicts of interest. This may include withdrawing from representation, obtaining informed consent from affected parties, or implementing safeguards to ensure impartiality and objectivity. The appropriate course of action will depend on the specific circumstances of each case.

4. **Seek Independent Advice**: In complex or challenging situations, legal professionals may seek advice from their peers, professional bodies, or ethics committees. Consulting with an independent third party can provide valuable insights and guidance on resolving conflicts of interest effectively and ethically.

5. **Document Actions Taken**: It is crucial to maintain a record of the steps taken to address conflicts of interest. Documentation helps demonstrate a commitment to ethical practice and provides transparency in case of future inquiries or disputes.

Legal professionals should be aware of the applicable laws, rules, and ethical standards governing conflicts of interest in their jurisdiction. Additionally, regular ethical training and continuing education can help legal professionals stay up-to-date with best practices for addressing conflicts of interest.

Example: Conflict of Interest in Corporate Representation

Consider a scenario where a law firm represents both a large corporation and an individual employee who is suing the same corporation for workplace discrimination. This situation presents an inherent conflict of interest as the law firm has a duty to represent both clients zealously while maintaining loyalty and objectivity.

To resolve this conflict, the law firm must take appropriate actions. They may choose to withdraw as counsel for one of the clients, obtain informed consent from both parties after disclosing the conflict, or implement safeguards to ensure the conflict does not compromise the fairness and integrity of the legal process.

To mitigate the conflict, the law firm could assign separate teams of attorneys to work on each client's case, ensuring that confidentiality and loyalty obligations are respected. By taking these measures, the law firm can effectively navigate the conflict of interest and provide ethical representation to both clients.

Additional Resources

Resolving conflicts of interest is an ongoing process that requires vigilance and adherence to ethical standards. Here are some additional resources that can provide further guidance on this topic:

+ American Bar Association (ABA) Model Rules of Professional Conduct: The ABA provides a comprehensive set of rules and guidelines for legal professionals, including specific provisions on conflicts of interest.

+ Legal Ethics Opinions: Many jurisdictions have ethics committees or organizations that issue opinions and guidelines on various ethical issues, including conflicts of interest. These opinions can provide valuable insights into resolving conflicts of interest in specific jurisdictions.

+ Legal Education Programs: Law schools and continuing legal education programs often offer courses and seminars on legal ethics, including conflicts of interest. These educational resources can help legal professionals stay informed and up-to-date on current ethical standards and best practices.

Remember, conflicts of interest are complex ethical issues, and each situation should be carefully evaluated on a case-by-case basis. By understanding the definition and types of conflicts of interest and taking appropriate steps to address them, legal professionals can uphold the highest standards of professional ethics and ensure justice and fairness in their practice.

Avoidance and Management of Conflict of Interest

Conflicts of interest are situations where individuals or organizations have multiple competing interests that could potentially influence their ability to act impartially. In the legal profession, conflicts of interest can arise in various contexts, such as legal representation, decision making, or financial relationships. It is crucial for legal professionals to identify, avoid, and effectively manage conflicts of interest to maintain ethical integrity and ensure the fair administration of justice.

Identifying Conflict of Interest

Identifying conflicts of interest requires a comprehensive understanding of the relationships and roles of the parties involved. Legal professionals should actively assess potential conflicts of interest in different situations such as:

- *Client representation*: When representing clients, lawyers need to determine if any personal, financial, or professional relationships may compromise their loyalty, independence, or objectivity. For example, if a lawyer represents a family member or has a personal interest in the outcome of a case, it may create a conflict of interest.

- *Law firm conflicts*: Law firms must establish procedures to identify conflicts of interest when taking on new clients or matters. This includes determining if any current or previous clients have adverse interests or if there are any relationships that could compromise the firm's ability to provide unbiased advice and representation.

- *Financial interests*: Legal professionals need to examine any financial interests they hold that may conflict with their professional responsibilities. For instance, if a lawyer or judge has a financial stake in a company involved in a legal matter they are handling, it can create a conflict of interest.

- *Personal relationships*: Personal relationships with individuals involved in a legal matter, such as family members, close friends, or business associates, can create conflicts of interest. Legal professionals must assess the potential impact of these relationships on their objectivity and ability to provide unbiased advice.

By proactively evaluating these and other relevant factors, legal professionals can identify potential conflicts of interest and take the necessary steps to address them.

Avoiding Conflict of Interest

The most effective way to manage conflicts of interest is to avoid them altogether. Avoidance strategies include:

+ *Screening procedures*: Law firms often implement screening procedures to prevent conflicts of interest from arising. This involves creating information barriers between lawyers or teams working on different matters to ensure confidential information is not shared inappropriately.

+ *Informed consent*: When a conflict of interest is identified, legal professionals can seek informed consent from all affected parties. This involves fully disclosing the potential conflict to the clients involved and obtaining their explicit consent to continue representation despite the conflict. However, informed consent may not always be sufficient, especially if the conflict of interest is significant or could compromise the lawyer's independence or loyalty to the client.

+ *Withdrawing representation*: In some cases, legal professionals may need to withdraw from or decline representation to avoid conflicts of interest. This can happen if the potential conflict is unavoidable, and adequate safeguards cannot be put in place to protect the client's interests.

+ *Structural safeguards*: Law firms can establish internal policies and procedures to prevent conflicts of interest. These may include regular conflict checks, training programs on conflict identification and management, and robust information management systems to track client engagements and relationships.

By implementing these avoidance strategies, legal professionals can mitigate the risks associated with conflicts of interest and uphold their ethical obligations.

Managing Conflict of Interest

In situations where conflicts of interest cannot be avoided, legal professionals must implement effective management strategies. Some approaches to managing conflicts of interest include:

+ *Disclosure and transparency*: Lawyers must disclose conflicts of interest to their clients and all relevant parties. Open communication is essential to ensure that affected parties have the opportunity to provide informed consent or take necessary steps to protect their interests.

+ *Obtaining independent advice*: In complex cases where conflicts of interest are present, legal professionals may recommend that their clients seek independent legal advice. This helps ensure that clients can make informed decisions while being aware of the potential impact of the conflict.

+ *Ethics opinions and professional guidance*: Legal professionals can consult ethics opinions, guidelines, and professional organizations' resources to seek guidance on managing conflicts of interest. These resources provide insights into best practices and ethical standards to help navigate complex situations.

+ *Supervision and oversight*: In law firms or organizational settings, implementing proper supervision and oversight mechanisms can help identify and address conflicts of interest in a timely manner. Senior lawyers or designated individuals can review potential conflicts, provide guidance, and monitor compliance with ethical obligations.

Effective management of conflicts of interest requires a combination of ethical judgment, careful consideration, and adherence to professional standards. By implementing these strategies, legal professionals can minimize the potential harm that conflicts of interest may pose to their clients and the overall integrity of the legal system.

Case Study: Conflict of Interest in Corporate Transactions

Consider a scenario where a law firm is advising both a seller and a buyer in a complex corporate transaction. The law firm has represented the seller for several years and has extensive knowledge of their operations and strategies. In the course of the transaction, the buyer expresses concerns about certain undisclosed liabilities and seeks guidance from the law firm.

In this situation, a conflict of interest arises due to the law firm's dual representation. To avoid or manage the conflict, the following steps can be taken:

1. Identify the Conflict: The law firm should recognize the conflicting interests between the seller and the buyer, as well as the potential risks associated with the dual representation.

2. Evaluate the Conflict's Significance: Assess the potential impact of the conflict on the advice and representation provided to both parties. Consider the confidentiality of information and the potential impairment of loyalty, independence, or objectivity.

3. Seek Informed Consent: If the conflict is deemed manageable, obtain informed consent from both parties after fully disclosing the conflict and its implications. Ensure that the clients understand the risks involved and provide explicit consent to proceed with the dual representation.

4. Implement Safeguards: Establish strict information barriers within the law firm to prevent the sharing of confidential information between the teams representing the seller and the buyer. This includes physical and digital separation of files, restricted access to certain documents, and supervision from designated individuals.

5. Monitor the Conflict: Continuously evaluate the ongoing representation to ensure that the conflict of interest does not compromise the quality of advice or representation provided to either party. If unforeseen complications or ethical concerns arise, consider withdrawing from the representation.

By diligently adhering to these steps, legal professionals can navigate conflicts of interest arising from corporate transactions and uphold their ethical duties to their clients.

Key Takeaways

Conflict of interest is a significant ethical concern in the legal profession, requiring careful identification, avoidance, and management. Here are the key takeaways from this section:

+ Conflict of interest can arise in various legal contexts, such as client representation, law firm engagements, financial interests, and personal relationships.

+ Identifying conflicts of interest requires a comprehensive assessment of relationships, roles, and potential influences.

+ Avoidance is the preferred strategy, achieved through screening procedures, informed consent, withdrawal from representation, and structural safeguards.

+ When conflicts of interest cannot be avoided, effective management involves disclosure, obtaining independent advice, seeking professional guidance, and implementing supervision and oversight.

+ Case-specific analysis and careful consideration are necessary to navigate conflicts of interest successfully.

By prioritizing ethical considerations, legal professionals can uphold their duty to act in the best interests of their clients and maintain the integrity of the legal system.

Ethical Implications of Conflicts of Interest

Conflicts of interest are a common ethical concern in various fields, including legal studies. A conflict of interest occurs when a person's professional or personal obligations or interests conflict with their duty to act in the best interests of a client, organization, or the public. In the legal profession, conflicts of interest can arise in different scenarios, such as representing multiple clients with opposing interests, personal relationships with clients or opposing parties, or financial interests impacting decision-making.

Understanding Conflicts of Interest

To grasp the ethical implications of conflicts of interest, it is important to first understand the concept itself. A conflict of interest can take different forms, including:

+ **Direct conflicts:** These arise when an individual's personal or financial interests directly contradict their professional obligations. For example, a lawyer representing a client in a case involving a company they have a personal investment in.

+ **Indirect conflicts:** These occur when an individual's actions or decisions could be influenced by external factors that compromise their objectivity or independence. For instance, a judge presiding over a case involving a close friend or family member.

+ **Perceived conflicts:** Even the appearance of a conflict of interest can be problematic, as it can erode public trust and confidence in the fairness or impartiality of legal proceedings. This can happen even if there is no actual conflict present, highlighting the importance of maintaining the perception of fairness.

It is crucial for legal professionals to identify and address conflicts of interest promptly to uphold their ethical responsibilities and preserve the integrity of the legal system.

Ethical Duties Involved

Conflicts of interest can fundamentally undermine the professional duties and ethical obligations of legal practitioners. Several important ethical principles are at stake when conflicts of interest emerge:

+ **Duty of loyalty:** Legal professionals have a duty to prioritize the best interests of their clients. Conflicts of interest compromise this duty and may result in a divergence from zealous representation. This can lead to inadequate advocacy or unjust outcomes.

+ **Independence and objectivity:** Legal practitioners are expected to exercise independent judgment and provide objective advice to clients. Conflicts of interest may impair their ability to fulfill these obligations, casting doubt on the integrity of their actions.

+ **Confidentiality:** Lawyers are required to maintain client confidentiality. However, when conflicts of interest arise, the confidential information of one client may be at odds with the interests of another client, potentially leading to breaches of professional confidentiality.

+ **Fairness and justice:** Conflicts of interest can compromise the fundamental principles of fairness and justice in legal proceedings. When a legal professional's personal or financial interests influence decision-making, it can undermine the impartiality and integrity of the legal system.

Addressing conflicts of interest is not only essential to meet ethical duties but also to maintain public trust in the legal profession.

Identifying and Managing Conflicts of Interest

To effectively address conflicts of interest, legal professionals should be vigilant in identifying potential conflicts and implementing suitable management strategies. Some steps that can be taken include:

+ **Conflict screening:** Lawyers should conduct thorough conflict checks before accepting a new client or case. This involves reviewing potential conflicts of interest, considering any past or present relationships, affiliations, or interests that may compromise objectivity.

+ **Client consent and waivers:** In some situations, if a conflict of interest arises but the client provides informed consent or a waiver, the legal professional may proceed with representation. However, it is crucial to ensure that the client understands the potential risks and implications of the conflict.

+ **Ethics committees and guidance:** Legal organizations and professional bodies often have ethics committees that can provide guidance and advice on managing conflicts of interest. Seeking such guidance can be helpful in navigating complex ethical dilemmas.

+ **Referral or withdrawal:** If a significant conflict of interest cannot be effectively managed, legal practitioners may need to consider referring the client to another lawyer or, if necessary, withdrawing from the representation altogether. This ensures that the conflicting interests do not compromise the legal professional's ethical obligations.

It is essential for legal professionals to document the steps taken to identify and manage conflicts of interest, demonstrating their commitment to ethical practice and accountability.

Case Study: Conflicts of Interest in Corporate Law

To illustrate the ethical implications of conflicts of interest, let's consider a case study in the field of corporate law. Imagine a law firm that represents both Company A and Company B, two direct competitors in the same industry. The lawyers in the firm are responsible for handling legal matters for both companies, including mergers and acquisitions.

In this scenario, a conflict of interest may arise if the lawyers have access to sensitive and confidential information from both Company A and Company B.

The lawyers must ethically navigate this situation to avoid compromising their duty of loyalty, confidentiality, and fair representation.

To manage this conflict, the law firm could consider the following actions:

1. Implement confidentiality policies: The law firm should establish strict protocols to ensure that lawyers who have access to confidential information from one client are prohibited from sharing that information with lawyers representing the other client.

2. Create separate legal teams: The law firm may assign separate legal teams to handle the legal matters of Company A and Company B. This reduces the risk of attorneys inadvertently using confidential information from one client to benefit the other.

3. Maintain transparency and client communication: The law firm should communicate openly with both clients about the potential conflict of interest and the measures put in place to manage it. This allows clients to make informed decisions and provide their consent to representation despite the conflict.

4. Review and update conflicts of interest regularly: It is crucial for the law firm to periodically review and update its conflicts of interest policies to adapt to changing circumstances. This ensures ongoing compliance with ethical standards and minimizes the risk of conflicts going unnoticed.

By proactively addressing conflicts of interest and implementing appropriate safeguards, the law firm can fulfill its ethical duties while effectively representing both clients.

Conclusion

Conflicts of interest are ethical concerns that legal professionals must navigate carefully. Understanding the concept of conflicts of interest, recognizing the ethical duties at stake, and effectively managing conflicts are crucial steps for upholding the integrity of the legal profession and ensuring fairness in legal proceedings. By being vigilant and proactive, legal practitioners can promote ethical decision-making and contribute to a more just and equitable world.

Additional Resources:

+ American Bar Association's Model Rules of Professional Conduct: https://www.americanbar.org/groups/professional_

```
responsibility/publications/model_rules_of_
professional_conduct/
```

- Legal Services Commission (UK) Guidance on Conflicts of Interest: `https://www.gov.uk/guidance/solicitors-conflicts-of-interest`

- Cornell Law School's Legal Information Institute on Conflicts of Interest: `https://www.law.cornell.edu/wex/conflict_of_interest`

Challenges in Identifying and Addressing Conflicts of Interest

Conflicts of interest are a pervasive issue in the legal profession and present significant challenges in maintaining ethical integrity. A conflict of interest arises when a lawyer's duties to one client are compromised by their obligations or interests in another matter or client. Identifying and addressing conflicts of interest require a comprehensive understanding of the complex relationships and potential ethical dilemmas that can arise.

Understanding Conflicts of Interest

A conflict of interest occurs when a lawyer's personal or financial interests conflict with their duty to act in the best interests of their client. It can also arise when a lawyer's duty to one client is in direct conflict with their duty to another client. Conflicts of interest can be classified into three main categories:

1. **Direct Conflict of Interest:** This occurs when a lawyer's loyalty to one client is directly opposed to their loyalty to another client in the same or a related matter. For example, representing both the buyer and the seller in a transaction might create a conflict of interest.

2. **Imputed Conflicts of Interest:** In some cases, a conflict of interest can be imputed from one lawyer to an entire firm or organization. This happens when the conflict arises from the personal interest of one lawyer, but the entire firm is affected due to the nature of their relationship.

3. **Appearance of Impropriety:** Even if there is no direct conflict of interest, a lawyer's actions or relationships may create the appearance of impropriety. This perception alone can erode public confidence in the legal profession and should be avoided.

Challenges in Identifying Conflicts of Interest

Identifying conflicts of interest is a critical step in ensuring ethical conduct in legal practice. However, it is not always an easy task due to several challenges that lawyers face. Some of the main challenges include:

1. **Complexity of Relationships:** The legal profession often involves complex relationships between lawyers, clients, and other parties. Identifying potential conflicts requires a thorough understanding of these relationships and the ability to recognize when competing interests may compromise a lawyer's obligations.

2. **Confidentiality Concerns:** Lawyers are bound by strict rules of confidentiality, which can make it challenging to identify conflicts of interest. Lawyers may have access to privileged information that could suggest a conflict, but they cannot disclose this information without proper authorization.

3. **Changing Circumstances:** Conflicts of interest can arise or evolve over time as circumstances change. A lawyer may not be aware of a potential conflict at the outset of a case or representation but may become aware of it during the course of their work. Staying vigilant and regularly reassessing potential conflicts is necessary.

4. **Subjectivity and Interpretation:** Determining whether a conflict of interest exists can sometimes be a subjective judgment. Different interpretations of professional rules and ethical guidelines can lead to disagreements among lawyers and professionals. This subjectivity can complicate the identification process.

5. **Limited Information:** In some cases, lawyers may not have access to all the necessary information to fully assess potential conflicts. Clients may not disclose important details or fail to recognize the relevance of certain relationships or interests. This limited information can hinder the identification process.

6. **Time Constraints:** Identifying conflicts of interest requires time for research, analysis, and consultation. However, lawyers often work under time constraints, and the pressure to meet deadlines can make it challenging to thoroughly identify and address potential conflicts.

Addressing Conflicts of Interest

Once a conflict of interest is identified, it must be appropriately addressed to ensure the lawyer's obligations are met and ethical integrity is maintained. Some strategies for addressing conflicts of interest include:

1. **Obtaining Informed Consent:** In some situations, a conflict of interest can be addressed by obtaining informed consent from the affected clients. This requires full disclosure of the conflict and its potential implications, allowing the clients to make an informed decision about whether to proceed with the representation.

2. **Screening and Disqualification:** In cases where obtaining consent is not possible, screening mechanisms can be put in place to segregate the affected lawyer or team from the matter. This helps prevent the flow of confidential information and minimizes the risk of the conflict adversely affecting the client's interests. If screening is not feasible or effective, disqualification may be necessary.

3. **Seeking Independent Legal Advice:** In complex situations, lawyers facing potential conflicts of interest may choose to seek independent legal advice to determine the best course of action. This can provide an objective perspective and help identify potential solutions that maintain ethical standards.

4. **Referral or Withdrawing from Representation:** In some cases, the only viable solution is for the lawyer to refer the client to another practitioner or withdraw from the representation entirely. This ensures that the affected client's interests are protected and prevents any potential harm resulting from the conflict.

5. **Documenting the Process:** It is crucial to document the steps taken to address conflicts of interest. This documentation serves as evidence that the lawyer has acted diligently and ethically in identifying and managing conflicts, providing protection in case of any disputes or claims.

Case Study: Conflicts of Interest in Corporate Mergers

To illustrate the challenges in identifying and addressing conflicts of interest, let us consider a case study involving conflicts of interest in corporate mergers. Suppose a law firm represents both Company A and Company B in separate legal matters. Company A approaches the law firm for advice on a potential merger with

Company B. The law firm must navigate potential conflicts of interest to ensure ethical compliance.

The challenges in this scenario could include the following:

+ Identifying conflicting interests that may arise due to the law firm's knowledge of both companies' confidential information.

+ Assessing the potential impact of the merger on the existing legal matters of both companies and whether it would compromise the interests of either client.

+ Determining whether obtaining informed consent from both Company A and Company B is feasible and sufficient to address the conflict.

+ Evaluating the current workload and capacity of the law firm to handle the additional legal work resulting from the merger.

Addressing these challenges may involve:

+ Conducting a thorough analysis of the potential conflicts by reviewing the relevant legal matters and confidential information of both Company A and Company B.

+ Seeking independent legal advice to ensure an objective evaluation of the conflict and the potential solutions.

+ Obtaining informed consent from both Company A and Company B after full disclosure of the potential conflicts and their implications.

+ Implementing screening mechanisms to segregate the teams working on the merger from those handling the existing legal matters of Company A and Company B.

+ Regularly reassessing the potential conflicts as the merger progresses to ensure ongoing ethical compliance.

By carefully considering the challenges and implementing appropriate strategies, lawyers can effectively identify and address conflicts of interest, safeguarding their ethical obligations and protecting their clients' interests.

Conclusion

Identifying and addressing conflicts of interest is a critical aspect of maintaining ethical integrity in the legal profession. The complexity of relationships, confidentiality concerns, changing circumstances, subjectivity in interpretation, limited information, and time constraints pose significant challenges in identifying conflicts. Once identified, conflicts of interest should be addressed through obtaining informed consent, screening, disqualification, seeking independent legal advice, referral or withdrawal from representation, and proper documentation of the process. By navigating these challenges and implementing appropriate strategies, lawyers can uphold their ethical obligations and ensure the best interests of their clients are prioritized.

Promoting Transparency and Accountability in Conflict of Interest

Conflicts of interest are a pervasive issue in the legal profession, as lawyers often find themselves in situations where their personal interests may conflict with their professional obligations. As such, promoting transparency and accountability is crucial in order to maintain the integrity of the legal profession and ensure that justice is served.

Understanding Conflicts of Interest

A conflict of interest occurs when a lawyer's personal, financial, or other interests interfere with their duty to act in their clients' best interests or undermine the fair administration of justice. These conflicts can arise in various scenarios, such as when a lawyer represents conflicting clients or when a lawyer's personal relationships or financial investments create biases that may compromise their objectivity.

To promote transparency and accountability, it is essential to first identify and understand the different types of conflicts of interest that can arise in legal practice. These include:

+ **Direct conflicts of interest:** These occur when a lawyer represents clients with opposing interests in the same matter. For example, if a lawyer represents both the plaintiff and the defendant in a civil case, it can create a conflict that compromises their ability to provide unbiased advice and representation to either party.

+ **Indirect conflicts of interest:** These arise when a lawyer's personal or financial interests may be affected by the outcome of a case. For instance, if a lawyer has a financial investment in a company involved in a legal dispute, it can create a conflict that influences their decision-making process.

+ **Imputed conflicts of interest**: These occur when a conflict of interest is imputed from one lawyer to another within the same law firm. This can happen when there is a close relationship between the lawyers involved or when the conflict arises from a lawyer's personal interests that are imputed to the entire firm.

By understanding these different types of conflicts of interest, legal professionals can better recognize and address potential conflicts before they create ethical dilemmas or hinder the fair administration of justice.

Roles and Responsibilities

To promote transparency and accountability in conflicts of interest, it is important to establish clear roles and responsibilities for legal professionals and the organizations they work for. This includes:

+ **Adopting robust conflict of interest policies**: Law firms and legal organizations should have clear policies in place that outline how conflicts of interest should be managed. This includes procedures for identifying conflicts, obtaining informed consent from affected clients, and implementing appropriate safeguards to mitigate potential biases.

+ **Regular training and education**: Legal professionals should receive regular training on conflict of interest rules and regulations, as well as ethical considerations surrounding conflicts. This helps ensure that lawyers are aware of their responsibilities and can effectively identify and manage conflicts as they arise.

+ **Establishing conflicts clearance procedures**: Law firms should have established procedures for reviewing potential conflicts of interest before taking on new clients or matters. This includes conducting thorough conflict checks to identify any potential conflicts and determining the appropriate steps to either avoid or mitigate those conflicts.

+ **Maintaining confidentiality and privacy**: When conflicts of interest are identified, it is essential to handle the information confidentially and ensure that client confidentiality is maintained throughout the conflict management process. This helps protect the integrity of the legal profession and maintain trust between lawyers and their clients.

+ **Implementing independent oversight:** To ensure accountability, legal organizations should establish independent oversight mechanisms to review and monitor conflicts of interest. This can include the creation of an ethics committee or the appointment of an ombudsperson who can impartially review conflicts and provide guidance on how to address them.

By clearly defining roles and responsibilities and implementing effective policies and procedures, legal professionals can help prevent conflicts of interest from compromising their duties to clients and the fair administration of justice.

Promoting Transparency and Disclosure

Transparency and disclosure are crucial in managing conflicts of interest and maintaining the public's trust in the legal profession. Legal professionals should strive to be transparent in their actions and disclose any potential conflicts to affected clients and relevant parties.

+ **Informed consent:** When a conflict of interest arises, legal professionals should obtain informed consent from affected clients after disclosing the conflict. This means explaining to clients the nature of the conflict, the potential risks, and how the conflict will be managed. Informed consent ensures that clients are aware of the conflict and can make informed decisions about whether to proceed with the representation.

+ **Conflicts disclosures:** Legal organizations should adopt a practice of regular and timely conflicts disclosures. This can include disclosing conflicts during the intake process, in engagement letters, or through ongoing communication with clients. By promptly disclosing conflicts, legal professionals demonstrate their commitment to transparency and enable affected parties to make informed decisions about their legal representation.

+ **Avoiding undisclosed conflicts:** Legal professionals must avoid undisclosed conflicts of interest at all costs. Failing to disclose a conflict not only compromises the fair administration of justice but also exposes lawyers to potential disciplinary action. Legal organizations should implement internal controls and monitoring systems to ensure that conflicts are promptly identified and disclosed.

+ **Promoting public awareness:** Legal organizations and professional associations should engage in public awareness campaigns to educate the general public about conflicts of interest and the importance of transparency in the legal profession. This can help build trust and confidence in the legal system by demonstrating the commitment of legal professionals to ethical conduct.

By promoting transparency and disclosure, legal professionals can effectively manage conflicts of interest and maintain the integrity of the legal profession.

Enforcement and Accountability

To ensure effective management of conflicts of interest, it is essential to have mechanisms in place for enforcing ethical standards and holding legal professionals accountable for their actions. This includes:

+ **Ethics committees and regulatory bodies:** Legal organizations and professional associations should have dedicated ethics committees or regulatory bodies responsible for enforcing ethical standards and handling complaints related to conflicts of interest. These bodies should have the authority to investigate allegations, impose disciplinary measures, and provide guidance on ethical considerations.

+ **Whistleblower protections:** Legal organizations should establish mechanisms to encourage and protect whistleblowers who report conflicts of interest or ethical misconduct. Whistleblower protection can help uncover potential conflicts and ensure that legal professionals are held accountable for their actions.

+ **Monitoring and audits:** Legal organizations should regularly monitor and audit their conflict of interest management practices to ensure compliance with ethical standards. This can involve conducting internal audits, seeking external reviews, or engaging third-party experts to assess the effectiveness of conflict management processes.

+ **Transparent disciplinary processes:** Disciplinary processes for conflicts of interest should be transparent and consistent, with clear guidelines on the types of sanctions that may be imposed. This promotes accountability and sends a clear message that conflicts of interest will not be tolerated within the legal profession.

By enforcing ethical standards and holding legal professionals accountable for their actions, the legal profession can ensure that conflicts of interest are effectively managed and that the interests of clients and the fair administration of justice are protected.

Case Study: Conflict of Interest in Corporate Representation

Consider the following scenario: A law firm represents a corporation in a lawsuit filed by a group of individuals who claim to have suffered injuries due to the corporation's products. The law firm also represents an individual plaintiff in a separate case against the same corporation, alleging similar injuries.

In this case, there is a direct conflict of interest as the law firm is simultaneously representing the corporation and an individual plaintiff in unrelated cases against the corporation. This creates a potential bias as the law firm's duty to zealously represent the corporation may conflict with its duty to act in the best interests of the individual plaintiff.

To promote transparency and accountability in this conflict of interest situation, the law firm should:

+ Promptly disclose the conflict of interest to both the corporation and the individual plaintiff, explaining the nature of the conflict and how it will be addressed.

+ Obtain informed consent from both parties after disclosing the conflict, ensuring that they understand the potential risks and any limitations that may arise due to the conflict.

+ Implement measures to mitigate the conflict, such as establishing separate teams within the firm to handle each case or transferring one of the cases to another law firm.

+ Document all actions taken to address the conflict of interest, including the disclosure process and any steps taken to mitigate the conflict. This provides a clear record of the firm's commitment to transparency and accountability.

By effectively managing conflicts of interest in this case, the law firm can maintain its integrity, fulfill its ethical obligations, and ensure that the interests of both the corporation and the individual plaintiff are protected.

Conclusion

Promoting transparency and accountability in conflicts of interest is essential to maintain the integrity of the legal profession and ensure that justice is served. By understanding the different types of conflicts, defining clear roles and responsibilities, promoting transparency and disclosure, enforcing ethical standards, and holding legal professionals accountable for their actions, the legal profession can effectively manage conflicts of interest and maintain public trust.

Conflicts of interest will continue to be a challenge in the legal profession, but with a commitment to ethical conduct and a proactive approach to conflict management, legal professionals can navigate these challenges and uphold the principles of justice, fairness, and equality.

Ethics in Legal Negotiation and Mediation

In this section, we will explore the ethical considerations that arise in the context of legal negotiation and mediation. Negotiation and mediation are alternative dispute resolution (ADR) methods used to resolve conflicts outside of the traditional legal process. These processes often involve parties working together to find mutually acceptable solutions, with the assistance of a neutral third party mediator or negotiator.

Importance of Ethics in Legal Negotiation and Mediation

Ethics play a crucial role in legal negotiation and mediation as these processes rely heavily on trust, fairness, and respect for the parties involved. Ethical behavior is essential to maintain the integrity of the process and ensure that all parties are treated fairly. In order to achieve a satisfactory resolution, it is important for legal professionals to adhere to a set of ethical standards that guide their conduct.

Confidentiality and Privacy

One of the fundamental ethical principles in legal negotiation and mediation is confidentiality. Parties must be able to freely and openly discuss their concerns, interests, and potential concessions without fear of their statements being used against them later in court or publicized without consent. Confidentiality promotes trust, open communication, and allows parties to explore potential solutions without the fear of prejudice. Legal professionals involved in negotiation and mediation are bound by strict rules of confidentiality and must ensure that sensitive information remains private.

Impartiality and Neutrality

Another key ethical principle in legal negotiation and mediation is the concept of impartiality and neutrality. The third-party mediator or negotiator must maintain a position of impartiality and refrain from favoring one party over another. This requires the mediator to avoid conflicts of interest, treat all parties with respect, and maintain a balanced approach throughout the process. Impartiality helps build trust and confidence in the mediator's ability to guide the negotiations towards a fair and just outcome.

Informed Consent

In legal negotiation and mediation, informed consent is a vital ethical consideration. All parties involved must fully understand the nature and process of negotiation or mediation and the potential outcomes before participating. It is the responsibility of the legal professionals to provide accurate and comprehensive information about the process, its advantages, and limitations. This ensures that parties enter into negotiation or mediation voluntarily and with a clear understanding of their rights and responsibilities.

Conflict of Interest

Ethical challenges can arise in legal negotiation and mediation when there is a conflict of interest. Legal professionals must avoid any situation where their personal or financial interests may compromise their ability to act in the best interests of the parties involved. This includes disclosing any potential conflicts of interest and recusing oneself from the process if necessary. It is imperative for the mediator or negotiator to maintain the trust and confidence of all parties by acting in their best interests.

Power Imbalance and Fairness

Legal negotiation and mediation often involve parties with differing levels of power and resources. Ethical considerations require legal professionals to ensure fairness by addressing power imbalances and facilitating equal participation. This can be achieved by providing opportunities for all parties to express their viewpoints, actively listening to their concerns, and ensuring that decisions are made based on fair and objective criteria. Mediators and negotiators should be vigilant in identifying and addressing any potential power imbalances to promote equitable outcomes.

Genuine Efforts and Good Faith

Ethics in legal negotiation and mediation demand genuine efforts and a commitment to acting in good faith. All parties should engage in the process sincerely and strive to reach a satisfactory resolution. This includes being honest and truthful in communications, refraining from misleading or deceptive tactics, and actively seeking common ground. Genuine efforts contribute to the overall integrity of the process and increase the likelihood of a successful outcome.

Ethical Decision-Making Framework

Legal professionals can employ an ethical decision-making framework to navigate the complex ethical considerations in negotiation and mediation. This framework involves:

1. Identifying the ethical dilemma: Recognize the specific ethical challenge or conflict that arises in a particular negotiation or mediation.

2. Gathering relevant information: Acquire all necessary facts and information related to the ethical dilemma to properly assess the situation.

3. Analyzing ethical principles and rules: Evaluate the ethical principles and rules that are applicable to determine the most appropriate course of action.

4. Exploring alternatives: Consider different courses of action and their potential consequences to determine the best way forward.

5. Making a decision: Based on the information and analysis, make an informed and ethically sound decision.

6. Implementing the decision: Take the necessary steps to put the decision into action and ensure ethical conduct throughout the negotiation or mediation process.

7. Reflecting on the decision: Continuously evaluate the outcomes of the decision and reflect on whether it aligns with ethical standards and principles.

Case Study: Addressing Power Imbalance in Mediation

To illustrate the ethical considerations in legal negotiation and mediation, let's consider a case study where there is a significant power imbalance between the parties involved. In this scenario, a large corporation is negotiating a settlement with a small business owner who has filed a lawsuit for breach of contract. The small business owner lacks the financial resources to continue the legal battle, while the corporation has the advantage of extensive funds and legal expertise.

The ethical challenge in this case is to ensure that the negotiation process is fair and equitable, despite the power imbalance. The mediator must take proactive steps to level the playing field and ensure the small business owner's interests are adequately represented. This could involve providing financial assistance to the business owner to cover legal costs, appointing pro bono legal representation, or encouraging the corporation to consider alternative forms of resolution, such as collaborative problem-solving or compromise outside of litigation.

By addressing the power imbalance and promoting fairness and equity, the mediator can facilitate a negotiation process that upholds ethical standards and allows for a just resolution.

Additional Resources and Further Reading

1. Fisher, R., Ury, W., & Patton, B. (2011). Getting to Yes: Negotiating Agreement Without Giving In. Penguin Books.

2. Menkel-Meadow, C., Pryor, L. A., & Schneider, A. K. (2006). Negotiation: Processes for Problem Solving. Wolters Kluwer Law & Business.

3. Riskin, L. L. (2007). Understanding Mediation: Using Theory to Inform Practice. Harvard University Press.

Conclusion

Ethics play a crucial role in legal negotiation and mediation. Upholding ethical principles such as confidentiality, impartiality, informed consent, and fairness is essential to ensure the integrity of the process and promote just outcomes. Legal professionals involved in negotiation and mediation should be guided by an ethical decision-making framework, considering the complexities of each situation and striving for genuine efforts and good faith. By maintaining high ethical standards, legal negotiation and mediation can effectively resolve disputes and contribute to a more equitable and just society.

Legal Ethics and Corporate Influence

In the realm of legal studies, the intersection between legal ethics and corporate influence is an area of great significance and scrutiny. Corporate influence refers to the power and impact that corporations exert over legal and ethical decision-making processes, often driven by their pursuit of profits and self-interest. This section explores the ethical dilemmas and challenges that arise when corporations hold significant power and influence within the legal system.

Understanding Corporate Influence

To understand the ethical implications of corporate influence, it is crucial to recognize the unique position that corporations hold in society. As legal entities, corporations have the ability to amass substantial financial resources and wield significant influence over legislation, policies, and legal proceedings. This power imbalance can create a host of ethical concerns, including:

- **Conflicts of interest:** Corporate influence can lead to situations where the interests of corporations conflict with the broader public interest or the rights of individuals. For example, a corporation may lobby for legislation that benefits its business at the expense of consumer protection or environmental sustainability.

- **Inequality and unfair advantage:** The disproportionate influence of corporations can contribute to inequality by enabling them to shape laws and regulations that favor their interests over those of smaller businesses or disadvantaged communities. This can undermine principles of fairness and justice within the legal system.

- **Erosion of public trust:** When corporations exert excessive influence over legal decision-making processes, it can erode public trust in the fairness and impartiality of the legal system. This can have long-term implications for the legitimacy and effectiveness of the legal system as a whole.

Ethical Challenges and Dilemmas

The presence of corporate influence in the legal system gives rise to a range of ethical challenges and dilemmas that legal professionals must navigate. Some of these challenges include:

- **Confidentiality and loyalty:** Legal professionals may face ethical dilemmas when their duty of loyalty to their corporate clients conflicts with their obligation to maintain client confidentiality. For example, if a corporate client engages in unethical behavior, the lawyer may be torn between their duty to the client and their ethical responsibility to report the misconduct.

- **Conflicts of interest:** Lawyers and legal professionals may encounter conflicts of interest when representing corporations that have relationships with other organizations or individuals. These conflicts can create ethical dilemmas as legal professionals strive to balance the interests of their corporate clients with their duty to act in the best interests of justice and the public.

+ **Transparency and accountability:** Corporate influence can undermine transparency and accountability within the legal system. Legal professionals may find it challenging to ensure that corporate interests do not compromise the integrity of legal processes and decision-making.

+ **Ethical decision-making:** When faced with legal dilemmas involving corporate influence, legal professionals must make ethical decisions that prioritize justice and the public interest over the desires of corporate clients. This requires a strong ethical framework and a commitment to professional integrity.

Addressing Ethical Concerns

Addressing the ethical concerns surrounding corporate influence in the legal system requires the implementation of various strategies and measures. Some approaches that can help mitigate the influence of corporations and uphold ethical standards include:

+ **Regulation and oversight:** Implementing robust regulations and mechanisms to monitor and control corporate influence is essential. This can involve stricter campaign finance laws, enhanced disclosure requirements, and transparent lobbying practices to ensure corporations cannot unduly sway legal decision-making processes.

+ **Ethical codes and professional guidelines:** Legal professional organizations should develop and enforce ethical codes and guidelines that explicitly address the challenges posed by corporate influence. These codes should provide clear guidance on how to navigate conflicts of interest, maintain confidentiality, and prioritize the public interest when dealing with corporate clients.

+ **Enhancing ethical education and training:** Legal education should incorporate comprehensive ethics training that equips future legal professionals with the tools to recognize and address ethical challenges related to corporate influence. This training should emphasize the importance of professional integrity and the ethical obligations of legal professionals.

+ **Promoting diversity and inclusivity:** Increasing diversity within the legal profession can help counteract the impacts of corporate influence. A diverse legal profession is better equipped to represent the interests of a broader range of stakeholders, promote fairness and justice, and challenge those aspects of corporate influence that perpetuate inequality and systemic biases.

Case Study: Ethical Issues in Corporate Lobbying

One notable example that highlights the ethical dilemmas posed by corporate influence is the practice of corporate lobbying. Lobbying involves attempts by corporations to shape legislation and regulations in their favor. While lobbying in itself is not inherently unethical, there are ethical concerns when lobbying efforts undermine the public interest or democratic processes.

For instance, pharmaceutical companies lobbying against regulations that aim to lower drug prices can raise ethical questions about their motivations and the impact on public health. Similarly, when corporations use their financial power to gain access and influence over policymakers, it can create an imbalance of power that undermines democratic principles.

To address such ethical concerns, transparency and accountability in corporate lobbying practices are crucial. Requiring corporations to disclose their lobbying activities, including financial contributions and meetings with policymakers, can help promote transparency and ensure that the public is aware of potential biases and conflicts of interest.

Conclusion

The ethical challenges presented by corporate influence in the legal system require careful consideration and proactive measures to maintain the integrity and fairness of the legal profession. Legal professionals must navigate conflicts of interest, uphold their duty of loyalty while prioritizing justice and the public interest. By implementing robust regulations, promoting transparency, and enhancing ethical education, the legal profession can strive to mitigate the negative impacts of corporate influence and uphold the principles of fairness, justice, and accountability.

Conclusion

In this section, we have explored the ethical issues that arise in the legal profession. We began by discussing the role and responsibilities of legal professionals, emphasizing the importance of professionalism and ethics in legal practice. We examined the ethical obligations that lawyers must adhere to, as outlined in professional codes of conduct and legal ethics.

One of the key ethical challenges in the legal profession is maintaining confidentiality and upholding attorney-client privilege. We examined the importance of confidentiality in legal practice and the limitations of attorney-client privilege. We also discussed the ethical dilemmas that arise in maintaining confidentiality and the need to balance it with other ethical obligations.

Conflict of interest is another ethical issue that legal professionals must navigate. We explored the definition and types of conflict of interest and discussed strategies for avoiding and managing conflicts. We highlighted the ethical implications of conflicts of interest and emphasized the importance of promoting transparency and accountability in this area.

Moving on, we delved into the moral foundations of law and justice. We explored different concepts of morality and justice, and examined the relationship between the two. We discussed various ethical theories that underpin legal systems, including natural law theory, legal positivism, legal realism, critical legal studies, and feminist legal theory.

Next, we explored the concept of legal rights and responsibilities. We defined rights and discussed different theories of legal rights. We also examined constitutional rights and liberties, and the ethical considerations that come into play when balancing individual rights with collective responsibilities. We stressed the importance of ethical enforcement of rights and the role of legal ethics in promoting human rights.

Throughout this section, we emphasized the interplay between ethics, social justice, and human rights. We discussed social justice theories, including egalitarianism, libertarianism, communitarianism, and feminist theories of social justice. We also explored the historical evolution of human rights and the international and domestic legal frameworks that protect and promote human rights.

Moreover, we examined social justice issues in the legal field, such as poverty, inequality, gender equality, racial and ethnic justice, LGBTQ+ rights, and environmental justice. We highlighted the ethical dimensions of these issues and the role of legal studies in addressing them. We also discussed the importance of access to justice and the ethical responsibility of legal professionals in ensuring equal access for marginalized communities.

In the context of criminal justice, we explored the ethics of the criminal justice system, including ethical principles, the role and responsibilities of criminal justice professionals, and the ethical dilemmas inherent in law enforcement, criminal prosecution, and the correctional system. We also examined the ethical controversies surrounding capital punishment and discussed alternatives, along with the ethical challenges in policing and maintaining public trust.

Finally, we touched upon the ethical issues that arise in the business and commerce sector. We discussed concepts of business ethics, ethical issues in corporate governance, corporate social responsibility, and ethical considerations in marketing and advertising. We examined the ethical dilemmas related to intellectual property rights and the balancing act between copyright protection and access to knowledge. We also explored the ethical challenges posed by globalization in the areas of international business, human rights, corruption, and environmental sustainability.

In conclusion, this section has provided an overview of the diverse ethical issues that emerge in the legal profession. By examining the moral foundations of law and justice, the ethical considerations in legal practice, and the interplay between ethics, social justice, and human rights, we have aimed to equip legal studies students with a solid understanding of the philosophical and ethical dimensions of their field. It is our hope that by engaging with these issues, students will be well-prepared to navigate the complex moral dilemmas they may encounter in their future careers and contribute to a more equitable, just, and sustainable world.

Social Justice and Human Rights

Theories of Social Justice

Egalitarianism and Distributive Justice

In the realm of social justice, egalitarianism and distributive justice play crucial roles in shaping a more equitable and just society. Egalitarianism is a philosophical belief that emphasizes equality and fairness, asserting that all individuals should have equal access to resources and opportunities. Distributive justice, on the other hand, is a framework that seeks to distribute resources and benefits in a fair and just manner.

Egalitarianism: Equality as a Fundamental Value

Egalitarianism is grounded in the principle that all individuals have inherent worth and deserve equal treatment and opportunities. This principle challenges social hierarchies and advocates for the elimination of unjust inequalities. Egalitarianism recognizes that certain inequalities, such as those based on race, gender, or socioeconomic status, can perpetuate systemic injustice and create barriers to equal opportunities.

One influential form of egalitarianism is John Rawls' theory of justice as fairness. Rawls argues that in a just society, individuals should have equal access to the basic social and political liberties, and inequalities should only be permitted if they benefit the least advantaged members of society. This concept, known as the difference principle, strives to address socioeconomic disparities and aims to uplift those most in need.

215

Distributive Justice: Balancing Fairness and Efficiency

Distributive justice is concerned with the fair allocation of resources and benefits within a society. It seeks to address how goods, services, opportunities, and burdens should be distributed among individuals. A key goal of distributive justice is to strike a balance between fairness and efficiency, ensuring that resources are allocated in a way that benefits society as a whole.

One commonly discussed principle of distributive justice is the principle of equal distribution. According to this principle, resources and benefits should be distributed equally among individuals, regardless of their contributions or needs. This principle promotes a sense of fairness and equality, treating all individuals as equals and rejecting any form of privilege or advantage.

Another principle is the principle of merit, which argues that resources should be distributed based on an individual's efforts, abilities, and contributions. This principle is often linked to the idea of rewarding individuals for their achievements and incentivizing productivity. While the principle of merit is appealing in its focus on individual agency, it can also perpetuate existing inequalities and disadvantage those who face structural barriers.

Challenges and Considerations in Egalitarianism and Distributive Justice

Egalitarianism and distributive justice face several challenges and considerations in practice. One challenge is determining the appropriate criteria for resource allocation. Should distribution be based solely on need, merit, or some combination of both? Striking the right balance can be difficult, as different individuals and societies may hold varying values and beliefs.

Another challenge involves addressing the tension between individual freedom and equality. Critics argue that strict egalitarianism may limit individual liberty and undermine incentives for innovation and productivity. Balancing these conflicting values is a complex task that requires careful consideration of social and economic dynamics.

Additionally, achieving egalitarian goals involves not only the distribution of resources but also addressing systemic barriers and discrimination. Simply focusing on equal outcomes may overlook the structural inequalities that perpetuate social injustices. It is vital to recognize and dismantle these barriers to create a more inclusive and just society.

Real-World Applications and Exercises

To better understand the concepts of egalitarianism and distributive justice, let's consider a real-world scenario:

Imagine a country where income inequality is high, with a significant wealth gap between the rich and the poor. Access to quality education is limited for low-income communities, leading to unequal opportunities for social mobility. As a legal studies professional, you are tasked with proposing strategies to promote egalitarianism and distributive justice in this society.

Exercise 1: Design a progressive taxation system that ensures wealthier individuals contribute a larger proportion of their income to fund public services and initiatives targeted at addressing social inequalities.

Exercise 2: Develop a policy framework that promotes equal access to education, addressing barriers such as funding disparities and inadequate resources in low-income communities.

Exercise 3: Advocate for the establishment of programs and initiatives that provide job training and employment opportunities for marginalized individuals and communities, aiming to reduce income disparities and enhance social mobility.

Remember, promoting egalitarianism and distributive justice requires a multifaceted approach that takes into account various factors, including economic realities, social dynamics, and structural inequalities.

Additional Resources

To deepen your understanding of egalitarianism and distributive justice, consider exploring the following resources:

- Book: "A Theory of Justice" by John Rawls

- Article: "Equality of Opportunity" by Elizabeth Anderson

- Documentary: "Inequality for All" directed by Jacob Kornbluth

- Podcast: "The Good Fight" hosted by Yascha Mounk

These resources provide valuable insights into the philosophical foundations, practical implications, and contemporary debates surrounding egalitarianism and distributive justice.

In conclusion, egalitarianism and distributive justice are essential frameworks for achieving a more equitable and just society. By embracing these principles and considering the challenges and considerations they present, legal studies professionals can play a crucial role in promoting social justice and shaping a more inclusive future.

Libertarianism and Individual Freedom

In this section, we will explore the concept of libertarianism and its relationship to individual freedom. Libertarianism is a political philosophy that emphasizes individual liberty and limited government intervention. It advocates for a free market economy, minimal state interference, and the protection of individual rights and freedoms. Let us delve into the key principles and ideas of libertarianism and how they promote individual freedom.

Principles of Libertarianism

At the core of libertarianism are the principles of individualism, self-ownership, and non-aggression. Libertarianism views individuals as autonomous beings capable of making their own decisions and pursuing their own interests without interference from the state. It recognizes that individuals have inherent rights and freedoms that should be respected and protected.

Individualism: Libertarianism places great importance on the individual as the primary unit of society. It asserts that individuals have the right to act in their own self-interest and have control over their own lives as long as they do not infringe upon the rights of others. Individualism emphasizes personal responsibility and self-reliance.

Self-Ownership: Libertarianism holds that individuals have the right to own themselves and their own bodies. This principle of self-ownership affirms that each person has the right to decide how to use their own body and the fruits of their labor. It rejects any form of coercion or force that could violate an individual's autonomy.

Non-Aggression: The principle of non-aggression is central to libertarianism. It asserts that individuals should not initiate force or fraud against others. It promotes peaceful and voluntary interactions among individuals and condemns any form of aggression, including physical force or coercion, as a violation of individual freedom.

Limited Government and Free Market

Libertarianism advocates for a limited role of government in society, with the primary function of protecting individual rights and maintaining law and order. It argues that excessive government intervention infringes upon individual freedom and stifles economic growth and innovation.

Limited Government: Libertarians believe in a minimal state that does not interfere in the personal choices and activities of individuals. They argue that government should be limited to the essential functions of maintaining a legal system, protecting property rights, enforcing contracts, and providing for national defense.

Free Market: Libertarianism strongly supports free market capitalism, viewing it as the most efficient and just economic system. It argues that voluntary exchanges and competition in the marketplace lead to prosperity and individual freedom. Libertarians advocate for the removal of government regulations and barriers to entry that hinder free trade and entrepreneurship.

Critiques and Challenges

While libertarianism presents a compelling case for individual freedom and limited government, it also faces critiques and challenges.

Income Inequality: One criticism of libertarianism is its potential to exacerbate income inequality. Critics argue that a free market system without government intervention may lead to concentration of wealth in the hands of a few, leaving the rest of society with limited opportunities.

Externalities and Public Goods: Libertarianism's emphasis on individual autonomy and limited government intervention raises concerns about the provision of public goods and addressing externalities. Public goods, such as defense or infrastructure, may not be adequately provided by the market alone, and addressing negative externalities, such as pollution, requires collective action.

Social Safety Net: Another challenge to libertarianism is the question of providing a social safety net for those in need. Critics argue that without government interventions, there may be insufficient support for vulnerable populations, leading to social injustices and disparities.

Examples and Applications

To better understand the practical implications of libertarianism, let's consider a few examples:

Legalization of Drugs: Libertarianism generally supports the decriminalization or legalization of drugs. It argues that individuals have the right to make decisions about their own bodies, including the use of recreational substances, as long as they do not harm others.

Deregulation in Industries: Libertarians advocate for reducing government regulations in various industries. They believe that excessive regulations stifle innovation, restrict market competition, and limit consumer choice. For example, they may argue for less government intervention in the healthcare or energy sectors.

Criminal Justice Reform: Libertarianism also finds application in criminal justice reform. It questions the effectiveness and ethical implications of punitive measures such as mandatory minimum sentences and the war on drugs. Instead, libertarians may support alternative approaches that prioritize rehabilitation and individual rights.

In conclusion, libertarianism promotes individual freedom through its principles of individualism, self-ownership, and non-aggression. It advocates for limited government intervention and the free market as key mechanisms to ensure individual autonomy and economic prosperity. While facing critiques and challenges, libertarianism offers a distinct perspective on the role of government and individual freedom in society.

Communitarianism and Common Good

Communitarianism is a philosophical and ethical theory that emphasizes the importance of community and the common good. It holds that individuals are not only autonomous beings with individual rights and interests, but also members of a community with social obligations and responsibilities. According to communitarianism, the well-being and flourishing of the community should be prioritized over individual interests.

Principles of Communitarianism

Communitarianism is rooted in the belief that human beings are social animals and that their well-being is intertwined with the well-being of the community. It emphasizes the following principles:

1. **Community as the source of values:** Communitarianism posits that moral values and principles are derived from communal traditions, practices, and shared experiences. It argues that individual values and rights should be understood within the context of the community.

2. **Emphasis on social responsibilities:** Communitarianism asserts that individuals have not only rights but also responsibilities towards the community. It stresses the importance of fulfilling these societal obligations for the betterment of the community as a whole.

3. **The common good:** Communitarianism places a significant emphasis on the common good, which refers to the well-being and welfare of the community as a whole. It argues that individual interests should be balanced and subordinated to the greater good of the community.

4. **Social cohesion and solidarity:** Communitarianism promotes social cohesion and solidarity among community members. It highlights the importance of shared values, mutual support, and cooperation for the stability and flourishing of the community.

Critiques of Communitarianism

While communitarianism offers valuable insights into community and social responsibilities, it has faced criticism from various perspectives. Some of the critiques include:

1. **Individual autonomy:** Critics argue that communitarianism places too much emphasis on community values and obligations, neglecting individual autonomy and freedom. They contend that individuals should have the right to pursue their own interests and define their own values, even if they differ from those of the community.

2. **Oppression of minority rights:** Communitarianism's focus on the common good and community values raises concerns about the potential suppression of minority rights and perspectives. Critics argue that the prioritization of

the majority's values and interests may lead to the marginalization of minority groups.

3. **Static and homogenous communities:** The notion of a unified and harmonious community, which communitarianism often idealizes, has been criticized as unrealistic. Critics contend that communities are diverse and consist of various subgroups with different values and interests, making it challenging to define a singular common good.

Application of Communitarianism in Legal Studies

In the field of legal studies, communitarianism offers a framework for examining and addressing ethical dilemmas and promoting social justice. It highlights the importance of considering the broader impact of legal decisions on the community and emphasizes the role of law in fostering social cohesion and the common good.

Case Study: Balancing Individual Rights and the Common Good   Let's consider a contemporary case study that illustrates the application of communitarianism in legal studies. Imagine a community facing an environmental crisis due to pollution caused by a local factory. The community members, driven by concerns for their health and well-being, demand stricter regulations and accountability for the factory owners.

In this scenario, a communitarian approach would involve balancing the individual rights of the factory owners to conduct business with the common good of the community's health and the environment. Legal scholars and policymakers would need to weigh the interests of the individuals against the potential harm inflicted on the community. They would aim to strike a balance that ensures social cohesion and the welfare of all community members.

Ethical Dilemma: Protecting Cultural Heritage   Another example of applying communitarianism in legal studies relates to the protection of cultural heritage. Imagine a situation where a community's cultural practices and traditions are threatened by urban development. Individuals within the community may have the right to sell their property for financial gain, but doing so would result in the destruction of cultural sites and practices.

In this case, a communitarian approach would involve considering the long-term consequences and the impact on the community's identity. Legal professionals and policymakers would need to balance individual property rights with the preservation of cultural heritage, taking into account the significance of cultural practices for community cohesion and well-being.

Resources and Further Reading

For a deeper understanding of communitarianism and its application in legal studies, the following resources are recommended:

+ *After the Rights Revolution: Reconceiving the Regulatory State* by Cass R. Sunstein.

+ *The Good Society: The Humane Agenda* by Robert Bellah et al.

+ *Law's Empire* by Ronald Dworkin.

+ *Communitarianism: A New Public Ethics* edited by Markate Daly.

+ *Between Past and Future: Eight Exercises in Political Thought* by Hannah Arendt.

These resources offer diverse perspectives on communitarianism, its principles, criticisms, and its relevance in legal studies. They provide a comprehensive foundation for exploring the concept further.

Key Takeaways

+ Communitarianism emphasizes the importance of community, social responsibilities, and the common good.

+ It posits that moral values are derived from communal traditions and shared experiences.

+ Communitarianism is critiqued for potentially neglecting individual autonomy, suppressing minority rights, and idealizing homogenous communities.

+ In legal studies, communitarianism provides a framework for addressing ethical dilemmas, considering the broader impact of legal decisions on the community, and promoting social justice.

In conclusion, communitarianism sheds light on the dynamic interplay between individual rights and social responsibilities, underscoring the importance of community values and the common good in legal studies. It encourages a balanced approach that considers both individual and communal interests for a more equitable and just society.

Feminist Theories of Social Justice

Feminist theories of social justice form a significant part of the broader discourse on social justice. These theories aim to address gender inequalities and promote equality and justice for marginalized genders within society. Feminist perspectives analyze power structures, social norms, and systemic biases that perpetuate gender inequality. In this section, we will explore the key concepts and principles of feminist theories of social justice, examine their relevance in legal studies, and discuss their implications for promoting a more equitable society.

Understanding Feminist Theories of Social Justice

Feminist theories provide a critical lens through which to examine social, political, and economic systems that oppress women and other marginalized genders. These theories challenge patriarchal structures and advocate for the recognition and inclusion of women's experiences, perspectives, and rights. Feminist theories of social justice are grounded in the belief that gender equality is essential for achieving a just society.

Feminist scholars have developed various theoretical frameworks to analyze gender inequality and social injustice. Some key feminist theories include liberal feminism, radical feminism, intersectional feminism, and postcolonial feminism. Each of these theories offers unique insights into the social construction of gender, power dynamics, and the intersectionality of oppressions.

Liberal Feminism

Liberal feminism focuses on achieving gender equality by challenging discriminatory laws, policies, and practices. It emphasizes equal rights, opportunities, and individual freedoms for women. Liberal feminists argue for legal reforms that address discrimination, such as removing barriers to women's participation in politics, education, and the workforce.

For example, liberal feminists have been instrumental in advocating for equal pay for equal work, reproductive rights, and the eradication of gender-based violence.

They argue that equal rights under the law are necessary to ensure social justice and promote gender equality in society.

Radical Feminism

Radical feminism seeks to challenge and dismantle the root causes of gender inequality. It views patriarchy as the primary source of oppression and advocates for a fundamental reorganization of society to eliminate gender-based hierarchies and power imbalances. Radical feminists argue that gender oppression is deeply ingrained in social institutions, cultural norms, and interpersonal relationships.

Radical feminist theory also highlights the importance of women's lived experiences and personal narratives. It calls for recognizing and valuing women's emotional labor, challenging traditional gender roles, and reimagining alternative visions of social organization. Radical feminists demand transformative change to create a society where all genders can thrive free from patriarchal constraints.

Intersectional Feminism

Intersectional feminism acknowledges that gender inequality intersects with other forms of oppression, such as racism, classism, ableism, and homophobia. Intersectional feminists argue that systems of power and oppression are interconnected and mutually reinforcing. They highlight the unique experiences and multiple identities of marginalized individuals and the compounding effects of discrimination.

Intersectional feminism emphasizes the importance of inclusive and diverse feminist movements that center the experiences of women from various racial, ethnic, socioeconomic, and cultural backgrounds. It calls for a more nuanced understanding of privilege and oppression, challenging the tendency to prioritize the experiences of privileged groups within feminist discourse.

Postcolonial Feminism

Postcolonial feminism examines the impact of colonialism and imperialism on gender relations and women's experiences in different cultural contexts. It critiques Western feminist theories for their ethnocentrism and failure to address how intersections of gender, race, and colonialism shape women's lives.

Postcolonial feminists argue for the decolonization of feminist discourse and the inclusion of diverse perspectives and knowledges. They seek to dismantle the dominance of Western feminist frameworks and highlight the agency and resistance of women in non-Western contexts.

Relevance in Legal Studies

Feminist theories of social justice have had a profound impact on legal studies, shaping the understanding of gender equality, women's rights, and social justice within the legal field. These theories have sparked critical debates on issues such as reproductive rights, domestic violence, sexual harassment, and discrimination.

In legal practice, feminist perspectives inform advocacy strategies, judicial decision-making, and policy development. Feminist legal scholars have contributed to the development of laws that address gender-based discrimination, promote women's rights, and enhance access to justice. They have also highlighted the limitations and biases within legal systems, calling for structural reforms to ensure gender justice.

Implications for a More Equitable Society

Feminist theories of social justice offer a framework for envisioning a society that is more equitable, just, and inclusive. By challenging gender norms, biases, and power imbalances, these theories seek to create spaces where all genders can participate fully and freely.

Implementing feminist principles in legal systems can help address systemic biases, promote gender-responsive laws, and enhance access to justice for marginalized genders. It also requires engaging in ongoing critical reflection and analysis of legal frameworks, policies, and practices to identify and rectify discriminatory and exclusionary practices.

Moreover, recognizing the intersectionality of oppressions and adopting an inclusive and diverse approach to feminist activism and advocacy can lead to more effective strategies for achieving social justice. This involves centering the experiences and needs of marginalized individuals in the fight against multiple forms of oppression.

Conclusion

Feminist theories of social justice provide valuable insights into the complex dynamics of gender inequality and oppression. By challenging traditional power structures, advocating for equal rights, and centering the experiences of marginalized genders, feminist theories contribute to the promotion of social justice in legal studies.

Understanding feminist perspectives is essential for legal professionals and scholars to address gender bias, advocate for women's rights, and contribute to the development of more equitable legal frameworks. By embracing feminist theories, we can work towards creating a society that values and respects the rights and dignity of all genders.

Multiculturalism and Social Justice

Multiculturalism and social justice are two interconnected concepts that play a crucial role in creating a more inclusive and equitable society. In this section, we will explore the relationship between multiculturalism and social justice, the challenges they present, and the potential solutions to promote social harmony and equality.

Understanding Multiculturalism

Multiculturalism refers to the coexistence of different cultures within a society, respecting and valuing each culture's unique characteristics. It recognizes and celebrates diversity, promoting equality and inclusion for all individuals, regardless of their cultural background.

Multiculturalism recognizes that each culture brings unique perspectives, values, and traditions, enriching the social fabric of a society. It aims to create an environment where individuals can maintain their cultural identities while interacting with others in a respectful and tolerant manner.

Social Justice and Equality

Social justice is the principle of fair and equitable distribution of resources, opportunities, and privileges within a society. It seeks to eliminate social inequalities and promote equal rights and opportunities for all individuals, regardless of their background.

In a multicultural society, social justice requires addressing the historical and structural inequalities faced by marginalized communities. It involves acknowledging and combating discrimination, prejudice, and systemic barriers that hinder equal access to education, healthcare, employment, and other essential services.

Multiculturalism and Social Justice

Multiculturalism and social justice go hand in hand, as promoting diversity and inclusivity is a fundamental aspect of achieving social justice. By recognizing and valuing cultural differences, multiculturalism contributes to a society that respects and upholds the rights and dignity of all individuals.

Multiculturalism plays a vital role in social justice by challenging dominant norms and promoting the representation and empowerment of underrepresented and marginalized groups. It encourages the recognition of cultural rights, linguistic diversity, and the promotion of cultural heritage, fostering a sense of belonging and identity.

At the same time, social justice ensures that multiculturalism is not merely tokenistic, but rather an authentic commitment to equity and fairness. It requires addressing power imbalances, dismantling systemic discrimination, and promoting opportunities for meaningful engagement between different cultural groups.

Challenges and Solutions

Despite its potential, multiculturalism faces several challenges in achieving social justice. These challenges include stereotyping, cultural assimilation, discrimination, and unequal power dynamics. Addressing these challenges requires a comprehensive and proactive approach.

Education and awareness are key to addressing stereotypes and promoting intercultural understanding. Incorporating multicultural perspectives in school curricula and promoting cultural exchange programs can help foster empathy and appreciation for diversity.

Legislation and policies that prohibit discrimination and promote equal opportunity are essential. Affirmative action measures can address historical inequities and provide marginalized groups with the opportunity to participate fully in society.

Community engagement and dialogue are crucial for building trust and understanding between diverse cultural groups. Creating spaces for open and honest conversations can help challenge biases and develop inclusive policies and practices.

It is also important to recognize and challenge systemic barriers that perpetuate inequality. This may involve restructuring institutions and systems to ensure equal access and representation for all individuals.

Examples and Real-World Applications

One example of the intersection between multiculturalism and social justice is the fight for indigenous rights. Many indigenous communities have faced historical and ongoing marginalization, land dispossession, and cultural suppression. Recognizing and respecting indigenous rights involves addressing past injustice and providing equitable opportunities for indigenous peoples in education, healthcare, and governance.

Another example is the inclusion of diverse voices in decision-making processes. Creating spaces for representation and participation for individuals from diverse cultural backgrounds ensures that policies and decisions are inclusive and consider the needs and perspectives of all members of society.

Further Resources and Activities

To delve deeper into the topic of multiculturalism and social justice, here are some recommended resources:

+ "Multiculturalism: A Very Short Introduction" by Ali Rattansi

+ "The Nature of Prejudice" by Gordon Allport

+ "Cultural Diversity and Education: Foundations, Curriculum, and Teaching" by James A. Banks

You can also engage in the following activities to enhance your understanding and promote multiculturalism and social justice:

1. Conduct research on the history and contributions of different cultural groups in your community.

2. Attend multicultural events or festivals to experience different cultures firsthand.

3. Engage in discussions or debates on the challenges and benefits of multiculturalism.

4. Volunteer with organizations that promote multicultural understanding and social justice.

Remember, promoting multiculturalism and social justice is an ongoing journey that requires continuous learning, empathy, and action. By embracing diversity and advocating for equality, we can contribute to a more just and inclusive society.

Conclusion

Multiculturalism and social justice are integral to creating a more equitable and inclusive society. Understanding and valuing cultural differences, promoting equal rights and opportunities, and addressing systemic barriers are essential in achieving social harmony and equality. By actively engaging with diverse cultural groups and challenging discriminatory practices, we can contribute to a society that embraces and celebrates the richness of its multicultural tapestry. Remember, promoting multiculturalism and social justice is an ongoing journey that requires continuous learning, empathy, and action. Let us work together to build a more just and inclusive world for all.

Social Justice and Equality

In this section, we will explore the crucial concepts of social justice and equality. These principles are at the core of legal studies and play a significant role in shaping a more equitable and just society. We will delve into the theories of social justice, discuss the challenges and discrimination faced by marginalized groups, and examine the importance of promoting equality in legal systems.

Defining Social Justice

Social justice refers to the fair and equitable distribution of resources, opportunities, and privileges in society. It encompasses the notion that all individuals should have equal access to basic rights, such as healthcare, education, employment, and justice. Social justice also involves addressing systemic inequalities and discrimination that hinder individuals' ability to live a dignified and fulfilling life.

Theories of Social Justice

Various theories have emerged to conceptualize and analyze social justice. Understanding these theories is crucial in evaluating the effectiveness of legal systems in promoting equality. Let's explore some of the major theories:

1. **Egalitarianism and Distributive Justice:** This theory asserts that resources and opportunities should be distributed equally among individuals, ensuring everyone has a fair share.

2. **Libertarianism and Individual Freedom:** Libertarianism emphasizes individual autonomy and limits the role of the state in redistributing

resources. It argues that people should be free to pursue their own interests and that a just society is one that respects individual freedoms.

3. **Communitarianism and Common Good:** Communitarianism highlights the importance of a strong community and collective well-being. It suggests that a just society is one that promotes the common good and maintains social cohesion.

4. **Feminist Theories of Social Justice:** Feminist theories explore the particular issues faced by women and advocate for equal rights and opportunities. They emphasize the need to address gender-based discrimination and create a more inclusive society.

5. **Multiculturalism and Social Justice:** Multiculturalism theory focuses on recognizing and valuing diverse cultural backgrounds. It promotes inclusivity, respect, and equal treatment for individuals from different racial, ethnic, and religious groups.

While these theories may have differing perspectives on how to achieve social justice, they all underscore the importance of equal treatment and opportunities for all members of society.

Promoting Equality in Legal Systems

Legal systems play a fundamental role in promoting and enforcing social justice and equality. Laws can shape social norms, protect the rights of individuals, and rectify historical injustices. Here are some essential aspects to consider in promoting equality within legal systems:

1. **Equal Protection Under the Law:** It is vital for legal systems to provide equal protection to all individuals, regardless of their race, gender, religion, or socioeconomic background.

2. **Anti-Discrimination Laws:** Laws prohibiting discrimination in employment, housing, education, and public accommodations contribute significantly to creating a more equitable society.

3. **Affirmative Action:** Affirmative action policies aim to address historical disadvantages and promote diversity by providing preferential treatment or quotas for underrepresented groups. Such policies play a crucial role in reducing inequalities and promoting inclusivity.

4. **Access to Justice:** Ensuring access to justice for all members of society, regardless of their financial resources, is essential. Legal aid programs, pro bono services, and streamlined court procedures are necessary to level the playing field.

While legal systems can institute measures to promote equality, it is important to acknowledge that achieving true social justice requires addressing underlying systemic issues and challenging societal biases.

Challenges and Discrimination Faced by Marginalized Groups

To fully understand the significance of social justice, we must address the challenges and discrimination faced by marginalized groups. These groups, including racial and ethnic minorities, women, LGBTQ+ individuals, and people with disabilities, often experience systemic barriers that impede their access to justice and equal opportunities.

Discrimination can occur at various levels, such as:

+ **Structural Discrimination:** Systems and institutions may perpetuate discriminatory practices, resulting in unequal treatment and limited access to resources for marginalized groups. For example, racial profiling by law enforcement or the gender pay gap.

+ **Institutional Discrimination:** Discrimination can be embedded in the policies, practices, and cultures of organizations, leading to biased decision-making and unequal treatment. This can be seen in discriminatory hiring practices or lack of accessibility for people with disabilities.

+ **Interpersonal Discrimination:** Individuals may experience direct discrimination in their interactions with others, such as being subjected to hate speech or harassment based on their identity.

Overcoming these challenges requires not only legal protections but also changes in societal attitudes and structures. It is imperative that legal professionals and policymakers work towards dismantling these barriers and promoting inclusivity and equal treatment for all.

Resources and Organizations

To gain a deeper understanding of social justice and equality, it is valuable to engage with resources offered by reputable organizations and institutions. Here are some recommendations:

+ **International:** United Nations Human Rights Council (UNHRC), International Labour Organization (ILO), World Health Organization (WHO).

+ **National:** Government agencies responsible for human rights, equality, and justice such as civil rights commissions or ombudsmen offices.

+ **Non-governmental Organizations (NGOs):** Amnesty International, Human Rights Watch, American Civil Liberties Union (ACLU), National Association for the Advancement of Colored People (NAACP), etc.

+ **Academic Institutions:** Many universities offer research centers, institutes, and programs focusing on social justice and equality.

Exploring these resources can provide valuable insights into ongoing initiatives, research, and advocacy efforts aimed at promoting social justice and equality.

Conclusion

Social justice and equality are essential elements in creating a more equitable and just society. Understanding the theories of social justice, promoting equal treatment within legal systems, and addressing the challenges faced by marginalized groups are vital steps towards achieving this goal. It is the responsibility of legal professionals, policymakers, and society as a whole to strive for social justice and equality for all individuals. By doing so, we contribute to a more inclusive and sustainable world.

Conclusion

In this section, we have explored the moral foundations of law and justice, delving into concepts of morality and justice, theories of law, and the definition and classification of legal rights. We have examined the role of ethics in legal practice, considering the ethical decision-making frameworks, principles, and values that guide legal professionals. We have also discussed the ethical issues that arise in the legal profession, such as confidentiality and attorney-client privilege, conflict of interest, and the responsibilities of legal professionals in promoting social justice and human rights.

From our exploration, it becomes evident that law and justice are intricately connected to morality and ethical principles. The principles of justice, fairness, and equality are the pillars on which legal systems are built. It is the ethical responsibility of legal professionals to uphold these principles and ensure that justice is accessible to all members of society.

We have examined various theories of law, including natural law theory, legal positivism, legal realism, critical legal studies, and feminist legal theory. Each theory provides a unique perspective on the nature and purpose of law, highlighting the importance of considering ethical implications in legal interpretation and application.

Legal rights and responsibilities play a crucial role in promoting justice and ensuring that individuals are treated fairly under the law. We have discussed the different types of legal rights, their theories, and the ethical considerations involved in balancing individual rights with collective responsibilities. Understanding the ethical dimensions of legal rights is essential for legal professionals to navigate complex legal dilemmas and promote justice.

The ethical issues in the legal profession are vast and encompass a wide range of challenges that legal professionals face in their daily practice. We have explored the ethical obligations and responsibilities of legal professionals, the importance of professional codes of conduct, and strategies for maintaining ethical integrity in legal practice. Confidentiality and attorney-client privilege present significant ethical challenges, as legal professionals must balance the duty of confidentiality with other ethical obligations. Conflict of interest is another critical issue that requires vigilance and transparency to avoid compromising ethical standards.

Social justice and human rights are essential considerations in legal studies. We have examined theories of social justice, the historical evolution of human rights, and the challenges in protecting and promoting human rights both domestically and internationally. Social justice issues, such as poverty, inequality, gender equality, racial and ethnic justice, LGBTQ+ rights, and environmental justice, demand attention and action from legal professionals to create a more equitable and just society.

Ethical issues in criminal justice pose unique challenges for legal professionals in law enforcement, criminal prosecution, and the correctional system. We have discussed the principles of criminal justice ethics, ethical dilemmas in the criminal justice system, and the ethical considerations involved in capital punishment. Policing and ethical challenges, such as the use of force, racial profiling, and police accountability, require ethical decision-making and a commitment to social justice.

Business and commerce are not exempt from ethical considerations. We have explored ethics in the business environment, corporate social responsibility, and the ethical dilemmas surrounding intellectual property rights and globalization. Legal professionals must navigate the ethical dimensions of business ethics, stakeholder management, and sustainable development to ensure ethical decision-making in the corporate world.

Law has the power to effect social change and reform. We have examined the role of law in social change, legal activism, and public interest law. The relationship between law, policy, and sustainable development highlights the importance of legal frameworks in promoting environmental regulation and addressing poverty. We have also discussed the ethical implications of technological advancements, privacy concerns in the digital age, and the intersection of technology with access to justice and social justice.

In conclusion, exploring philosophical and ethical issues in legal studies equips legal professionals with the knowledge and skills needed to navigate moral dilemmas, promote justice, and shape a more equitable, just, and sustainable world. Understanding the moral foundations of law and justice, along with the ethical considerations in legal practice, provides a solid foundation for legal professionals to uphold the principles of justice, fairness, and equality in their work. By engaging with these issues, legal professionals can contribute to the development of a society where the rule of law is upheld, human rights are protected, and social justice is advanced.

Human Rights and Legal Protection

Historical Evolution of Human Rights

Human rights, as we understand them today, have a rich and complex history that spans centuries. The idea of human rights emerged as a response to various forms of abuse, oppression, and injustice faced by individuals and communities throughout history. Understanding the historical evolution of human rights allows us to appreciate their significance and the progress made in promoting and protecting the rights and dignity of all individuals.

Ancient Civilizations and Early Notions of Rights

The concept of human rights can be traced back to ancient civilizations, where certain rights and freedoms were recognized, although not always universally. In ancient Mesopotamia, the Code of Hammurabi (c. 1754 BCE) established principles of justice and fairness, although these principles were primarily applied to maintaining social order rather than protecting individual rights. Similarly, ancient Greek and Roman societies recognized certain fundamental rights, such as the concept of natural law and the right to a fair trial.

Influence of Religion and Philosophy

Religion and philosophy played a significant role in shaping early notions of human rights. Religious teachings and scriptures provided moral and ethical guidance, emphasizing the inherent worth and dignity of every individual. For example, in Judaism, the concept of "tzelem Elohim" (image of God) underscored the equal worth and dignity of all human beings. In Christianity, the teachings of love, compassion, and the golden rule informed the understanding of human rights. Similarly, in Islam, the concept of "Ummah" emphasized the unity and equality of all believers.

Philosophical traditions also contributed to the development of human rights. The Stoics, for instance, stressed the importance of reason and equality among all humans, regardless of social status. The Enlightenment period witnessed the emergence of philosophical ideas that profoundly influenced the development of human rights. Thinkers such as John Locke, Jean-Jacques Rousseau, and Immanuel Kant asserted the inherent rights and freedoms of individuals, including the rights to life, liberty, and property.

Emergence of Human Rights Documents

The recognition and codification of human rights began to take shape in the modern era with the advent of written constitutions, bills of rights, and international instruments. One of the pivotal documents in the history of human rights is the Magna Carta (1215), which established principles of justice, due process, and limitations on the power of the monarchy in medieval England.

The Enlightenment ideals also influenced the American Declaration of Independence (1776) and the United States Constitution (1787), which enshrined fundamental rights and liberties. The French Revolution led to the adoption of the Declaration of the Rights of Man and of the Citizen (1789), which proclaimed the equal rights of all citizens.

The 20th century witnessed significant advancements in international human rights law. The Universal Declaration of Human Rights (UDHR) was adopted by the United Nations General Assembly in 1948, in response to the atrocities committed during World War II. The UDHR is a milestone document that sets out a range of civil, political, economic, social, and cultural rights that all individuals are entitled to, without distinction of any kind.

Expansion and Challenges of Human Rights

Since the adoption of the UDHR, the recognition and protection of human rights have continued to expand. Numerous international human rights treaties and conventions have been established, addressing specific rights issues such as gender equality, racial discrimination, torture, and the rights of children, among others. Regional human rights systems, such as the European Convention on Human Rights and the Inter-American system, have also played a crucial role in protecting and promoting human rights.

However, the history of human rights has also been marked by challenges and setbacks. The implementation of human rights standards is not always straightforward, and violations continue to occur in various parts of the world. Conflicts, political considerations, and cultural differences often pose significant obstacles to the realization of human rights. Furthermore, emerging issues, such as the impact of new technologies on privacy and digital rights, highlight the ongoing need to adapt and evolve human rights frameworks to new contexts.

Key Takeaways

The historical evolution of human rights reveals a gradual progression towards recognizing the inherent dignity and worth of every individual. From ancient civilizations to religious teachings, philosophy, and the rise of human rights documents, the idea of human rights has become deeply ingrained in our collective consciousness. However, the journey towards achieving universal respect for human rights is an ongoing one, requiring ongoing effort, vigilance, and commitment from individuals, governments, and organizations worldwide.

Further Reading

1. Glendon, M. A. (2001). A World Made New: Eleanor Roosevelt and the Universal Declaration of Human Rights. Random House. 2. Forsythe, D. P. (2012). Human Rights in International Relations. Cambridge University Press. 3. Morsink, J. (2009). The Universal Declaration of Human Rights: Origins, Drafting, and Intent. University of Pennsylvania Press.

Discussion Questions

1. How does the historical evolution of human rights intersect with the development of legal systems? 2. Discuss the impact of religious teachings and philosophical traditions on the concept of human rights. 3. What are some of the

challenges faced in the implementation of human rights standards? 4. How can emerging technologies both enable and pose challenges to the protection of human rights? 5. What role can individuals and communities play in promoting and protecting human rights in their respective contexts?

Exercises

1. Research the historical evolution of human rights in your own country and identify key milestones and challenges. 2. Conduct a case study on a specific human rights violation and explore the legal and ethical implications surrounding it. 3. Form a discussion group to explore the impact of new technologies on privacy and human rights, examining both positive and negative aspects. 4. Analyze a recent human rights report from an international or regional human rights organization and identify the major challenges highlighted. 5. Interview a local human rights advocate or activist and discuss their experiences in promoting and protecting human rights.

Universal Declaration of Human Rights

The Universal Declaration of Human Rights (UDHR) is a historic document that was adopted by the United Nations General Assembly on December 10, 1948. It serves as an international framework for the protection and promotion of human rights. The UDHR consists of 30 articles that outline fundamental human rights and freedoms that all individuals are entitled to, regardless of their nationality, race, gender, or any other status. In this section, we will explore the key principles and provisions of the UDHR, its significance in the realm of human rights, and its impact on shaping legal systems globally.

Background and Objectives

The UDHR was a response to the atrocities committed during World War II and the recognition of the need for a comprehensive set of principles to safeguard the dignity and rights of every human being. It was drafted by representatives from different cultural, legal, and philosophical backgrounds, reflecting a collective effort to unite nations around a common set of values.

The main objectives of the UDHR are to establish a universal standard of human rights, promote respect for human rights and fundamental freedoms, and provide a foundation for the development of international law. It reaffirms the inherent dignity and worth of all human beings and sets out the basic principles that should guide the conduct of individuals, governments, and international organizations.

Key Principles and Provisions

The UDHR encompasses a wide range of civil, political, economic, social, and cultural rights. Some of the key principles and provisions of the UDHR include:

1. **Universality:** The UDHR applies to all individuals, regardless of their citizenship, nationality, or any other status. It recognizes that all human beings are born free and equal in dignity and rights.

2. **Inalienability:** The rights enshrined in the UDHR are inherent to every human being and cannot be taken away or transferred. They cannot be waived, even voluntarily.

3. **Indivisibility:** The UDHR recognizes that human rights are interconnected and interdependent. Civil, political, economic, social, and cultural rights are mutually reinforcing and must be treated as a whole.

4. **Non-Discrimination:** The UDHR prohibits discrimination based on race, color, sex, language, religion, political or other opinion, national or social origin, property, birth, or any other status. All individuals are entitled to equal protection under the law.

5. **Rights and Responsibilities:** The UDHR acknowledges that the exercise of rights carries responsibilities. While individuals are entitled to their rights, they also have a duty to respect the rights of others.

Significance and Influence

The UDHR has had a profound impact on the development of human rights standards globally. It has provided a common framework and language for discussing human rights and has influenced the drafting of national and international laws, as well as constitutions.

The principles enshrined in the UDHR have been incorporated into various international human rights treaties, including the International Covenant on Civil and Political Rights (ICCPR) and the International Covenant on Economic, Social and Cultural Rights (ICESCR). These treaties further specify and elaborate on the rights and freedoms outlined in the UDHR, emphasizing the binding nature of the obligations they entail.

The UDHR has also inspired the establishment of regional human rights systems, such as the European Convention on Human Rights (ECHR) and the African Charter on Human and Peoples' Rights. These regional systems have played a crucial role in advancing the protection and promotion of human rights within their respective jurisdictions.

Moreover, the UDHR has served as a moral compass and advocacy tool for human rights activists and organizations worldwide. Its principles have been invoked in countless legal cases, policy debates, and social movements, promoting greater awareness and accountability in the field of human rights.

Contemporary Challenges and Critiques

While the UDHR has made significant progress in promoting and protecting human rights, there are several challenges and critiques that need to be addressed. These include:

1. **Cultural Relativism:** Some argue that the UDHR reflects Western values and fails to account for cultural and religious diversity. They contend that universal human rights should be adapted to different cultural contexts.

2. **Implementation Gap:** Despite its widespread ratification, the full realization of the rights enshrined in the UDHR remains a challenge. Many countries struggle to effectively implement and enforce human rights protections, leading to ongoing human rights abuses.

3. **Emerging Issues:** The UDHR was drafted well before the advent of modern technologies, such as the internet and social media. New challenges, such as privacy rights, online freedom of expression, and artificial intelligence, require further examination within the framework of the UDHR.

Addressing these challenges requires continued dialogue, engagement, and cooperation among governments, civil society organizations, and individuals. It is essential to ensure that the principles of the UDHR remain relevant and applicable in a rapidly changing world.

Conclusion

The Universal Declaration of Human Rights represents a milestone in the history of human rights, providing a universal framework for the protection and promotion of human dignity and freedom. Its principles and provisions continue to inspire individuals, shape legal systems, and advance the cause of human rights globally. While challenges and critiques persist, the UDHR remains a powerful symbol of human aspiration and a guidepost for creating a more just and equitable world. It is our collective responsibility to uphold and defend the principles enshrined in the UDHR, ensuring that every person can live a life free from discrimination, oppression, and injustice.

International Human Rights Instruments

International human rights instruments are legal frameworks established at the international level to protect and promote human rights. These instruments play a crucial role in establishing universal standards and norms for the protection of human rights across different countries and regions. In this section, we will examine the significance of international human rights instruments, their historical evolution, major conventions and treaties, and their impact on human rights protection worldwide.

Significance of International Human Rights Instruments

International human rights instruments are essential for ensuring that human rights are respected and protected globally. They serve as a foundation for establishing legal obligations and responsibilities of states in promoting and safeguarding human rights. These instruments provide a framework for accountability, allowing individuals and organizations to hold states accountable for human rights violations. Moreover, they facilitate international cooperation and collaboration in addressing human rights issues and promoting a culture of respect for human dignity.

Historical Evolution of International Human Rights Instruments

The history of international human rights instruments dates back to the aftermath of World War II. The atrocities committed during the war led the international community to recognize the urgent need for a comprehensive framework to protect human rights. As a result, the United Nations (UN) was established, and its founding charter, the UN Charter, included the promotion and protection of human rights as one of its core principles.

Over the years, a series of international conventions and treaties have been adopted to address specific aspects of human rights. These instruments have been developed and refined through negotiations involving various stakeholders, including states, civil society organizations, and individuals. The adoption of these instruments has led to the gradual expansion of human rights protection and the recognition of new rights.

Major Conventions and Treaties

Several major conventions and treaties form the foundation of international human rights law. These instruments outline rights and obligations in various areas of human rights, including civil, political, economic, social, and cultural rights. Some of the notable conventions and treaties include:

+ **Universal Declaration of Human Rights (UDHR):** Adopted in 1948, the UDHR is a landmark document that sets out fundamental human rights to be universally protected. It covers civil, political, economic, social, and cultural rights, and serves as a cornerstone for subsequent human rights instruments.

+ **International Covenant on Civil and Political Rights (ICCPR):** Adopted in 1966, the ICCPR focuses on civil and political rights, such as the right to life, freedom of speech, and the right to a fair trial. It establishes legal obligations for states to respect and protect these rights.

+ **International Covenant on Economic, Social and Cultural Rights (ICESCR):** Also adopted in 1966, the ICESCR recognizes economic, social, and cultural rights, such as the right to education, the right to work, and the right to an adequate standard of living. It highlights states' responsibilities in ensuring the enjoyment of these rights.

+ **Convention on the Elimination of All Forms of Discrimination Against Women (CEDAW):** Adopted in 1979, CEDAW is a comprehensive treaty that addresses gender-based discrimination and promotes gender equality. It outlines specific obligations for states to eliminate discrimination against women in various spheres of life.

+ **Convention against Torture and Other Cruel, Inhuman or Degrading Treatment or Punishment (CAT):** Adopted in 1984, CAT prohibits the use of torture and other forms of cruel, inhuman, or degrading treatment or punishment. It requires states to take effective measures to prevent, investigate, and provide redress for acts of torture.

+ **Convention on the Rights of the Child (CRC):** Adopted in 1989, the CRC is a comprehensive treaty that sets out the rights of children, including their right to survival, development, protection, and participation. It places obligations on states to ensure that children's rights are respected and protected.

These are just a few examples of the numerous international human rights instruments that exist. Each instrument addresses specific rights and obligations, reflecting the evolving understanding of human rights and the needs of different populations.

Impact of International Human Rights Instruments

International human rights instruments have had a significant impact on human rights protection worldwide. They have contributed to the development of a global human rights framework and created legal obligations for states to respect, protect, and fulfill human rights. The impact of these instruments can be seen in various aspects:

- **Legislation and Policy Development:** International human rights instruments provide a basis for the development of national legislation and policies on human rights. States are required to align their domestic laws with the provisions of these instruments, ensuring the protection of human rights at the national level.

- **Judicial Decisions:** International human rights instruments have influenced judicial decisions in national courts. Courts often refer to these instruments when interpreting laws and deciding cases involving human rights issues. This helps to promote consistent interpretation and application of human rights standards.

- **Advocacy and Activism:** International human rights instruments have provided a rallying point for advocacy and activism by civil society organizations, human rights defenders, and grassroots movements. These instruments have been used to raise awareness, mobilize support, and challenge human rights violations around the world.

- **Promotion of Human Rights Standards:** International human rights instruments have facilitated the development of human rights standards and norms. They provide a framework for dialogue and exchange of best practices among states, encouraging the adoption of common approaches to human rights issues.

- **Institutional Mechanisms:** International human rights instruments have led to the establishment of specialized bodies and mechanisms to monitor and enforce compliance with human rights standards. For example, the UN Human Rights Council and treaty bodies oversee the implementation of specific conventions and treaties.

Despite these positive impacts, challenges remain in terms of ensuring effective implementation and enforcement of international human rights instruments. Some states may fail to fulfill their obligations, and there is often limited awareness of human rights among certain populations. Additionally, the changing global landscape presents new challenges that require continuous adaptation and innovation in the field of human rights protection.

Conclusion

International human rights instruments play a crucial role in promoting universal respect for and protection of human rights. They provide a framework for establishing legal obligations and standards at the international and national levels. These instruments have had a significant impact on human rights protection, influencing legislation, policy development, judicial decisions, and advocacy efforts. While challenges persist, international human rights instruments continue to shape the discourse on human rights and contribute to a more just and equitable world.

Domestic Implementation of Human Rights

In this section, we will explore the domestic implementation of human rights within legal systems. Human rights are fundamental rights and freedoms that every individual is entitled to, regardless of their nationality, race, religion, or any other characteristic. The international community has recognized the importance of human rights and has developed numerous legal instruments and frameworks to protect and promote these rights. However, the challenge lies in implementing and enforcing these rights at the domestic level.

Legal Framework for Domestic Implementation

Domestic implementation of human rights requires a comprehensive legal framework that incorporates international human rights standards into national laws. This framework typically includes:

1. **Constitutional Protection:** Many countries incorporate human rights provisions into their constitutions, guaranteeing individuals certain fundamental rights and freedoms. A constitution serves as the supreme law of the land and provides a legal foundation for the protection of human rights.

2. **Legislation:** Governments must enact specific laws that protect human rights and ensure their implementation. These laws can cover a wide range of areas, such as civil and political rights, economic, social and cultural rights, labor rights, and environmental rights.

3. **Judicial Remedies:** A robust judicial system is crucial for the effective implementation of human rights. Courts play a vital role in interpreting and applying laws, resolving disputes, and providing remedies for human rights violations.

4. **Administrative Mechanisms:** Administrative bodies, such as human rights commissions or ombudsman offices, play a significant role in monitoring and promoting human rights. They investigate complaints, conduct inquiries, and make recommendations to ensure the protection of rights.

These components work together to establish a legal framework that protects and promotes human rights at the domestic level.

Challenges in Domestic Implementation

While the legal framework provides a foundation for the implementation of human rights, several challenges exist in practice. These challenges may include:

1. **Lack of Awareness and Education:** Many individuals may not be aware of their rights or how to effectively exercise them. Effective implementation requires awareness-raising campaigns and educational programs to ensure that individuals understand their rights and how to protect them.

2. **Inadequate Resources:** Implementing human rights often requires financial, human, and infrastructure resources. Governments may face resource constraints, limiting their ability to fully implement and enforce human rights laws.

3. **Political Will and Compliance:** The implementation of human rights can be hindered by political factors. Governments may lack the political will to fully

implement human rights laws, and individuals responsible for enforcing these laws may not comply with their obligations.

4. **Discrimination and Social Bias:** Discrimination and social biases can undermine the effective implementation of human rights. Prejudices based on factors such as race, gender, religion, or sexual orientation can result in unequal treatment and denial of rights to certain individuals or groups.

Addressing these challenges requires a multi-faceted approach, involving collaboration between government institutions, civil society organizations, and international bodies.

Promoting Domestic Implementation

To promote the effective domestic implementation of human rights, various strategies can be employed:

1. **Capacity Building:** Governments should invest in capacity-building programs to strengthen the knowledge and skills of judges, lawyers, law enforcement officials, and other relevant stakeholders. This ensures that they have the necessary tools to effectively implement human rights laws.

2. **Awareness and Education:** Public awareness campaigns and educational programs can help individuals understand their rights and responsibilities. These initiatives can be carried out through various channels, including media, schools, and community organizations.

3. **Accountability Mechanisms:** Establishing robust mechanisms to hold individuals and institutions accountable for human rights violations is crucial. This includes conducting impartial investigations, prosecuting perpetrators, and providing remedies for victims.

4. **Engagement with Civil Society:** Governments should actively engage with civil society organizations, human rights defenders, and grassroots movements. Collaboration with these entities can provide valuable insights, expertise, and monitoring mechanisms to ensure effective implementation.

In addition to these strategies, international cooperation and support can also play a crucial role in promoting domestic implementation of human rights.

Case Study: Domestic Implementation of the Right to Freedom of Expression

To illustrate the domestic implementation of human rights, let's focus on the right to freedom of expression. This right is enshrined in various international human rights instruments, such as the Universal Declaration of Human Rights and the International Covenant on Civil and Political Rights.

In a fictional country called "Alpha," the government has ratified these international treaties and incorporated the right to freedom of expression into its constitution. However, the practical implementation of this right faces challenges due to political, cultural, and social factors.

To address these challenges, the government of Alpha takes several steps. Firstly, it launches a nationwide campaign to raise awareness about the right to freedom of expression. This campaign includes public service announcements, educational programs in schools, and workshops for journalists, bloggers, and social media influencers.

Secondly, Alpha establishes an independent media regulatory body tasked with ensuring that media organizations uphold ethical standards and respect freedom of expression. This body provides guidelines and regulations, conducts investigations into complaints, and imposes penalties for violations.

Thirdly, the government creates a legal aid program to provide assistance to individuals or groups whose freedom of expression has been violated. This program funds legal representation, facilitates access to justice, and supports individuals in seeking appropriate remedies.

Lastly, Alpha actively engages with civil society organizations, journalists' associations, and human rights defenders to establish a collaborative platform for dialogue and consultation on freedom of expression issues. This platform serves as a space for sharing best practices, identifying challenges, and finding collaborative solutions.

Through these initiatives, Alpha strives to promote the domestic implementation of the right to freedom of expression, ensuring that individuals can freely express their opinions, ideas, and beliefs without fear of censorship or reprisals.

Conclusion

The domestic implementation of human rights is a complex and multi-dimensional process. It requires a comprehensive legal framework, awareness-raising, capacity-building, accountability mechanisms, and collaboration among various stakeholders. Despite challenges, effective implementation of human rights is essential for fostering a just and equitable society where individuals can live with dignity, equality, and freedom. Governments, civil society organizations, and individuals all have a role to play in promoting and protecting these fundamental rights.

Challenges and Controversies in Human Rights Protection

Human rights are fundamental rights and freedoms that every individual is entitled to, regardless of their nationality, race, gender, religion, or any other status. While the recognition and protection of human rights are essential for maintaining a just and equitable society, there are numerous challenges and controversies that arise in this process. In this section, we will explore some of these challenges and controversies in human rights protection.

Intersectionality and Inclusive Rights

One of the significant challenges in human rights protection is ensuring inclusivity and recognizing the intersectionality of different forms of discrimination. Intersectionality refers to the interconnected nature of social categorizations, such as race, class, gender, and sexuality, as they create overlapping and interdependent systems of discrimination. It recognizes that individuals may face multiple forms of discrimination simultaneously, and these intersecting identities shape their experience of human rights.

For instance, a person of a minority racial or ethnic group and a member of the LGBTQ+ community may face compounded forms of discrimination and violations of their human rights. The challenge lies in developing frameworks and policies that adequately address the needs and experiences of individuals with intersecting identities, ensuring that their rights are protected in an inclusive manner.

Cultural Relativism vs. Universalism

Another controversial issue in human rights protection is the tension between cultural relativism and universalism. Cultural relativism suggests that human rights are culturally and socially constructed and may vary across different societies and cultures. It argues that the understanding and interpretation of human rights should take into account the cultural context and values of a particular community.

On the other hand, universalism posits that human rights are inherent to all individuals by virtue of being human, regardless of cultural or societal differences. It emphasizes the universality and indivisibility of human rights, arguing that certain fundamental rights should be universally upheld and protected.

This debate raises questions about how to address human rights abuses in cultural contexts where practices may conflict with universal human rights standards. Striking a balance between respecting cultural diversity and upholding universal human rights principles is a complex challenge that requires nuanced approaches and dialogue.

Enforcement and Accountability

Ensuring the effective enforcement and accountability for human rights violations is another crucial challenge. While international human rights instruments, such as treaties and conventions, establish legal frameworks for the protection of human rights, their enforcement mechanisms vary.

In some cases, states may lack the political will or capacity to enforce human rights obligations, resulting in a lack of accountability for violations. Additionally, human rights abuses committed by non-state actors, such as armed groups or multinational corporations, pose challenges in terms of identifying responsible parties and holding them accountable.

Addressing this challenge requires strengthening domestic legal systems, promoting the rule of law, and establishing effective monitoring and reporting mechanisms. It is also important to encourage international cooperation and coordination in investigating and addressing human rights violations, ensuring that those responsible are held accountable.

Emerging Human Rights Issues

Human rights protection is not static and continuously faces new challenges due to the evolving nature of society and advancements in technology. New and emerging human rights issues require ongoing assessment and adaptation of legal frameworks and policies.

For instance, issues related to privacy and data protection in the digital age, the impact of artificial intelligence on human rights, and the influence of social media on freedom of expression present new challenges for human rights protection. These issues require careful consideration and a proactive approach to ensure that human rights frameworks remain relevant and effective in addressing contemporary challenges.

Examples of Controversies in Human Rights

To further illustrate the challenges and controversies in human rights protection, let's consider some real-world examples:

1. Freedom of Expression and Hate Speech: Balancing the protection of freedom of expression and the prevention of hate speech poses a challenge. Determining where the line is drawn between protected speech and speech that incites violence or discrimination requires careful consideration of the context and potential harm caused.

2. Right to Privacy and National Security: Balancing the right to privacy with the need for national security measures, such as surveillance, raises concerns. Ensuring that surveillance practices are proportionate, necessary, and subject to appropriate safeguards is essential to protect human rights while addressing security threats.

3. Women's Rights and Cultural Practices: Protecting women's rights while respecting cultural practices that may discriminate against women poses a challenge. For example, addressing issues such as forced marriages, female genital mutilation, or honor-based violence requires engaging with communities and finding culturally sensitive solutions.

4. Economic, Social, and Cultural Rights: Ensuring equitable access to basic necessities, such as healthcare, education, and housing, poses challenges due to resource constraints and societal inequalities. Balancing these rights with competing priorities in economic and social development requires policy interventions and resource allocation strategies.

Resources and Recommendations

To navigate the challenges and controversies in human rights protection, it is crucial to rely on various resources and consider different perspectives. Here are some recommendations:

1. Universal Declaration of Human Rights: The foundational international human rights document provides a set of principles and standards that can guide human rights protection efforts. Familiarize yourself with its provisions and use it as a reference point.

2. United Nations Human Rights Council: Stay informed about the work of the UN Human Rights Council, which addresses human rights violations globally. Their reports, resolutions, and recommendations can provide valuable insights into contemporary challenges and responses.

3. Non-Governmental Organizations (NGOs): NGOs, such as Amnesty International, Human Rights Watch, and local human rights organizations, are valuable sources of information and advocacy. Explore their publications, reports, and campaigns to better understand specific human rights issues.

4. Engage in Dialogue: Engage in conversations and dialogue with diverse individuals and groups to better comprehend different perspectives and develop well-rounded approaches to human rights protection. This can include discussions with experts, activists, community members, and affected individuals.

5. Case Studies and Experiential Learning: Analyze real-world case studies and engage in experiential learning opportunities to deepen your understanding of the challenges and controversies in human rights protection. This could involve participating in simulations, internships, or workshops in relevant fields.

Remember that addressing challenges and controversies in human rights protection is an ongoing process that requires collective efforts and continuous reflection. By critically examining these issues, engaging with diverse perspectives, and advocating for human rights, we can contribute to building a more just and inclusive society.

Human Rights and Social Justice

In this section, we will explore the important connection between human rights and social justice. Human rights are fundamental rights and freedoms to which every individual is inherently entitled. Social justice, on the other hand, refers to the fair and equitable distribution of resources, opportunities, and privileges within a society. Both human rights and social justice are crucial aspects of a just and inclusive society, and they are closely interrelated.

The Relationship between Human Rights and Social Justice

Human rights and social justice are intertwined concepts that reinforce each other. Human rights provide the moral and legal framework for promoting social justice. They ensure that every individual is treated with dignity, equality, and fairness, and that their basic needs are met. Social justice, on the other hand, seeks to address systemic inequalities and barriers that prevent individuals from enjoying their human rights.

Human rights and social justice go hand in hand in achieving a more equitable society. Social justice initiatives aim to eliminate discrimination, poverty, and other injustices, which are key obstacles to the realization of human rights. By promoting social justice, we can create a society that upholds human rights for all.

The Role of Human Rights in Advancing Social Justice

Human rights provide a framework for advocating and advancing social justice. They establish legal obligations for governments and institutions to uphold the rights and well-being of individuals. Human rights principles, such as non-discrimination, equality, and participation, guide policies and actions that foster social justice.

For example, the right to education ensures that all individuals have equal access to quality education, regardless of their social or economic background. By guaranteeing this right, societies can promote social justice by reducing inequality and enhancing opportunities for all.

Similarly, the right to health ensures that everyone has access to adequate healthcare services. This right plays a crucial role in addressing health disparities and promoting social justice by ensuring that vulnerable populations receive the care and support they need.

Human rights also play a vital role in combating discrimination and promoting equality. Rights such as the right to non-discrimination and the right to equal protection under the law provide a legal basis for challenging discriminatory practices and policies. By addressing systemic inequalities, societies can create a more just and inclusive environment for all individuals.

Challenges in Promoting Human Rights and Social Justice

While human rights and social justice are essential principles, there are various challenges in their promotion and realization. These challenges include:

1. Lack of awareness: Many individuals may not be aware of their rights or the importance of social justice. Lack of awareness can hinder efforts to promote and protect human rights and achieve social justice.

2. Discrimination and inequality: Discrimination and inequality are prevalent in many societies, posing significant obstacles to achieving social justice. Addressing deep-rooted biases and structural barriers is crucial for creating a more inclusive society.

3. Political resistance: Advancing human rights and social justice can face resistance from those in power who may benefit from maintaining the status quo. Overcoming political resistance requires strong advocacy and public support.

4. Limited resources: Adequate resources are necessary to address social injustices and realize human rights. Limited funding and competing priorities can hinder efforts to promote social justice effectively.

5. Implementation and enforcement: While human rights are enshrined in international and national laws, their implementation and enforcement can be challenging. Governments, institutions, and organizations need to ensure that laws and policies are effectively implemented and enforced to protect human rights and promote social justice.

Case Study: Human Rights, Social Justice, and Gender Equality

One area where human rights and social justice intersect is gender equality. Gender equality is a fundamental human right and a key aspect of social justice.

Promoting gender equality involves challenging social norms, stereotypes, and practices that perpetuate discrimination and inequality based on gender. It involves ensuring equal opportunities, access to resources, and challenging gender-based violence and discrimination.

For example, laws promoting gender equality can address issues such as pay gaps, gender-based violence, and access to education and healthcare. Implementing and enforcing these laws can help create a more just and equitable society where individuals' rights are respected and protected.

Promoting gender equality is not only a human rights issue but also a social justice imperative. By empowering women, addressing gender inequalities, and challenging discriminatory practices, societies can foster social justice and create a more inclusive and equitable society for everyone.

Conclusion

Human rights and social justice are inseparable. Human rights provide the normative framework for promoting social justice, while social justice initiatives aim to eliminate systemic inequalities and injustice that hinder the realization of human rights. By understanding and promoting the relationship between human rights and social justice, we can work towards creating a more equitable, just, and sustainable world for all individuals.

Human Rights and Globalization

In today's interconnected world, globalization has emerged as a force that transcends geographical boundaries and connects people, economies, and cultures. While globalization offers numerous benefits, it also poses significant challenges to human rights. This section explores the complex relationship between human rights and globalization, examining the impact of globalization on human rights and the role of human rights in shaping globalization.

Understanding Globalization

Globalization refers to the increasing interconnectedness and interdependence of countries through the exchange of goods, services, information, technology, and ideas. It is driven by advancements in transportation, communication, and technology, enabling rapid movement of people and goods across borders.

Globalization is characterized by the expansion of multinational corporations, the growth of international trade, and the integration of financial markets. It has facilitated the flow of capital, labor, and resources across countries, leading to economic integration and the creation of global supply chains.

Impact on Human Rights

While globalization has brought economic growth and development to many parts of the world, it has also presented new challenges for the protection and promotion of human rights. The impact of globalization on human rights can be analyzed in various dimensions:

1. Economic Dimension: Globalization has contributed to economic inequality both within and between countries. While it has lifted many out of poverty, it has also marginalized and disadvantaged vulnerable groups. The expansion of global supply chains has often resulted in exploitative labor practices, including low wages, long working hours, and poor working conditions. Moreover, economic globalization has led to the concentration of wealth and power in the hands of a few, exacerbating social disparities.

2. Social Dimension: Globalization has influenced social structures and cultural norms, often leading to the erosion of traditional values and practices. Cultural globalization has brought increased interaction between different cultures, but it has also led to cultural homogenization and the loss of cultural diversity. Furthermore, globalization has contributed to the rise of consumerism and materialism, impacting social values and priorities.

3. Political Dimension: Globalization has influenced the power dynamics between states and has presented challenges to national sovereignty. International trade agreements and economic integration have limited the ability of states to regulate their economies and implement policies that protect human rights. Global governance structures often prioritize economic interests over human rights considerations, leaving marginalized communities and individuals without adequate protection.

Role of Human Rights

Despite the challenges posed by globalization, human rights play a critical role in shaping and guiding the process of globalization. Human rights provide a normative framework that ensures the protection and promotion of dignity, freedom, equality, and justice.

1. Normative Framework: Human rights principles, enshrined in international human rights instruments, set the standards for the treatment of individuals and communities. These principles include the right to life, liberty, and security of person, the right to a fair trial, the right to freedom of expression, and the right to equal treatment. Human rights provide a foundation for addressing the negative impacts of globalization and promoting a more equitable and just global order.

2. Accountability: Human rights norms create obligations for states and other actors to respect, protect, and fulfill human rights. States have a responsibility to regulate and monitor the impact of globalization on human rights. International human rights mechanisms, such as treaty monitoring bodies and special rapporteurs, play a crucial role in holding states accountable for their human rights obligations. Non-state actors, including multinational corporations, also have a responsibility to respect human rights in their business operations.

3. Advocacy and Activism: Human rights advocates and activists play a crucial role in raising awareness about the human rights implications of globalization. They work to highlight the voices of marginalized groups and advocate for policy changes to promote human rights in the context of globalization. Grassroots movements, such as the global fair trade movement and campaigns against sweatshop labor, have emerged to address the negative impacts of globalization on human rights.

Challenges and Opportunities

The intersection of human rights and globalization presents both challenges and opportunities for promoting a more just and equitable world order. Some of the key challenges include:

1. Power Imbalance: The unequal distribution of power and resources in the era of globalization poses challenges to the effective realization of human rights. Powerful states and multinational corporations often wield disproportionate influence, undermining efforts to address human rights violations.

2. Regulatory Gaps: Globalization has revealed regulatory gaps in addressing human rights violations that occur beyond national borders. International human rights frameworks often lack enforceable mechanisms to hold non-state actors accountable for human rights abuses.

3. Cultural Relativism: The clash of cultural norms and values in the context of globalization raises questions about the universality of human rights. Cultural relativism arguments challenge the application of human rights principles in diverse cultural contexts.

However, globalization also presents opportunities for advancing human rights:

1. Collaboration and Solidarity: Globalization has facilitated greater collaboration and solidarity among states, civil society organizations, and individuals committed to promoting human rights. Networking and information sharing have empowered advocacy efforts and fostered global movements for change.

2. Technology and Communication: Advances in technology and communication have created new avenues for raising awareness about human rights violations and mobilizing support for human rights causes. Social media platforms have played a significant role in amplifying marginalized voices and promoting human rights activism.

3. Economic Interdependence: Economic globalization has blurred national boundaries, making it increasingly difficult to ignore human rights concerns. Human rights violations can have reputational and economic consequences for states and corporations, creating incentives for improved human rights practices.

Conclusion

As globalization continues to shape our world, the promotion and protection of human rights become increasingly crucial. The interplay between human rights and globalization highlights the need for a human rights-based approach to address the challenges and harness the opportunities presented by globalization. By recognizing the inherent dignity and worth of every individual and ensuring the universality of human rights principles, we can strive towards a more equitable and just global order that upholds the rights and well-being of all.

Conclusion

In this section, we have explored the ethical issues surrounding social justice and human rights within the context of legal studies. We began by discussing the theories of social justice, including egalitarianism, libertarianism, communitarianism, and feminist theories. We also examined the concept of human rights and the international and domestic frameworks that protect these rights.

One of the key takeaways from this section is the recognition of the interconnectedness between social justice and human rights. Social justice is essential for creating a society in which everyone has equal opportunities and access to resources and services. Human rights provide the legal and moral framework for protecting individuals' dignity, freedom, and well-being.

We have also explored specific social justice issues within legal studies, such as poverty and inequality, gender equality, racial and ethnic justice, LGBTQ+ rights, and environmental justice. These issues highlight the inequalities that persist in our society and the responsibility of legal professionals to address them through the application of ethical principles.

Furthermore, we examined the ethical considerations within the criminal justice system, including the principles of criminal justice ethics, the role of law enforcement, ethical challenges in criminal prosecution, and issues related to capital punishment and policing. These topics underscore the importance of ethical decision-making and the need for accountability within the criminal justice system.

In the realm of business and commerce, we delved into the ethical issues that arise in the business environment, such as corporate governance, corporate social responsibility, and intellectual property rights. We also discussed the ethical implications of globalization, including human rights in global supply chains and environmental sustainability.

Lastly, we emphasized the role of law in social change and reform. We explored how law can be used as a tool for social change through legal activism, impact litigation, and policy advocacy. We also discussed the connection between law, policy, and sustainable development, as well as the ethical challenges posed by technological advancements.

Throughout this section, we have emphasized the importance of ethical decision-making, professionalism, and the pursuit of social justice within the legal profession. By understanding the ethical considerations inherent in legal studies, legal professionals can navigate moral dilemmas, promote justice, and contribute to the creation of a more equitable, just, and sustainable world.

In conclusion, the study of philosophical and ethical issues in legal studies is crucial for developing a deep understanding of the moral complexities and responsibilities within the legal profession. By embracing ethical principles and promoting social justice, legal professionals can play a pivotal role in shaping a better future for society. As future legal practitioners and scholars, it is our duty to continuously reflect on these issues and strive for a more just and equitable society through the application of ethics and morality in legal practice.

Social Justice Issues in Legal Studies

Poverty, Inequality, and Economic Justice

In this section, we will explore the ethical issues surrounding poverty, inequality, and economic justice. These are crucial topics within the field of legal studies as they address the fundamental questions of fairness, distributive justice, and the role of law in addressing social and economic disparities.

Understanding Poverty and Inequality

To begin our analysis, let us first define poverty and inequality. Poverty refers to the state of lacking the basic necessities for a decent standard of living. This includes access to food, clean water, shelter, healthcare, and education. Inequality, on the other hand, refers to the unequal distribution of resources, opportunities, and wealth among individuals and groups in society.

In many countries, poverty and inequality are closely linked. Economic inequality, for instance, can perpetuate and exacerbate poverty by limiting access to essential resources and opportunities for those who are already marginalized. It is crucial for legal scholars and practitioners to understand the root causes and consequences of poverty and inequality in order to develop effective strategies for promoting economic justice.

Theories of Economic Justice

Various theories of economic justice provide a framework for understanding and addressing poverty and inequality. Let us explore three prominent theories in this section: utilitarianism, egalitarianism, and capabilities approach.

Utilitarianism holds that the most ethical outcome is the one that maximizes overall happiness and well-being in society. From a utilitarian perspective, reducing poverty and inequality can be seen as beneficial for society as a whole. However, critics argue that utilitarianism may overlook the interests and needs of disadvantaged individuals in the pursuit of aggregate happiness.

Egalitarianism, on the other hand, emphasizes the equal distribution of resources and opportunities among all members of society. Proponents of egalitarianism argue that reducing poverty and inequality is essential for achieving a just and fair society. However, critics raise concerns about individual effort and merit being disregarded in a purely egalitarian system.

The capabilities approach, developed by economist Amartya Sen, focuses on individuals' abilities to function in society. It emphasizes the importance of providing individuals with the necessary resources and freedoms to pursue their own goals and aspirations. This approach recognizes that poverty and inequality limit people's capabilities and seeks to address these systemic obstacles.

Legal Strategies for Economic Justice

Legal studies play a crucial role in identifying and implementing strategies for addressing poverty, inequality, and promoting economic justice. Let us explore some key legal strategies in this regard:

1. Social safety nets: Governments can establish and enforce social safety net programs to provide a basic level of support and protection for individuals living in poverty. These programs may include welfare benefits, unemployment assistance, and healthcare provisions.

2. Progressive taxation: Tax policies can play a role in reducing economic inequality by implementing progressive tax systems, where the wealthy contribute a larger percentage of their income compared to those with lower incomes. This approach seeks to redistribute wealth and resources more equitably.

3. Labor rights and protections: Ensuring fair labor practices, such as minimum wages, safe working conditions, and protection against discrimination, can help address economic inequality and empower workers to achieve economic security.

4. Access to education: Legal frameworks can promote equal access to quality education, which is essential for breaking the cycle of poverty. Policies that address the barriers to education, such as discrimination, lack of resources, and unequal distribution of educational opportunities, can help reduce inequality.

5. Consumer protection and financial regulation: Strong consumer protection laws and financial regulations can help prevent exploitation and predatory practices that disproportionately affect individuals living in poverty. These laws can promote transparency, fairness, and accountability in economic transactions.

Case Study: Universal Basic Income

One innovative approach to addressing poverty and inequality is the concept of a universal basic income (UBI). UBI is a system in which every individual receives a regular, unconditional sum of money from the government, regardless of their income or employment status.

Advocates argue that UBI has the potential to alleviate poverty, reduce inequality, and provide individuals with the necessary resources to meet their basic needs and pursue opportunities. Critics, however, raise concerns about the potential disincentive to work and the significant costs associated with implementing UBI.

UBI has gained traction in recent years, with pilot programs and experiments being conducted in different parts of the world. Legal scholars and policymakers play a crucial role in analyzing the ethical implications, feasibility, and impact of UBI as a tool for economic justice.

Conclusion

Poverty, inequality, and economic justice are complex issues that require interdisciplinary approaches and innovative legal strategies. By understanding the theories of economic justice, exploring legal frameworks, and analyzing case studies, legal scholars and practitioners can contribute to the creation of a more equitable and just society. It is through the intersection of legal studies, ethics, and social activism that meaningful progress in addressing poverty and inequality can be achieved.

Gender Equality and Women's Rights

In this section, we will explore the complex issues surrounding gender equality and women's rights within the legal framework. Achieving gender equality is not just a matter of social justice, but also a fundamental human right and a prerequisite for sustainable development. We will examine the historical context, legal principles, and challenges faced in promoting gender equality, as well as explore the legal tools and strategies used to protect women's rights.

Historical Context

To understand the current status of gender equality and women's rights, it is crucial to examine the historical context. Throughout history, women have faced systemic discrimination and marginalization in various aspects of life, including education, employment, politics, and personal autonomy. Traditional gender roles and stereotypes have perpetuated inequality and limited opportunities for women.

The feminist movement, which emerged in the late 19th and early 20th centuries, played a significant role in advocating for gender equality and women's rights. The suffrage movement fought for women's right to vote, paving the way for broader recognition and protection of women's rights. The United Nations has also played a crucial role in promoting gender equality through international legal instruments and frameworks.

Legal Principles

Gender equality and women's rights are protected under various legal frameworks and international human rights treaties. The Universal Declaration of Human Rights, adopted by the United Nations General Assembly in 1948, recognizes the principles of equality and non-discrimination. The Convention on the Elimination of All Forms of Discrimination Against Women (CEDAW), adopted in 1979, is another essential instrument that provides a comprehensive framework for addressing gender-based discrimination.

Key legal principles that underpin gender equality and women's rights include:

+ Non-discrimination: Women should enjoy equal rights and opportunities without any form of discrimination based on gender.

+ Equal participation: Women have the right to participate fully and equally in all spheres of life, including politics, education, employment, and decision-making processes.

+ Gender-based violence: States have an obligation to prevent, investigate, and address gender-based violence, including domestic violence, sexual harassment, and trafficking.

+ Access to justice: Women should have equal access to justice, including legal aid and effective remedies for gender-based discrimination or violence.

+ Reproductive rights: Women have the right to make informed decisions about their reproductive health and access to reproductive healthcare services.

Challenges in Promoting Gender Equality

Despite the legal protections and principles in place, numerous challenges persist in achieving gender equality and promoting women's rights. These challenges stem from deep-rooted societal norms, cultural barriers, and structural inequalities. Some of the key challenges include:

+ Gender stereotypes: Traditional gender roles and stereotypes perpetuate unequal power dynamics and limit women's opportunities for advancement in various spheres.

+ Gender-based violence: Women continue to face various forms of gender-based violence, including domestic violence, sexual assault, and harmful practices like female genital mutilation and child marriage.

+ Intersectionality: Women from marginalized and minority communities, including women of color, LGBTQ+ women, and women with disabilities, face compounded forms of discrimination and exclusion.

+ Unequal economic opportunities: Women often face wage gaps, limited access to credit and financial resources, and discrimination in the workplace.

+ Limited political representation: Women are underrepresented in political leadership roles, which hinders their ability to influence policy decisions and enact meaningful change.

Legal Tools and Strategies

To address these challenges and promote gender equality, various legal tools and strategies have been employed at the national and international levels. These include:

+ Legislation: Governments enact laws and regulations to criminalize gender-based discrimination and violence, promote equal opportunities, and provide legal remedies for women.

+ Quotas and affirmative action: Many countries have implemented gender quotas and affirmative action policies to increase women's representation in politics, corporate boards, and leadership positions.

+ Gender mainstreaming: Governments and organizations adopt gender mainstreaming strategies to ensure that gender perspectives are incorporated into policy development, legislation, and decision-making processes.

+ Awareness and education: Promoting gender equality requires raising awareness and educating the public about women's rights and the consequences of gender-based discrimination.

+ Advocacy and activism: Grassroots organizations, NGOs, and women's rights activists play a crucial role in advocating for policy changes, raising awareness, and holding governments accountable.

Real-World Example: The Fight for Equal Pay

Equal pay for equal work is a fundamental principle of gender equality. However, gender wage gaps continue to persist in many countries, with women earning significantly less than their male counterparts for the same work. This issue has gained renewed attention and sparked public debate in recent years.

One real-world example of the fight for equal pay is the case of the U.S. Women's National Soccer Team (USWNT). In 2019, the team filed a gender discrimination lawsuit against the U.S. Soccer Federation, alleging pay disparities and unequal working conditions compared to the men's team. The case highlighted the pervasive issue of gender pay gaps in professional sports and brought broader attention to the need for equal pay.

The USWNT case exemplifies the importance of legal advocacy in challenging gender-based discrimination and seeking redress for unequal treatment. It also underscores the significance of public support, media attention, and collective action in driving social change.

Conclusion

Gender equality and women's rights are essential elements of a just and equitable society. While progress has been made in promoting gender equality, challenges persist in various spheres. Legal frameworks, principles, and strategies play a crucial role in addressing these challenges and advancing women's rights. Continued efforts are needed at all levels to dismantle gender-based discrimination, challenge harmful social norms, and build a more inclusive and equal future for all. Remember, gender equality is not just a women's issue—it is a human rights issue that benefits society as a whole.

Racial and Ethnic Justice

Racial and ethnic justice is a critical area of study within legal studies. It addresses the inequalities and injustices faced by marginalized racial and ethnic groups, and seeks to develop strategies and approaches to rectify these disparities. In this section, we will explore the principles, challenges, and solutions related to racial and ethnic justice.

Understanding Racial and Ethnic Justice

Racial and ethnic justice focuses on the fair treatment of individuals and groups, regardless of their racial or ethnic background. It seeks to eliminate discrimination, prejudice, and biases that hinder the progress and well-being of marginalized communities.

Historically, racial and ethnic minority groups have faced systemic discrimination and social disadvantages in many societies. This has manifested in various forms, such as racial profiling, unequal access to employment and education, disproportionate representation in the criminal justice system, and limited political participation.

Racial and ethnic justice aims to challenge and address these inequalities by promoting equal opportunities,representation, rights, and dignity for all individuals, irrespective of their racial or ethnic identity.

Legal Frameworks for Racial and Ethnic Justice

Many legal frameworks exist to protect and promote racial and ethnic justice. Here, we will discuss some key legal principles and tools that contribute to the pursuit of racial and ethnic justice.

Civil Rights Act of 1964:   The Civil Rights Act of 1964 is a landmark piece of legislation in the United States that prohibits discrimination on the basis of race, color, religion, sex, or national origin in public accommodations, employment, and federally funded programs. It established the Equal Employment Opportunity Commission (EEOC) to investigate and enforce compliance with anti-discrimination laws.

Equal Protection Clause: The Equal Protection Clause, found in the Fourteenth Amendment of the U.S. Constitution, ensures that all individuals are granted equal protection under the law. It prohibits the government from denying any person within its jurisdiction equal protection of the laws. This clause has been instrumental in challenging discriminatory policies and practices.

International Conventions and Treaties: Internationally, several conventions and treaties address racial and ethnic discrimination. The International Convention on the Elimination of All Forms of Racial Discrimination (ICERD), adopted by the United Nations General Assembly in 1965, aims to eliminate racial discrimination and ensure equal treatment for all races and ethnicities. It requires state parties to prohibit racial discrimination and take measures to promote understanding, tolerance, and equality among different racial and ethnic groups.

Challenges in Achieving Racial and Ethnic Justice

Despite the existence of legal frameworks, achieving racial and ethnic justice faces numerous challenges. Here, we will explore some of the obstacles and complexities involved.

Implicit Bias: Implicit biases are unconscious attitudes, beliefs, and stereotypes that affect our understanding and interactions with individuals from different racial and ethnic backgrounds. These biases can influence decision-making processes, perpetuating discriminatory practices even when explicit laws exist against such behavior.

Structural Racism: Structural racism refers to the ways in which societal systems, institutions, and policies disproportionately disadvantage racial and ethnic minority groups. It is embedded in the very fabric of social, economic, and political structures, making it challenging to identify and eradicate.

Intersectionality: Intersectionality acknowledges that individuals may experience overlapping forms of discrimination and oppression based on their race, ethnicity, gender, sexuality, socio-economic status, and other identities.

Recognizing and addressing the complexities of intersecting identities is essential in achieving racial and ethnic justice.

Promoting Racial and Ethnic Justice

Efforts to promote racial and ethnic justice require a multi-faceted approach. Here are some strategies, initiatives, and areas of focus that contribute to the advancement of racial and ethnic justice.

Community Engagement: Engaging with communities and empowering voices from racial and ethnic minority groups is crucial in shaping policies and practices that address their unique needs and challenges. Community-based organizations, grassroots movements, and advocacy groups play a vital role in raising awareness, mobilizing support, and driving policy change.

Education and Awareness: Education is a powerful tool in combating racial and ethnic discrimination. Incorporating diverse perspectives in educational curricula, promoting cultural competence, and raising awareness about historical and contemporary racism can foster understanding and empathy among individuals.

Policy Reform: Advocating for policy reforms that address systemic barriers and discrimination is essential for achieving racial and ethnic justice. Reforms may include criminal justice reforms, educational equity, affordable housing, voting rights protections, and employment opportunities.

Data Collection and Analysis: Collecting disaggregated data on race and ethnicity can help identify disparities, monitor progress, and inform evidence-based policies. Analyzing data through an intersectional lens is essential in understanding the unique challenges faced by different racial and ethnic minority groups and developing effective solutions.

Case Study: Affirmative Action

Affirmative action is a policy that seeks to promote equal opportunities for historically marginalized groups, including racial and ethnic minorities, in education and employment. By considering an individual's race or ethnicity as a factor in decision-making, affirmative action aims to address historical and ongoing discrimination.

Proponents argue that affirmative action is essential in creating a more equitable society by providing opportunities for those who have faced systemic barriers. Critics contend that it perpetuates reverse discrimination and undermines meritocracy.

The Supreme Court of the United States has issued several rulings on the constitutionality of affirmative action. In the landmark case of Grutter v. Bollinger (2003), the Court upheld the use of race as one factor among many in college admissions, as long as it was used for the purpose of achieving a diverse student body. However, subsequent decisions have placed limitations on the extent to which race can be considered in admissions processes.

The debate surrounding affirmative action raises important questions about the balance between promoting racial and ethnic justice and the principles of fairness and meritocracy. It also highlights the challenges and complexities involved in addressing historical disparities and creating inclusive opportunities for marginalized communities.

Conclusion

Racial and ethnic justice is a crucial component of legal studies. This section has explored the principles, challenges, and strategies involved in promoting racial and ethnic justice. By understanding the legal frameworks, identifying obstacles, and implementing effective strategies, we can work towards a more equitable and just society that values and supports individuals from all racial and ethnic backgrounds.

LGBTQ+ Rights and Social Justice

In this section, we will explore the ethical issues surrounding LGBTQ+ rights and the pursuit of social justice. The lesbian, gay, bisexual, transgender, and queer (LGBTQ+) community has faced significant challenges throughout history, including legal discrimination, social stigma, and limited access to rights and privileges. However, there have been significant advancements in recognizing and protecting the rights of LGBTQ+ individuals in recent years. We will discuss the moral and ethical foundations for LGBTQ+ rights, as well as the ongoing struggles and concerns faced by this community.

The Moral and Ethical Foundations of LGBTQ+ Rights

The fight for LGBTQ+ rights is rooted in principles of equality, non-discrimination, and human rights. The moral argument in favor of LGBTQ+ rights asserts that all individuals, regardless of their sexual orientation or gender identity, should be treated with dignity, respect, and equal protection under the law. Furthermore, LGBTQ+ individuals have the right to live authentically and express their identities without fear of discrimination or harm.

Ethical theories that support LGBTQ+ rights include:

+ **Utilitarianism:** This ethical theory emphasizes maximizing overall happiness and well-being. From a utilitarian perspective, granting LGBTQ+ individuals equal rights and protections would promote greater happiness and well-being for society as a whole.

+ **Rights-based ethics:** This ethical framework recognizes that all individuals have inherent rights, including the right to life, liberty, and the pursuit of happiness. From a rights-based perspective, LGBTQ+ individuals have the same fundamental rights as anyone else and should be afforded equal protection and opportunities.

+ **Social contract theory:** This theory asserts that individuals agree to live within a society and follow certain rules and norms in exchange for the benefits provided by that society. From a social contract perspective, LGBTQ+ individuals are entitled to the same rights and privileges as other members of society.

Legal Advances in LGBTQ+ Rights

Over the past few decades, there have been significant legal advancements in LGBTQ+ rights around the world. Some key legal developments include:

+ **Decriminalization of homosexuality:** Many countries have decriminalized consensual same-sex sexual activity, overturning archaic laws that criminalized homosexuality.

+ **Recognition of same-sex marriage:** A growing number of countries have legalized same-sex marriage, granting LGBTQ+ couples the same legal rights and benefits as heterosexual couples.

+ **Protection against discrimination:** Laws have been enacted in various jurisdictions to protect LGBTQ+ individuals from discrimination in employment, housing, healthcare, and other areas.

+ **Gender identity recognition:** Some countries have implemented legal frameworks to legally recognize and protect the gender identity of transgender and non-binary individuals.

Despite these legal advancements, challenges and inequalities persist. Many countries still have laws that criminalize same-sex relationships, transgender individuals face significant barriers in obtaining legal recognition of their gender identity, and LGBTQ+ individuals continue to face discrimination and violence in their everyday lives.

Current Challenges and Concerns

While progress has been made in securing legal rights and protections for LGBTQ+ individuals, there are ongoing challenges and concerns that need to be addressed. Some of these include:

- **Violence and discrimination:** LGBTQ+ individuals, particularly transgender women of color, continue to face disproportionate rates of violence and discrimination. Hate crimes, harassment, and bullying are still prevalent issues that need to be addressed.

- **Healthcare disparities:** LGBTQ+ individuals often face barriers to accessing quality healthcare, including prejudice from healthcare providers and limited access to culturally competent care.

- **Conversion therapy:** Many jurisdictions still allow or tolerate the practice of conversion therapy, which seeks to change an individual's sexual orientation or gender identity. This practice has been widely discredited by medical and psychological professionals and poses significant risks to the well-being of LGBTQ+ individuals.

- **Intersectionality:** LGBTQ+ individuals also intersect with other marginalized identities, such as race, ethnicity, socioeconomic status, and disability. It is crucial to recognize and address the unique challenges faced by LGBTQ+ individuals who experience multiple forms of discrimination.

Promoting LGBTQ+ Rights and Social Justice

Promoting LGBTQ+ rights and social justice requires a multi-faceted approach. Some strategies that can be adopted include:

- **Legislative reforms:** Advocacy for the enactment of comprehensive anti-discrimination laws that protect LGBTQ+ individuals in all aspects of life, including employment, housing, education, and healthcare.

+ **Education and awareness:** Promoting education and awareness about LGBTQ+ issues, including providing accurate information about sexual orientation, gender identity, and the impacts of discrimination and stigma.

+ **Combatting stereotypes:** Challenging and dismantling negative stereotypes and biases through media representation, education programs, and public outreach.

+ **Supporting LGBTQ+ organizations:** Supporting organizations that provide resources, support, and advocacy for LGBTQ+ individuals can make a significant impact in advancing their rights and promoting social justice.

+ **Intersectional approach:** Recognizing and addressing the intersecting forms of discrimination faced by LGBTQ+ individuals who also belong to other marginalized communities.

Case Study: Marriage Equality

Marriage equality has been one of the most significant advancements in LGBTQ+ rights globally. The recognition of same-sex marriage has provided legal and societal benefits to thousands of LGBTQ+ couples. This case study explores the ethical considerations surrounding marriage equality.

One of the primary ethical arguments in favor of marriage equality is the principle of equal treatment. Denying same-sex couples the right to marry is seen as a form of discrimination based on sexual orientation, which goes against the principles of equality and non-discrimination.

Opponents of marriage equality often cite religious or cultural beliefs to justify their stance. They argue that marriage should be reserved for heterosexual couples based on traditional interpretations of religious texts or societal norms. However, proponents of marriage equality counter that legal marriage is a civil institution and should not be dictated by religious or cultural beliefs.

The fight for marriage equality has involved legal challenges, public campaigns, and advocacy efforts. Ultimately, the recognition of same-sex marriage not only affirms the rights of LGBTQ+ individuals but also contributes to a more inclusive and equitable society.

Conclusion

The struggle for LGBTQ+ rights and social justice is an ongoing battle. It requires a commitment to promoting equality, challenging discrimination, and advocating for the rights and well-being of LGBTQ+ individuals. By recognizing the moral and ethical foundations of LGBTQ+ rights and addressing the current challenges and concerns, we can work towards creating a society that embraces diversity, promotes equality, and ensures social justice for all.

Environmental Justice and Sustainable Development

Environmental justice and sustainable development are two interconnected concepts that play a crucial role in addressing the environmental challenges of our time. This section will explore the principles, issues, and initiatives related to environmental justice and sustainable development, focusing on their significance in the field of legal studies and the broader society.

Understanding Environmental Justice

Environmental justice refers to the fair distribution of environmental benefits and burdens among all members of society, regardless of their race, socioeconomic status, or other characteristics. It recognizes that marginalized communities often bear a disproportionate burden of environmental hazards and lack access to environmental resources and amenities.

Environmental Injustice Examples   To illustrate the concept of environmental injustice, consider the following examples:

- **Toxic Waste Disposal:** Historically, low-income communities and communities of color have been more likely to be located near hazardous waste sites and incinerators, leading to increased exposure to toxic pollutants.

- **Air Pollution:** Poorer neighborhoods and communities with predominantly minority populations often experience higher levels of air pollution due to the presence of industrial facilities and traffic congestion.

- **Limited Access to Clean Water:** In some regions, marginalized communities may lack access to clean and safe drinking water, while more affluent communities have abundant water resources.

These examples highlight the inequities in the distribution of environmental resources and the disproportionate burden of environmental risks faced by marginalized communities.

Principles of Environmental Justice

Environmental justice is guided by several key principles, which serve as a foundation for addressing environmental inequalities and promoting social equity. These principles are:

- **Fairness:** Environmental benefits and burdens should be distributed equitably among all members of society, without discrimination or bias.

- **Inclusion:** Marginalized communities should have meaningful participation in decision-making processes related to environmental policies and projects that affect their well-being.

- **Accountability:** Individuals and organizations responsible for environmental harm should be held accountable for their actions and provide remedies to affected communities.

- **Precaution:** Precautionary measures should be taken to prevent harm to public health and the environment, especially when scientific evidence is uncertain or incomplete.

These principles serve as a framework for developing policies, laws, and initiatives that aim to rectify environmental injustices and promote environmental equity.

Sustainable Development and Environmental Justice

Sustainable development is an approach that seeks to balance economic growth, social well-being, and environmental protection to meet the needs of the present generation without compromising the ability of future generations to meet their own needs. It recognizes the complex interconnections between society, the economy, and the environment.

The Three Pillars of Sustainable Development   Sustainable development is often conceptualized based on three interconnected pillars:

- **Environmental Pillar:**   This pillar emphasizes the protection and conservation of natural resources, the mitigation of environmental degradation, and the promotion of sustainable resource management practices.

+ **Social Pillar:** The social pillar focuses on equity, inclusivity, and social well-being, ensuring that economic development benefits all members of society and leaves no one behind.

+ **Economic Pillar:** The economic pillar emphasizes the need for sustainable economic growth, which takes into account environmental limits and internalizes the costs of resource use and pollution.

The integration of these three pillars is essential for achieving sustainability and addressing the challenges posed by environmental degradation and societal inequities.

Environmental Justice and Sustainable Development Initiatives

Various initiatives and frameworks have been developed to promote environmental justice and sustainable development. These initiatives aim to address the unequal distribution of environmental benefits and burdens, promote access to environmental resources, and foster long-term sustainability. Some of these initiatives include:

Environmental Impact Assessments Environmental Impact Assessments (EIAs) are a widely used tool to assess the potential environmental, social, and health impacts of proposed projects or policies. EIAs help ensure that decision-makers consider potential impacts on marginalized communities and involve public participation in the decision-making process. They provide an opportunity for affected communities to voice their concerns and propose alternatives that minimize negative impacts.

Community-Based Environmental Management Community-based environmental management approaches involve actively engaging communities in the decision-making processes related to environmental issues. These approaches recognize that communities possess valuable traditional knowledge and insights about their local ecosystems. By involving communities in resource management, policy development, and conservation efforts, these initiatives empower marginalized groups and promote environmental justice.

Environmental Laws and Regulations Environmental laws and regulations play a crucial role in ensuring environmental justice and sustainable development. These laws set standards for pollution control, natural resource management, and environmental impact assessments. They also provide legal mechanisms for holding polluters accountable and protecting the rights of affected communities. Strengthening and enforcing environmental laws and regulations are essential steps towards achieving environmental justice.

Current Challenges

Despite the progress made in addressing environmental justice and promoting sustainable development, several challenges persist. Some of the key challenges include:

Inadequate Implementation and Enforcement The implementation and enforcement of environmental laws and regulations often face challenges due to resource constraints, lack of capacity, and limited political will. This can lead to inequalities in environmental protection and a disproportionate burden on marginalized communities.

Climate Change and Disproportionate Impacts Climate change exacerbates existing environmental injustices, as marginalized communities are often more vulnerable to its impacts. Climate change-related events, such as extreme weather events and sea-level rise, can lead to displacement, loss of livelihoods, and exacerbate socio-economic disparities.

Lack of Access to Environmental Information Access to accurate and timely environmental information is essential for effective decision-making and meaningful public participation. However, marginalized communities often lack access to such information, limiting their ability to engage in environmental decision-making processes.

Conclusion

Environmental justice and sustainable development are integral components of a just and equitable society. Recognizing the importance of fair distribution of environmental benefits and burdens and promoting sustainable practices can contribute to a more inclusive and sustainable future. By addressing the challenges and working towards meaningful solutions, we can ensure a more equitable and sustainable world for current and future generations.

Social Justice and Access to Justice

In this section, we will explore the important connection between social justice and access to justice. Social justice is the concept of fairness and equality in society, while access to justice refers to the availability and affordability of legal services and resources. Together, they contribute to creating a more equitable and just society. We will discuss the challenges and barriers to access to justice, examine strategies for promoting access to justice, and highlight the role of technology in enhancing access to justice.

Challenges to Access to Justice

Access to justice is a fundamental principle of a fair legal system. However, there are various challenges and barriers that prevent individuals and marginalized communities from accessing justice. Some of these challenges include:

1. **Financial Barriers:** The cost of legal services can be prohibitively high, making it difficult for low-income individuals to seek legal assistance. Legal fees, court costs, and other expenses associated with legal proceedings can create a significant financial burden.

2. **Geographical Barriers:** Many individuals, particularly those living in remote areas, face geographical barriers when it comes to accessing legal services. Limited availability of legal professionals and courts can make it challenging for individuals to access justice.

3. **Language and Cultural Barriers:** Language and cultural differences can act as barriers to accessing justice. Limited availability of legal services in languages other than the official language of a country can hinder access. Additionally, cultural norms and traditions may impact an individual's willingness to seek legal assistance.

4. **Lack of Legal Awareness and Education:** Limited awareness about one's legal rights and the legal system can prevent individuals from seeking justice. Lack of legal education and information contributes to a power imbalance, making it difficult for individuals to navigate the legal system.

5. **Discrimination and Bias:** Systemic discrimination and bias can create barriers to accessing justice, particularly for marginalized communities. Discrimination based on race, gender, ethnicity, religion, or socioeconomic status can result in unequal treatment within the legal system.

Strategies for Promoting Access to Justice

To promote access to justice and ensure social justice, various strategies and initiatives have been developed. These strategies aim to address the challenges mentioned earlier and create a more inclusive and equitable legal system. Some of these strategies include:

1. **Legal Aid Programs**: Legal aid programs provide free or low-cost legal services to individuals who cannot afford legal representation. These programs help bridge the financial gap and ensure access to justice for low-income individuals.

2. **Pro Bono Services**: Pro bono services involve lawyers providing free legal assistance to individuals in need. Pro bono work helps expand access to justice by leveraging the skills and expertise of legal professionals to support marginalized communities.

3. **Community Legal Education**: Community legal education initiatives aim to increase awareness and understanding of legal rights among the general public. These programs provide information about the legal system, available resources, and avenues for seeking justice.

4. **Technology and Online Legal Services**: Technology, particularly digital platforms and online services, can enhance access to justice. Online legal platforms provide information, resources, and assistance, making legal services more accessible to individuals who face geographical or financial barriers.

5. **Legal Empowerment of Marginalized Communities**: Empowering marginalized communities through legal education and resources is crucial for promoting access to justice. Community-based organizations and NGOs play a vital role in providing legal support and empowering individuals to advocate for their rights.

Role of Technology in Access to Justice

Technology has revolutionized many aspects of our lives, including access to justice. It has the potential to address several barriers and enhance access to justice for individuals and communities. Here are some ways technology is being used for access to justice:

1. **Online Legal Information and Resources:** Digital platforms provide access to comprehensive legal information, resources, and self-help tools. Individuals can access legal documents, guidelines, and educational materials to better navigate the legal system.

2. **Virtual Legal Services:** Virtual legal services, such as online consultations and videoconferencing, enable individuals to consult with legal professionals without geographical limitations. This is particularly beneficial for individuals in remote areas or those with mobility constraints.

3. **Electronic Filing and Case Management:** Electronic filing systems and digital case management platforms streamline legal processes, reducing paperwork and administrative burdens. This improves efficiency and access to court services.

4. **Legal Chatbots and AI-Assisted Services:** AI-powered chatbots and virtual assistants can provide basic legal guidance and support, ensuring access to justice for individuals who cannot afford legal representation. These tools can help answer common legal questions and provide information on available legal resources.

5. **Online Dispute Resolution:** Online dispute resolution platforms offer an alternative to traditional court proceedings, providing a more accessible and cost-effective means of resolving legal disputes. These platforms facilitate negotiation, mediation, and arbitration processes online.

While technology offers significant opportunities for enhancing access to justice, it is essential to address the digital divide and ensure that marginalized communities have the necessary resources and skills to benefit from these advancements.

Conclusion

Access to justice is a crucial aspect of social justice and an essential requirement for a fair and equitable society. Addressing the challenges to access to justice and implementing strategies for promoting access to justice is vital for creating a legal system that is inclusive and responsive to the needs of all individuals and communities. Technology, when used effectively and equitably, can play a significant role in enhancing access to justice and bridging the gap between marginalized communities and the legal system. By promoting social justice and ensuring access to justice, we can work towards creating a more equitable, just, and sustainable world for everyone.

Social Justice and Marginalized Communities

In the pursuit of a more equitable and just world, it is imperative to address the specific challenges faced by marginalized communities. Throughout history, certain groups have been systematically disadvantaged and have faced discrimination and oppression based on factors such as race, gender, sexuality, socioeconomic status, disability, and more. This section will explore the ethical issues surrounding social justice and the plight of marginalized communities, as well as the legal strategies and initiatives aimed at addressing these challenges.

Understanding Marginalized Communities

To effectively advocate for social justice, it is important to first understand the concept of marginalized communities. Marginalization refers to the social, economic, and political exclusion experienced by certain groups due to their identity or characteristics that are considered outside the societal norm. Marginalized communities often face structural disadvantages, limited access to resources, discrimination, and social stigmatization.

Examples of marginalized communities include racial and ethnic minorities, indigenous populations, LGBTQ+ individuals, women, people with disabilities, immigrants and refugees, and individuals experiencing poverty. Understanding the unique struggles faced by these communities is crucial in developing targeted solutions and advocating for their rights.

Social Justice and Intersectionality

In the pursuit of social justice for marginalized communities, it is important to recognize the intersecting nature of identities and oppressions. Intersectionality, a concept popularized by scholar Kimberlé Crenshaw, emphasizes that individuals can experience multiple forms of oppression simultaneously, resulting in unique and compounded disadvantages.

For instance, a woman of color may face discrimination based on both her race and gender, and the resulting intersectional oppression can have a profound impact on various aspects of her life, including access to education, healthcare, employment, and housing. Recognizing intersectionality is crucial in addressing the multifaceted challenges faced by marginalized communities and ensuring that efforts to promote social justice are inclusive and comprehensive.

Challenges Faced by Marginalized Communities

Marginalized communities face a myriad of challenges that hinder their ability to access justice, resources, and opportunities. Some key challenges include:

1. **Systemic Discrimination:** Marginalized communities often bear the brunt of systemic discrimination, which affects their access to education, employment, healthcare, housing, and justice. Discriminatory practices and policies perpetuate social and economic inequalities.

2. **Poverty and Socioeconomic Inequality:** Marginalized communities are disproportionately affected by poverty and experience higher levels of socioeconomic inequality. Limited access to education, healthcare, and employment opportunities perpetuate cycles of poverty and exclusion.

3. **Violence and Discrimination:** Many marginalized communities face higher rates of violence, including hate crimes, police brutality, and domestic violence. Discrimination and prejudice based on race, gender, and sexuality contribute to these alarming statistics.

4. **Health Disparities:** Marginalized communities often experience significant health disparities. Factors such as limited access to healthcare, environmental inequalities, and discrimination contribute to higher rates of chronic illnesses, mental health issues, and shorter life expectancies.

5. **Education Inequity:** Marginalized communities often confront educational inequities, including disparities in funding, resources, and quality of education. This perpetuates existing social and economic inequalities and limits opportunities for upward mobility.

Legal Strategies for Social Justice

To address the challenges faced by marginalized communities and promote social justice, legal strategies play a crucial role. Here are some key approaches and initiatives:

1. **Anti-Discrimination Laws:** Governments can enact and enforce laws that protect marginalized communities from discrimination. These laws prohibit discrimination in various domains such as employment, housing, and public accommodations, and may also cover factors such as race, gender, disability, and sexual orientation.

2. **Affirmative Action:** Affirmative action policies seek to address historical disadvantages faced by marginalized communities by promoting equal opportunities in education and employment. These policies aim to counteract systemic discrimination and create a level playing field.

3. **Human Rights Advocacy:** International and domestic human rights frameworks provide a basis for advocating for the rights of marginalized communities. Human rights organizations, activists, and legal professionals play a crucial role in holding governments accountable for human rights violations and promoting social justice.

4. **Community-Based Legal Services:** Providing marginalized communities with access to legal representation and resources is vital. Community-based legal services, such as legal aid clinics and pro bono programs, offer assistance to individuals who might not otherwise afford legal representation.

5. **Intersectional Policy Approaches:** Recognizing the intersecting identities and oppressions experienced by marginalized communities, policymakers can adopt intersectional approaches that address the specific needs and challenges faced by each community. This involves taking into account the unique experiences of individuals at the intersections of race, gender, sexuality, and other identities.

6. **Empowering Marginalized Voices:** Inclusive decision-making processes and effective representation of marginalized communities are crucial in promoting social justice. Empowering marginalized voices involves giving them a seat at the table, amplifying their perspectives, and involving them in shaping policies and initiatives that affect their lives.

Promoting Social Justice in Practice

Promoting social justice for marginalized communities requires collective action and a commitment to change. Here are some practical steps that individuals, organizations, and communities can take:

1. **Education and Awareness:** Educate yourself and others about the challenges faced by marginalized communities. Raise awareness about the importance of social justice and the impact of systemic discrimination.

2. **Advocacy and Activism:** Stand up against injustices and advocate for policy changes that promote equality and social justice. Support grassroots organizations and initiatives that work towards empowering marginalized communities.

3. **Promote Inclusivity:** Foster inclusive spaces that value diversity and promote equal opportunities. Challenge discriminatory practices and biases within your personal and professional spheres.

4. **Allyship:** Use your privilege to amplify the voices of marginalized communities. Act as an ally by supporting and advocating alongside marginalized individuals and communities.

5. **Legislative Engagement:** Engage with the legislative process by staying informed about proposed policies and legislation that impact marginalized communities. Contact your elected representatives to voice your support for social justice initiatives.

6. **Support Marginalized-Owned Businesses:** Recognize and support businesses owned by individuals from marginalized communities. Economic empowerment can contribute to breaking cycles of poverty and exclusion.

By working collectively to address the unique challenges faced by marginalized communities, we can foster a more equitable and just society. Promoting social justice requires ongoing commitment, continuous advocacy, and a willingness to challenge existing power structures and systems of oppression.

Further Reading

1. Crenshaw, Kimberlé. *Demarginalizing the Intersection of Race and Sex: A Black Feminist Critique of Antidiscrimination Doctrine, Feminist Theory and Antiracist Politics*. University of Chicago Legal Forum, 1989, pp. 139-167.

2. Davis, Angela Y. *Women, Race & Class*. Vintage, 1983.

3. United Nations Human Rights. *Racial and Ethnic Discrimination*. Office of the High Commissioner for Human Rights.

4. MacKinnon, Catharine A. *Toward a Feminist Theory of the State*. Harvard University Press, 1989.

5. Human Rights Watch. *World Report 2021*. Human Rights Watch, 2021.

6. Sen, Amartya. *Development as Freedom*. Anchor Books, 1999.

Exercises

1. Research and analyze a real-life case where a marginalized community successfully advocated for their rights. What strategies did they employ, and what were the outcomes?

2. Explore the legal and ethical implications of a specific social justice issue affecting marginalized communities, such as racial profiling, gender-based violence, or indigenous land rights. Consider the key principles and legal frameworks that can be applied to address the issue.

3. Identify a public policy or legislative proposal that can positively impact a marginalized community. Develop an advocacy plan to promote this proposal and engage with relevant stakeholders.

4. Conduct a comparative analysis of different countries' approaches to promoting social justice for marginalized communities. Consider their legal frameworks, policy initiatives, and outcomes.

Conclusion

Promoting social justice and advocating for the rights of marginalized communities is essential for creating a more equitable and just society. By understanding the challenges faced by these communities, recognizing intersecting oppressions, and employing targeted legal strategies, we can work towards dismantling systemic discrimination and creating a world where everyone has equal opportunities and access to justice. It is our collective responsibility to stand up against injustice and actively contribute to the ongoing fight for social justice.

Ethical Issues in Criminal Justice

Ethics and the Criminal Justice System

Principles of Criminal Justice Ethics

In the field of legal studies, understanding the principles of criminal justice ethics is essential when examining the ethical considerations that guide the behavior of individuals within the criminal justice system. Criminal justice ethics encapsulate the moral guidelines that criminal justice professionals, such as law enforcement officers, attorneys, and correctional officers, must adhere to while performing their duties. These principles serve as the foundation for maintaining integrity, fairness, and justice within the criminal justice system.

Integrity

Integrity is a fundamental principle of criminal justice ethics. It refers to the adherence to moral and ethical principles, honesty, and the consistent demonstration of ethical behavior. Criminal justice professionals must act with integrity to earn and maintain public trust. This involves conducting themselves in a manner that upholds the highest standards of honesty and truthfulness. Acting without integrity can lead to a breakdown of trust in the criminal justice system, hindering its ability to effectively serve the community.

Justice

Justice is another key principle that guides criminal justice ethics. It entails ensuring fairness, equality, and impartiality in the treatment of individuals involved in the criminal justice system. The principle of justice requires that criminal justice professionals uphold the rights of both victims and offenders and ensure that the punishment fits the crime. Criminal justice professionals must be objective and impartial in their decision-making, refraining from any bias or discrimination based on race, gender, social status, or any other irrelevant factors.

Accountability

Accountability is a principle that holds criminal justice professionals responsible for their actions and decisions. It requires individuals within the criminal justice system to answer for their conduct and accept the consequences of their actions. Accountability fosters transparency, trust, and public confidence in the criminal justice system. Criminal justice professionals are responsible for their responsibilities and obligations and must be willing to accept any criticism or consequences when their actions deviate from ethical standards.

Respect for Law and Due Process

Respect for law and due process is a principle that underpins the criminal justice system. Criminal justice professionals must uphold the rule of law, ensuring that all individuals are treated fairly, regardless of their guilt or innocence. This principle requires adherence to legal procedures and protections, such as the presumption of innocence, the right to legal representation, and fair and timely trials. Respecting due process safeguards the rights of individuals and maintains the integrity of the criminal justice system.

Professionalism

Professionalism is an essential principle of criminal justice ethics. It involves maintaining a high level of competence, expertise, and ethical behavior in all professional interactions. Criminal justice professionals must demonstrate professionalism by adhering to professional codes of conduct, maintaining confidentiality, and continually developing their skills and knowledge. Professionalism promotes trust and confidence in the criminal justice system and promotes the effective and ethical delivery of justice.

Use of Force

The use of force is a complex and delicate area within criminal justice ethics. While criminal justice professionals may need to use force to protect themselves or others, it must be done responsibly and within the limits of the law. The use of force should always be a last resort, employed only when necessary and proportional to the threat faced. Criminal justice professionals must be trained in de-escalation techniques to minimize the need for force and ensure that force is used ethically and judiciously.

Ethical Decision-Making

Ethical decision-making is a crucial skill for criminal justice professionals. They often encounter situations that require them to make difficult choices that have ethical implications. To make ethical decisions, criminal justice professionals should consider the principles outlined above, weigh the potential consequences of their actions, consult with colleagues, and adhere to professional codes of conduct. Ethical decision-making ensures that criminal justice professionals act in the best interest of justice and the community they serve.

Challenges in Criminal Justice Ethics

Criminal justice professionals face numerous challenges when attempting to adhere to the principles of ethics. These challenges can include the pressure to prioritize conviction rates over fairness, the temptation to abuse power or engage in corrupt practices, and the difficulties associated with maintaining personal biases in the decision-making process. Additionally, the use of new technologies and social media can present unforeseen ethical dilemmas. Criminal justice professionals must be aware of these challenges and actively work to address them to uphold the principles of criminal justice ethics.

Case Study: Body-Worn Cameras

One contemporary example highlighting the intersection of criminal justice ethics and technology is the use of body-worn cameras by law enforcement officers. Body-worn cameras have been introduced to increase transparency, accountability, and to improve the trust between law enforcement and the communities they serve. However, the ethical implications of body-worn cameras are multifaceted.

On one hand, body-worn cameras can help protect the integrity of the criminal justice system by providing an accurate account of interactions between law enforcement officers and the public. This can help ensure that individuals' rights are respected, inappropriate use of force is minimized, and accusations of misconduct are thoroughly investigated.

On the other hand, the use of body-worn cameras raises concerns about privacy rights, the potential for selective editing or misinterpretation of footage, and the impact on vulnerable and marginalized communities. Balancing the need for transparency and accountability with privacy rights and the potential for unintended consequences requires careful consideration and clear policies regarding the proper use, storage, and access to body-worn camera footage.

Criminal justice professionals and policymakers must engage in ongoing ethical discussions to address these concerns and develop guidelines and protocols that prioritize the principles of criminal justice ethics while effectively utilizing new technologies in law enforcement.

Resources for Further Reading

1. Banks, C. (2020). Criminal Justice Ethics: Theory and Practice. Sage Publications. 2. Pollock, J. M. (2020). Ethical Dilemmas and Decisions in Criminal Justice. Cengage Learning. 3. Peak, K. J. (2017). Justice Administration: Police, Courts, and Corrections Management. Pearson.

Key Terms

1. Integrity 2. Justice 3. Accountability 4. Respect for Law and Due Process 5. Professionalism 6. Use of Force 7. Ethical Decision-Making 8. Body-Worn Cameras

Self-Reflection Questions

1. How can criminal justice professionals balance the need for justice with the ethical consideration of fairness? 2. What steps can be taken to promote accountability within the criminal justice system? 3. How does the use of body-worn cameras impact the principles of criminal justice ethics? 4. Why is ethical decision-making important in the criminal justice field? 5. What challenges do criminal justice professionals face when attempting to uphold ethical standards?

Role and Responsibilities of Criminal Justice Professionals

In the field of criminal justice, professionals play a critical role in maintaining law and order, protecting the rights of individuals, and upholding the principles of justice. Criminal justice professionals, including law enforcement officers, prosecutors, defense attorneys, judges, and correctional officers, have distinct roles and responsibilities that contribute to the effective functioning of the criminal justice system. In this section, we will explore the various roles and responsibilities of these professionals and discuss the ethical considerations involved in their work.

Law Enforcement Officers

Law enforcement officers are on the front lines of the criminal justice system. They are responsible for preventing and investigating crimes, apprehending suspects, and maintaining public safety. The role of law enforcement officers includes:

+ **Crime Prevention:** Law enforcement officers strive to prevent crimes by actively patrolling their assigned areas, conducting surveillance, and engaging with the community. They may implement community policing strategies to build trust and establish cooperative partnerships with community members.

+ **Crime Investigation:** When a crime occurs, law enforcement officers are responsible for conducting thorough investigations. They collect evidence, interview witnesses and suspects, and ensure that all relevant information is documented accurately.

+ **Apprehension of Suspects:** Law enforcement officers have the authority to apprehend individuals suspected of committing crimes. They must exercise caution and ensure the safety of both the individuals involved and themselves.

+ **Protecting Public Safety:** Maintaining public safety is one of the primary responsibilities of law enforcement officers. They respond to emergencies, address public disturbances, and enforce laws to prevent harm to individuals and property.

The role of law enforcement officers requires ethical decision-making and adherence to professional standards. They must respect the rights of individuals, use appropriate force only when necessary, and uphold the principles of fairness and impartiality.

Prosecutors

Prosecutors play a critical role in the criminal justice system by representing the government in criminal cases. Their primary responsibility is to seek justice and ensure that the guilty are held accountable. The role of prosecutors includes:

+ **Case Evaluation:** Prosecutors review evidence, statements from witnesses, and any other relevant information to determine whether there is enough evidence to proceed with a criminal case. They must assess the strength of the case and decide whether to pursue charges.

+ **Case Preparation:** Prosecutors gather and organize evidence, interview witnesses, and develop a strategy for presenting the case in court. They work closely with law enforcement officers to ensure a thorough investigation.

+ **Courtroom Representation:** Prosecutors represent the government's interests in court. They present evidence, examine witnesses, and make arguments to convince the judge or jury of the defendant's guilt. They must also ensure that the defendant's rights are protected during the trial.

+ **Negotiating Plea Bargains:** Prosecutors have the authority to negotiate plea bargains with defendants. They may offer reduced charges or sentencing recommendations in exchange for the defendant's guilty plea. This allows for more efficient use of resources within the criminal justice system.

Prosecutors have a duty to seek justice and act in the best interests of the public. They must uphold ethical standards, ensure fairness in the criminal justice process, and protect the rights of both victims and defendants.

Defense Attorneys

Defense attorneys serve as advocates for individuals accused of committing crimes. Their role is to protect the rights of their clients and ensure a fair legal process. The responsibilities of defense attorneys include:

+ **Legal Advice and Counsel:** Defense attorneys provide legal advice to their clients and explain their rights throughout the criminal justice process. They assess the evidence against their clients and strategize the best course of action.

+ **Investigation and Discovery:** Defense attorneys investigate the charges against their clients, gather evidence, and examine the evidence presented by the prosecution. They may hire investigators or experts to support their case.

+ **Courtroom Representation:** Defense attorneys represent their clients in court proceedings. They cross-examine witnesses, challenge the prosecution's evidence, and present a defense strategy aimed at casting doubt on their client's guilt.

+ **Negotiating Plea Bargains:** Defense attorneys negotiate with prosecutors to secure the best possible outcome for their clients. They may advocate for reduced charges or sentencing recommendations, or negotiate for alternative resolutions such as diversion programs or community service.

Defense attorneys have a duty to zealously represent their clients, protect their rights, and ensure a fair legal process. They must maintain client confidentiality, avoid conflicts of interest, and act ethically in their interactions with prosecutors and the court.

Judges

Judges play a crucial role in the criminal justice system by ensuring fair and impartial adjudication. They have the power to interpret and apply the law, make determinations on legal issues, and impose appropriate sentences. The responsibilities of judges include:

+ **Case Management:** Judges oversee criminal cases from initial appearances to sentencing. They review motions and evidence, make decisions on pre-trial release or detainment, and manage the court calendar.

+ **Legal Decision-Making:** Judges apply the law to the facts of a case and make legal decisions. They rule on admissibility of evidence, resolve legal disputes, and issue rulings on motions brought by the prosecution or defense.

+ **Presiding over Trials:** Judges ensure that the trial proceedings are fair, orderly, and follow legal procedures. They rule on objections, provide jury instructions, and oversee the conduct of the trial.

+ **Sentencing:** Judges determine appropriate sentences for individuals convicted of crimes. They consider factors such as the severity of the offense, the defendant's criminal history, and any mitigating or aggravating circumstances.

Judges have a duty to be impartial, fair, and ensure the integrity of the legal process. They must apply the law objectively, protect the rights of all parties involved, and maintain public trust in the judiciary.

Correctional Officers

Correctional officers work in correctional facilities and are responsible for the custody, care, and control of incarcerated individuals. Their role focuses on maintaining safety and security within correctional institutions. The responsibilities of correctional officers include:

+ **Inmate Supervision:** Correctional officers monitor and supervise the activities of inmates within the facility. They enforce rules and regulations, prevent disturbances, and respond to emergencies.

+ **Safety and Security:** Correctional officers ensure the safety and security of the facility by conducting searches, maintaining order, and preventing escapes. They may also use appropriate force to maintain control in situations that pose a threat to the safety of inmates or staff.

+ **Rehabilitation and Reintegration:** Correctional officers play a role in the rehabilitation and reintegration of inmates. They may facilitate educational programs, vocational training, and counseling services to help prepare inmates for successful reentry into society.

+ **Record-Keeping:** Correctional officers document incidents, daily activities, and interactions with inmates. Accurate record-keeping is essential for maintaining accountability and ensuring the safety of both inmates and staff.

Correctional officers must uphold ethical standards and treat inmates with dignity and respect. They must also ensure their own safety and well-being while carrying out their responsibilities in a challenging and potentially dangerous environment.

In summary, criminal justice professionals play distinct roles and have specific responsibilities within the criminal justice system. Whether they are law enforcement officers, prosecutors, defense attorneys, judges, or correctional officers, these professionals must adhere to ethical principles, protect individual rights, and contribute to the pursuit of justice. Their work is essential in maintaining a fair and effective criminal justice system that serves the needs of society.

5. Ethical Issues in Criminal Justice

5.1 Ethical Dilemmas in Law Enforcement

Law enforcement agencies and individuals within these agencies often face complex ethical dilemmas in their day-to-day work. These ethical dilemmas arise due to the nature of their duties and the challenging situations they encounter. In this section, we will explore some of the common ethical dilemmas faced by law enforcement professionals and discuss potential strategies for addressing them.

Definition of Ethical Dilemmas in Law Enforcement

Ethical dilemmas in law enforcement refer to situations where law enforcement professionals encounter conflicting moral principles or obligations. These dilemmas often arise when an officer is confronted with a decision that could have conflicting outcomes, where adhering to one moral principle could result in violating another. For example, an officer may be faced with the dilemma of using force to subdue a suspect who poses a threat to public safety. While using force may be necessary to protect the public, it could also result in potential harm to the suspect.

Examples of Ethical Dilemmas in Law Enforcement

1. Use of Force: One of the most significant ethical dilemmas in law enforcement is the use of force. Officers are often faced with situations where they must make split-second decisions about using force to protect themselves or others. However, determining the appropriate level of force can be challenging, and officers may face dilemmas about whether to escalate or de-escalate the situation.

2. Racial Profiling: Another ethical dilemma that law enforcement professionals face is racial profiling. When officers engage in racial profiling, they unfairly target individuals based on their race or ethnicity. This poses a significant ethical issue as it violates the principles of fairness, justice, and equal treatment under the law.

3. Corruption and Bribery: Law enforcement professionals may also encounter ethical dilemmas related to corruption and bribery. They may be offered bribes or incentives to overlook or participate in illegal activities. Making the decision to act ethically and maintain their integrity in such situations can be challenging, especially if there are temptations of personal gain or pressures from colleagues.

Addressing Ethical Dilemmas in Law Enforcement

1. Training and Education: Providing law enforcement professionals with comprehensive training and education on ethics is crucial. By equipping officers with the knowledge and skills to navigate ethical dilemmas, they are better prepared to make informed decisions. This training should include scenario-based exercises, case studies, and discussions about ethical principles and their application in real-life situations.

2. Ethical Decision-Making Models: Implementing ethical decision-making models can provide guidance to law enforcement professionals when faced with ethical dilemmas. Models such as the Ethical Decision-Making Framework, which involves steps like gathering information, considering alternatives, and evaluating

consequences, can help officers analyze the ethical implications of their actions and make principled decisions.

3. Code of Ethics: Law enforcement agencies should have a clear and comprehensive code of ethics that outlines the expected standards of conduct for officers. This code should address specific ethical dilemmas commonly faced in law enforcement and provide guidelines for ethical decision-making. It should also include mechanisms for reporting ethical violations and protecting whistleblowers.

4. Supervision and Accountability: Supervisors in law enforcement agencies play a vital role in addressing ethical dilemmas. They should provide guidance and support to officers, conduct regular reviews of their actions, and hold them accountable for ethical misconduct. This includes implementing systems for reporting and addressing ethical violations, as well as providing opportunities for officers to seek guidance on ethical dilemmas.

5. Community Engagement: Building strong relationships between law enforcement agencies and the communities they serve is essential for addressing ethical dilemmas. Developing community-oriented policing practices can help foster trust, transparency, and accountability. Engaging in dialogue with community members and involving them in decision-making processes can provide valuable insights and perspectives on ethical issues.

Case Study: Use of Force

Consider a case where a law enforcement officer is called to respond to a domestic violence incident. Upon arrival, the officer encounters a highly agitated individual who is threatening to harm their partner with a weapon. The officer must quickly assess the situation and make a decision about the use of force.

In this scenario, the officer faces an ethical dilemma. On one hand, they have a duty to protect the potential victim and ensure public safety. On the other hand, using force could potentially result in harm or even death to the individual exhibiting violent behavior.

To address this dilemma, the officer should consider employing de-escalation techniques and attempting to defuse the situation by engaging in verbal communication. They can also consider backup or alternative strategies, such as calling in a specialized crisis intervention team. The officer should weigh the potential risks and benefits of using force and utilize the principles of proportionality, necessity, and reasonableness to guide their decision.

Resources and Further Reading

1. National Institute of Justice: "Ethics for Law Enforcement: Becoming an Ethical Police Officer" 2. Police Executive Research Forum: "Building Trust between the Police and the Citizens They Serve" 3. The Atlantic: "The Thorny Relationship Between Cops and Black Barbershops" 4. American Civil Liberties Union: "Racial Profiling" 5. U.S. Department of Justice: Community Oriented Policing Services

Key Takeaways

- Ethical dilemmas in law enforcement arise when conflicting moral principles or obligations are encountered. - Examples of ethical dilemmas in law enforcement include use of force, racial profiling, and corruption. - Addressing ethical dilemmas requires training, ethical decision-making models, codes of ethics, supervision and accountability, and community engagement. - The use of force is a significant ethical dilemma in law enforcement, and officers must consider de-escalation techniques, proportionality, and reasonableness when making decisions. - Further reading and resources are available to deepen understanding of ethical dilemmas in law enforcement.

5.2 Capital Punishment and Ethical Controversies

5.3 Policing and Ethical Challenges

Ethical Issues in Criminal Prosecution

In the field of legal studies, the ethical issues surrounding the practice of criminal prosecution are complex and multi-faceted. These ethical dilemmas arise from the fundamental responsibility of prosecutors to pursue justice while simultaneously upholding the rights of defendants. This section will explore some of the key ethical issues faced by prosecutors and provide insights into navigating these challenges.

Prosecutorial Discretion

Prosecutorial discretion refers to the power vested in prosecutors to make decisions regarding the initiation, continuation, and resolution of criminal cases. While this discretion allows prosecutors to prioritize cases and allocate resources effectively, it also presents ethical concerns. The exercise of discretion must be guided by principles of fairness, equality, and impartiality.

One ethical issue related to prosecutorial discretion is the potential for bias and discrimination. Prosecutors must ensure that their decisions are not influenced by factors such as race, gender, socioeconomic status, or political affiliations. Unconscious biases can lead to selective prosecution and injustice. To mitigate this issue, prosecutors can undergo implicit bias training and implement policies to promote unbiased decision-making.

Another ethical consideration is the appropriate use of prosecutorial discretion in cases involving non-violent offenses or minor infractions. The application of harsh penalties in such cases can disproportionately impact disadvantaged individuals and perpetuate social inequalities. Prosecutors should consider alternative approaches, such as diversion programs or restorative justice, to promote rehabilitation and reduce the burden on the criminal justice system.

Ensuring Due Process

Prosecutors have a constitutional obligation to uphold the due process rights of defendants, ensuring fairness and protecting against miscarriages of justice. However, ethical dilemmas arise when prosecutors encounter conflicting priorities, such as securing a conviction versus safeguarding the rights of the accused.

One ethical issue is the obligation to disclose exculpatory evidence. The landmark Supreme Court case Brady v. Maryland established that prosecutors must provide the defense with any evidence that is favorable to the accused and material to guilt or punishment. Failing to disclose this evidence can result in wrongful convictions and undermine public trust in the criminal justice system. Prosecutors must prioritize the pursuit of truth over the desire for a conviction and adhere to comprehensive disclosure practices.

Additionally, prosecutorial misconduct poses a significant ethical concern. This includes actions such as withholding evidence, coercing witnesses, or making false statements. Such behavior undermines the integrity of the legal process and threatens the principles of fairness and justice. It is crucial for prosecutors to abide by ethical rules and professional codes of conduct, and for appropriate disciplinary actions to be taken when misconduct occurs.

Ethical Considerations in Plea Bargaining

Plea bargaining commonly occurs in criminal prosecutions as a means of resolving cases through negotiated pleas instead of going to trial. While plea bargaining can expedite the legal process and reduce the burden on the courts, it raises ethical concerns regarding coercion, fairness, and the proper administration of justice.

One ethical issue is the pressure on defendants to accept pleas due to resource constraints or prosecutorial tactics. Defendants who are unable to afford a strong defense may feel compelled to accept a plea deal, even if they believe in their innocence. It is essential for prosecutors to ensure that defendants fully understand the implications of the plea agreement and that they are not coerced into giving up their rights.

Another ethical consideration is the potential for disparities in plea bargaining outcomes based on factors such as race, socioeconomic status, or legal representation. Studies have shown that certain groups, particularly minorities and the economically disadvantaged, are more likely to receive harsher plea offers and suffer from plea coercion. Prosecutors must be vigilant in avoiding these disparities and promoting fairness in plea negotiations.

Ethics in High-Profile Cases

High-profile cases, often involving public figures or controversial issues, present unique ethical challenges for prosecutors. These cases receive significant media attention and public scrutiny, requiring prosecutors to balance their ethical duties with public expectations and their own ambition for career advancement.

One ethical issue involves the media's influence on prosecutorial decisions. Media pressure can create a risk of overzealous prosecution or the pursuit of high-profile cases for personal or political gain. Ethical prosecutors must resist these pressures and base their decisions on the merits of the case, not on public opinion.

Furthermore, prosecutors must consider the potential impact of high-profile cases on the lives and reputations of the accused. In these cases, the presumption of innocence and the right to a fair trial are critical. Prosecutors must ensure that the pursuit of justice does not trample on the rights and dignity of the defendants.

Resources and Ethical Constraints

Another significant ethical concern for prosecutors is the allocation of limited resources. Prosecutorial offices often face constraints in terms of staffing, budget, and time. These resource limitations can create ethical dilemmas, such as whether to pursue less serious cases or to prioritize cases that have a higher likelihood of conviction.

Prosecutors must strive to strike a balance between resource allocation and ethical obligations. They should prioritize cases that involve serious harm to individuals or society while considering alternative approaches such as diversion or rehabilitation programs for non-violent offenses. Collaboration with law enforcement, community organizations, and stakeholders can help optimize resource utilization while fulfilling ethical responsibilities.

In conclusion, ethical issues in criminal prosecution require prosecutors to navigate a complex terrain where justice, fairness, and the protection of rights intersect. By embracing principles of fairness, impartiality, and transparency, prosecutors can contribute to a criminal justice system that is more equitable and just.

Ethical Challenges in the Correctional System

The correctional system plays a crucial role in society by administering justice and providing rehabilitation for individuals who have been convicted of crimes. However, like any system, it is not without its ethical challenges. In this section, we will explore some of the key ethical issues that arise within the correctional system and discuss possible solutions and considerations.

Overcrowding and Inhumane Conditions

One of the most pressing ethical challenges in the correctional system is the issue of overcrowding and inhumane conditions within prisons. Overcrowded prisons can lead to a range of problems, including increased violence, lack of access to healthcare and education, and limited resources for rehabilitation programs.

To address this challenge, there is a need for systemic change and a comprehensive approach. Firstly, it is crucial to invest in alternative sentencing options, such as community service or electronic monitoring, for non-violent offenders. This can help alleviate overcrowding and ensure that prison space is reserved for those who pose a significant risk to society. Moreover, policymakers should focus on implementing evidence-based practices, such as risk assessment tools, to determine the appropriate level of custody and reduce unnecessary incarceration.

In addition, improving living conditions within prisons is imperative. This includes providing adequate healthcare, nutritious meals, and access to education and vocational training programs. Collaborating with nonprofit organizations and community partners can also play a significant role in enhancing the rehabilitative aspects of the correctional system.

Use of Solitary Confinement

Solitary confinement refers to the practice of isolating individuals in a small cell for 22 to 24 hours per day, often for extended periods. While it is primarily intended for disciplinary purposes or to protect the safety of others, the use of solitary confinement raises ethical concerns.

Extended periods of isolation can have severe psychological and emotional effects on individuals, including increased risk of depression, anxiety, and even suicide. Moreover, the use of solitary confinement may not effectively address the underlying causes of problematic behavior and can impede the rehabilitation process.

To address these ethical challenges, correctional institutions should limit the use of solitary confinement to exceptional circumstances and for the shortest duration necessary. There should be strict guidelines and oversight in place to ensure that individuals in solitary confinement receive adequate mental health support and are regularly evaluated for their readiness to reenter the general population.

Prisoner Rehabilitation

Another ethical challenge in the correctional system revolves around the focus and effectiveness of prisoner rehabilitation programs. The ultimate goal of these programs should be to facilitate the successful reintegration of individuals into society upon their release. However, inadequate resources, limited access to education and job training, and a lack of individualized treatment plans can hinder the successful rehabilitation of prisoners.

To address these challenges, correctional institutions should prioritize the development and implementation of evidence-based rehabilitation programs. These programs should address the unique needs and circumstances of each individual, with a focus on providing education, vocational training, mental health treatment, and substance abuse counseling.

Collaboration between correctional institutions, community organizations, and employers is crucial to ensure that individuals have access to quality educational and employment opportunities upon their release. By investing in comprehensive rehabilitation programs, society can promote a more equitable and just correctional system that prioritizes the successful reintegration of individuals.

Ethical Treatment of Staff

Ethical challenges in the correctional system are not limited to the treatment of prisoners but also encompass the ethical treatment of correctional staff.

Correctional officers and staff often face demanding and potentially dangerous situations, which can lead to stress, burnout, and ethical dilemmas.

To address these challenges, correctional institutions should prioritize the well-being of their staff by providing comprehensive training, mental health support, and regularly evaluating their workload and work-life balance. Moreover, there should be opportunities for staff to report unethical conduct within the correctional system without fear of retaliation. By fostering a supportive and ethical work environment, correctional institutions can enhance staff morale, reduce turnover, and ultimately improve the overall functioning of the system.

Conclusion

In this section, we have explored some of the key ethical challenges within the correctional system. These challenges range from overcrowding and inhumane conditions to the ethical use of solitary confinement, prisoner rehabilitation, and the ethical treatment of correctional staff. By addressing these challenges, society can work towards creating a more just and humane correctional system that promotes rehabilitation, reduces recidivism, and ensures the fair treatment of all individuals involved. It is imperative that policymakers, correctional institutions, and the broader community collaborate to implement sustainable solutions that prioritize ethics and social justice.

Criminal Justice and Social Justice

In the field of legal studies, criminal justice is a fundamental aspect that addresses the enforcement of laws and the administration of justice in society. It involves the detection, apprehension, prosecution, and punishment of individuals who violate the law. However, it is essential to examine the intersection of criminal justice with social justice, as this relationship has profound ethical implications.

Understanding Criminal Justice

Criminal justice is a multifaceted system that encompasses various entities, including law enforcement agencies, the judiciary, correctional institutions, and rehabilitation programs. The primary goal of criminal justice is to maintain public order, protect individual rights, and promote the well-being and safety of society as a whole.

The Principles of Social Justice

On the other hand, social justice is a concept rooted in ethics and human rights. It advocates for the fair and equitable distribution of resources, opportunities, and benefits in society. Social justice aims to address systemic inequalities and promote equality and inclusivity for all individuals, regardless of their socioeconomic status, race, gender, or other characteristics.

The Relationship between Criminal Justice and Social Justice

Criminal justice and social justice are closely intertwined, as the criminal justice system plays a significant role in upholding or undermining social justice principles. On one hand, criminal justice can act as a tool for social change by combating systemic discrimination, protecting the vulnerable, and holding individuals accountable for their actions. On the other hand, if the criminal justice system is biased, discriminatory, or selectively enforced, it can perpetuate injustice and contribute to social inequalities.

Ethical Considerations in the Criminal Justice System

When examining the relationship between criminal justice and social justice, it is crucial to consider several ethical considerations:

1. **Equal Treatment:** The principle of equal treatment states that all individuals, regardless of their social standing or personal characteristics, should be treated fairly and impartially by the criminal justice system. This means that law enforcement agencies, prosecutors, and judges should not discriminate or show bias based on race, gender, socioeconomic status, or other factors.

2. **Due Process:** Due process is a fundamental principle in which individuals accused of committing a crime have the right to a fair and impartial trial. This includes the right to legal representation, the presumption of innocence until proven guilty, and the opportunity to present evidence and witness testimony in their defense.

3. **Rehabilitation and Reintegration:** Another ethical consideration is the focus on rehabilitation and reintegration into society. Criminal justice systems should prioritize efforts to rehabilitate offenders, address the root causes of criminal behavior, and provide individuals with the necessary support and resources to successfully reintegrate into their communities.

4. **Restorative Justice:** Restorative justice is an approach that focuses on repairing the harm caused by criminal behavior. It emphasizes dialogue, mediation, and reconciliation between victims, offenders, and the community, in

addition to traditional punitive measures. Restorative justice aims to promote healing, accountability, and a sense of community empowerment.

Ethical Challenges in Criminal Justice

Despite the principles outlined above, criminal justice systems worldwide face numerous ethical challenges that impede the achievement of social justice:

1. **Racial and Ethnic Disparities:** One of the most pressing issues is the presence of racial and ethnic disparities within the criminal justice system. Studies consistently show that marginalized communities, particularly people of color, are disproportionately affected by law enforcement practices, harsher sentencing, and inequitable access to legal representation.

2. **Wrongful Convictions:** Wrongful convictions pose a significant ethical challenge within the criminal justice system. Innocent individuals may be wrongly identified, charged, and convicted of crimes, leading to severe consequences, including imprisonment, loss of reputation, and emotional trauma.

3. **Overcriminalization and Mass Incarceration:** The increasing trend of overcriminalization and mass incarceration raises concerns about the fairness and effectiveness of the criminal justice system. Overly punitive laws, mandatory minimum sentences, and the warehousing of individuals in correctional facilities can perpetuate cycles of poverty, exacerbate social inequalities, and hinder rehabilitation efforts.

4. **Police Misconduct and Abuse of Power:** Instances of police misconduct, excessive use of force, and abuse of power undermine public trust and confidence in the criminal justice system. These incidents highlight the need for comprehensive police reform, accountability mechanisms, and increased transparency to ensure fair and just law enforcement practices.

Promoting Social Justice in Criminal Justice

To address the ethical challenges in the criminal justice system and promote social justice, several measures can be implemented:

1. **Police Reform and Training:** Enhancing police training, de-escalation tactics, and community policing initiatives can foster positive relationships between law enforcement and the communities they serve. Implementing technology and body-worn cameras can also increase police accountability and transparency.

2. **Sentencing Reform:** Reforming sentencing policies to promote proportionality, fairness, and rehabilitation can help mitigate the issues of overcriminalization and mass incarceration. Alternative sentencing programs, such

as diversion and rehabilitation programs, can provide individuals with opportunities for personal growth and reintegration into society.

3. Addressing Systemic Bias: Criminal justice systems must actively address and combat systemic biases that contribute to racial and ethnic disparities. This can be achieved through implicit bias training, diverse recruitment of law enforcement personnel, and the implementation of evidence-based practices that ensure equitable treatment for all individuals.

4. Restorative Justice Practices: Incorporating restorative justice approaches into the criminal justice system can foster healing, community cohesion, and accountability. By engaging victims, offenders, and the community in the resolution process, restorative justice can empower individuals and address the underlying causes of criminal behavior.

Case Study: The Movement for Criminal Justice Reform in the United States

The United States has been at the forefront of a significant grassroots movement advocating for criminal justice reform. This movement aims to address the systemic issues within the criminal justice system and promote social justice.

One significant aspect of this movement is the focus on ending racial and ethnic disparities in the criminal justice system. Activists argue that racism and racial bias are embedded in various stages of the criminal justice process, from policing practices to sentencing decisions. They push for comprehensive reforms that promote equity, fairness, and accountability in law enforcement and the administration of justice.

Furthermore, criminal justice reform advocates in the United States emphasize the importance of reducing mass incarceration and implementing sentencing reforms. They argue that lengthy prison sentences, particularly for nonviolent offenses, contribute to overcrowded prisons and hinder rehabilitation efforts. The movement calls for alternatives to incarceration, such as diversion programs, drug courts, and community-based sentencing, to address the root causes of crime and promote reintegration into society.

The movement for criminal justice reform also highlights the need for police accountability and transparency. Activists demand increased oversight of law enforcement practices, policies that limit the use of excessive force, and mechanisms to address instances of police misconduct. They argue that building trust between law enforcement agencies and the communities they serve is essential for fostering effective and just policing.

In conclusion, the intersection of criminal justice and social justice is a crucial consideration in the field of legal studies. Understanding the ethical implications and challenges within the criminal justice system is essential for promoting social equality, fairness, and a more just society. By addressing systemic biases, promoting rehabilitation, and implementing restorative justice practices, we can work towards a criminal justice system that upholds the principles of social justice and ensures equal treatment for all individuals.

Criminal Justice and Rehabilitation

In the field of criminal justice, rehabilitation plays a crucial role in ensuring that offenders can reintegrate into society and lead productive, law-abiding lives. It focuses on addressing the root causes of criminal behavior, providing necessary support and guidance, and promoting positive behavioral change. This section will discuss the principles and approaches of rehabilitation in the context of criminal justice, including various programs and strategies employed to facilitate successful reintegration.

Principles of Rehabilitation

Rehabilitation is founded on the principles of individualization, treatment, and reintegration. These principles recognize that each offender is unique and requires personalized interventions to address their specific needs. The individualization principle emphasizes the importance of tailoring rehabilitation programs to target the underlying factors that contribute to criminal behavior, such as substance abuse, mental health issues, or lack of education.

Additionally, the treatment principle recognizes that offenders often require therapeutic interventions to address their criminogenic needs effectively. This may involve cognitive-behavioral therapy, substance abuse treatment, anger management programs, vocational training, or educational programs. By addressing these needs, rehabilitation aims to equip offenders with the necessary skills and tools to make positive changes in their lives.

The reintegration principle highlights the importance of preparing offenders for a successful return to society. This involves providing support, guidance, and opportunities for skill-building to facilitate their reintegration into the workforce, family, and community. It also emphasizes the need for collaboration between criminal justice agencies, social service providers, and community organizations to ensure a seamless transition and reduce the risk of recidivism.

Approaches to Rehabilitation

Various approaches to rehabilitation have been developed, each with its focus and strategies. Three common approaches in criminal justice are the risk-needs-responsivity (RNR) model, restorative justice, and therapeutic jurisprudence.

The RNR model is based on the principles of risk assessment, targeted interventions, and responsivity to treatment. It involves conducting a thorough risk assessment to identify an offender's level of risk to reoffend. This assessment helps determine the appropriate level of treatment and supervision required. The model then focuses on addressing the criminogenic needs (e.g., substance abuse, antisocial attitudes) that are most strongly associated with reoffending. Finally, responsivity refers to tailoring treatment approaches to the learning style, motivation, and characteristics of the individual offender.

Restorative justice takes a victim-centered approach and seeks to repair the harm caused by the offender's actions. It involves facilitating dialogue and engagement between the victim, offender, and community to hold the offender accountable, promote healing, and support the reintegration of the offender. Instead of focusing solely on punishment, restorative justice emphasizes the principles of accountability, reparation, and reintegration.

Therapeutic jurisprudence recognizes that interactions within the criminal justice system can have psychological and emotional impacts on offenders. It seeks to minimize potential harm and promote positive outcomes by integrating therapeutic and rehabilitative elements into legal processes. This approach aims to create procedural justice, enhance the well-being of offenders, and reduce the likelihood of reoffending.

Rehabilitation Programs and Strategies

Numerous rehabilitation programs and strategies have been implemented to facilitate the successful reintegration of offenders. Let's explore a few examples:

1. Cognitive-Behavioral Therapy (CBT): CBT is a common therapeutic approach used in rehabilitation. It focuses on identifying and modifying dysfunctional thinking patterns and behaviors that contribute to criminal behavior. By promoting positive cognitive restructuring and teaching new coping strategies, CBT helps offenders develop pro-social skills and reduce the risk of reoffending.

2. Vocational Training and Education Programs: Lack of education and job skills can be barriers to successful reintegration. Vocational training and education programs provide offenders with opportunities to acquire marketable skills and

qualifications, increasing their chances of employment upon release. These programs range from basic literacy courses to specialized vocational training in fields such as construction, culinary arts, or information technology.

3. Substance Abuse Treatment: Substance abuse is a common underlying factor associated with criminal behavior. Rehabilitation programs often include substance abuse treatment to address addiction and reduce the risk of relapse. These programs may involve detoxification, counseling, group therapy, and aftercare support to help offenders overcome substance abuse issues and maintain sobriety.

4. Community-Based Programs: Community-based programs offer support and supervision to offenders as they transition back into society. These programs may include halfway houses, day reporting centers, or intensive probation and parole supervision. By providing a structured environment and access to support services, community-based programs help offenders establish stable living arrangements, gain employment, and access necessary resources for successful reintegration.

5. Restorative Justice Circles: Restorative justice circles bring together victims, offenders, and community members in a facilitated discussion to address the harms caused by the offense. These circles aim to promote healing, foster empathy, and facilitate dialogue between all parties involved. Through active participation and accountability, offenders have the opportunity to understand the consequences of their actions and work towards repairing the harm done.

Challenges and Innovations

While rehabilitation programs have shown promising results, they are not without challenges. One major challenge is the lack of resources and funding for comprehensive rehabilitation services. Many correctional institutions face budgetary constraints, limiting the availability and quality of rehabilitation programs. Moreover, ensuring continuity of care and support upon release can be challenging, as offenders may face limited access to resources and support services in the community.

Innovations in technology and research have the potential to address these challenges and enhance the effectiveness of rehabilitation programs. For example, virtual reality-based therapy programs have shown promise in treating psychological disorders, such as post-traumatic stress disorder, among offenders. E-learning platforms and online educational resources can also expand access to education and vocational training programs, particularly in remote areas or correctional facilities with limited resources.

Furthermore, collaborations between criminal justice agencies, community organizations, and employers can create opportunities for transitional employment and reduce barriers to reintegration. By providing job placements, mentorship programs, and support networks, these collaborations help offenders secure stable employment, earn a living wage, and establish a sense of purpose and belonging.

In conclusion, rehabilitation is an essential component of the criminal justice system. By focusing on individualized treatment, reintegration, and addressing the criminogenic needs of offenders, rehabilitation programs aim to reduce recidivism and promote positive behavioral change. Through various approaches, such as the RNR model, restorative justice, and therapeutic jurisprudence, offenders are given the opportunity to rebuild their lives and contribute positively to society. However, challenges persist, and continued efforts in resource allocation, innovations, and collaborations are necessary to enhance the effectiveness of rehabilitation strategies and ensure the successful reintegration of offenders.

Conclusion

In this chapter, we have explored the various ethical issues in the field of criminal justice. We have examined the principles of criminal justice ethics, the role and responsibilities of criminal justice professionals, and the ethical dilemmas they face in their work. We have also discussed the ethical issues in law enforcement, criminal prosecution, and the correctional system.

One of the key principles of criminal justice ethics is the principle of fairness and impartiality. Criminal justice professionals are tasked with upholding this principle and ensuring that all individuals are treated equally under the law. However, they often face ethical dilemmas when faced with conflicting interests or pressures.

In law enforcement, ethical challenges arise in the form of the use of force and racial profiling. Police officers need to make split-second decisions in high-pressure situations, and these decisions can have serious consequences. Balancing the need to protect the public with the duty to respect individual rights is a constant challenge.

In the field of criminal prosecution, ethical issues can arise in the pursuit of justice. Prosecutors have a duty to seek the truth and uphold the law, but they also have an obligation to protect the rights of the accused. This can sometimes create conflicts of interest or ethical dilemmas.

Within the correctional system, ethical challenges include issues such as rehabilitation and social justice. As society's understanding of crime and punishment evolves, the ethical considerations surrounding incarceration are constantly changing. There is a growing recognition of the importance of rehabilitation and reducing recidivism rates.

Criminal justice is not only about punishment but also about promoting social justice. It is crucial to acknowledge that the criminal justice system has historically disproportionately affected marginalized communities, racial and ethnic minorities, and those living in poverty. Addressing these inequalities and working towards a more equitable system is essential.

Capital punishment is a topic that raises significant ethical controversies. Arguments for and against it often revolve around issues of human rights, morality, and the value of human life. While some argue that it serves as a deterrent and a just punishment for heinous crimes, others raise concerns about the possibility of wrongful convictions and the inherent cruelty of taking a life.

To address these concerns, there have been calls for alternatives to capital punishment, such as life imprisonment without parole. These alternatives aim to protect human rights while still holding individuals accountable for their actions.

Another significant ethical challenge in criminal justice is the need for police accountability and transparency. Recent events have highlighted the need for reform and increased scrutiny over law enforcement practices. Building trust between the police and the communities they serve is crucial for maintaining public safety and promoting social justice.

In conclusion, ethical issues in criminal justice are complex and multifaceted. Criminal justice professionals must navigate these challenges while upholding principles of fairness, justice, and respect for human rights. Addressing these ethical dilemmas requires ongoing dialogue, reform, and a commitment to social justice. By embracing ethical principles and striving for a more just and equitable system, we can work towards a more ethical and effective criminal justice system for all.

Capital Punishment and Ethical Controversies

Arguments For and Against Capital Punishment

Capital punishment, also known as the death penalty, is a highly controversial and ethically complex issue. It involves the state-sanctioned execution of individuals who have been convicted of committing serious crimes, such as murder. Advocates of capital punishment argue that it serves as a powerful deterrent, provides justice to the victims and their families, and ensures the safety of society. On the other hand, opponents of capital punishment assert that it is inherently cruel and inhumane, fails to deter crime effectively, and risks the possibility of executing innocent individuals. This section examines the arguments for and against capital punishment, exploring the ethical, practical, and philosophical considerations involved.

Arguments For Capital Punishment

1. **Deterrence:** Proponents of capital punishment argue that it deters potential criminals from committing heinous acts. The threat of facing the ultimate punishment may dissuade individuals from engaging in serious crimes, thus ensuring the safety and security of society.

2. **Deserved Punishment:** Supporters of capital punishment believe that individuals who commit heinous crimes deserve to be punished with the highest possible penalty. They argue that capital punishment provides a just retribution for the pain and suffering caused to the victims and their families.

3. **Closure and Justice:** Advocates of capital punishment argue that it brings closure to the victims' families by providing a sense of justice. The execution of the convicted perpetrator can bring a measure of emotional relief and closure to those affected by the crime.

4. **Cost and Resource Allocation:** Proponents of capital punishment contend that it is more cost-effective than keeping offenders in prison for life. They argue that the financial resources saved by carrying out executions can be allocated to other areas such as crime prevention and victim support.

5. **Public Opinion:** Supporters of capital punishment often cite public opinion polls that indicate a significant percentage of the population supports the death penalty. They argue that the implementation of capital punishment aligns with the will of the people and democratic principles.

Arguments Against Capital Punishment

1. **Inhumane and Cruel:** Opponents of capital punishment argue that it violates the fundamental right to life and constitutes a form of cruel and unusual punishment. They assert that no government or authority should have the power to decide who lives and who dies.

2. **Risk of Executing Innocent Individuals:** Critics of capital punishment highlight the inherent risk of executing innocent individuals. Despite advancements in forensic science, wrongful convictions do occur, and the irreversible nature of the death penalty leaves no room for rectification in case of a mistake.

3. **Ineffectiveness as a Deterrent:** Opponents of capital punishment contend that empirical evidence does not support the claim that it effectively deters crime. They argue that the potential consequence of execution does not outweigh the motivations and circumstances that lead individuals to commit serious crimes.

4.   **Racial and Socioeconomic Disparities:** Critics point out that capital punishment disproportionately affects minority and economically disadvantaged individuals.   Studies have shown significant disparities in the application of the death penalty, raising concerns about systemic bias and an unequal justice system.

5.   **Possibility of Rehabilitation:** Opponents argue that capital punishment denies the possibility of rehabilitation and redemption for offenders. They believe that individuals convicted of heinous crimes should be given an opportunity for rehabilitation and reintegration into society.

The Complexity of Capital Punishment

The debate over capital punishment is complex and often emotionally charged. It encompasses not only moral and ethical considerations but also practical and legal implications.   Understanding the arguments for and against capital punishment requires a comprehensive examination of the social, cultural, and historical factors that shape attitudes towards punishment and justice.

It is important to note that the arguments presented here are not exhaustive and that there are diverse perspectives within both supporters and opponents of capital punishment. The ongoing discourse surrounding this issue emphasizes the need for critical analysis, informed dialogue, and a deeper understanding of the complexities inherent in the administration of justice.

Ethical Implications of Capital Punishment

Capital punishment, also known as the death penalty, is a highly controversial and emotionally charged topic that raises significant ethical considerations. This section explores the ethical implications of capital punishment from various philosophical and ethical perspectives, examines the arguments for and against it, and highlights the broader societal impacts of this form of punishment.

The Utilitarian Perspective

Utilitarianism is a consequentialist ethical theory that focuses on maximizing overall happiness or utility. From a utilitarian perspective, the ethical implications of capital punishment can be evaluated based on its impact on society as a whole.

Supporters of capital punishment argue that it serves as a deterrent and prevents potential criminals from committing heinous crimes. They believe that the threat of death penalty acts as a powerful deterrent, ultimately reducing the overall crime rate. Utilitarian proponents argue that this serves the greater good by promoting public safety and protecting potential victims.

However, opponents of capital punishment raise several concerns from a utilitarian standpoint. They argue that the death penalty does not effectively deter crime, as empirical evidence fails to establish a clear causal relationship between capital punishment and reduced crime rates. Furthermore, they argue that the costs associated with capital punishment, such as lengthy legal proceedings, appeals, and incarceration on death row, are exorbitant and divert resources from other crime prevention and rehabilitation efforts.

The Retributive Perspective

Retributive justice focuses on the concept of punishment as a form of retribution for wrongdoing. Proponents of capital punishment from this perspective argue that it provides a just response to the most serious crimes, ensuring that offenders receive the punishment they deserve. They believe that justice demands a proportional punishment for crimes such as murder, and that the severity of the offense justifies the ultimate penalty.

Opponents of capital punishment, however, question the notion of retribution as a justifiable basis for punishment. They argue that the death penalty violates the principle of proportionality, as it involves taking a human life and fails to consider the potential for wrongful convictions. They also highlight the inherent risk of executing innocent individuals, which raises serious ethical concerns and undermines the legitimacy of retribution as a justification for capital punishment.

The Human Rights Perspective

From a human rights perspective, capital punishment is seen as a violation of the right to life and dignity. The Universal Declaration of Human Rights and other international human rights instruments recognize the inherent right to life and prohibit cruel and inhumane treatment.

Opponents of capital punishment argue that it is a form of state-sanctioned violence and an irreversible punishment that denies individuals the opportunity for rehabilitation, redemption, and the possibility of rectifying miscarriages of justice. They also highlight the arbitrary nature of capital punishment, as it is often influenced by factors such as race, socioeconomic status, and quality of legal representation.

Supporters of capital punishment, on the other hand, argue that certain crimes are so heinous and morally repugnant that they warrant the ultimate punishment. They believe that the death penalty is a just response to these crimes and fulfills society's need for justice and closure.

The Abolitionist Movement

The ethical implications of capital punishment have sparked a global abolitionist movement. The movement seeks to end the use of the death penalty worldwide, advocating for a shift towards more humane and rehabilitative forms of punishment.

Abolitionists argue that capital punishment is fundamentally flawed and irreconcilable with the principles of fairness, justice, and human rights. They highlight the potential for wrongful convictions, the discriminatory application of the death penalty, and the failure to address the underlying causes of crime. They argue for alternative approaches, such as life imprisonment without parole, that provide opportunities for rehabilitation, protect human rights, and address the root causes of criminal behavior.

Contemporary Issues and Challenges

The ethical implications of capital punishment continue to be subject to intense debate and scrutiny. Advances in DNA technology have led to the exoneration of individuals who were wrongfully convicted, raising concerns about the potential for irreversible errors in capital cases. The racial and socioeconomic disparities in the application of the death penalty have also come under scrutiny, challenging the perception of equal justice under the law.

Moreover, the international community has increasingly called for the abolition of capital punishment, viewing it as a human rights violation. Many countries have abolished the death penalty, while others retain it but impose moratoriums or significantly restrict its use.

Conclusion

The ethical implications of capital punishment encompass a range of philosophical and ethical perspectives. Utilitarian considerations revolve around the impact on overall societal well-being, while retributive justice focuses on proportionate punishment. From a human rights standpoint, capital punishment is seen as a violation of the right to life and dignity. The abolitionist movement seeks to end the use of the death penalty, advocating for more humane and rehabilitative approaches to punishment. Despite ongoing debates and challenges, the ethical implications of capital punishment highlight the need for a comprehensive examination of its fairness, effectiveness, and compatibility with societal values.

Alternatives to Capital Punishment

Capital punishment, also known as the death penalty, has been a controversial issue for many years. It involves the execution of individuals who have been convicted of certain crimes deemed to be the most heinous, such as murder. However, there are ethical concerns surrounding the use of capital punishment, including the risk of executing innocent individuals and the potential for arbitrary or discriminatory application of the penalty. As a result, there has been a growing interest in exploring alternatives to capital punishment that can still serve the goals of justice and public safety. In this section, we will discuss some of these alternatives and their implications.

Life Imprisonment without Parole

One of the most common alternatives to capital punishment is a sentence of life imprisonment without the possibility of parole. This means that the convicted individual will spend the remainder of their life in prison without any chance of release. Proponents of this alternative argue that it achieves the goals of punishment and public safety without the irreversible nature of capital punishment. Life imprisonment without parole allows for the opportunity for rehabilitation and possible redemption, while still ensuring that dangerous individuals are kept out of society.

However, critics argue that life imprisonment without parole does not truly provide an alternative to the death penalty, as it still involves the permanent deprivation of liberty. They argue that it may be arbitrarily applied, and that the costs of maintaining a large population of lifers in prison are burdensome to the state. Additionally, there are concerns about the potential for wrongful convictions, as individuals sentenced to life imprisonment without parole may later be exonerated.

Restorative Justice

Restorative justice is an alternative approach to punishment that focuses on repairing the harm caused by criminal behavior. Instead of an adversarial process centered around punishment, restorative justice seeks to involve all parties affected by the crime in a dialogue aimed at reconciliation and resolution. This may involve meeting with the victim, offender, and community members to discuss the impact of the crime and develop a plan for restitution and reintegration.

Proponents of restorative justice argue that it emphasizes healing and rehabilitation, rather than punishment. By addressing the underlying causes of criminal behavior and promoting accountability, it aims to prevent future crimes. Restorative justice also prioritizes the needs and voices of the victims, allowing them to participate in the process and potentially find closure.

However, critics of restorative justice express concerns about its effectiveness in cases involving serious crimes. They argue that it may not adequately address the severity of certain offenses, and that it could lead to re-victimization or unequal outcomes. Critics also note that restorative justice requires a high level of community support and resources to be successful, making it difficult to implement on a large scale.

Rehabilitation and Reformation Programs

Another alternative to capital punishment is the implementation of rehabilitation and reformation programs within correctional systems. These programs aim to address the underlying causes of criminal behavior and provide individuals with the skills and support necessary to reintegrate into society successfully. They may include educational programs, vocational training, counseling, and substance abuse treatment.

Proponents of rehabilitation and reformation programs argue that they offer a more humane and effective approach to addressing criminal behavior. By focusing on rehabilitation rather than punishment, these programs aim to reduce recidivism rates and promote long-term societal safety. They also align with the principle of providing individuals with an opportunity for personal growth and transformation.

However, critics of rehabilitation and reformation programs express concerns about their effectiveness and potential for abuse. They argue that some individuals may not be motivated to participate fully in these programs, and that resources may be limited, resulting in inadequate treatment. Critics also highlight the need for sufficient monitoring and support to ensure individuals successfully reintegrate into society and do not pose a risk to public safety.

Community-Based Sentencing

Community-based sentencing is an alternative approach that emphasizes the participation of the community in the criminal justice process. Instead of traditional incarceration, individuals may be sentenced to community service, probation, or alternative forms of supervision. Restorative justice principles often underpin community-based sentencing, as it aims to involve the community in the rehabilitation and reintegration of offenders.

Proponents of community-based sentencing argue that it allows individuals to maintain ties with their community, increasing the chances of successful rehabilitation and reintegration. This approach also promotes accountability and provides individuals with an opportunity to make amends for their actions. Additionally, community-based sentencing may be more cost-effective than incarceration, as it reduces the strain on correctional facilities.

However, critics express concerns about the potential for unequal treatment in community-based sentencing. They argue that marginalized communities may bear a disproportionate burden and that there may be a lack of resources or support for community-based programs. Critics also highlight the need for careful monitoring and supervision to ensure compliance and public safety.

Conclusion

In conclusion, there is a growing interest in exploring alternatives to capital punishment that can still promote justice and public safety. Life imprisonment without parole, restorative justice, rehabilitation and reformation programs, and community-based sentencing are some of the alternatives that have been proposed. Each alternative has its own strengths and weaknesses, and their implementation requires careful consideration of ethical, practical, and resource-related factors. As the debate on capital punishment continues, these alternatives offer avenues for discussion and potential reform in the criminal justice system.

International Perspectives on Capital Punishment

Capital punishment, also known as the death penalty, is a highly controversial and divisive issue around the world. While some countries have abolished capital punishment, others continue to practice it, leading to a wide range of perspectives on the matter. In this section, we will explore the international perspectives on capital punishment, examining the arguments for and against its use, as well as the diverse approaches taken by different countries.

Arguments for Capital Punishment

Proponents of capital punishment argue that it serves as a deterrent to crime, ensuring public safety and protecting society from dangerous individuals. They believe that the fear of facing the ultimate punishment can discourage potential criminals from committing heinous offenses, thereby reducing crime rates. Additionally, advocates often claim that capital punishment provides a sense of closure and justice to the victims' families, offering them a form of retribution.

Another argument put forth is that capital punishment is a necessary tool for maintaining law and order. In societies where the criminal justice system is perceived as inadequate or ineffective, the death penalty is seen as a means of restoring faith in the system and upholding the rule of law. Proponents of capital punishment also argue that it serves as a form of proportional punishment for crimes that are considered the most morally reprehensible.

Arguments against Capital Punishment

Opponents of capital punishment raise several ethical, moral, and practical concerns. One of the main arguments against capital punishment is the potential for wrongful convictions and the irreversible nature of the punishment. The risk of executing innocent individuals is a significant factor that has led many countries to abolish or impose a moratorium on the death penalty. Furthermore, the arbitrary application of capital punishment, often influenced by factors such as race, socioeconomic status, and inadequate legal representation, raises concerns about fairness and justice.

Another argument against capital punishment is its failure to address the root causes of crime. Critics argue that investments in preventive measures, rehabilitation programs, and social support systems would be more effective in reducing crime rates and promoting a safer society than the use of the death penalty. Additionally, opponents contend that capital punishment violates the inherent right to life and constitutes a form of cruelty and inhumane treatment.

International Approaches

The global perspective on capital punishment varies significantly from country to country. According to Amnesty International, as of 2021, over two-thirds of countries worldwide have abolished the death penalty in law or practice. Europe, in particular, has become a stronghold for the abolitionist movement, with all 27 member states of the European Union having abolished capital punishment.

In contrast, several countries, such as the United States, China, Iran, Saudi Arabia, and Japan, continue to retain capital punishment. However, even among retentionist countries, there is a wide range of approaches and practices. For example, some countries limit the scope of capital punishment to specific crimes such as murder or treason, while others employ it for a broader range of offenses, including drug trafficking and apostasy.

International human rights law plays a crucial role in shaping the global discourse on capital punishment. The Universal Declaration of Human Rights (UDHR), adopted by the United Nations General Assembly in 1948, emphasizes the right to life and the prohibition of cruel, inhumane, or degrading treatment or punishment. Regional human rights treaties, such as the European Convention on Human Rights and the American Convention on Human Rights, also contain provisions safeguarding the right to life.

Challenges and Reforms

The use of capital punishment continues to face numerous challenges and calls for reform. One significant challenge is ensuring fairness and impartiality in the application of the death penalty. Human rights organizations and advocates argue that racial disparities, inadequate legal representation, and discriminatory practices undermine the legitimacy and fairness of capital punishment. Efforts to address these concerns include the requirement for mandatory review and appeals, the provision of effective legal representation, and greater transparency in the criminal justice system.

Another key challenge is striking a balance between respecting national sovereignties and promoting universal human rights standards. The retentionist countries often assert that the use of capital punishment is a matter of national sovereignty and represents the will of their citizens. On the other hand, abolitionist countries and human rights organizations stress the need for a global consensus on the abolition of the death penalty to protect the inherent right to life.

Reforms in the area of capital punishment focus on promoting alternatives to the death penalty, such as life imprisonment without parole or restorative justice approaches. Some countries have introduced legislation to limit the scope of capital offenses, restrict the methods of execution, or establish safeguards to prevent wrongful convictions. Moreover, international organizations, civil society groups, and legal scholars continue to advocate for the worldwide abolition of the death penalty, emphasizing the value of human dignity, equal justice, and respect for human rights.

Case Study: The Global Trend Towards Abolition

The trend towards the abolition of capital punishment has gained considerable momentum in recent decades. The number of countries that have abolished the death penalty has steadily increased, reflecting evolving societal attitudes and a growing adherence to human rights principles.

As an example, let us consider the case of Canada. Canada abolished the death penalty for murder in 1976 and completely abolished it from the criminal code in 1998. The decision to abolish capital punishment followed an ongoing public debate and a series of legal challenges that highlighted concerns about the discriminatory application of the death penalty, the risk of executing innocent individuals, and the violation of the right to life. The abolition of capital punishment in Canada was seen as a significant step towards embracing a more inclusive and humane approach to justice.

Similarly, in recent years, several countries have abolished the death penalty or imposed a moratorium on its use. For instance, Burkina Faso abolished the death penalty in 2018, becoming the 20th country in Africa to do so. In 2020, Kazakhstan ratified the Second Optional Protocol to the International Covenant on Civil and Political Rights, aiming at the abolition of the death penalty. These examples demonstrate the growing global consensus against capital punishment and the acknowledgment of its incompatibility with human rights standards.

Resources for Further Exploration

1. Amnesty International - https://www.amnesty.org/ 2. United Nations Office of the High Commissioner for Human Rights - https://www.ohchr.org/EN/Issues/Pages/ListOfIssues.aspx 3. Death Penalty Information Center - https://deathpenaltyinfo.org/ 4. The Innocence Project - https://www.innocenceproject.org/ 5. European Coalition to End the Death Penalty - https://www.ecpm.org/

Key Takeaways

1. Capital punishment is a highly controversial and divisive issue, with arguments both for and against its use. 2. The international perspectives on capital punishment vary significantly, with some countries abolishing it while others retaining or practicing it. 3. Human rights standards and regional agreements play a crucial role in shaping the global discourse on capital punishment. 4. Challenges in the application of capital punishment include ensuring fairness, preventing wrongful convictions, and addressing disparities and discriminatory practices. 5. The trend towards abolition reflects an evolving understanding of human rights principles and a growing consensus against the death penalty.

Exercises

1. Select a retentionist country and an abolitionist country. Compare and contrast their approaches to capital punishment, including the offenses for which it is applied and any safeguards in place. 2. Debate the ethical implications of capital punishment, considering arguments for and against its use. Evaluate the

effectiveness of the death penalty as a deterrent to crime. 3. Research a case of a wrongful conviction in a capital punishment case. Discuss the implications of such cases on the legitimacy and fairness of capital punishment. 4. Explore the impact of international human rights treaties and agreements on the use of capital punishment.   Assess the role of regional human rights bodies in promoting abolition. 5. Evaluate the effectiveness of alternatives to the death penalty, such as life imprisonment without parole or restorative justice approaches. Analyze the factors that contribute to their success or failure.

Additional Readings

1. Bedau, H. A., & Cassell, P. G. (Eds.). (2020). *Debating the Death Penalty: Should America Have Capital Punishment?*. Oxford University Press. 2. Hood, R. (2015). *The Death Penalty: A Worldwide Perspective* (5th ed.). Oxford University Press. 3. Sarat, A., Boulanger, C., & Simon, J. (Eds.). (2017). *The Palgrave Handbook of the Death Penalty and the United States*. Palgrave Macmillan. 4. Zimring, F. E. (2015). *The City That Became Safe: New York's Lessons for Urban Crime and Its Control*. Oxford University Press. 5. Zimring, F. E., & Johnson, G. (2017). *The Next Frontier: National Development, Political Change, and the Death Penalty in Asia*. Oxford University Press.

Reforms and Policy Recommendations in Capital Punishment

Capital punishment, also known as the death penalty, has long been a subject of ethical controversy and debate.   As society progresses, there is a growing recognition of the need for reforms and policy recommendations in this area. This section discusses some of the key issues surrounding capital punishment and proposes possible reforms to address these concerns.

The Ethics of Capital Punishment

Before delving into reforms and policy recommendations, it is important to briefly revisit the ethical arguments surrounding capital punishment. Proponents of capital punishment argue that it serves as a deterrent to crime and provides a sense of justice for the victims and their families. However, opponents argue that it violates the inherent right to life, is applied disproportionately to marginalized populations, and risks executing innocent individuals.

Reforming the Capital Punishment Process

1. **Improving Legal Representation:** One of the most pressing issues in capital punishment cases is the quality of legal representation for defendants. Many defendants facing the death penalty do not have access to competent and well-resourced defense attorneys. To address this, it is crucial to invest in public defender programs and provide adequate resources for the defense.

    2. **Ensuring Procedural Fairness:** Capital punishment cases must be subject to rigorous scrutiny to ensure procedural fairness. This includes providing defendants with access to forensic experts, ensuring fair jury selection processes, and eliminating racial bias in the application of the death penalty.

    3. **Reducing Delays:** The lengthy and costly appeals process in capital cases often leads to significant delays in carrying out the punishment. To address this, reforms should focus on streamlining the legal process while still maintaining crucial safeguards.

Policy Recommendations

1. **Moratorium on Executions:** Consider implementing a moratorium on executions to allow for a thorough review of the capital punishment system. This would provide an opportunity to assess the ethical implications, study the impact on marginalized communities, and consider alternatives.

    2. **Mandatory Review of Wrongful Convictions:** Establish a mandatory review process for all cases involving capital punishment to identify potential wrongful convictions. This could involve DNA testing, revisiting eyewitness testimonies, and considering new evidence. The goal is to prevent the irreversible punishment of innocent individuals.

    3. **Transparency and Accountability:** Enhance transparency and accountability in the administration of capital punishment by requiring detailed documentation of the decision-making process and implementation of the death penalty. This could involve annual reporting on capital punishment cases, providing access to data for researchers, and conducting independent audits of the process.

    4. **International Law Compliance:** Ensure compliance with international human rights standards in the application of capital punishment. This includes adopting measures to prohibit the execution of juvenile offenders, individuals with mental disabilities, and those convicted of non-violent offenses.

    5. **Promote Alternatives to Capital Punishment:** Increase support for alternatives to capital punishment, such as life without parole or restorative justice

programs.   These alternatives allow for accountability while avoiding the irreversible consequences of executing individuals.

Case Study: The Innocence Project

The Innocence Project is a prime example of an organization that advocates for reforms in the criminal justice system, with a specific focus on wrongful convictions in capital cases. Through post-conviction DNA testing, the Innocence Project has helped to exonerate numerous individuals who were wrongly sentenced to death. This highlights the importance of reform measures, including mandatory reviews and access to new evidence, in preventing miscarriages of justice.

Conclusion

Reforming capital punishment requires a comprehensive approach that addresses the ethical concerns, improves the fairness of the legal process, and promotes alternatives to the death penalty. By implementing the proposed reforms and policy recommendations, society can move towards a more just and equitable criminal justice system that upholds human rights and prevents the irreversible punishment of innocent individuals.

Capital Punishment and Human Rights

Capital punishment, also known as the death penalty, is a highly controversial and debated topic worldwide. It raises significant ethical and human rights concerns, as it involves taking a person's life as a punishment for a serious crime. This section explores the intersection of capital punishment with human rights, examining the ethical challenges and implications associated with this practice.

Historical Background

The use of the death penalty dates back to ancient times, where it served as a form of punishment for various crimes. Throughout history, societies have employed this extreme penalty to deter crime, seek retribution, and enforce justice. However, as our understanding of human rights has evolved, so has the debate surrounding capital punishment.

In recent years, there has been a global trend towards abolition, with a significant number of countries abolishing capital punishment either in law or practice. The movement towards abolition is primarily rooted in the recognition of the inherent dignity and right to life of every individual, as enshrined in international human rights instruments.

Human Rights Perspective

From a human rights perspective, capital punishment raises several fundamental concerns. The right to life is a universally recognized human right, protected by various international human rights treaties and conventions. The Universal Declaration of Human Rights, for example, asserts the right to life as a fundamental principle, without any discrimination.

The death penalty also encompasses other human rights concepts, such as the prohibition of torture and cruel, inhuman, or degrading treatment or punishment. The methods used in capital punishment, including lethal injection, hanging, and firing squad, can be seen as violating these rights, as they cause unnecessary suffering and pain.

International Legal Framework

The international legal framework provides significant guidance on the relationship between capital punishment and human rights. The Second Optional Protocol to the International Covenant on Civil and Political Rights (ICCPR), aiming at the abolition of the death penalty, prohibits the imposition of the death penalty for all crimes within the jurisdiction of states parties to the protocol.

Furthermore, regional human rights instruments, such as the European Convention on Human Rights and the American Convention on Human Rights, also place restrictions on the use of capital punishment. These instruments emphasize the importance of protecting the right to life and ensuring that the death penalty is implemented sparingly, for the most serious crimes and with adequate safeguards.

Ethical Considerations

The ethical considerations surrounding capital punishment extend beyond the legal and human rights frameworks. Supporters argue that capital punishment serves as a deterrent to crime, promotes public safety, and provides closure to victims' families. However, opponents argue that it is irreversible, prone to error, and does not effectively deter crime.

Moreover, questions of morality and personal beliefs come into play when discussing capital punishment. Some argue that taking a life, regardless of the circumstances, is inherently wrong and violates the principles of human dignity.

Others contend that certain crimes are so heinous that the death penalty is the only just punishment.

Contemporary Challenges

Capital punishment faces ongoing challenges and controversies in contemporary society. One of the key concerns is the potential for wrongful convictions and the risk of executing innocent individuals. Numerous cases have emerged, highlighting flaws in the justice system, such as inadequate legal representation, racial bias, and unreliable evidence.

Another issue is the arbitrary application of the death penalty, where it may disproportionately affect marginalized and vulnerable groups in society. Studies have shown that individuals from racial and ethnic minorities, as well as those facing socioeconomic disadvantage, are more likely to receive the death penalty.

Alternative Approaches

In response to these challenges, many countries have chosen to abolish capital punishment or implement moratoriums on its use.   Instead, they focus on alternative approaches to justice, such as life imprisonment without the possibility of parole, restorative justice, and rehabilitation programs.

These alternative approaches prioritize the protection of human rights, while still ensuring that offenders are held accountable for their actions. They provide opportunities for rehabilitation and reintegration into society, recognizing the possibility of reform and second chances.

Conclusion

Capital punishment and human rights intersect in complex and profound ways. The ongoing debate surrounding the death penalty raises critical questions about the inherent value of human life, the role of punishment in society, and the significance of justice and human rights.

As societies continue to evolve, so too must our understanding of justice and the principles that underpin it. By critically examining the ethical considerations and human rights implications of capital punishment, we can contribute to the ongoing dialogue on creating a more just and humane society.

Capital Punishment and Deterrence

In this section, we will explore the complex and controversial topic of capital punishment, specifically focusing on the concept of deterrence. Capital punishment, also known as the death penalty, refers to the practice of legally executing individuals who have been convicted of committing certain heinous crimes. Deterrence, on the other hand, is the idea that the threat of punishment can prevent potential offenders from engaging in criminal behavior.

Background

Capital punishment has a long history and is rooted in the belief that certain crimes merit the ultimate punishment. Proponents argue that it serves as a deterrent, protecting society from dangerous individuals and delivering justice to the victims and their families. Opponents, however, raise concerns about the ethics, effectiveness, and potential for wrongful convictions associated with capital punishment.

The Deterrence Theory

The deterrence theory posits that individuals are less likely to commit crimes if they believe they will face severe punishment, such as the death penalty. It is based on the assumption that human beings are rational actors who weigh the potential costs and benefits before engaging in criminal activities.

Rational Choice Theory: One of the foundations of deterrence theory is the rational choice theory. According to this theory, individuals make rational decisions by considering the potential risks and rewards of their actions. If the perceived costs of committing a crime outweigh the benefits, individuals will be deterred from engaging in criminal behavior.

Empirical Evidence

The effectiveness of capital punishment as a deterrent has been the subject of extensive research and debate. Many studies have attempted to examine the relationship between the existence or use of the death penalty and crime rates.

Statistical analysis: Researchers often employ statistical methods to analyze the impact of capital punishment on deterrence. These studies typically compare crime rates between states or countries with and without the death penalty, or before and after the implementation or abolition of capital punishment.

Mixed findings: The findings of empirical studies on capital punishment and deterrence have been mixed. Some studies have found a deterrent effect, suggesting that the presence of the death penalty leads to lower murder rates. However, other studies have found no significant correlation or even a positive relationship between capital punishment and crime rates.

Challenges and Limitations

Deterrence theory and research face several challenges and limitations that complicate the understanding of the relationship between capital punishment and deterrence.

Causal inference: Establishing a causal relationship between capital punishment and deterrence is inherently challenging. Researchers must account for various factors that may influence crime rates, such as socioeconomic conditions, law enforcement strategies, and societal changes.

Deterrence vs. incapacitation: Critics argue that the purpose of capital punishment is primarily incapacitation - the permanent removal of dangerous individuals from society - rather than deterrence. They contend that the death penalty focuses on punishment rather than prevention.

Controversies and Ethical Considerations

The use of capital punishment raises a host of ethical considerations and controversies.

Human rights: Capital punishment is viewed by many as a violation of the right to life, as enshrined in international human rights law. Critics argue that the death penalty is a cruel and inhumane practice that should be abolished.

Risk of wrongful convictions: One of the significant concerns with capital punishment is the potential for wrongful convictions. The irreversible nature of the death penalty means that any errors or miscarriages of justice cannot be undone.

Disproportionate application: Another ethical concern is the disproportionate application of the death penalty, particularly along racial and socioeconomic lines. Studies have shown disparities in the application of capital punishment, raising questions of fairness and justice.

Case Study: The United States

The United States provides an interesting case study in the discussion of capital punishment and deterrence. While the death penalty remains legal in some states, its use has been declining in recent years. Several factors contribute to this shift, including concerns about the fairness of the process, the risk of wrongful convictions, and changing public attitudes towards capital punishment.

Conclusion

The debate surrounding capital punishment and deterrence is highly complex and contentious. While deterrence theory suggests that the death penalty can serve as a deterrent to crime, empirical evidence on the effectiveness of capital punishment in deterring crime is inconclusive. Moreover, ethical considerations regarding human rights, risk of wrongful convictions, and the disproportionate application of the death penalty further complicate the issue. As societies continue to grapple with these challenges, the discussion on the role and efficacy of capital punishment in promoting deterrence and justice remains ongoing.

Conclusion

In conclusion, the ethical issues surrounding capital punishment are complex and multifaceted. Throughout this section, we have delved into the arguments for and against capital punishment, examined its ethical implications, discussed alternatives, and explored international perspectives and reforms in this area.

We began by examining the principles and moral justifications behind capital punishment. Proponents argue that it serves as retribution, a deterrent, and a means of protecting society. Opponents, on the other hand, contend that it violates human rights, fails to deter crime effectively, and carries the risk of wrongful convictions and executions.

We explored the ethical implications of capital punishment and highlighted the various concerns associated with it. One of the main concerns is the potential for the punishment to be administered unfairly, with a disproportionate impact on certain demographics. Racial, economic, and geographic disparities have been widely documented, raising questions about the fairness and equity of the death penalty system.

Moreover, the irreversibility of capital punishment poses a significant ethical dilemma. The risk of executing an innocent person raises serious moral concerns and challenges the ethical justification for this form of punishment. The case of wrongful convictions, such as that of Cameron Todd Willingham and many others, serves as a powerful reminder of the fallibility of the criminal justice system.

We delved into the international perspectives on capital punishment, highlighting the significant variations in its use and acceptance across countries. Some countries have abolished the death penalty altogether, while others continue to employ it as a legal punishment. The global trend towards abolition reflects an increasing recognition of the ethical and human rights implications of capital punishment.

Alternatives to capital punishment were explored, including life imprisonment without parole, restorative justice, and rehabilitation programs. These alternatives provide opportunities for accountability, remorse, and the possibility of reform, while avoiding the irreversible and morally troubling consequences of execution.

Additionally, we discussed the role of human rights in the context of capital punishment. The principles of human dignity, respect for life, and the prohibition of cruel and inhuman treatment provide a foundation for critiquing the use of capital punishment. International human rights instruments, such as the Universal Declaration of Human Rights, reinforce the view that the death penalty is incompatible with the fundamental rights and values enshrined in these documents.

Reforms and policy recommendations were also explored in this section. In recent years, there has been a growing movement towards limiting the use of capital punishment, imposing stricter safeguards, and enhancing procedural fairness in capital cases. These include measures such as the elimination of mandatory death sentences, ensuring effective legal representation for defendants, and conducting thorough and unbiased investigations.

It is important to note that the death penalty is a deeply divisive and controversial issue, and there are passionate arguments on both sides. The concluding message we can draw from this section is that the ethical considerations surrounding capital punishment demand careful reflection and examination. As society evolves and our understanding of justice and human rights deepens, it becomes imperative to critically evaluate the ethical implications of this form of punishment.

In order to shape a more equitable, just, and sustainable world, it is essential to engage in informed discussions and debates around capital punishment. Students and practitioners in legal studies have a crucial role to play in exploring alternatives, advocating for reforms, and contributing to the ongoing dialogue about the ethical underpinnings of the criminal justice system.

We hope that this section has provided a comprehensive overview of the ethical controversies surrounding capital punishment. By grappling with these complex issues, we can collectively work towards a legal system that upholds the principles of justice, fairness, and respect for human rights.

Policing and Ethical Challenges

Police Use of Force and Ethical Dilemmas

The use of force by police officers is a complex and controversial issue that raises numerous ethical dilemmas. It is crucial to understand the principles and considerations underlying police use of force in order to navigate these dilemmas and promote justice. In this section, we will explore the ethical aspects of police use of force, the challenges it presents, and potential solutions to ensure the appropriate and ethical application of force.

Understanding Police Use of Force

Police use of force refers to the application of physical or psychological force by law enforcement officers in carrying out their duties. It is essential for maintaining public order, protecting lives, and ensuring the safety of both the officers and the community. However, it also comes with ethical responsibilities and limitations.

The principles of legality, necessity, proportionality, and reasonableness are integral to understanding the ethical standards for police use of force. Legality dictates that force must be exercised within the boundaries of the law. Necessity requires officers to use force only when it is necessary to achieve a legitimate objective, such as overcoming resistance or preventing harm. Proportionality means that the force applied should be proportional to the threat faced. Reasonableness emphasizes that officers should act based on the facts and circumstances at hand, considering the perspectives of a reasonable officer in a similar situation.

Ethical Dilemmas in Police Use of Force

While the principles mentioned above provide a framework for ethical decision-making, the practical application of police use of force often presents dilemmas. Let us explore some of the ethical dilemmas commonly encountered by law enforcement officers:

1. Use of Deadly Force: One of the most significant dilemmas is the use of deadly force, particularly in situations where there is a threat to life. Officers must balance their duty to protect themselves and the community with the obligation to preserve life. Determining when deadly force is necessary and whether it was proportionate can be challenging.

2. Discretion and Bias: The discretionary power of police officers allows them to make judgment calls on when and how to use force. However, this discretion can

be influenced by unconscious bias, leading to disproportionate or unjustified use of force against certain individuals or communities. Addressing biases and promoting fair and unbiased decision-making is crucial.

3. De-Escalation vs. Immediate Response: Another dilemma arises when officers have to decide between employing de-escalation techniques to resolve a situation peacefully or using force for immediate control. Balancing the need for immediate action to protect lives with the potential risks associated with escalation requires ethical judgment.

4. Public Perception and Accountability: Police use of force often attracts public scrutiny and can undermine trust between law enforcement and the community. The ethical dilemma here is to balance the need for transparency and accountability while protecting the reputation and safety of involved officers. Ensuring that investigations are thorough, fair, and independent can help address this dilemma.

Addressing Ethical Dilemmas in Police Use of Force

To navigate ethical dilemmas in police use of force, a comprehensive approach involving training, policies, and accountability measures is necessary. Here are some strategies and considerations:

1. Training and Education: Police departments should provide comprehensive training on use of force, emphasizing ethical decision-making, de-escalation techniques, and recognizing biases. Continuous education on emerging best practices can help officers make informed choices.

2. Clear Use of Force Policies: Departments should establish clear and concise use of force policies that align with ethical principles. These policies should outline the circumstances where force may be used, the level of force permissible, and the obligation to provide medical assistance after the use of force.

3. Accountability and Review Mechanisms: Independent oversight bodies or review boards can play a crucial role in ensuring accountability and transparency. These bodies should have the power to investigate use of force incidents, review policies, and make recommendations for improvement.

4. Community Engagement: Building trust and reducing bias starts with community engagement efforts. Police departments should actively involve community members in the development of policies, training programs, and oversight mechanisms. This collaboration fosters a sense of ownership and shared responsibility.

5. Technology and Innovation: Harnessing technology, such as body-worn cameras and advanced training simulators, can provide valuable evidence and

insights into use of force incidents. Leveraging innovative solutions can improve accountability, training, and decision-making processes.

Case Study: The Implementation of De-Escalation Tactics

To further illustrate the ethical considerations in police use of force, let us examine the implementation of de-escalation tactics. De-escalation involves using strategies to reduce tension and avoid the use of force whenever possible. One example of successful de-escalation tactics is the Crisis Intervention Team (CIT) model.

The CIT model integrates specialized training for officers to effectively respond to individuals experiencing a mental health crisis. It emphasizes communication, active listening, empathy, and the use of non-lethal force options. By employing de-escalation techniques, officers can better manage potentially volatile situations while prioritizing the preservation of life.

However, the implementation of de-escalation tactics faces challenges. These include insufficient resources, limited training opportunities, and resistance to change within law enforcement agencies. Overcoming these obstacles requires a commitment to proper funding, ongoing training, and a proactive organizational culture that prioritizes de-escalation strategies.

Conclusion

Police use of force and the ethical dilemmas it entails are critical issues in contemporary society. Understanding the principles of legality, necessity, proportionality, and reasonableness helps guide ethical decision-making. By addressing biases, implementing proper training, establishing clear policies, fostering accountability, and promoting community engagement, we can strive for a more just and ethical approach to police use of force. It is through these efforts that we can shape a more equitable, just, and sustainable world while ensuring the safety and well-being of both law enforcement officers and the communities they serve.

Police Bias and Racial Profiling

In the field of criminal justice, one of the most pressing ethical issues that arises is police bias and racial profiling. This issue raises questions about the fairness and impartiality of law enforcement practices, and it has significant implications for social justice and human rights. In this section, we will explore the concept of police bias, examine the phenomenon of racial profiling, discuss its ethical implications, and consider strategies to address this problem.

Understanding Police Bias

Police bias refers to the tendency of law enforcement officers to hold preconceived notions or prejudices against certain individuals or groups based on characteristics such as race, ethnicity, religion, or socioeconomic status. This bias can influence their decision-making processes, leading to discriminatory practices in law enforcement.

It is important to note that police bias is not limited to intentional acts of discrimination, but also includes unconscious biases that may be ingrained in individuals due to societal conditioning. These biases can affect the way officers perceive, interact with, and treat individuals from different backgrounds.

Racial Profiling: Definition and Scope

Racial profiling is a specific form of police bias that refers to the practice of targeting individuals for law enforcement scrutiny solely based on their race, ethnicity, or national origin. This practice assumes that certain racial or ethnic groups are more likely to engage in criminal activity, leading to disproportionate surveillance and targeting of these groups.

Racial profiling can take various forms, including traffic stops, pedestrian stops, searches, arrests, and use of force. It can occur both on the streets and within other domains of law enforcement, such as airport security or immigration enforcement. Racial profiling not only violates the principles of equality and fairness but also undermines trust between law enforcement agencies and the communities they serve.

Ethical Implications of Police Bias and Racial Profiling

Police bias and racial profiling raise significant ethical concerns, as they violate the principles of fairness, equality, and non-discrimination. These practices perpetuate systemic racism and contribute to the marginalization and stigmatization of certain racial or ethnic groups.

First and foremost, police bias and racial profiling undermine the right to equal treatment before the law. They result in the unequal distribution of police resources and attention, leading to the over-policing of certain communities while neglecting others. This unequal treatment erodes trust and diminishes the legitimacy of law enforcement.

Furthermore, police bias and racial profiling can have devastating social and psychological consequences for individuals who are targeted. It can create a hostile environment, foster feelings of fear and mistrust towards law enforcement, and perpetuate stereotypes and prejudices. These practices not only harm individuals but also contribute to broader social inequalities and perpetuate social divisions.

Addressing Police Bias and Racial Profiling

Addressing police bias and racial profiling requires a multifaceted approach that involves changes in policies, training, and community engagement. Here are some strategies that can help mitigate these problems:

1.   Training and Education: Law enforcement agencies should provide comprehensive training on implicit bias, cultural sensitivity, and de-escalation techniques. Officers need to be aware of their biases and learn effective strategies for fair and impartial policing.

2. Data Collection and Analysis: Collecting data on police stops, searches, and arrests is crucial for identifying patterns of racial profiling. Agencies should regularly analyze this data to identify disparities and take corrective measures.

3. Accountability and Oversight: Establishing independent civilian oversight boards or review mechanisms can help ensure accountability and transparency in addressing allegations of police bias and racial profiling. These oversight bodies should have the authority to investigate complaints and recommend disciplinary actions.

4. Community Policing: Promoting community engagement and collaboration between law enforcement agencies and communities can foster trust, understanding, and cooperation. It is essential to involve community members in the development of policing policies and practices to ensure they are responsive to community needs.

5.   Body-worn Cameras: The implementation of body-worn cameras can provide an objective record of police-citizen interactions, promoting accountability and transparency. Research has shown that body-worn cameras can reduce incidents of misconduct and increase public trust in law enforcement.

6. Bias-Free Policing Policies: Law enforcement agencies should develop and enforce explicit policies that explicitly prohibit racial profiling and provide clear guidelines for fair and impartial policing.

7. Officer Diversity: Increasing the diversity of law enforcement agencies can help reduce police bias and improve community relations. Hiring officers from different racial, ethnic, and cultural backgrounds can enhance understanding, empathy, and cultural competence within police departments.

8.   Collaboration with Community Organizations: Engaging community organizations and leaders in dialogue and collaborative problem-solving can help bridge the gap between law enforcement and communities affected by bias and profiling.

Conclusion

Addressing police bias and racial profiling requires a comprehensive and systematic approach that encompasses changes in policies, training, and community engagement. By recognizing and actively working to eliminate these biases, we can promote fairness, equality, and social justice in law enforcement practices. It is crucial to foster an environment where every individual, regardless of their race or ethnicity, feels safe, respected, and protected by the law.

Police Accountability and Transparency

Police accountability and transparency are crucial aspects of ensuring a just and fair criminal justice system. The actions and conduct of law enforcement agencies have a significant impact on the trust and confidence that the public places in them. When there is a lack of accountability and transparency, it undermines the legitimacy of the police and erodes public trust. This section will examine the importance of police accountability and transparency, the challenges in achieving them, and potential solutions to promote accountability and transparency.

Importance of Police Accountability

Police accountability refers to the mechanisms and processes through which law enforcement agencies are held responsible for their actions and behaviors. It is essential for maintaining the integrity and legitimacy of the police force. Here are some reasons why police accountability is crucial:

- **Ensuring fair justice system:** Police accountability ensures that the criminal justice system operates fairly and impartially. It helps prevent abuses of power, corruption, and misconduct, ensuring that individuals are treated justly and without bias.

- **Building trust with communities:** Accountability fosters trust between law enforcement agencies and the communities they serve. When the police are held accountable for their actions, it demonstrates a commitment to upholding the rights and well-being of the public.

- **Reducing misconduct:** Accountability measures help deter police misconduct. Knowing that their actions will be scrutinized and consequences will be imposed, police officers are more likely to adhere to ethical standards and professional conduct.

- ✦ **Promoting professionalism:** Accountability promotes professionalism within the police force. It encourages officers to continuously improve their skills and knowledge, adhere to ethical guidelines, and maintain high standards of integrity.

- ✦ **Preventing systemic biases:** Through accountability, systemic biases and discriminatory practices within law enforcement can be identified and addressed. By holding individuals accountable for their actions, the focus can shift towards ensuring fair and unbiased treatment for all.

Fostering police accountability is not only essential for the well-being and trust of communities but also contributes to the effectiveness and efficiency of law enforcement operations.

Challenges in Achieving Police Accountability

While the importance of police accountability is indisputable, there are several challenges that hinder its realization. These challenges include:

- ✦ **Opaque disciplinary processes:** In many cases, the disciplinary processes within law enforcement agencies lack transparency. This lack of transparency can lead to a perception of cover-ups or favoritism, eroding trust in the system.

- ✦ **Limited access to information:** Obtaining accurate and timely information about police activities, investigations, and disciplinary action can be challenging. Limited access to information creates barriers to holding law enforcement accountable for their actions.

- ✦ **Lack of independent oversight:** Without independent oversight, there is a risk of conflict of interest and bias in investigations into police misconduct. Independent oversight bodies play a crucial role in ensuring impartiality and fairness.

- ✦ **Resistance to change:** Resistance to reform and the status quo within law enforcement agencies can impede efforts to improve accountability. A culture of silence, fear, or loyalty can hinder the reporting and addressing of misconduct.

- ✦ **Inadequate resources:** Limited funding and resources can hamper the implementation of accountability measures. Adequate resources are needed to invest in training, technology, and independent oversight to ensure effective accountability.

These challenges necessitate innovative solutions and a comprehensive approach to address police accountability effectively.

Promoting Police Accountability and Transparency

To promote police accountability and transparency, a multi-faceted approach is needed. Here are some key strategies and measures that can be implemented:

- **Independent oversight:** Establishing independent oversight bodies with the power to investigate complaints and allegations of misconduct can enhance accountability.

- **Transparency in disciplinary processes:** Making disciplinary processes more transparent can build trust and ensure public confidence. Disciplinary actions, along with explanations, should be publicized to foster transparency.

- **Body-worn cameras:** Equipping police officers with body-worn cameras can provide an objective record of interactions between law enforcement and the public. This can serve as evidence in investigations and promote accountability.

- **Community engagement:** Engaging with the community through regular meetings, forums, and collaborations can help build trust and establish a two-way communication channel. This community input can contribute to holding law enforcement accountable.

- **Training and education:** Providing comprehensive training on ethical conduct, cultural sensitivity, and de-escalation techniques can equip police officers with the necessary skills to uphold accountability.

- **Whistleblower protection:** Implementing robust whistleblower protection mechanisms can encourage law enforcement personnel to report misconduct without fear of retaliation.

- **Enhanced data collection and analysis:** Collecting and analyzing data on police encounters, use of force incidents, and officer complaints can help identify patterns or biases that require attention.

+ **Community oversight boards:** Establishing community oversight boards comprised of representatives from diverse backgrounds can provide an additional layer of accountability.

By implementing these strategies and measures, law enforcement agencies can enhance accountability and transparency, fostering public trust in the police.

Case Study: Civilian Review Boards

One example of a mechanism for enhancing police accountability and transparency is the establishment of civilian review boards. Civilian review boards are independent bodies comprised of community members who review complaints against law enforcement officers. They serve as a bridge between the community and the police department and provide an extra layer of oversight.

Civilian review boards have several functions, including:

+ **Investigating complaints:** Civilian review boards investigate complaints of misconduct filed by community members against law enforcement officers.

+ **Reviewing internal investigations:** They review internal investigations conducted by law enforcement agencies to assess the thoroughness and fairness of these investigations.

+ **Recommendations for discipline:** Based on their investigations, civilian review boards make recommendations for disciplinary actions against officers found to have engaged in misconduct.

+ **Policy recommendations:** They can also make recommendations to the police department on policies and procedures to improve transparency, accountability, and community relations.

Civilian review boards empower the community by allowing them to actively participate in holding law enforcement accountable. They contribute to transparency by providing an independent assessment of complaints and investigations, ensuring that law enforcement agencies are held responsible for their actions.

Conclusion

Police accountability and transparency are essential for promoting justice, protecting individual rights, and building trust between law enforcement agencies and the communities they serve. Achieving accountability requires a comprehensive approach that includes independent oversight, transparency in disciplinary processes, technological advancements, community engagement, and continuous training and education. By implementing these measures, society can work towards a criminal justice system that values integrity, fairness, and the well-being of all its members.

Community Policing and Ethical Engagement

In recent years, the relationship between law enforcement agencies and the communities they serve has faced intense scrutiny. Instances of police misconduct, excessive use of force, and racial profiling have eroded trust and undermined the legitimacy of the criminal justice system. In response, there has been a growing movement towards community policing, an approach that emphasizes collaboration between the police and community members to address crime and ensure public safety. This section will explore the concept of community policing and its ethical implications in promoting trust, transparency, and accountability.

Understanding Community Policing

Community policing is a philosophy and organizational strategy that aims to make the police more accessible, accountable, and responsive to the needs and concerns of the community. It recognizes that the police cannot effectively address crime and maintain public safety without the cooperation and support of the community. Community policing shifts the focus from reactive law enforcement to proactive problem-solving, with an emphasis on building partnerships, enhancing communication, and promoting community engagement.

The key elements of community policing include:

- Community Partnerships: Law enforcement agencies work collaboratively with community members, organizations, and other stakeholders to identify and address public safety issues.

- Problem-Solving Orientation: Police officers engage in problem-solving activities to identify the root causes of crime and develop strategies to prevent and reduce it.

- Proactive Policing: Instead of simply responding to calls for service, police officers take a proactive approach by conducting targeted patrols, engaging in community outreach, and working to prevent crime before it occurs.

- Organizational Transformation: Law enforcement agencies undergo organizational changes to support community policing, including training officers in communication and problem-solving skills, reallocating resources, and reevaluating performance metrics.

- Accountability and Transparency: Police departments are accountable to the community and adhere to transparent practices, such as providing clear and timely information, conducting internal investigations, and holding officers accountable for their actions.

Ethical Considerations in Community Policing

Community policing inherently raises ethical considerations that must be carefully addressed to ensure trust, fairness, and justice. The following ethical principles are particularly important in the context of community policing:

1. **Respect for Individuals' Rights and Dignity:** Community policing requires law enforcement officers to respect the rights and dignity of all individuals, regardless of their race, ethnicity, gender, or socio-economic status. Officers should avoid discriminatory practices and bias-based policing, treating everyone they interact with fairly and with respect.

2. **Proportional Use of Force:** Police officers must use force only when necessary and in proportion to the threat faced. They should prioritize de-escalation techniques and nonviolent strategies to resolve conflicts peacefully. Unnecessary or excessive use of force erodes trust and can lead to violations of individuals' rights.

3. **Integrity and Accountability:** Community policing requires police officers to maintain the highest levels of integrity and accountability. They should act ethically, uphold the law impartially, and promptly address any misconduct or violations within their ranks. Transparency in investigations and disciplinary actions is crucial to maintain public trust.

4. **Confidentiality and Privacy:** Law enforcement agencies must respect individuals' privacy rights and maintain confidentiality when interacting with the community. The information shared by community members should be protected and used only for legitimate law enforcement purposes. Unauthorized disclosure or misuse of private information undermines the trust essential for community policing.

5. **Transparency and Communication:** Open and honest communication is vital for community policing. Law enforcement agencies should provide clear and accessible information to the community, including policies, procedures, and crime statistics. Regular community meetings, public forums, and social media engagement can enhance transparency and foster meaningful dialogue between the police and the public.

6. **Fairness and Equal Treatment:** Community policing demands that law enforcement agencies treat all individuals fairly, without discrimination or bias. Officers should be aware of their own biases and actively work to overcome them. Promoting procedural justice, ensuring due process, and addressing systemic inequities are essential to building trust and legitimacy in the community.

Challenges and Ethical Dilemmas in Community Policing

Implementing community policing faces several challenges and ethical dilemmas that require careful consideration and resolution. Some of these challenges include:

+ **Building Trust:** Establishing trust between the police and the community can be challenging, especially if there is a history of strained relations or past incidents of misconduct. Law enforcement agencies must invest time and effort to engage with community members, address their concerns, and demonstrate their commitment to fair and just practices.

+ **Accountability and Oversight:** Maintaining accountability and ensuring effective oversight mechanisms are crucial for community policing. Independent civilian oversight boards, body-worn cameras, and civilian complaint review processes can help hold law enforcement accountable for their actions. However, striking the right balance between police autonomy and civilian oversight can be complex.

+ **Training and Education:** Equipping police officers with the necessary skills and knowledge to engage in community policing is essential. Training should focus on de-escalation techniques, cultural competence, bias awareness, and ethical decision-making. Providing ongoing professional development opportunities for officers ensures they stay updated on best practices and emerging issues.

+ **Resource Allocation:** Implementing community policing requires adequate resources, including personnel, training, technology, and community support services. Limited resources can hinder the effective implementation of community policing strategies, potentially straining the relationship between the police and the community.

◆ **Resistance to Change:** Some law enforcement agencies may be resistant to change and reluctant to embrace community policing. Factors such as organizational culture, resistance to new practices, and the influence of police unions can impede the successful adoption of community policing principles.

Case Study: Success of Community Policing in Camden, New Jersey

One example that showcases the potential of community policing is the transformation of the Camden Police Department in New Jersey. Faced with high crime rates, community distrust, and budget constraints, the city disbanded its police department in 2012 and rebuilt it from scratch with the principles of community policing at its core.

The Camden Police Department prioritized community engagement, increased the number of officers on foot patrols, established partnerships with community organizations, and introduced regular community meetings. The department also implemented de-escalation training, revised use-of-force policies, and adopted body-worn cameras to enhance accountability and transparency.

As a result of these efforts, Camden saw a significant reduction in violent crime, improved community trust, and increased cooperation between the police and the public. The success of the Camden model highlights the potential of community policing to address crime and foster positive relationships between law enforcement and the community.

Conclusion

Community policing offers a promising approach to address the ethical challenges and build trust between law enforcement agencies and the communities they serve. By emphasizing collaboration, problem-solving, transparency, and accountability, community policing can enhance public safety while respecting individuals' rights and dignity. However, implementing community policing requires sustained commitment, adequate resources, and careful attention to ethical considerations. By prioritizing community engagement and ethical practices, law enforcement agencies can work towards a more just and equitable society.

Ethical Decision Making in Law Enforcement

Ethical decision making is a crucial aspect of law enforcement as it involves making choices that align with moral principles and values. Law enforcement professionals often encounter complex situations that require careful consideration of ethical implications. In this section, we will explore the process of ethical decision making in law enforcement, key ethical principles to consider, and challenges that arise in this context.

Understanding Ethical Decision Making

Ethical decision making involves evaluating different options and choosing the course of action that best adheres to ethical principles. In law enforcement, ethical decision making is particularly important due to the significant impact that the decisions can have on individuals and communities.

To make sound ethical decisions in law enforcement, it is essential to follow a systematic decision-making process. This process includes the following steps:

1. Identify the ethical dilemma: Law enforcement professionals should be able to recognize situations where ethical issues are at play. This requires an understanding of ethical principles and an awareness of potential conflicts between competing values.

2. Gather information: To make an informed decision, law enforcement professionals must gather all relevant information related to the ethical dilemma. This includes understanding the facts of the situation, considering the perspectives of all parties involved, and consulting legal mandates and departmental policies.

3. Identify alternative courses of action: Once the information is gathered, it is necessary to generate multiple options to address the ethical dilemma. This step encourages critical thinking and creativity in exploring various solutions.

4. Evaluate the alternatives: Law enforcement professionals should assess each alternative by analyzing the potential consequences, both positive and negative. Consideration should be given to the impact on stakeholders, the adherence to ethical principles, and the long-term implications of each option.

5. Make a decision: Based on the evaluation of alternatives, law enforcement professionals must make a decision that reflects ethical considerations. This decision should be well-reasoned and aligned with the principles of justice, fairness, and integrity.

6. Implement the decision: Once a decision is made, it is necessary to put the chosen course of action into practice. This requires effective communication, coordination with relevant stakeholders, and careful execution.

7. Reflect and learn: After implementing the decision, it is crucial to reflect on the outcome and learn from the experience. Evaluation helps in identifying strengths and weaknesses, improving decision-making processes, and refining ethical judgment.

Key Ethical Principles in Law Enforcement

Law enforcement professionals should be guided by a set of ethical principles that inform their decision making. These principles provide a framework for evaluating moral dilemmas and acting in the best interest of justice and the community. Some key ethical principles include:

1. Integrity: Upholding integrity involves acting honestly, demonstrating trustworthiness, and maintaining strong moral principles. It requires law enforcement professionals to be accountable for their actions and to avoid conflicts of interest.

2. Justice: The principle of justice emphasizes treating all individuals fairly and equally. Law enforcement professionals should strive for impartiality, ensuring that the law is applied without prejudice or discrimination.

3. Respect: Respect entails valuing the dignity, rights, and autonomy of all individuals. Law enforcement professionals should treat everyone with respect, even in challenging or confrontational situations.

4. Courage: Courage is crucial in law enforcement, as it involves the willingness to do what is right, even in the face of adversity. Law enforcement professionals should exhibit moral courage and stand up against unethical practices.

5. Confidentiality: Maintaining confidentiality is essential in building trust and protecting sensitive information. Law enforcement professionals must respect the privacy and confidentiality of individuals unless there are legal obligations or exceptions.

6. Accountability: Law enforcement professionals should be accountable for their actions and decisions. This involves taking responsibility for the consequences of their actions, admitting mistakes, and actively seeking to rectify any harm caused.

7. Transparency: Transparency promotes trust and legitimacy in law enforcement. Professionals should be open and honest in their interactions, providing accurate and timely information to the public.

Challenges in Ethical Decision Making

Ethical decision making in law enforcement is not without challenges. The following are some common challenges that law enforcement professionals may face:

1. Conflicting obligations: Law enforcement professionals often face situations where multiple ethical obligations appear to be in conflict. For example, maintaining public safety may conflict with respecting individual rights. Balancing these conflicting obligations requires careful analysis and consideration of all relevant factors.

2. High-stress environments: Law enforcement professionals work in high-stakes and high-stress environments, which can impact their decision-making ability. Stressors can impair judgment and lead to unethical decision making. Awareness of these challenges is crucial for mitigating their impact.

3. Groupthink: In situations where decision making involves a group of individuals, there is a risk of groupthink, where the desire for consensus outweighs independent critical thinking. This can lead to unethical decisions. Encouraging independent thought, diversity of perspectives, and constructive dissent can help mitigate this challenge.

4. Code of silence: Law enforcement professionals may feel pressured to remain silent or withhold information about unethical practices within their organization. Breaking the code of silence can be difficult and can have personal and professional consequences. Creating a culture that encourages reporting and provides protection for whistleblowers is essential.

5. Limited resources: Law enforcement agencies often face resource constraints, which can create ethical dilemmas. For example, limited resources may require prioritizing certain cases over others. Finding ethical solutions that maximize the use of available resources requires careful consideration and strategic planning.

Case Study: Use of Force Dilemma

Consider the following case study to illustrate the challenges and complexities of ethical decision making in law enforcement:

Officer Smith is called to a domestic disturbance in a residential neighborhood. Upon arrival, he encounters an agitated individual who appears to be under the influence of drugs. The individual becomes increasingly aggressive and refuses to comply with Officer Smith's commands.

Officer Smith must decide whether to use force to subdue the individual and maintain control of the situation. He recognizes the potential risks of using force, as well as the need to protect himself and others. However, he is also aware of the ethical principles of proportionality, necessity, and fairness in the use of force.

To make an ethical decision in this situation, Officer Smith should:

1. Assess the threat: Officer Smith must evaluate the level of threat posed by the individual. Is the individual armed? Are there others at risk? This assessment will help determine the necessity and proportionality of the use of force.

2. Consider alternative approaches: Officer Smith should consider whether there are less intrusive options available to de-escalate the situation. Can he call for backup? Are there verbal tactics that might calm the individual? Exploring non-violent alternatives is crucial.

3. Follow departmental policies and legal guidelines: Officer Smith should be familiar with departmental policies and legal guidelines regarding the use of force. These policies provide a framework for decision making and help ensure consistency and accountability.

4. Document the decision-making process: Officer Smith should document the factors considered, the reasoning behind the decision, and the actions taken during the incident. This documentation serves as evidence of his adherence to ethical standards.

5. Seek post-incident review: After the incident, Officer Smith should participate in a post-incident review process to assess the effectiveness and ethics of his decision. This review provides an opportunity for learning and improvement.

By following these steps, Officer Smith can navigate the ethical challenges of this use of force dilemma while upholding his duty to protect and serve the community.

Resources for Ethical Decision Making in Law Enforcement

Law enforcement professionals can utilize various resources to enhance their understanding and application of ethical decision-making principles. Some valuable resources include:

1. Code of Ethics: Many law enforcement agencies have a code of ethics that outlines the expected standards of conduct for their personnel. These codes serve as a guide for ethical decision making and provide a set of principles to follow.

2. Training and Education: Ongoing training programs and educational opportunities are essential for law enforcement professionals to develop the knowledge and skills necessary for ethical decision making. These programs can cover topics such as ethical theories, procedural justice, and cultural competency.

3. Professional Associations and Organizations: Law enforcement professionals can join professional associations and organizations that provide resources, guidance, and networking opportunities. These groups often offer ethics committees, conferences, and publications that focus on ethical decision making in law enforcement.

4. Legal and Ethical Experts: Consulting with legal and ethical experts can provide valuable insights and guidance in navigating complex ethical decision-making scenarios. These experts can offer perspectives based on legal precedence, ethical theories, and professional standards.

5. Case Studies and Simulations: Reviewing real-world case studies and engaging in simulated scenarios can help law enforcement professionals practice ethical decision making in a controlled and educational environment. These exercises can enhance critical thinking, problem-solving, and moral reasoning skills.

By utilizing these resources, law enforcement professionals can enhance their ethical decision-making skills and contribute to the promotion of justice and fairness in their practice.

Conclusion

Ethical decision making is of paramount importance in law enforcement. By following a systematic decision-making process and adhering to key ethical principles, law enforcement professionals can navigate complex moral dilemmas and promote justice. Despite the challenges present in this field, the commitment to ethical decision making contributes to building trust, maintaining integrity, and upholding the principles of a just and equitable society.

Policing and Social Justice

Policing is an essential function of society, aimed at maintaining law and order and ensuring the safety of communities. However, the interactions between the police and the community can also raise significant ethical and social justice concerns. This section explores the challenges and dilemmas that arise in the context of policing and social justice and examines ways to address them.

The Role of Police in Promoting Social Justice

The role of the police extends beyond enforcing laws; they also have a responsibility to promote social justice within their communities. Social justice entails the fair distribution of resources, opportunities, and benefits to all members of society, irrespective of their race, gender, socio-economic background, or other characteristics.

While the primary duty of the police is to maintain order and protect public safety, they should also uphold the principles of social justice in their daily interactions with the community. This involves treating all individuals with respect and dignity, ensuring equal protection under the law, and addressing any biases or biases that may exist.

Addressing Police Bias and Racial Profiling

One of the most significant ethical challenges in policing is the issue of bias, particularly racial profiling. Racial profiling occurs when law enforcement officers target individuals based on their race or ethnicity rather than on evidence of criminal behavior. This practice is not only discriminatory but also undermines the principles of social justice and equality.

To address police bias and racial profiling, police departments can implement various measures. These include:

1. Training: Providing thorough and ongoing training to officers on bias awareness, cultural competence, and the importance of treating all individuals fairly and without prejudice.

2. Community Engagement: Actively engaging with community members, organizations, and leaders to foster understanding, trust, and cooperation. This can also involve recruiting police officers from diverse backgrounds to reflect the community's demographics.

3. Use of Data and Technology: Implementing data-driven strategies and technological tools to monitor and identify patterns of bias in policing practices. This can help identify problematic areas and guide interventions.

4. Accountability and Oversight: Establishing robust accountability mechanisms, such as civilian review boards, to investigate complaints of bias and misconduct. Holding officers accountable for their actions is crucial to building trust and promoting social justice.

Ensuring Police Accountability and Transparency

Transparency and accountability are essential principles in maintaining public trust and ensuring social justice. Police departments must be accountable for their actions and responsible for addressing any misconduct or abuses of power. This requires clear policies and procedures for reporting and investigating complaints against officers and holding them accountable when necessary.

To enhance police accountability and transparency, the following measures can be implemented:

1. Body-worn Cameras: Equipping police officers with body-worn cameras can provide an objective record of interactions with the public and serve as a valuable tool for review and accountability.

2. Independent Oversight: Establishing independent oversight bodies with the authority to investigate complaints, review policies, and make recommendations for improvements. These bodies should have civilian representation and be granted sufficient resources and powers.

3. Data Collection and Analysis: Collecting data on police activities, such as stops, searches, and use of force, and analyzing this information for patterns of bias or misconduct. This data should be made accessible to the public to ensure transparency.

4. Internal Affairs Units: Strengthening internal affairs units within police departments to ensure timely and thorough investigations of complaints against officers. This includes whistleblower protections for officers who report misconduct within the department.

Community Policing and Social Justice

Community policing emphasizes building trust and collaboration between the police and the community they serve. It aims to address the root causes of crime, prevent conflicts, and promote social justice. By actively engaging with community members and organizations, community policing can foster a sense of ownership, empowerment, and shared responsibility for public safety.

Community policing strategies for promoting social justice include:

1. Problem-Oriented Policing: Identifying and addressing underlying issues that contribute to crime and social inequality within communities. This involves partnerships with social service agencies, community organizations, and residents to develop comprehensive solutions.

2. Procedural Justice: Implementing fair and transparent procedures during police interactions, such as respectful communication, active listening, and explanation of decisions. This helps build trust and legitimacy in the community.

3. Restorative Justice: Using restorative justice principles to address minor offenses and repair harm within the community. This approach focuses on repairing relationships, promoting accountability, and preventing future conflicts.

4. Community Engagement: Actively involving community members in decision-making processes, such as developing policies, setting priorities, and evaluating the effectiveness of policing strategies. This ensures that the diverse voices and needs of the community are considered.

It is important to note that while community policing can be an effective strategy for promoting social justice, its success relies on genuine collaboration, meaningful engagement, and a commitment to addressing systemic issues.

Conclusion

Policing and social justice are interconnected. Policing practices deeply impact the lives of individuals and communities, and therefore, it is crucial that ethical considerations and social justice principles guide police actions. By addressing issues of bias, promoting accountability and transparency, and adopting community policing strategies, police departments can work towards building trust, promoting social justice, and ensuring the safety and well-being of all members of society.

Policing and Public Trust

When it comes to maintaining law and order in a society, the police play a crucial role. However, this role comes with a great responsibility to uphold the law, protect citizens, and ensure justice. Policing is not just about enforcing laws, but also about building trust and maintaining a positive relationship with the public. This section will explore the concept of policing and the importance of public trust in the context of ethical issues in legal studies.

Understanding Policing

Policing refers to the activities carried out by law enforcement agencies to maintain public order, prevent and detect crimes, and ensure the safety and security of the community. It involves various tasks such as patrolling, investigation, crime prevention, and community engagement. However, the effectiveness of policing is not solely measured by crime rates or arrest statistics but also by the level of trust and confidence that the public has in the police.

The Importance of Public Trust

Public trust is the foundation of effective policing. When the community trusts the police, they are more likely to cooperate, provide information, and work together to prevent and solve crimes. Trust also leads to increased confidence in the criminal justice system, ensuring that it operates fairly and impartially.

Without public trust, the legitimacy of the police is undermined, making it harder for them to carry out their duties effectively. Suspicion and fear can lead to the breakdown of community-police relationships, hindering efforts to establish a safe and secure society. It is crucial for police departments to strive to build public trust and maintain it through ethical practices and transparency.

Ethical Challenges in Policing

Maintaining public trust in policing is not without its challenges. In recent years, there have been numerous cases of police misconduct, excessive use of force, racial profiling, and a lack of accountability. These incidents have eroded public trust and heightened tensions between law enforcement and marginalized communities. Police departments around the world are grappling with ethical challenges to restore public trust and redefine their relationship with the communities they serve.

Police Accountability and Transparency

One key aspect of building public trust is ensuring police accountability and transparency. Police departments should have robust systems in place to investigate complaints against officers, address misconduct, and take appropriate disciplinary action when necessary. This includes implementing civilian oversight boards, independent review mechanisms, and transparent reporting of police activities.

By holding officers accountable for their actions and ensuring transparency in investigations, police departments can demonstrate their commitment to fairness, justice, and trustworthiness. Regular communication and engagement with the public, including open forums and community meetings, are also vital in promoting transparency and fostering a sense of accountability.

Community Policing and Ethical Engagement

Community policing is an approach that emphasizes collaboration between the police and the community in addressing crime and maintaining public order. It shifts the focus from a reactive response to proactive engagement, with officers working closely with community members to identify and solve problems.

Ethical engagement with the community is a fundamental component of community policing. This involves developing relationships, listening to community concerns, and tailoring policing strategies based on the unique needs and values of the community. By involving the community in decision-making processes and problem-solving, police can enhance public trust and cooperation.

Ethical Decision Making in Law Enforcement

Ethical decision making is crucial for police officers in a variety of situations they encounter on a daily basis. Officers must navigate complex moral dilemmas, balancing the need for public safety with the protection of individual rights and liberties. Ethical decision-making frameworks, such as the ethical decision triangle (EDT), can assist officers in making sound ethical choices.

The EDT consists of three components: duty, character, and consequences. It requires officers to consider their duty to uphold the law and protect citizens, their own moral character in terms of integrity and ethical behavior, and the potential consequences of their actions. By using this framework, officers can approach ethical dilemmas in a systematic and principled manner.

Building Trust through Proactive Measures

To overcome the challenges to public trust and establish a positive relationship with the community, police departments can take proactive measures. Some approaches include:

1. Training and education: Continuous training on ethics, cultural sensitivity, de-escalation techniques, and community policing principles can equip officers with the skills and knowledge necessary to engage with the public ethically.

2. Diverse recruitment and representation: Police departments should strive to reflect the diversity of the communities they serve. Recruiting officers from different backgrounds helps build trust and understanding across diverse populations.

3. Collaborative problem-solving: Engaging community members in identifying and addressing issues enhances trust and cooperation. Police departments can work with community organizations, schools, and local leaders to develop initiatives that address the root causes of crime and build safer communities.

4. Use of technology and data: Transparency and accountability can be enhanced through the use of technology, such as body-worn cameras, to capture interactions between officers and the public. Data collection and analysis can enable police departments to identify and address patterns of misconduct or bias.

5. Restorative justice practices: Emphasizing restorative justice principles, such as mediation and reconciliation, can help repair harm, promote healing, and restore trust between the police and the community.

Conclusion

Public trust is a vital component of effective policing. Maintaining trust requires ethical decision making, accountability, transparency, and proactive engagement with the community. By addressing the ethical challenges in policing and implementing strategies to build trust, police departments can ensure public safety while promoting justice and social harmony.

Conclusion

In this chapter, we have explored the ethical challenges faced in the criminal justice system. We examined the principles of criminal justice ethics, the role and responsibilities of criminal justice professionals, and the ethical dilemmas encountered in law enforcement, prosecution, and the correctional system. We also discussed the intersection between criminal justice and social justice, as well as the importance of rehabilitation in the criminal justice process.

One of the key ethical issues in the criminal justice system is the use of force by law enforcement officers. This issue has gained significant attention in recent years, with numerous cases of excessive force and police brutality coming to light. As a society, we must navigate the balance between ensuring public safety and protecting the civil rights and well-being of individuals. It is crucial for law enforcement agencies to have robust training programs that emphasize de-escalation techniques and emphasize the importance of respect for human rights.

Another ethical dilemma in criminal justice is the issue of capital punishment. The question of whether the death penalty is morally justifiable has long been a topic of debate. While some argue that it serves as a deterrent and provides closure to victims' families, others argue that it violates the right to life and can lead to the execution of innocent individuals. It is essential for society to engage in a thoughtful and informed discussion about the effectiveness, fairness, and morality of capital punishment.

Policing biases and racial profiling are further ethical challenges in the criminal justice system. The unjust targeting of individuals based on their race or ethnicity erodes trust between law enforcement agencies and the communities they serve. Implementing policies and training programs to address implicit bias and promote equitable policing can help reduce these concerns and foster a sense of justice and fairness.

Furthermore, as criminal justice professionals, it is vital to uphold ethical standards in all aspects of their work. This includes maintaining confidentiality, avoiding conflicts of interest, and adhering to professional codes of conduct. Striving for transparency, accountability, and integrity is essential to ensure public trust and confidence in the criminal justice system.

To promote social justice within the criminal justice system, we must also focus on rehabilitation and reintegration. The goal should be to address the underlying causes of criminal behavior and provide individuals with the support and resources needed to rebuild their lives. By focusing on rehabilitation rather than solely punishment, we can work towards breaking the cycle of crime and helping individuals become productive members of society.

In conclusion, ethical issues in the criminal justice system are complex and require careful consideration. It is crucial for criminal justice professionals to navigate these dilemmas with integrity, empathy, and a commitment to justice and fairness. By promoting ethical practices and embracing social justice principles, we can work towards a criminal justice system that promotes rehabilitation, protects human rights, and ensures a more equitable and just society.

Legal and Ethical Issues in Business and Commerce

Ethics in Business Environment

Concept of Business Ethics

In today's complex business landscape, the concept of business ethics plays a vital role in guiding organizations towards ethical decision making and responsible practices. Ethics in business refers to the moral principles and values that govern the behavior and actions of individuals and organizations in the commercial sphere. It encompasses a range of ethical considerations, including honesty, integrity, fairness, transparency, and social responsibility.

Importance of Business Ethics

Business ethics is not merely a theoretical concept; it is of utmost significance in the practical world. There are several reasons why business ethics is important:

1. Enhancing Reputation and Building Trust: Ethical business practices contribute to the establishment of a strong reputation and help build trust among customers, employees, and stakeholders. Organizations that act ethically are more likely to attract loyal customers and long-term business partnerships.

2. Fostering Employee Morale and Engagement: When employees work in an environment that prioritizes ethical behavior, it fosters a sense of pride, morale, and engagement. Ethical guidelines provide employees with a clear framework for making decisions and ensure a fair and respectful work culture.

3. Promoting Lawful Operations: Ethical business practices go hand in hand with legal compliance. By adhering to ethical standards, organizations minimize the risk of legal violations and protect themselves from legal consequences, such as fines, lawsuits, and damage to their reputation.

4.   Nurturing Customer Loyalty: Ethical businesses prioritize customer satisfaction and strive to deliver products and services of high quality.   By considering the interests and well-being of customers, organizations build loyalty, which can lead to repeat business and positive word-of-mouth recommendations.

5.   Contributing to Social and Environmental Well-being: Business ethics extends beyond profitability and encompasses responsible practices towards society and the environment.   Ethical businesses actively engage in activities that promote social welfare, such as philanthropy, community development, and environmental sustainability.

Ethical Principles in Business

To operationalize business ethics, several ethical principles serve as guiding frameworks for decision making:

1. Integrity: Business integrity entails honesty, truthfulness, and reliability. It means conducting business in a transparent manner, maintaining consistency between words and deeds, and honoring commitments made to stakeholders.

2. Fairness: Fairness involves treating all stakeholders impartially and without discrimination. Organizations should ensure fair practices in areas such as hiring, promotions, compensation, and customer interactions.

3.   Responsibility: Business responsibility refers to the obligation of organizations to consider the well-being of society and the environment.   This includes actions such as ethical sourcing, sustainable manufacturing practices, and minimizing the negative impact on local communities and the environment.

4. Respect for Others: Respect for others is a fundamental ethical principle that emphasizes treating individuals with dignity, valuing diversity, and promoting inclusivity.   It entails respecting the rights, opinions, and perspectives of all stakeholders,   including   employees,   customers,   suppliers,   and   the   wider community.

5. Accountability: Accountability involves taking responsibility for one's actions and decisions. Ethical organizations are accountable to their stakeholders and are willing to accept the consequences of their actions. This includes being transparent in communication, admitting mistakes, and taking steps to rectify them.

Challenges and Dilemmas in Business Ethics

Implementing ethical practices in business is not without challenges and ethical dilemmas. Some common challenges include:

1.   Conflicting Interests: Organizations often face situations where the interests of different stakeholders, such as shareholders, employees, customers, and the community, may conflict. Balancing these interests ethically can be complex and require careful consideration.

2.   Globalization and Cultural Differences: In a globalized business environment, organizations operate in diverse cultural contexts with varying ethical norms and values.   Finding common ground and ensuring ethical consistency across international operations can be challenging.

3. Corporate Social Responsibility vs. Profitability: The pursuit of profit sometimes creates tension with corporate social responsibility. Organizations must navigate the fine line between profitability and ethical responsibility, seeking sustainable business models that prioritize both economic and societal well-being.

4. Ethical Decision Making: Ethical decision making can be complex and subjective.   It often requires considering multiple factors, assessing potential consequences, and making choices that prioritize ethical principles. This process can be challenging and lead to ethical dilemmas.

Real-World Example: The Enron Scandal

The Enron scandal serves as a notable example of the consequences of unethical business practices.   Enron, once considered one of the world's leading energy companies, collapsed in 2001 due to fraudulent accounting practices and a lack of ethical oversight.

Enron executives engaged in activities such as inflating profits, hiding debts, and manipulating financial statements to deceive investors and boost stock prices. These unethical practices ultimately led to the downfall of the company, significant financial losses for shareholders, and the dissolution of Arthur Andersen, Enron's accounting firm.

The Enron scandal highlights the importance of ethical behavior in business and the severe consequences that can arise from a lack of ethical oversight. It serves as a reminder of the need for strong ethical principles, transparency, and accountability in the corporate world.

Additional Resources

1. Business Ethics: Managing Corporate Citizenship and Sustainability in the Age of Globalization by Andrew Crane and Dirk Matten.

2.   Ethics in the Workplace: Tools and Tactics for Organizational Transformation by Craig E. Johnson.

3.   The   Center   for   Business   Ethics   at   Bentley   University:
www.bentley.edu/centers/center-for-business-ethics
4. The Ethics Resource Center: www.ethics.org
5. The Business Ethics Blog: www.businessethicsblog.com

Key Takeaways

- Business ethics refers to the moral principles and values that guide ethical decision making and responsible practices in the commercial sphere.

- Ethical business practices enhance reputation, build trust, foster employee morale, and contribute to social and environmental well-being.

- Ethical principles in business include integrity, fairness, responsibility, respect for others, and accountability.

- Challenges in business ethics arise from conflicting interests, globalization, the balance between profitability and social responsibility, and complex ethical decision making.

- The Enron scandal serves as a cautionary tale, illustrating the severe consequences of unethical business practices.

Remember, in the world of business, ethics are not just a matter of choice but a necessity for long-term success and positive societal impact.

Ethical Issues in Corporate Governance

Corporate governance refers to the system of rules, practices, and processes by which a company is directed and controlled. It encompasses the relationships among a company's management, its board of directors, its shareholders, and other stakeholders, and provides a framework for achieving the company's objectives and ensuring accountability.

Ethics plays a crucial role in corporate governance as it sets the standards for responsible and ethical behavior within an organization. Ethical issues in corporate governance arise when there is a conflict between the interests of different stakeholders, or when there is a breach of ethical principles and values. In this section, we will explore some of the key ethical issues in corporate governance and their implications.

Conflict of Interest

One of the most significant ethical issues in corporate governance is conflict of interest. A conflict of interest occurs when a person or entity has multiple interests, one of which could potentially compromise their judgment or loyalty to another party.

In the context of corporate governance, conflicts of interest can arise in various ways. For example, a director may have a personal financial interest in a transaction that the company is considering, or an executive may use confidential information for personal gain. These conflicts can undermine the integrity of decision-making and lead to actions that are not in the best interest of the company or its stakeholders.

To address conflicts of interest, companies should establish and enforce comprehensive policies and procedures. These policies should require directors, executives, and employees to disclose any actual or potential conflicts of interest and recuse themselves from decision-making where conflicts exist. Transparency and accountability are essential in managing conflicts of interest and maintaining the trust of stakeholders.

Executive Compensation

Another ethical issue in corporate governance is executive compensation. Excessive executive compensation, especially when it is not aligned with the company's performance, can raise concerns about fairness and transparency.

In recent years, there have been numerous instances where executives of financially struggling companies received significant bonuses while employees were laid off or shareholders suffered losses. This misalignment between executive pay and company performance can lead to public outrage and damage the reputation of the company.

To address this issue, companies should adopt compensation practices that are based on performance and aligned with the long-term interests of shareholders. This can include tying executive compensation to the achievement of specific financial and non-financial goals, as well as implementing clawback provisions that allow the company to recover compensation in the event of misconduct or poor performance.

In addition, companies should improve transparency and disclosure regarding executive compensation. This can help shareholders and other stakeholders understand the rationale behind compensation decisions and hold the company accountable for its practices.

Whistleblowing and Corporate Culture

Whistleblowing is an important mechanism for uncovering wrongdoing and promoting transparency and accountability in corporate governance.

Whistleblowers are individuals who report illegal or unethical activities within their organization.

Ethical issues arise when companies fail to create a culture that supports and protects whistleblowers. In some cases, whistleblowers face retaliation or suffer adverse consequences for speaking up. This can discourage others from reporting misconduct and allow unethical behavior to go unchecked.

To foster an ethical corporate culture, companies should establish policies and mechanisms to encourage whistleblowing. This can include anonymous reporting channels, protections against retaliation, and a commitment to thoroughly investigate and address complaints. By creating a culture that values integrity and accountability, companies can help prevent unethical behavior and protect the interests of stakeholders.

Corporate Social Responsibility

Corporate social responsibility (CSR) refers to a company's commitment to addressing social, economic, and environmental issues in its operations and interactions with stakeholders. Ethical issues arise when companies fail to fulfill their CSR obligations or engage in practices that harm society or the environment.

For example, companies may engage in unethical labor practices, exploit natural resources without regard for sustainability, or contribute to environmental pollution. These actions can damage the reputation of the company, lead to legal and regulatory issues, and alienate stakeholders.

To address CSR issues, companies should adopt ethical practices that prioritize the well-being of society and the environment. This can include implementing sustainable business practices, promoting diversity and inclusion, supporting community development initiatives, and being transparent about their social and environmental impact.

Companies should also engage with stakeholders and listen to their concerns and expectations. By incorporating stakeholder perspectives into their decision-making processes, companies can ensure that their actions align with ethical principles and contribute to the greater good.

Conclusion

Ethical issues in corporate governance are critical considerations for companies seeking to establish a framework for responsible and ethical behavior. Conflict of interest, executive compensation, whistleblowing, and corporate social responsibility are just a few of the many ethical issues that can arise in corporate governance.

To address these issues, companies must prioritize transparency, accountability, and a commitment to ethical principles. By doing so, companies can not only protect the interests of their stakeholders but also build a reputation for integrity and earn the trust of their customers, employees, and the wider society. Effective corporate governance requires ongoing attention to ethical issues, continuous improvement, and a dedication to creating a more equitable and sustainable world.

Corporate Social Responsibility

Corporate Social Responsibility (CSR) is a concept that refers to a company's voluntary commitment to manage its economic, social, and environmental impacts in a responsible manner. It goes beyond legal compliance and aims to contribute to sustainable development and societal well-being. In this section, we will explore the importance of CSR, its key principles, challenges in implementation, and the benefits it can bring to businesses and society.

Importance of Corporate Social Responsibility

The significance of CSR has grown rapidly in recent years as businesses are expected to operate in a socially and environmentally responsible manner. Here are some reasons why CSR is important:

- **Enhancing reputation:** Engaging in CSR initiatives can help improve a company's reputation and build trust with stakeholders, including customers, employees, investors, and communities. By demonstrating a commitment to ethical practices and sustainability, companies can attract more customers and retain their loyalty.

- **Risk management:** Adopting CSR practices can help companies identify and mitigate potential risks, such as legal violations, negative public perception, and supply chain disruptions. By proactively addressing these risks, companies can protect their brand and avoid potential financial, legal, and reputational damages.

- **Stakeholder engagement:** CSR initiatives provide opportunities for companies to engage with their stakeholders and address their concerns. By involving stakeholders in decision-making processes and considering their perspectives, companies can build stronger relationships and foster collaboration.

+ **Long-term sustainability:** Embracing CSR allows companies to align their business strategies with long-term sustainable development goals. By considering the social and environmental impacts of their operations, companies can contribute to the well-being of communities and preserve the planet's resources for future generations.

Overall, CSR is essential for companies to create value beyond financial performance and to demonstrate their commitment to being responsible corporate citizens.

Principles of Corporate Social Responsibility

Corporate social responsibility is guided by several key principles that serve as a framework for responsible business practices. Here are some fundamental principles:

1. **Sustainable development:** Companies should conduct their business in a way that meets the needs of the present without compromising the ability of future generations to meet their own needs. This involves considering the environmental, social, and economic impacts of business activities and striving for long-term sustainability.

2. **Ethics and integrity:** Companies should uphold the highest standards of ethical behavior and integrity. This includes practicing transparency, honesty, and fairness in all business dealings and complying with applicable laws and regulations.

3. **Respect for human rights:** Companies should respect and support the protection of internationally recognized human rights. This involves avoiding complicity in human rights abuses and ensuring that their activities do not infringe upon the rights of individuals or communities.

4. **Environmental responsibility:** Companies should minimize their environmental footprint by adopting environmentally friendly practices and technologies. This includes reducing greenhouse gas emissions, conserving natural resources, and promoting waste reduction and recycling.

5. **Stakeholder engagement:** Companies should actively engage with and consider the interests and concerns of their stakeholders, including employees, customers, suppliers, communities, and investors. This involves

creating mechanisms for feedback, dialogue, and collaboration to inform decision-making processes.

These principles provide a guiding framework for companies to integrate social and environmental considerations into their day-to-day operations.

Challenges in Implementing Corporate Social Responsibility

Implementing CSR initiatives can present several challenges for businesses. It requires a comprehensive understanding of the organization's impact on society and the environment, as well as a commitment to address any negative impacts. Here are some common challenges in implementing CSR:

+ **Resource allocation:** Implementing CSR initiatives often requires financial and human resources. Companies may face challenges in allocating sufficient resources to CSR activities while balancing other business needs and priorities. Finding a balance between economic objectives and social/environmental objectives can be a complex task.

+ **Measuring impact:** Assessing the impact of CSR initiatives can be challenging. Companies need to develop effective metrics and measurement systems to evaluate the outcomes and impact of their CSR efforts. This can be particularly difficult when measuring intangible benefits, such as improved brand reputation or employee satisfaction.

+ **Complex supply chains:** Companies with global supply chains face challenges in ensuring that their suppliers and business partners adhere to responsible practices. Managing and monitoring the social and environmental performance of suppliers throughout the supply chain can be complex and resource-intensive.

+ **Greenwashing:** Some companies may engage in greenwashing, which is the practice of making false or misleading claims about the environmental or social benefits of their products or practices. Avoiding greenwashing requires transparency and clear communication about the company's actual CSR efforts.

Overcoming these challenges requires strong leadership, organizational commitment, and a systematic approach to CSR implementation.

Benefits of Corporate Social Responsibility

While implementing CSR initiatives can be challenging, it can also bring numerous benefits to businesses and society. Here are some key benefits of CSR:

- **Enhanced brand reputation and competitive advantage:** Companies that demonstrate a strong commitment to CSR can enhance their brand reputation, attract more customers, and differentiate themselves from competitors. CSR can serve as a competitive advantage by building trust and loyalty among stakeholders.

- **Improved employee engagement and retention:** CSR initiatives can contribute to a positive work environment and enhance employee satisfaction. Companies that prioritize CSR often attract and retain talent more effectively, leading to improved productivity and reduced recruitment costs.

- **Risk mitigation and cost savings:** By proactively addressing social and environmental issues, companies can reduce the risk of legal violations, reputational damage, and operational disruptions. CSR initiatives can also lead to cost savings through energy efficiency, waste reduction, and improved resource management.

- **Innovation and business opportunities:** Embracing CSR can drive innovation by encouraging companies to develop sustainable products, services, and business models. CSR initiatives can also open up new business opportunities, such as partnerships with socially and environmentally conscious organizations.

- **Positive societal impact:** Through CSR, companies can contribute to solving social and environmental challenges, such as poverty alleviation, education, and environmental conservation. By actively engaging with communities, companies can make a tangible difference and create shared value.

Overall, CSR can lead to a positive impact on both business performance and society, creating a win-win situation.

Examples of Corporate Social Responsibility

To better understand CSR in practice, let's explore a few examples of companies that have embraced CSR initiatives:

1. **Patagonia:** This outdoor clothing and gear company has implemented a range of CSR initiatives, including promoting fair labor practices, reducing its environmental footprint, and supporting environmental advocacy. Patagonia's commitment to sustainability has helped build a loyal customer base and fostered a strong brand identity.

2. **Unilever:** Unilever, a multinational consumer goods company, has integrated sustainability into its business strategy through initiatives such as the Sustainable Living Plan. The plan focuses on reducing the company's environmental impact, improving the well-being of employees and communities, and enhancing the social and environmental sustainability of its supply chain.

3. **TOMS:** TOMS, a shoe and eyewear company, follows a "One for One" model, where for every product sold, the company donates a pair of shoes or helps restore sight to a person in need. This social impact initiative has resonated with customers and has helped TOMS position itself as a socially responsible brand.

These examples showcase how companies from different industries and sizes can incorporate CSR into their business strategies and create positive impacts.

Conclusion

Corporate Social Responsibility is a critical aspect of modern business that goes beyond profit-making and aims to ensure sustainable development and societal well-being. Implementing CSR can pose challenges for companies, but the benefits are substantial, including enhanced reputation, improved employee engagement, risk mitigation, and positive societal impact. By adhering to the principles of sustainability, ethics, human rights, environmental responsibility, and stakeholder engagement, companies can contribute to a more equitable and sustainable world while achieving long-term business success.

Ethical Considerations in Marketing and Advertising

In today's highly competitive and consumer-driven world, marketing and advertising play a significant role in promoting products and services to target audiences. However, with this power comes responsibility. Ethical considerations in marketing and advertising are crucial to ensure fair and honest practices that respect consumer rights and uphold social values. In this section, we will explore the ethical issues that marketers and advertisers face, examine the principles that guide their decision-making, and discuss strategies to maintain ethical integrity in this field.

Ethics in Marketing and Advertising

Marketing and advertising ethics revolve around the moral principles and values that govern the actions and behavior of marketers and advertisers. At the heart of ethical considerations in this realm is the idea of transparency, honesty, and respect for consumer autonomy. Marketers and advertisers have a responsibility to provide accurate and truthful information, avoid deceptive tactics, and protect consumers from harm.

Moreover, ethical marketing and advertising involve recognizing and respecting the rights and dignity of consumers. This includes avoiding discriminatory practices, ensuring privacy and data protection, and refraining from exploiting vulnerable individuals or groups. Ethical marketers also strive to contribute to the overall well-being of society and engage in social and environmental responsibility.

Principles of Ethical Marketing and Advertising

Several principles guide ethical decision-making in marketing and advertising:

1. **Truth and Accuracy:** Marketers should ensure that their claims and representations about products or services are truthful and supported by evidence. Exaggeration, false testimonials, and misleading statements should be avoided.

2. **Transparency and Disclosure:** Marketers should provide clear and accurate information about the features, benefits, and limitations of the products or services they promote. Material information that could significantly affect consumers' decisions should be disclosed.

3. **Respect for Consumer Privacy:** Marketers should respect consumer privacy rights and obtain explicit consent for using personal data. They should implement strong data protection measures and comply with relevant laws and regulations.

4. **Fairness and Non-Discrimination:** Marketers should treat all consumers fairly and avoid engaging in discriminatory practices based on characteristics such as race, gender, religion, or age. Inclusivity and diversity should be valued and promoted.

5. **Social and Environmental Responsibility:** Marketers should consider the social and environmental impact of their marketing decisions and strive to contribute positively to societal well-being. They should promote sustainable practices, support social causes, and avoid engaging in harmful activities.

Challenges and Ethical Dilemmas

The field of marketing and advertising presents several challenges and ethical dilemmas that marketers and advertisers must navigate. These include:

1. **Deceptive Advertising:** Marketers may be tempted to use misleading or exaggerated claims to attract consumers. Balancing the desire to grab attention with the need for ethical communication is a constant challenge.

2. **Targeting Vulnerable Audiences:** Marketers must be careful not to exploit vulnerable individuals, such as children or the elderly, who may be more susceptible to manipulative advertising tactics.

3. **Privacy and Data Protection:** With the rise of digital marketing, the collection and use of consumer data raise ethical concerns. Marketers must ensure that they handle personal information responsibly and respect privacy rights.

4. **Stereotyping and Discrimination:** Marketers should avoid perpetuating stereotypes or engaging in discriminatory practices in their advertising content. They should promote diversity and inclusivity.

5. **Socially Irresponsible Messaging:** Marketers should be mindful of the potential impact of their messaging on societal values and norms. Ethical issues can arise when advertising promotes harmful behaviors or perpetuates negative social attitudes.

Strategies for Ethical Marketing and Advertising

To promote ethical marketing and advertising practices, several strategies can be employed:

1. **Ethics Training and Education:** Marketers and advertisers should receive comprehensive training on ethical principles and practices. Continuing education programs can help professionals stay updated on the latest ethical considerations in the field.

2. **Strong Codes of Conduct:** Organizations should establish and enforce strong codes of conduct and ethics policies that outline expected behavior and consequences for non-compliance. These codes should address specific ethical issues in marketing and advertising.

3. **Consumer Engagement and Feedback:** Marketers should actively engage with consumers, listen to their feedback, and address their concerns. Creating opportunities for open dialogue builds trust and helps identify and rectify ethical issues.

4. **Self-Regulation and Compliance:** Marketers and advertisers should adhere to industry standards and guidelines. Self-regulatory bodies, such as advertising

associations, play a vital role in enforcing ethical practices and addressing complaints.

5. **Due Diligence in Partnerships**: Marketers should carefully vet and select business partners, agencies, and endorsers to ensure their ethical standards align. Close monitoring of advertising campaigns and regular audits can help maintain ethical integrity.

Addressing Unconventional Challenges: Dark Patterns

One unconventional challenge in marketing and advertising ethics is the use of "dark patterns." Dark patterns refer to design techniques or user interfaces that manipulate users into making decisions they may not have otherwise made, often leading to unintended consequences or harm. Examples include tricking users into unknowingly signing up for subscriptions or purchasing products.

To address this challenge, marketers and advertisers should prioritize user autonomy and respect in their design choices. Providing clear and explicit choices, avoiding manipulative tactics, and seeking user feedback can help mitigate the negative effects of dark patterns.

Conclusion

Ethical considerations in marketing and advertising are essential for building trust, maintaining consumer satisfaction, and upholding social values. Marketers and advertisers must adhere to principles of truth, transparency, fairness, and respect for privacy and diversity. By prioritizing ethical practices and embracing strategies to address challenges, professionals can contribute to an industry that promotes integrity, social responsibility, and the well-being of consumers and society as a whole.

Ethical Decision Making in Business

Ethics plays a crucial role in the world of business. As individuals and organizations navigate complex and ever-changing economic landscapes, it becomes imperative to consider ethical implications and make sound decisions that align with moral values. In this section, we will explore the process of ethical decision making in the context of business and delve into various frameworks that can guide individuals and organizations in their pursuit of ethical excellence.

Understanding Ethical Decision Making

Ethical decision making involves analyzing a situation, considering different perspectives and ethical theories, and choosing a course of action that is morally acceptable. In the realm of business, ethical decision making entails evaluating the potential impact of a decision on stakeholders, including employees, customers, shareholders, and the broader society.

There are several steps involved in ethical decision making:

1. **Identify the ethical issue:** The first step is to clearly identify the ethical problem at hand. This requires a comprehensive understanding of the facts and circumstances surrounding the decision.

2. **Gather information:** Once the issue is identified, it is important to gather all the relevant information related to the decision. This may involve conducting research, consulting experts, and seeking different perspectives.

3. **Evaluate alternative actions:** Next, it is necessary to identify and assess various alternative courses of action that could be taken. Each option should be evaluated based on its potential ethical implications, considering factors such as fairness, honesty, and the overall well-being of stakeholders.

4. **Consider ethical theories:** Ethical theories provide frameworks for analyzing and evaluating different moral perspectives. These theories, such as utilitarianism, deontology, and virtue ethics, offer principles and guidelines that can inform ethical decision making in business.

5. **Apply ethical principles:** With an understanding of ethical theories, it is important to apply relevant ethical principles to the decision-making process. These principles may include concepts such as honesty, fairness, respect, and social responsibility.

6. **Make a decision:** After thoroughly evaluating the alternatives and considering ethical theories and principles, a decision can be made. The chosen course of action should be one that aligns with ethical values and demonstrates a commitment to responsible and moral conduct.

7. **Reflect on the decision:** Reflecting on the decision and its outcomes is an essential step in the ethical decision-making process. This reflection helps individuals and organizations learn from their experiences, adapt their ethical frameworks, and make improvements in future decision-making processes.

Frameworks for Ethical Decision Making

There are several frameworks and models available to guide ethical decision making in the business environment. Let us explore some of the most commonly used frameworks:

1. **Utilitarianism:** Utilitarianism is a consequentialist ethical theory that suggests making decisions based on the greatest overall happiness for the greatest number of people. In the context of business, this framework focuses on maximizing the benefits and minimizing the harms to all stakeholders.

2. **Deontology:** Deontological ethics emphasizes the adherence to moral duties and obligations. This framework suggests that ethical decisions should be guided by categorical imperatives or universal principles, regardless of the consequences. In business, deontological approaches prioritize principles such as honesty, fairness, and respect for individual rights.

3. **Virtue Ethics:** Virtue ethics focuses on developing moral character traits and emphasizes the importance of personal virtues in decision making. This framework suggests that individuals should strive to cultivate virtues such as honesty, integrity, and compassion. In business, virtue ethics can guide decision making by considering the long-term development of moral character within organizations.

4. **Justice Ethics:** Justice ethics is concerned with fairness and social justice. This framework suggests that ethical decisions should be made based on principles of distributive justice, equality, and fairness. In the business context, justice ethics calls for equal treatment of employees, customers, and the communities in which businesses operate.

Challenges in Ethical Decision Making

Ethical decision making in business is not without its challenges. The following are some common challenges individuals and organizations may face:

+ **Conflicting interests:** Business decisions often involve balancing the interests of different stakeholders, which can lead to conflicting ethical considerations. For example, a decision that benefits shareholders financially may negatively impact employees or the environment.

+ **Pressure and temptation:** Individuals in business may face pressures and temptations that can compromise their ethical judgment. The pursuit of financial gain, competition, and professional advancement can sometimes overshadow moral considerations.

+ **Uncertainty and complexity:** Ethical decision making can be challenging in situations where there is ambiguity or complexity. Sometimes, the consequences of a decision may be uncertain, making it difficult to assess the potential ethical implications accurately.

+ **Lack of awareness and training:** Many individuals in business may not have sufficient ethical awareness or training to navigate complex ethical dilemmas. This can result in a lack of understanding of the consequences of their decisions and actions.

Ethical Decision Making in Practice

To enhance ethical decision making in business, organizations can implement several strategies and practices:

+ **Ethics training and education:** Providing ongoing ethics training and education can help employees develop a sound understanding of ethical principles and decision-making frameworks. This can empower individuals to make ethical choices and act with integrity.

+ **Developing a strong ethical culture:** Organizations should cultivate a strong ethical culture that promotes transparency, accountability, and ethical conduct. This can be achieved through the development and enforcement of ethical codes of conduct, policies, and procedures.

+ **Ethics committees and advisors:** Establishing ethics committees and appointing ethics advisors can provide a platform for individuals to seek guidance and advice when facing ethical dilemmas. These structures can help ensure that decisions are subject to ethical scrutiny and review.

+ **Whistleblower protection:** Creating mechanisms to protect whistleblowers encourages the reporting of unethical behavior. It is important to establish policies that safeguard individuals who speak up against wrongdoing and prevent retaliation.

+ **Stakeholder engagement:**   Engaging with stakeholders can provide organizations with valuable insights into their concerns and ethical expectations.   This dialogue can inform decision making and enable organizations to consider a broader range of perspectives.

Case Study: Ethical Decision Making in Supply Chain Management

Consider a multinational corporation that sources its raw materials from suppliers in developing countries. The corporation discovers that one of its suppliers is employing child labor in hazardous conditions. The ethical dilemma arises when the corporation must decide whether to sever ties with this supplier or work with the supplier to improve labor conditions.

To address this ethical dilemma, the corporation could follow the following steps:

1. **Identify the ethical issue:** The issue at hand is the use of child labor in hazardous conditions.

2. **Gather information:** The corporation gathers information about the specific labor practices within the supplier's facility and assesses the working conditions and potential harms to the child laborers.

3. **Evaluate alternative actions:** The corporation considers alternative actions, such as terminating the contract with the supplier or working collaboratively with the supplier to improve labor conditions.

4. **Apply ethical theories and principles:** The corporation applies ethical theories, such as utilitarianism and justice ethics, to evaluate the potential consequences and fairness of each alternative. It recognizes the harms caused by child labor and the responsibilities it has toward the children involved.

5. **Make a decision:** Based on the evaluation, the corporation decides to work with the supplier to improve labor conditions. This decision is guided by the belief that collaboration can lead to long-term positive change and improve the lives of the child laborers.

6. **Reflect on the decision:** The corporation reflects on the decision and monitors the progress made in improving labor conditions. It reassesses its relationships with suppliers and implements measures to prevent similar ethical issues in the future.

This case study highlights the importance of ethical decision making in supply chain management. By actively considering ethical implications and taking responsibility for the welfare of all stakeholders, businesses can contribute to a more just and sustainable global economy.

Conclusion

Ethical decision making in business requires thoughtful reflection, consideration of relevant ethical theories, and a commitment to responsible conduct. By following a systematic process, utilizing ethical frameworks, and implementing strategies to promote ethical behavior, individuals and organizations can navigate the complexities of the business world while upholding moral values.

Developing ethical decision-making skills cultivates a culture of integrity, enhances stakeholders' trust, and contributes to a more equitable and sustainable business environment. Embracing ethical considerations in business decisions is not only morally right but also beneficial for long-term success and the overall well-being of society.

Business Ethics and Professionalism

In the world of business, ethical conduct and professionalism are paramount for fostering trust, maintaining reputation, and creating a sustainable and responsible environment. Business ethics refers to the moral principles and values that guide ethical decision-making and behavior in a business context. Professionalism, on the other hand, encompasses the standards of behavior, competence, and integrity that govern the conduct of professionals in their respective fields. In this section, we will explore the importance of business ethics and professionalism, discuss key principles and practices, and examine the challenges and opportunities that arise in the business world.

Importance of Business Ethics

Business ethics plays a crucial role in shaping the behavior and practices of individuals and organizations within the business realm. It provides a framework for ethical decision-making that ensures fairness, honesty, and accountability. By adhering to ethical principles, businesses can enhance their reputation, build trust with stakeholders, and contribute to the overall well-being of society. Furthermore, ethical behavior fosters a positive corporate culture, attracting and retaining employees who value integrity and social responsibility.

Principles of Business Ethics

To navigate the complexities of ethical decision-making in business, it is important to understand and apply key principles of business ethics. Some of these principles include:

1. **Integrity:** Upholding honesty, truthfulness, and consistency in all business dealings.

2. **Respect for Others:** Recognizing and valuing the rights, dignity, and worth of all individuals.

3. **Fairness:** Ensuring equal treatment, impartiality, and justice in business practices.

4. **Transparency:** Providing clear and accurate information to stakeholders, promoting openness and accountability.

5. **Accountability:** Taking responsibility for one's actions and their consequences.

6. **Social Responsibility:** Considering the impact of business decisions on society and the environment, and acting in a manner that promotes the well-being of stakeholders and the greater community.

By embracing these principles, businesses can establish an ethical foundation that guides their day-to-day operations and long-term strategic decisions.

Ethical Issues in Business

Despite efforts to promote ethical conduct, businesses face various ethical challenges. Some common ethical issues in the business world include:

1. **Corporate Governance:** Ensuring proper oversight, accountability, and transparency in the decision-making processes of organizations.

2. **Conflict of Interest:** Managing situations where personal interests or relationships compromise objectivity and impartiality.

3. **Fair Competition:** Striving to maintain a level playing field and avoid unfair advantage in the marketplace.

4. **Whistleblowing:** Encouraging employees to report unethical behavior without fear of retaliation.

5. **Environmental Responsibility:** Balancing economic goals with environmental sustainability, minimizing negative impact on the planet.

6. **Consumer Protection:** Ensuring the safety, truthfulness, and fairness of products and services provided to customers.

Addressing these ethical issues requires a proactive approach, including the development of ethical guidelines, training programs, and effective monitoring mechanisms.

Ethical Decision-Making in Business

Ethical decision-making in business involves considering the potential consequences of actions and evaluating them against ethical principles and values. The following steps can guide professionals in making ethical decisions:

1. **Identify the ethical dilemma:** Recognize that an ethical issue exists and the conflicting values or interests involved.

2. **Gather information:** Collect relevant facts, consult experts, and consider different perspectives to better understand the situation.

3. **Evaluate alternative actions:** Identify and evaluate various courses of action, considering their ethical implications and potential consequences.

4. **Make a decision:** Choose the course of action that aligns with ethical principles and values.

5. **Implement and reflect:** Put the decision into action and reflect on the outcome, seeking feedback and learning from the experience.

By following a systematic approach to ethical decision-making, professionals can navigate challenging situations and uphold ethical standards in their business practices.

Professionalism in Business

Professionalism is essential in business as it sets expectations for behavior, competence, and integrity. Some key attributes of professionalism include:

1. **Ethical Conduct:** Demonstrating high moral standards and adhering to professional codes of ethics.

2. **Competence:** Mastering the skills and knowledge required in the specific business field.

3. **Reliability:** Fulfilling commitments, meeting deadlines, and delivering quality work.

4. **Accountability:** Taking responsibility for one's actions and being answerable for the outcomes.

5. **Communication:**   Effectively   conveying   information   and   ideas, demonstrating active listening and respect for others.

6. **Professional Image:**   Presenting   oneself   in   a   manner   that   reflects professionalism and credibility.

By embodying these qualities, professionals can build trust, foster positive relationships, and achieve success in their respective fields.

Challenges and Opportunities

Business ethics and professionalism face both challenges and opportunities in the ever-changing business landscape. Technological advancements, globalization, and evolving societal expectations present new ethical dilemmas and complexities. However, they also offer opportunities for businesses to integrate ethical considerations into their operations, embrace innovation, and create sustainable, socially responsible solutions. Moreover, businesses can seize the opportunity to collaborate with stakeholders, adopt best practices, and contribute to a more ethical and inclusive business environment.

Conclusion

Business ethics and professionalism are crucial for creating an ethical business environment that promotes trust, accountability, and sustainable growth. By adhering to ethical principles, professionals can navigate the complexities of the business world, make sound decisions, and contribute to the well-being of society at large. Embracing professionalism and ethical conduct enables businesses to build strong relationships, maintain a positive reputation, and achieve long-term success in an ever-changing global marketplace.

Business Ethics and Stakeholder Management

In the world of business, ethical considerations play a crucial role in maintaining trust, building a reputation, and fostering sustainable relationships. Business ethics refers to the moral principles and values that guide the behavior and decision-making processes of individuals and organizations in the business environment. Stakeholder management, on the other hand, involves identifying and addressing the needs and interests of various parties who are affected by or have a stake in the business.

Ethics in Business

Ethics in business serves as a framework for responsible and ethical decision making, ensuring that businesses operate in a manner that is fair, just, and in compliance with legal and societal norms. Good business ethics are essential for long-term success and sustainability, as they contribute to public trust, customer loyalty, and employee engagement.

Ethical considerations in business encompass a broad range of issues, including honesty, integrity, fairness, respect, transparency, and social responsibility. Businesses are expected to adhere to ethical standards not only in their internal operations but also in their relationships with stakeholders, the community, and the environment.

Stakeholder Management

Stakeholders are individuals or groups that have an interest in or are affected by the activities of a business. These may include employees, customers, shareholders, suppliers, communities, government agencies, and the environment. Effective stakeholder management involves identifying key stakeholders, understanding their needs and concerns, and developing strategies to engage and address their interests.

The primary objective of stakeholder management is to create value for all stakeholders while ensuring the long-term success and sustainability of the business. By prioritizing the needs of stakeholders and considering their interests, businesses can build trust, enhance reputation, and foster mutually beneficial relationships.

Balancing Stakeholder Interests

Balancing the interests and needs of various stakeholders can be a challenging task for businesses. Different stakeholders often have divergent interests and expectations, making it necessary to find a middle ground that satisfies as many stakeholders as possible. It is crucial to consider the ethical implications and consequences of business decisions on all stakeholders.

The stakeholder management process involves identifying, analyzing, and prioritizing stakeholders based on their influence, power, legitimacy, and urgency. This helps businesses determine the key stakeholders and their respective interests and develop strategies to address their concerns.

To effectively balance stakeholder interests, businesses can implement mechanisms such as regular communication, stakeholder engagement programs, and feedback mechanisms. By involving stakeholders in decision-making processes and actively seeking their input, businesses can enhance transparency, trust, and collaboration.

Ethical Challenges in Stakeholder Management

Stakeholder management is not without its challenges and ethical dilemmas. Businesses often face conflicting stakeholder interests and must navigate complex situations where satisfying one stakeholder may result in disappointing another. Some common ethical challenges in stakeholder management include:

1. **Conflicting stakeholder interests:** Businesses must find ways to address the needs and expectations of stakeholders while ensuring fairness and avoiding favoritism.

2. **Power imbalances:** Certain stakeholders may have more power or influence than others, potentially leading to situations where the interests of powerful stakeholders overshadow those of others. Businesses need to ensure fairness, inclusivity, and equal opportunities for all stakeholders.

3. **Transparency and accountability:** Businesses must be transparent in their decision-making processes and accountable for their actions. This includes providing accurate and timely information to stakeholders and being open to feedback and criticism.

4. **Social and environmental responsibility:** Balancing economic considerations with social and environmental concerns is a significant challenge. Businesses need to take responsibility for their impact on society

and the environment, considering the long-term sustainability and well-being of stakeholders and the planet.

5. **Global stakeholder management:** In a globalized world, businesses operate across borders and deal with diverse stakeholders from different cultural, social, and regulatory contexts. Understanding and respecting varying cultural norms and values is crucial for ethical stakeholder management.

Case Study: Starbucks and Stakeholder Engagement

Starbucks, the global coffee chain, is widely recognized for its commitment to ethical business practices and stakeholder engagement. By actively involving various stakeholders in decision-making processes, Starbucks has built a strong reputation for social responsibility and sustainability.

One example of their stakeholder engagement initiatives is the Starbucks Shared Planet program. This program involves partnerships with Fairtrade organizations, ensuring fair compensation for coffee farmers and promoting sustainable farming practices. Through these partnerships, Starbucks addresses the interests of both coffee suppliers and socially conscious consumers.

Starbucks also prioritizes employee welfare, offering competitive wages, benefits, and career development opportunities. By valuing their employees, Starbucks maintains a motivated and engaged workforce, leading to higher customer satisfaction.

Furthermore, Starbucks takes its environmental responsibilities seriously by implementing sustainable practices, such as reducing waste and promoting recycling. These initiatives align with the interests of environmentally conscious customers and contribute to the long-term sustainability of the business.

By effectively managing its stakeholders and incorporating their interests into business decisions, Starbucks has created a positive brand image and built a loyal customer base.

Conclusion

Business ethics and stakeholder management are interconnected aspects of responsible and sustainable business practices. Ethical considerations provide a moral compass for businesses, helping them make decisions that balance the interests of stakeholders and society at large. Stakeholder management ensures that businesses actively engage with and address the needs and concerns of their stakeholders.

While challenges and ethical dilemmas may arise in stakeholder management, businesses can navigate these complexities by prioritizing transparency, fairness, accountability, and social responsibility. By doing so, businesses can foster trust, build strong relationships, and contribute positively to society and the environment.

Resources:

+ Crane, A., Matten, D., Glozer, S., & Spence, L. (2019). *Business Ethics: Managing Corporate Citizenship and Sustainability in the Age of Globalization.* Oxford University Press.

+ Freeman, R. E., Harrison, J. S., Wicks, A. C., Parmar, B., & De Colle, S. (2019). *Stakeholder Theory: The State of the Art.* Cambridge University Press.

+ Velasquez, M. G. (2019). *Business Ethics: Concepts and Cases.* Pearson.

+ Starbucks Global Responsibility Report:

  `https://www.starbucks.com/responsibility/global-report`

Exercises:

1. Choose a well-known company and analyze its approach to stakeholder management. Identify the key stakeholders and discuss how the company addresses their needs and concerns.

2. Think of a situation where a business faces conflicting stakeholder interests. Propose a strategy for the business to address these conflicting interests while maintaining ethical standards.

3. Research a case study on a company that faced a stakeholder-related ethical dilemma. Analyze the situation, identify the ethical issues involved, and suggest alternative courses of action for the company.

4. Imagine you are a business owner who wants to improve stakeholder engagement and ethical practices. Develop a stakeholder management plan outlining the steps you would take to identify and address the needs of various stakeholders.

Important Note: Business ethics and stakeholder management are complex topics that require continuous reflection and adaptation to changing business landscapes. It is essential to stay updated with the latest research, trends, and legal frameworks to ensure ethical practices in the business environment.

Conclusion

In this section, we have explored the ethical issues in the business and commerce sector. We began by discussing the concept of business ethics and its importance in the modern business environment. We examined various ethical issues that arise in corporate governance, such as conflicts of interest and the role of corporate social responsibility. We also explored the ethical considerations in marketing and advertising, emphasizing the need for transparency and honesty in business practices.

One key ethical dilemma in business and commerce is the protection of intellectual property rights. We delved into the challenges associated with balancing the need for copyright protection with the accessibility of knowledge. We discussed how emerging technologies and digital platforms have created new complexities and ethical dilemmas in this area.

Globalization also presents ethical challenges in the business world. We examined the ethical considerations in international business, focusing on human rights in global supply chains, bribery and corruption, and environmental sustainability. We emphasized the need for ethical leadership and responsible global business practices to ensure social justice and protect human rights.

Furthermore, we discussed the role of law in social change and reform, both within the business sector and beyond. We explored how law can be a powerful tool for social change, with examples of legal activism and impact litigation. We also examined the role of law in promoting sustainable development, particularly in the context of environmental regulation and climate change. Additionally, we highlighted the ethical implications of technological advancements in the legal field, such as artificial intelligence, cybersecurity, and privacy protection.

It is important for legal professionals and business leaders to recognize and address these ethical issues in their practice. By adhering to ethical principles and codes of conduct, they can establish trust, maintain integrity, and contribute to a more equitable and sustainable world. Seeking collaboration, accountability, and transparency in decision-making processes can help mitigate ethical dilemmas in the business and commerce sector.

In conclusion, ethical considerations are crucial in navigating the complex landscape of business and commerce. By integrating ethical thinking into decision-making processes, businesses can contribute to the promotion of justice and social equality. Legal professionals, business leaders, and policymakers must work together to address ethical challenges, advocate for human rights, and shape a more equitable, just, and sustainable world.

Intellectual Property Rights and Ethical Dilemmas

Understanding Intellectual Property Rights

Intellectual property rights are a crucial aspect of the legal landscape in modern society. They are designed to protect the creations of the human mind, such as inventions, artistic works, and symbols, from unauthorized use or exploitation. In this section, we will explore the concept of intellectual property rights, their significance, and the key principles that govern them.

Definition and Scope of Intellectual Property Rights

Intellectual property refers to intangible creations of the human intellect, such as inventions, artistic works, trademarks, and trade secrets. Intellectual property rights are legal rights that grant creators and owners exclusive rights to use, reproduce, or distribute their creations. These rights are crucial incentives for innovation, creativity, and economic growth.

The scope of intellectual property rights encompasses various forms of creative works and innovations. Some of the main categories include:

+ Patents: Grants exclusive rights to inventors for new and useful inventions, such as processes, machines, or compositions of matter.

+ Copyrights: Protect original works of authorship, such as literary, artistic, and musical works, from unauthorized copying, distribution, or adaptation.

+ Trademarks: Provide protection for recognizable signs, symbols, or logos that distinguish goods or services from those of others.

+ Trade Secrets: Safeguard undisclosed information, such as formulas, processes, or other proprietary business information that derives value from being secret.

Rationale for Intellectual Property Rights

The rationale behind intellectual property rights lies in the recognition and reward of human creativity, innovation, and investment. By granting exclusive rights to creators and owners, intellectual property rights aim to incentivize the generation of new ideas and ensure the fair exploitation of these creations. They also serve to promote economic growth, stimulate competition, and benefit society as a whole.

Intellectual property rights provide creators and innovators with the ability to control the use and commercial exploitation of their creations. This control is crucial for artists, inventors, entrepreneurs, and businesses to protect their investments, reap the rewards of their efforts, and maintain a competitive edge in the marketplace.

Principles of Intellectual Property Rights

Several principles underpin the legal framework of intellectual property rights. Understanding these principles is essential for navigating the complex landscape of intellectual property law. Some key principles include:

- Exclusive rights: Intellectual property rights grant exclusive rights to creators and owners, allowing them to control the use, reproduction, and distribution of their creations.

- Limited duration: Intellectual property rights are generally time-limited. The duration varies depending on the type of intellectual property, ensuring a balance between rewarding creators and promoting broader societal benefits.

- Public interest: Intellectual property rights aim to strike a balance between protecting the rights of creators and promoting the broader public interest. This includes considerations such as access to knowledge, public health, cultural preservation, and technological advancement.

- Fair use and exceptions: Intellectual property laws often include provisions for fair use or exceptions, allowing limited use of copyrighted works for purposes such as education, research, criticism, or commentary.

- International obligations: Intellectual property rights are subject to international obligations and treaties, such as the World Intellectual Property Organization (WIPO) agreements, which facilitate global harmonization and cooperation in the protection of intellectual property.

Challenges and Controversies in Intellectual Property Rights

Intellectual property rights are not without challenges and controversies. Balancing the protection of individual rights with the societal benefits and ensuring access to knowledge and innovation can be complex. Some key challenges include:

- Digital piracy and infringement: The rise of digital technologies has made it easier to reproduce and distribute copyrighted works, leading to concerns about piracy and infringement.

- Patent trolls: Some entities misuse the patent system by acquiring patents solely for the purpose of suing others for infringement, rather than actively using or developing the inventions.

- Access to essential medicines: The protection of pharmaceutical patents can sometimes hinder access to life-saving drugs and treatments, particularly in developing countries.

- Open source movement: The open-source movement challenges traditional notions of intellectual property, advocating for the free sharing and collaboration of creative works and innovations.

Ethical Considerations in Intellectual Property

Ethical considerations play a crucial role in intellectual property rights. Fairness, equity, and societal well-being should be weighed alongside the interests of creators and innovators. Some ethical considerations in intellectual property include:

- Balancing exclusive rights: Striking a balance between granting exclusive rights to creators and promoting the public interest, such as access to knowledge, cultural diversity, and scientific progress.

- Patent quality: Ensuring the quality and validity of patents to prevent the granting of overly broad or trivial patents that may hinder innovation or impede competition.

- Ethical use of copyrighted works: Respecting the rights of creators and obtaining proper permissions for the use of copyrighted works, particularly in the digital age where infringement is prevalent.

- Ethical licensing and technology transfer: Ensuring fair and equitable licensing agreements that maximize the societal benefits and promote the dissemination of knowledge and technology.

Conclusion

Understanding intellectual property rights is crucial in a world driven by creativity, innovation, and knowledge. These rights incentivize and reward creators and innovators, while also benefiting society as a whole. By balancing the rights of individuals with the broader public interest, intellectual property rights contribute to economic growth, technological progress, and cultural development. However, challenges and ethical considerations persist, necessitating ongoing dialogue and careful examination of the intellectual property landscape.

Ethical Issues in Intellectual Property Protection

Intellectual property refers to the legal rights that are granted to individuals or organizations for their creative and innovative works. These rights are intended to provide incentives for the creation and dissemination of knowledge, as well as to reward individuals for their intellectual efforts. However, the protection of intellectual property can give rise to a number of ethical issues that need to be carefully considered.

1. Balancing competing interests

One of the key ethical challenges in intellectual property protection is striking the right balance between the interests of creators and innovators, and the interests of society as a whole. On one hand, granting exclusive rights to creators can incentivize creativity and innovation. On the other hand, overly restrictive intellectual property laws can hinder the free flow of knowledge and impede further innovation.

For example, consider the patent system, which grants inventors exclusive rights to their inventions for a limited period of time. While patents encourage innovation by providing inventors with a monopoly over their inventions, they can also lead to high costs for consumers and restrict access to essential medicines or technologies. Balancing the interests of inventors and the public is crucial in addressing this ethical dilemma.

2. Ethical implications of enforcement

The enforcement of intellectual property rights can raise ethical concerns, particularly when it comes to digital piracy and copyright infringement. While it is important to protect the rights of creators and prevent unauthorized use of their work, stringent enforcement measures can also limit individuals' access to information and impede the free exchange of ideas.

In the digital age, where information can be easily copied and disseminated, the enforcement of intellectual property rights becomes a complex ethical issue. Striking a balance between protecting creators' rights and promoting access to knowledge is a key challenge for policymakers and legal professionals.

3. Patenting of life forms and biotechnology

The patenting of life forms and biotechnological innovations raises significant ethical questions. Patenting living organisms can be seen as commodifying nature and the genetic resources of indigenous communities. It can also give rise to concerns related to bio-piracy and the exploitation of biodiversity for commercial gain.

Additionally, the patenting of genetic material and biotechnological inventions can have implications for global health and food security. Access to life-saving medical treatments, such as essential drugs or gene therapies, can be limited due to high costs associated with patented technologies. Ethical considerations must be taken into account when deciding whether and how to grant patents in the field of biotechnology.

4. Ethics of intellectual property licensing

The licensing of intellectual property rights raises ethical issues related to fairness, distribution of benefits, and access to knowledge. Licensing agreements can be used to restrict competition, create monopolies, and limit access to essential technologies or cultural works.

For example, the practice of "evergreening" in the pharmaceutical industry involves obtaining new patents for minor modifications of existing drugs in order to extend exclusivity and prevent the entry of generic competitors. This practice can limit access to affordable medications and raise concerns about the ethics of intellectual property licensing.

5. Intellectual property and cultural heritage

The protection of intellectual property can sometimes clash with the preservation and promotion of cultural heritage. Intellectual property laws, particularly copyright, can restrict the use and dissemination of traditional knowledge, folklore, and indigenous cultural expressions.

For indigenous communities, sharing and passing on traditional knowledge is a fundamental part of their cultural identity. The application of intellectual property laws to cultural heritage can be seen as a form of cultural appropriation and can undermine communities' rights to their own cultural heritage.

To address these ethical issues, legal frameworks such as the Nagoya Protocol aim to recognize and protect the rights of indigenous communities and ensure that they are fairly compensated for the use of their traditional knowledge and genetic resources.

In conclusion, ethical issues in intellectual property protection arise from the tension between the interests of creators and innovators, and the broader societal interests. Balancing these competing interests, considering the implications of enforcement, and addressing concerns related to biotechnology, licensing, and cultural heritage are crucial in promoting a fair and sustainable intellectual property system. It is essential to continuously evaluate and refine intellectual property laws and practices to ensure that they align with ethical principles and promote the greater good.

Balancing Copyright Protection and Access to Knowledge

In the digital age, the tension between copyright protection and access to knowledge has become increasingly significant. Copyright laws aim to incentivize creativity and protect the rights of creators, while access to knowledge is essential for the progress and development of society. Finding the right balance between these two goals is crucial to foster innovation and ensure equitable access to information.

Copyright Protection: A Brief Overview

Copyright is a legal concept that grants exclusive rights to authors and creators over their original works. These rights include the right to reproduce, distribute, display, and perform their creations. Copyright protection encourages creators to invest time, effort, and resources into producing valuable content, such as books, music, films, and software.

The duration of copyright protection varies across jurisdictions, but it generally lasts for the author's lifetime plus a certain number of years after their death. During this period, copyright holders have the right to control how their works are used and to receive financial compensation for their use.

Access to Knowledge: The Importance of Information Sharing

Access to knowledge is a fundamental aspect of education, research, and cultural development. It enables individuals to learn, explore new ideas, and contribute to the advancement of society. Free access to knowledge promotes creativity, innovation, and the democratization of information.

The digital revolution has made it easier than ever to share and access information. The internet, open educational resources, and digital libraries have expanded opportunities for learning and research. However, access to knowledge is not evenly distributed globally, and many barriers, such as copyright restrictions and high subscription fees for scholarly journals, limit access to valuable information.

Challenges in Balancing Copyright Protection and Access to Knowledge

Balancing copyright protection and access to knowledge poses several challenges. One challenge is the tension between the need to protect creators' rights and the desire to promote innovation and creativity. Striking the right balance ensures that creators are rewarded for their work while still allowing for the free flow of ideas and information.

Another challenge is the rapid advancement of technology, which has made it easier to reproduce and distribute copyrighted materials. The ease of digital copying and online sharing has led to widespread copyright infringement, particularly in the context of digital media. Finding effective methods to prevent unauthorized sharing while not unduly restricting legitimate access is a complex task.

Furthermore, there is a need to address the issue of fair compensation for creators while still facilitating access to knowledge for educational, research, and public interest purposes. The rise of open access models and creative commons licenses has provided alternative approaches to copyright, encouraging the sharing and reuse of creative works while respecting the rights of content creators.

Approaches to Balancing Copyright Protection and Access to Knowledge

To strike a balance between copyright protection and access to knowledge, various approaches have been proposed and implemented. These include:

1. **Fair Use Doctrine:** Fair use is a legal doctrine that allows limited use of copyrighted material without permission from the copyright holder. It allows for the use of copyrighted works for purposes such as criticism, comment, news reporting, teaching, scholarship, and research. The fair use doctrine provides flexibility in interpreting copyright law and allows for transformative uses that benefit society.

2. **Creative Commons Licenses:** Creative Commons licenses provide a framework for creators to grant permissions beyond the scope of traditional copyright. These licenses allow creators to choose the rights they want to retain and those they are willing to waive. By using Creative Commons licenses, creators can enable others to share, remix, and build upon their work, while still providing proper attribution and respecting the original creator's rights.

3. **Open Access:** Open access is a movement that promotes free and unrestricted access to scholarly and scientific research. It advocates for the removal of financial and legal barriers that limit access to knowledge by providing free online access to research articles and academic publications. Open access models, such as those supported by institutional repositories and open access journals, aim to ensure that research findings are widely accessible, fostering collaboration and innovation.

4. **Digital Rights Management (DRM):** DRM refers to technologies and strategies used to prevent unauthorized copying and distribution of digital content. It has been utilized to protect copyrighted material, such as music, movies, and e-books. However, DRM systems have been criticized for their potential to restrict access to content even for legitimate purposes and

impede users' fair use rights. Striking a balance between DRM's protective measures and users' rights remains a challenge.

Real-World Examples and Case Studies

To illustrate the challenges and potential solutions in balancing copyright protection and access to knowledge, let's examine a few real-world examples:

1. **Open Educational Resources (OER):** OER are freely available educational materials that can be used, adapted, and shared by educators and learners. These resources, such as open textbooks and online courses, provide access to quality educational materials without the financial barriers associated with traditional textbooks. The OER movement promotes open licenses and collaborative content creation to ensure equitable access to educational resources.

2. **Software Licensing and Open Source Movement:** The open-source movement has revolutionized the software industry by promoting collaborative development and sharing of software source code. Open-source licenses, such as the GNU General Public License (GPL), allow users to access, modify, and distribute software freely. This approach facilitates innovation and knowledge sharing while still respecting copyright and encouraging contributions to a common pool of knowledge.

3. **Digital Streaming and Copyright Issues:** The rise of digital streaming services, such as Netflix and Spotify, has changed how we access and consume digital content. These services provide legal alternatives to piracy by offering affordable access to a vast library of movies, TV shows, and music. However, licensing agreements and regional restrictions can limit the availability of content in certain countries, highlighting the need for global solutions to facilitate access to knowledge.

Conclusion

Balancing copyright protection and access to knowledge is a complex task that requires careful consideration of the rights of creators and the needs of society. Striking the right balance fosters creativity, promotes innovation, and ensures equitable access to information. By embracing approaches such as fair use, Creative Commons licenses, open access, and open-source models, we can navigate the ethical and legal challenges in the digital age and shape a more equitable and knowledge-rich world.

Emerging Challenges in Intellectual Property Rights

Intellectual property rights (IPR) are legal rights that protect the creations of the human mind, such as inventions, literary and artistic works, trademarks, and designs. They provide creators and innovators with the exclusive rights to use, sell, and benefit from their creations. However, with the rapid advancement of technology and globalization, the field of intellectual property faces several emerging challenges. In this section, we will explore these challenges and their implications for the protection of intellectual property rights.

Digital Piracy and Copyright Infringement

One of the most pressing challenges in intellectual property rights today is the proliferation of digital piracy and copyright infringement. With the advent of the internet, it has become easier than ever to reproduce and distribute copyrighted material without permission. This poses a significant threat to copyright holders, who may experience financial losses and a decline in their market share.

The rise of peer-to-peer file sharing networks, online streaming platforms, and torrent websites has made it convenient for users to access copyrighted content, such as music, movies, software, and books, for free or at a much lower cost. This not only affects the revenue of creative industries but also undermines the incentive for content creators to produce new works.

Various legal and technological measures have been implemented to combat digital piracy. Copyright laws have been strengthened, enforcement agencies have been established, and digital rights management (DRM) technologies have been developed to protect digital content. However, these measures often face criticism for being overly restrictive and infringing on users' rights to access information and engage in cultural exchange.

Open Source and Creative Commons Licensing

Another emerging challenge in intellectual property rights is the increasing popularity of open-source software and Creative Commons licensing. Open-source software refers to computer programs whose source code is available to the public, allowing users to study, modify, and distribute the software freely. This model of collaboration and sharing has gained significant traction in the software development community.

Similarly, Creative Commons licensing provides a framework for creators to share their works while retaining some rights and control over their use. It allows creators to choose from a range of permissions to define how their work can be shared, reused, and remixed by others. This licensing approach has fostered a culture of collaboration and innovation, particularly in industries such as music, art, and literature.

While open-source and Creative Commons licensing promote the free exchange of ideas and knowledge, they present challenges for traditional intellectual property regimes. The concepts of ownership and exclusivity are reconsidered in favor of collective creation and community-driven innovation. As a result, creators and rights holders must navigate a complex landscape of licensing models to protect their interests.

Patenting in Emerging Technologies

Technological advancements in fields such as biotechnology, artificial intelligence, and blockchain present unique challenges in patenting. These emerging technologies are often characterized by rapid development, uncertainty, and overlapping claims. The complexity and interdisciplinary nature of these innovations require a reassessment of patenting criteria and processes.

For example, the patentability of genetic sequences and genetically engineered organisms has raised ethical concerns regarding the ownership and control of life forms. Similarly, artificial intelligence algorithms and inventions have sparked debates about the extent to which machines can be considered inventors and whether they should be eligible for patent protection.

Furthermore, blockchain technology, which underpins cryptocurrencies and decentralized applications, challenges traditional notions of centralized control and ownership. The distributed nature of blockchain networks and the open-source philosophy behind many blockchain projects make it difficult to establish and enforce patent rights.

To address these challenges, patent offices and policymakers need to adapt to the evolving landscape of technology and formulate guidelines and regulations that strike a balance between promoting innovation and protecting the public interest.

Globalization and Cross-Border Enforcement

With the globalization of markets and the ease of digital communication, intellectual property rights face challenges in terms of cross-border enforcement. While intellectual property laws are generally territorial, infringing activities can easily transcend national borders through online platforms, making enforcement more complex and costly.

Different countries have varying levels of intellectual property protection, enforcement mechanisms, and cultural attitudes towards intellectual property rights. This can create discrepancies in the level of protection experienced by rights holders in different jurisdictions.

International agreements, such as the World Intellectual Property Organization (WIPO) treaties and bilateral or multilateral trade agreements, aim to harmonize intellectual property laws and facilitate cooperation between nations. However, reaching a consensus on issues such as copyright duration, fair use exceptions, and technological protection measures remains a challenge.

Additionally, the rise of counterfeit goods and trade in pirated products exacerbates the challenges in cross-border enforcement. Counterfeiters take advantage of weak intellectual property regimes in some countries to produce and distribute fake products, resulting in significant economic losses for legitimate businesses and risks to consumer health and safety.

Addressing these challenges requires stronger coordination and collaboration among international stakeholders, including governments, industry associations, and intergovernmental organizations. Effective cross-border enforcement mechanisms and capacity-building initiatives in developing countries are crucial to safeguarding intellectual property rights in a globalized world.

Emerging Challenges in Intellectual Property Rights: Summary

In summary, the field of intellectual property rights faces several emerging challenges in the digital age. Digital piracy and copyright infringement, open-source and Creative Commons licensing, patenting in emerging technologies, and globalization and cross-border enforcement all present unique complexities and require innovative approaches.

As technology continues to evolve and reshape the way we create, share, and consume information and creative works, the protection of intellectual property rights will remain a dynamic and evolving field. Balancing the interests of rights holders, users, and the broader public will be essential in shaping a more equitable and sustainable intellectual property system.

Ethical Responsibilities of Intellectual Property Professionals

In the field of intellectual property (IP), professionals have a crucial role in protecting and managing the rights of creators and inventors. However, along with these responsibilities, they also have ethical obligations to uphold. This section explores the ethical considerations that intellectual property professionals should be mindful of in their practice.

Defining Intellectual Property

Before delving into the ethical responsibilities of IP professionals, it is important to understand what intellectual property entails. Intellectual property refers to the legal rights granted to individuals or organizations for their creations or inventions. It includes patents, copyrights, trademarks, and trade secrets.

Balancing Interests and Fair Use

One of the key ethical responsibilities of IP professionals is to balance the interests of rights holders and promote fair use. While IP laws provide exclusive rights to creators and inventors, they also recognize the importance of access to knowledge and cultural expression. IP professionals should strive to strike a balance between protecting the rights of creators and allowing for legitimate uses by others.

For example, in the realm of copyright, IP professionals should advise clients on the appropriate use and limitations of copyrighted materials. They should educate clients about fair use provisions, which allow for the use of copyrighted works without permission in certain circumstances, such as criticism, commentary, or education.

Avoiding Plagiarism and Misrepresentation

Another ethical responsibility of IP professionals is to ensure that their clients' work is original and free from plagiarism. They should encourage clients to create new and innovative works rather than copying or imitating existing ones. This not only promotes ethical conduct but also helps clients avoid legal disputes and reputational damage.

IP professionals should also refrain from misrepresenting their clients' work to gain an unfair advantage. They should provide accurate and truthful information about the intellectual property to be protected, avoiding any misleading or false statements.

Protecting Confidential Information

In the course of their work, IP professionals often come across confidential information related to their clients' intellectual property. Maintaining the confidentiality of such information is a critical ethical responsibility. IP professionals should take appropriate measures to protect confidential information and avoid unauthorized disclosure.

For example, when drafting patent applications, IP professionals should ensure that the application discloses the invention adequately while safeguarding any sensitive information. They should also have proper procedures in place to handle confidential client information securely.

Ethical Considerations in Licensing and Transactions

IP professionals often play a role in negotiating licensing agreements and other IP-related transactions. In these situations, they should prioritize fairness, transparency, and informed decision-making.

Ethical considerations include ensuring that all parties involved have a clear understanding of the terms and conditions of the agreement, including any potential limitations or restrictions. IP professionals should promote open and honest communication throughout the negotiation process and provide clients with accurate and unbiased advice.

Addressing Ethical Challenges

IP professionals may encounter ethical challenges in their practice. For instance, they may face conflicts of interest when representing clients with competing or conflicting interests. It is essential for IP professionals to identify and address such conflicts, ensuring that they act in the best interests of each client while maintaining their ethical obligations.

Additionally, emerging technologies and digital advancements present new ethical dilemmas for IP professionals. For example, issues related to online piracy, unauthorized sharing of copyrighted materials, and infringement in the digital realm require IP professionals to adapt their ethical practices to address these evolving challenges.

Professional Development and Ethical Education

To fulfill their ethical responsibilities, IP professionals should engage in ongoing professional development and ethical education. Staying abreast of developments in IP laws, regulations, and best practices is crucial for providing effective and ethical representation to clients.

Professional organizations and associations, such as the International Trademark Association and the American Intellectual Property Law Association, offer resources, training programs, and opportunities for networking and knowledge sharing. IP professionals should take advantage of these resources to enhance their ethical understanding and practices.

Conclusion

Ethical responsibilities are integral to the practice of intellectual property professionals. Upholding ethical standards not only ensures their own professional integrity but also contributes to a fair and balanced intellectual property system. By balancing the interests of rights holders and promoting fair use, avoiding plagiarism and misrepresentation, protecting confidential information, addressing ethical challenges, and continuing professional development, IP professionals can fulfill their ethical obligations and promote ethical conduct in the field of intellectual property.

Intellectual Property and Innovation

In the modern world, innovation plays a crucial role in driving economic growth and societal progress. Intellectual property (IP) laws are designed to protect and incentivize innovation by granting exclusive rights to creators and inventors. This section will explore the relationship between intellectual property and innovation, examining the principles and challenges involved in this dynamic field.

Understanding Intellectual Property

Intellectual property refers to creations of the mind, such as inventions, artistic works, designs, and symbols. These creations can be protected under various forms of IP rights, including patents, copyrights, trademarks, and trade secrets. These rights provide legal protection and control over the use, distribution, and reproduction of intellectual creations.

Importance of Intellectual Property

Intellectual property protection is essential for promoting innovation and creativity. It provides inventors and creators with the exclusive rights to their work, allowing them to profit from their efforts and investments. This protection also encourages the sharing of knowledge and ideas, as inventors are more willing to disclose their innovations when they have legal safeguards in place.

Patents

Patents are a crucial form of IP protection for inventions and technological innovations. They grant inventors exclusive rights to their inventions for a limited period, typically 20 years. To obtain a patent, an invention must be new, non-obvious, and useful. The patent system encourages innovation by providing inventors with a monopoly over their inventions, allowing them to recoup their investments and reap the benefits of their ingenuity.

However, the patent system is not without its challenges. Patent trolls, for example, acquire patents not to innovate or create new products, but to sue others for infringement. This practice stifles innovation and hinders competition. The issue of patent quality is also a concern, as overly broad or vague patents can impede progress and hinder follow-on innovation.

Copyright

Copyright is another vital form of IP protection that safeguards original creative works, such as books, music, movies, and software. Copyright grants authors exclusive rights to reproduce, distribute, and display their works for a limited period, typically the author's lifetime plus 70 years.

While copyright protection is crucial for incentivizing creativity, the digital age has presented new challenges. The ease of copying and distributing digital content has led to issues of piracy and unauthorized use. Striking a balance between protecting copyright holders and promoting access to knowledge and creativity has become increasingly complex in the digital era.

Trademarks

Trademarks protect distinctive signs, such as logos, names, and symbols, that distinguish goods and services in the marketplace. They provide consumers with a guarantee of quality and help companies build brand recognition and reputation. Trademarks can be renewed indefinitely, as long as they are actively used and defended against infringement.

In the age of globalization and e-commerce, trademark issues have become more complex. With the rise of online marketplaces, counterfeit goods and trademark infringement have become significant problems. Companies must actively monitor and enforce their trademarks to protect their brand image and consumer trust.

Trade Secrets

Trade secrets refer to confidential and valuable information that gives a business a competitive edge. Trade secret protection does not require registration, unlike patents or trademarks. Instead, businesses must take reasonable measures to protect the secrecy of the information.

Trade secret issues have gained prominence in recent years, particularly with regards to cybersecurity and employee mobility. Theft or misappropriation of trade secrets can have severe consequences for businesses, leading to financial loss and damage to their competitive position.

Balancing IP Protection and Innovation

While IP protection is crucial for promoting innovation, striking the right balance is essential. Overly restrictive IP laws can hinder follow-on innovation and limit access to knowledge. On the other hand, weak IP protection may discourage inventors and creators from investing time and resources into new ideas.

Efforts to find this balance include shorter patent terms for rapidly evolving industries such as technology and pharmaceuticals, as well as increased flexibility in copyright laws for educational and research purposes. Open-source movements and creative commons licenses have also emerged as alternatives to traditional IP models.

Emerging Challenges in IP and Innovation

The rapid pace of technological advancements has brought about new challenges for IP and innovation. Issues such as 3D printing, artificial intelligence, and digital platforms have raised questions about the boundaries of IP protection and the role of traditional IP laws in the digital age.

Additionally, the global nature of innovation and commerce has created challenges in harmonizing IP laws across different jurisdictions. Cross-border enforcement, harmonization of patent standards, and addressing the needs of developing countries are ongoing issues in the field of IP and innovation.

Conclusion

The intersection of intellectual property and innovation is a complex and evolving landscape. Effective IP protection is crucial for incentivizing creativity and driving economic growth. However, finding the right balance between protection and access to knowledge poses ongoing challenges. As technology advances and global markets continue to expand, evolving IP laws and strategies will be vital for fostering innovation and ensuring a fair and sustainable future.

Intellectual Property and Cultural Heritage

In this section, we will explore the connection between intellectual property rights and cultural heritage. Cultural heritage refers to the tangible and intangible aspects of a society's history, including artifacts, traditions, customs, languages, and knowledge systems. These elements are essential for preserving a community's identity and promoting cultural diversity.

Understanding Intellectual Property Rights

First, let's delve into the concept of intellectual property (IP) rights. Intellectual property refers to creations of the mind, such as inventions, literary and artistic works, symbols, names, and designs, used in commerce. The World Intellectual Property Organization (WIPO) defines IP as a means to encourage innovation and creativity by granting exclusive rights to creators and inventors.

There are several types of intellectual property rights, including patents, copyrights, trademarks, industrial designs, and geographical indications. Each of these rights serves as a legal framework to protect different categories of intellectual creations.

Preserving Cultural Heritage

Cultural heritage is an invaluable asset that must be preserved and protected for future generations. However, there is often a tension between the protection of intellectual property rights and the need to safeguard cultural heritage. This tension arises when cultural expressions or traditional knowledge are subject to commercially driven intellectual property claims.

For instance, indigenous communities have unique traditional knowledge, practices, and cultural expressions passed down through generations. These traditional forms of knowledge are often intertwined with nature and the environment. However, the exploitation of these cultural expressions by unauthorized individuals or entities can lead to misappropriation and even commercialization without benefit to the communities.

Challenges and Ethical Considerations

One of the challenges associated with intellectual property and cultural heritage is the difficulty in defining and protecting traditional knowledge and cultural expressions. These forms of knowledge and expressions are often collectively owned by communities and are not easily categorized within existing legal frameworks. This poses a problem when it comes to demonstrating originality and novelty required for intellectual property protection.

Another ethical consideration is the potential for infringement on the rights and cultural autonomy of communities. When intellectual property rights are granted to individuals or entities outside the cultural group, it can undermine the cultural integrity and self-determination of the community from which the knowledge or expression originates.

Balancing Intellectual Property Rights and Cultural Heritage

To strike a balance between intellectual property rights and cultural heritage, it is crucial to develop legal frameworks and mechanisms that respect and protect traditional knowledge and cultural expressions. One approach is the incorporation of cultural safeguards within intellectual property laws.

For example, the concept of "prior informed consent" can be integrated into intellectual property systems. This means that before any commercial use of traditional knowledge or cultural expressions, the community from which it originates must give their informed consent. This ensures that community members have the ability to control the use and dissemination of their cultural heritage.

Additionally, creating mechanisms for benefit-sharing is essential. This involves sharing of the economic benefits derived from the use of traditional knowledge or cultural expressions with the communities that hold the intellectual property rights. Benefit-sharing can contribute to the preservation and revitalization of cultural heritage, supporting the cultural autonomy and well-being of the communities involved.

Case Study: Traditional Medicinal Knowledge

To illustrate the complexities of intellectual property and cultural heritage, let us consider the case of traditional medicinal knowledge. Indigenous communities across the world have rich knowledge of medicinal plants and their healing properties. This knowledge is often passed down orally from generation to generation.

However, this traditional medicinal knowledge is increasingly being exploited by pharmaceutical companies for commercial purposes, without consent or benefit-sharing with the indigenous communities. This raises questions about the ethical implications of profiting from traditional knowledge without acknowledging and compensating the cultural contributors.

To address this issue, countries like India have established systems to protect traditional medicinal knowledge. The Traditional Knowledge Digital Library (TKDL) in India documents traditional medicinal knowledge in a searchable database, making it accessible for patent examiners to prevent the grant of patents based on traditional knowledge that is already in the public domain.

Conclusion

The intersection of intellectual property rights and cultural heritage demands careful consideration to ensure the protection and preservation of traditional knowledge and cultural expressions. By developing legal frameworks that respect the rights and autonomy of the cultural communities, while also incentivizing creativity and innovation, we can strike a balance that supports cultural diversity and promotes a more equitable world. It is essential to promote dialogue and collaboration between different stakeholders, including indigenous communities, governments, and international organizations, to create sustainable solutions for the protection of cultural heritage.

Conclusion

In this chapter, we have explored the ethical issues that arise in the realm of business and commerce. We have examined the concept of business ethics and discussed its importance in the modern business environment. We have also delved into the ethical considerations in areas such as corporate governance, corporate social responsibility, marketing and advertising, and decision making.

One of the key findings of this chapter is the recognition that businesses have a responsibility to go beyond profit-making and take into account the impact of their actions on society, the environment, and other stakeholders. This concept, known as corporate social responsibility, emphasizes the need for businesses to balance economic goals with social and environmental concerns.

We have discussed the ethical issues related to intellectual property rights, particularly in the age of digital information sharing. Balancing the protection of intellectual property with the promotion of access to knowledge is a challenge that businesses face today. The chapter provides insights into the ethical responsibilities of intellectual property professionals and the importance of innovation and cultural heritage.

Globalization, another critical aspect of business and commerce, brings about its own set of ethical challenges. We have examined some of the ethical considerations in international business, including the protection of human rights in global supply chains, corruption and bribery, and environmental sustainability. The chapter highlights the need for ethical leadership and responsible business practices in the context of globalization.

In conclusion, ethical issues in business and commerce play a significant role in shaping our society and the global economy. Businesses are increasingly being held accountable for their actions, and there is a growing recognition of the importance of ethical behavior in the business world. It is essential for individuals and organizations to understand the ethical implications of their decisions and actions and strive to create a more equitable, just, and sustainable business environment. By incorporating ethical principles into business practices, we can work towards a more socially responsible and ethical business landscape.

To further explore the ethical dimensions of business and commerce, I encourage readers to engage in discussions, case studies, and ethical dilemmas that arise in the real world. By actively participating in these debates and reflecting on the ethical challenges faced by businesses, we can develop a deeper understanding of the ethical issues in this field and contribute to the creation of a more ethical and responsible business community.

Throughout this book, we have covered a wide range of philosophical and ethical issues in legal studies. From the fundamentals of legal studies and the relationship between philosophy and ethics to the ethical decision-making frameworks in legal practice, we have explored the various concepts, theories, and principles that underpin the field.

We have examined the moral foundations of law and justice, including the concepts of morality, justice, and the relationship between them. We have also discussed the different theories of law, such as natural law theory, legal positivism, legal realism, critical legal studies, and feminist legal theory. Furthermore, we have examined legal rights and responsibilities, constitutional rights and liberties, and the ethics of rights and responsibilities.

The book has delved into the ethical issues in the legal profession, including professionalism and ethics, confidentiality and attorney-client privilege, and conflicts of interest. We have explored the role of ethics in criminal justice, with a focus on the principles of criminal justice ethics, capital punishment, and ethical challenges in law enforcement.

Additionally, we have discussed social justice and human rights, including theories of social justice, the historical evolution of human rights, and social justice issues in legal studies. Lastly, we have examined the role of law in social change and reform, as well as the intersection of law, policy, and sustainable development.

By gaining a deep understanding of these philosophical and ethical issues, we can navigate moral dilemmas, promote justice, and contribute to a more equitable, just, and sustainable world. As future legal professionals, policymakers, and advocates, it is crucial to be ethically informed and engaged in order to shape a better future.

I hope that this book has provided you with a solid foundation in the philosophical and ethical issues in legal studies. I encourage you to continue exploring these topics, engaging in critical thinking, and grappling with the challenging ethical questions that will arise throughout your legal careers. Together, we can work towards a more just and ethical society.

Globalization and Ethical Challenges

Ethical Considerations in International Business

In today's globalized world, businesses operate across borders, engaging in trade and investment activities that span different countries and cultures. As international business expands, ethical considerations become increasingly important. Ethical behavior in international business involves making choices that are morally and socially responsible, taking into account the impact of business decisions on various stakeholders, including employees, consumers, local communities, and the environment. In this section, we will explore important ethical considerations in international business and discuss strategies for promoting ethical behavior.

Understanding the Ethical Dimensions of International Business

International business presents unique ethical challenges due to cultural differences, legal frameworks, political systems, and economic disparities. Businesses must navigate these complexities while upholding ethical principles. Some of the key ethical considerations in international business include:

1. **Human rights and labor standards:** Companies operating globally must ensure that their operations respect and protect human rights, including the rights of workers. Ethical violations such as child labor, forced labor, and unsafe working conditions can damage a company's reputation and lead to legal consequences.

2. **Corruption and bribery:** Doing business in certain countries may involve navigating corrupt practices, such as bribery and favoritism. Ethical businesses must resist engaging in such activities and promote fair and transparent business practices.

3. **Environmental sustainability:** International businesses have a responsibility to minimize their environmental impact. This includes reducing carbon emissions, conserving natural resources, and implementing sustainable practices throughout the supply chain.

4. **Fair trade and supply chain ethics:** International businesses should ensure that their supply chains are free from exploitative labor practices, promote fair trade, and respect the rights of local communities.

5. **Respecting cultural diversity:** International businesses operate in diverse cultural contexts. It is essential to understand and respect local customs, traditions, and values while conducting business.

These ethical considerations require businesses to go beyond legal compliance and adopt ethical standards that promote social responsibility and sustainability.

Promoting Ethical Behavior in International Business

Promoting ethical behavior in international business involves a combination of organizational policies, individual actions, and external regulations. Here are some approaches to promoting ethical behavior:

1. **Developing a code of conduct:** Businesses should establish a code of conduct that outlines the ethical principles and values to guide employees' behavior. This code should address issues such as bribery, human rights, labor standards, and environmental sustainability.

2. **Training and awareness programs:** Companies should provide comprehensive training programs to educate employees about ethical considerations in international business. These programs should raise awareness about the potential ethical dilemmas employees may encounter and help them develop the skills to make ethical decisions.

3. **Corporate social responsibility:** Embracing corporate social responsibility (CSR) principles can help businesses integrate ethical considerations into their core values and strategies. CSR initiatives can include philanthropy, community engagement, and environmental sustainability efforts.

4. **Due diligence in the supply chain:** Businesses should conduct rigorous due diligence to verify that their suppliers and partners adhere to ethical practices. This includes screening suppliers for labor violations, working towards fair trade practices, and ensuring environmental sustainability throughout the supply chain.

5. **Collaboration and partnerships:** Businesses can collaborate with local communities, non-governmental organizations (NGOs), and other stakeholders to address ethical challenges. Engaging with stakeholders can lead to innovative solutions and enhance social and environmental outcomes.

6. **Transparency and accountability:** Businesses should be transparent about their operations and report on their ethical performance. This includes providing clear information about labor practices, environmental impacts, and corporate governance, demonstrating a commitment to accountability.

By adopting these strategies, businesses can foster a culture of ethical behavior and contribute to a more sustainable and equitable global business environment.

Case Study: Ethical Considerations in the Fashion Industry

The fashion industry is a prominent example of the ethical considerations in international business. The industry faces ethical challenges related to labor rights, environmental sustainability, and supply chain practices. For instance, some fast fashion brands have been criticized for their exploitation of workers in developing countries, with reports of low wages, long working hours, and unsafe working conditions. Additionally, the fashion industry is known for its significant environmental impact, including water pollution, waste generation, and greenhouse gas emissions.

To address these ethical challenges, some fashion brands have taken proactive steps. They have implemented fair trade practices, promoted sustainable sourcing of materials, and ensured transparency throughout their supply chains. Furthermore, consumer awareness and demand for ethically produced fashion have led to the rise of sustainable and ethical fashion brands.

However, ethical considerations in the fashion industry remain complex, and there is still work to be done. Businesses must continuously assess their practices, align them with ethical standards, and engage in collaborations to drive industry-wide change.

Conclusion

Ethical considerations in international business are crucial for creating a sustainable and responsible business environment. Businesses must recognize the ethical dimensions of their operations and take proactive steps to address them. By adopting ethical principles, promoting transparency, and engaging with stakeholders, businesses can contribute to a more equitable and just global economy. It is essential for individuals, organizations, and governments to work together to ensure that ethical considerations are at the forefront of international business practices.

Human Rights in Global Supply Chains

Global supply chains play a significant role in the production and distribution of goods around the world. However, the complex and often opaque nature of these supply chains can give rise to numerous human rights concerns. This section explores the ethical challenges associated with human rights in global supply chains and examines the role of law and regulations in addressing these issues.

Understanding Global Supply Chains

A global supply chain refers to the network of organizations and activities involved in the production, distribution, and consumption of goods or services. It involves the coordination of various stages, including sourcing of raw materials, manufacturing, transportation, warehousing, and retailing. Supply chains are often global in nature, spanning across different countries and involving multiple stakeholders, such as suppliers, manufacturers, distributors, and retailers.

Human Rights Violations in Global Supply Chains

The globalization of supply chains has resulted in increased outsourcing and offshoring of production to countries with lower labor costs. While this has led to economic benefits for businesses, it has also heightened the risk of human rights violations. Some of the common human rights concerns in global supply chains include:

- **Forced labor and modern slavery:** Many workers, particularly in industries such as textiles, electronics, and agriculture, are subjected to exploitative working conditions, including forced labor, debt bondage, and human trafficking.

- **Child labor:** Despite efforts to eliminate child labor, it still persists in some supply chains, depriving children of their right to education and exposing them to hazardous work.

- **Unsafe working conditions:** Lack of safety standards and inadequate worker protection measures in certain industries can lead to accidents, injuries, and even fatalities.

- **Wage and labor rights violations:** Some supply chains engage in unfair labor practices, such as paying below minimum wage, denying workers their right to form unions or engage in collective bargaining, and imposing excessive working hours.

Legal Framework for Protecting Human Rights in Supply Chains

Addressing human rights violations in global supply chains requires a robust legal framework at both domestic and international levels. Several legal instruments and initiatives aim to hold businesses accountable for their impact on human rights. These include:

- **United Nations Guiding Principles on Business and Human Rights (UNGPs):** The UNGPs outline the responsibilities of businesses to respect human rights and provide guidance on how to prevent, address, and remedy human rights abuses. They emphasize the need for due diligence in supply chains and the importance of access to remedy for affected individuals.

- **International Labor Organization (ILO) Conventions:** The ILO has established numerous conventions that cover various aspects of labor rights, including freedom of association, collective bargaining, forced labor, and child labor. These conventions provide a common framework for protecting workers' rights and serve as a basis for national legislation.

- **National legislation:** Many countries have enacted laws that require companies to disclose information about their supply chains and to take steps to address human rights risks. Examples include the California Transparency in Supply Chains Act and the UK Modern Slavery Act.

Challenges in Ensuring Human Rights Compliance

Despite the existence of legal frameworks, enforcing human rights compliance in global supply chains is challenging. Some of the key obstacles include:

+ **Lack of transparency:** Supply chains often involve multiple tiers of suppliers, making it difficult to monitor and trace the origin of products and identify potential human rights abuses.

+ **Weak governance:** Some countries have limited capacity or political will to enforce labor and human rights laws, allowing violations to go unchecked.

+ **Power imbalances:** Imbalances in power between buyers and suppliers can result in unfair and exploitative practices, as suppliers may be pressured to meet unrealistic production targets at the expense of workers' rights.

+ **Complexity of supply chains:** Global supply chains are highly complex, involving numerous stakeholders with different legal systems, cultural norms, and business practices. Coordinating efforts to address human rights issues can be challenging.

Promoting Human Rights in Global Supply Chains

Efforts to promote human rights in global supply chains require a multi-stakeholder approach, involving collaboration among governments, businesses, civil society organizations, and consumers. Some strategies to enhance human rights compliance include:

+ **Supply chain transparency:** Companies should strive to enhance transparency by mapping their supply chains, conducting risk assessments, and disclosing relevant information to the public. This enables stakeholders to identify potential risks and hold companies accountable for human rights violations.

+ **Due diligence:** Businesses have a responsibility to conduct due diligence to identify, prevent, and mitigate human rights risks in their supply chains. This involves assessing suppliers' human rights performance, providing training and capacity building, and implementing effective grievance mechanisms.

+ **Collaboration and engagement:** Governments, businesses, and civil society organizations should collaborate to share best practices, develop common standards, and address systemic issues. Engaging with suppliers, workers, and local communities is crucial for understanding and addressing human rights challenges.

+ **Consumer awareness and advocacy**: Consumers can play a vital role in driving change by making informed choices and supporting businesses with responsible supply chains. Increased consumer awareness and advocacy can encourage companies to adopt ethical practices and create market demand for ethically produced goods.

Case Study: The Rana Plaza Factory Collapse

The Rana Plaza tragedy, which occurred in Bangladesh in 2013, serves as a stark reminder of the human rights risks associated with global supply chains. The collapse of the factory building, which housed multiple garment factories, resulted in the deaths of over 1,100 workers and injured thousands more. The incident highlighted the need for greater transparency, improved labor conditions, and increased accountability in the garment industry.

In response to the Rana Plaza disaster, various stakeholders, including brands, retailers, and labor rights organizations, came together to establish the Accord on Fire and Building Safety in Bangladesh. The Accord aimed to improve factory safety standards, conduct inspections, provide training to workers, and establish grievance mechanisms. This collaborative initiative demonstrated the importance of multi-stakeholder engagement in addressing human rights issues in supply chains.

Conclusion

Protecting human rights in global supply chains is a complex and multifaceted challenge. It requires a combination of legal, regulatory, and voluntary measures to ensure that businesses respect and uphold the rights of workers throughout the supply chain. By promoting transparency, conducting due diligence, and fostering collaboration, stakeholders can work towards creating a more ethical and sustainable global supply chain system that respects human rights.

Corruption and Bribery in Global Commerce

In the realm of global commerce, corruption and bribery pose significant challenges to ethical business practices and the promotion of a fair and just economic system. Corruption refers to the abuse of entrusted power for personal gain, while bribery involves offering, giving, receiving, or soliciting something of value as a means to influence the actions or decisions of individuals in positions of power. These unethical practices undermine the principles of fairness, transparency, and equality in the business world and have far-reaching consequences for economic growth, social development, and global justice.

Understanding Corruption and Bribery

Corruption and bribery can take various forms and occur at different levels within global commerce. They can involve public officials, private sector entities, or individuals engaging in illegal practices for personal or organizational gains. Common forms of corruption in global commerce include embezzlement, kickbacks, nepotism, and fraud. On the other hand, bribery can manifest in the form of financial incentives, lavish gifts, or favors offered or received in exchange for preferential treatment, contracts, or regulatory advantages.

To address the issue of corruption and bribery effectively, it is crucial to understand the underlying causes and consequences of these unethical practices. Economic inequality, weak governance structures, lack of accountability, and cultural norms that tolerate or encourage corrupt behavior are some of the factors that contribute to the prevalence of corruption and bribery in global commerce. The consequences of corruption and bribery are severe, including distorted markets, reduced foreign investment, compromised business ethics, and compromised the rule of law.

International Legal Frameworks and Instruments

To combat corruption and bribery in global commerce, international legal frameworks and instruments have been established to guide and regulate business practices. The United Nations Convention against Corruption (UNCAC) is a comprehensive global framework that aims to prevent, detect, and deter corruption across different sectors. It provides guidelines for legal, institutional, and preventive measures to ensure accountability and transparency in public and private sectors.

Additionally, the Organisation for Economic Co-operation and Development (OECD) has developed the Anti-Bribery Convention, which sets standards for combating bribery and promoting integrity in international business transactions. The convention requires member countries to criminalize bribery of foreign public officials and implement measures to prevent and detect such acts.

Furthermore, regional organizations such as the European Union and the African Union have also implemented legal instruments and initiatives to address corruption and bribery within their respective jurisdictions. These frameworks emphasize the importance of cooperation, information exchange, and mutual legal assistance in combating corruption and bribery.

Challenges and Solutions

Combatting corruption and bribery in global commerce poses significant challenges due to the complexity and clandestine nature of these practices. However, several strategies and solutions can help mitigate these challenges and promote ethical business conduct.

1. Strengthening Legal Frameworks: Countries need to enact and enforce robust anti-corruption laws that criminalize corruption and bribery in all their forms. These laws should provide for severe penalties and strengthen mechanisms for asset recovery and confiscation.

2. Enhancing Transparency and Reporting Mechanisms: Organizations should establish and promote effective systems for reporting corruption and bribery, including whistleblower protection mechanisms. Transparent financial practices, open procurement processes, and public access to information can also help in reducing opportunities for corruption.

3. Promoting Ethical Business Practices: Businesses should adopt strong ethical codes of conduct that prohibit corruption and bribery. Regular training and awareness programs can educate employees about the risks and consequences associated with engaging in these practices.

4. International Cooperation: Collaboration between countries, international organizations, and regional bodies is essential to address corruption and bribery issues effectively. Joint investigations, mutual legal assistance, and information sharing mechanisms can help in detecting and prosecuting cross-border corruption cases.

5. Promoting a Culture of Integrity: Governments, businesses, civil society, and individuals need to work together to foster a culture of integrity and accountability. This can be achieved through education, awareness campaigns, and promoting ethical values at all levels of society.

Case Study: The Siemens Scandal

One of the most prominent examples of corruption and bribery in global commerce is the Siemens scandal that unfolded in the mid-2000s. Siemens, a German multinational conglomerate, was found to have engaged in widespread bribery to secure lucrative contracts in several countries.

The company's corrupt practices involved bribing government officials, political parties, and employees of state-owned enterprises to gain an unfair advantage in the competitive market. The bribes were often disguised as consulting fees, commissions, or charitable donations.

The Siemens scandal highlighted the far-reaching consequences of corruption, including tarnished reputation, financial losses, legal penalties, and erosion of trust. It also served as a wake-up call for the need to strengthen international efforts against corruption in global commerce.

In response to the scandal, Siemens underwent significant reforms and implemented comprehensive anti-corruption measures. These included establishing an independent compliance department, enhancing internal controls, and encouraging a culture of ethical behavior among employees. The case of Siemens illustrates the importance of proactive measures to prevent and address corruption and bribery within organizations.

Conclusion

Corruption and bribery in global commerce represent significant challenges to the principles of fairness, transparency, and equality in economic systems. To combat these unethical practices effectively, it is essential to strengthen international legal frameworks, enhance transparency, promote ethical business practices, foster international cooperation, and promote a culture of integrity.

Addressing corruption and bribery requires a multi-faceted approach involving governments, businesses, civil society, and individuals. By working together and implementing robust measures, we can create a more equitable and just global business environment that promotes sustainable economic growth and social development.

Environmental Sustainability and Global Trade

Environmental sustainability is a crucial concern in today's world, as the impacts of human activities on the environment continue to grow. Global trade, on the other hand, has become increasingly interconnected, with goods and services being exchanged across borders at an unprecedented scale. In this section, we will explore the relationship between environmental sustainability and global trade, examining the challenges and opportunities that arise when balancing economic growth with environmental protection.

The Environmental Impacts of Global Trade

Global trade has undoubtedly contributed to worldwide economic growth and development. However, it has also led to various environmental challenges. The expansion of international transportation networks has increased greenhouse gas emissions, contributing to climate change. The extraction of natural resources to meet global demand has led to deforestation, habitat destruction, and biodiversity loss. Industrial production for export often results in high levels of pollution and the generation of hazardous waste.

These environmental impacts are not limited to any particular region but have ripple effects across the globe. For instance, the emissions produced from the burning of fossil fuels for transportation during the global shipping of goods contribute to air pollution and climate change in both exporting and importing countries. Therefore, it is vital to address the environmental consequences of global trade to promote sustainable development.

International Environmental Agreements

To tackle global environmental challenges, international cooperation is essential. Several multilateral environmental agreements (MEAs) have been established to address specific environmental issues. These agreements aim to promote sustainable development and mitigate the negative impacts of global trade on the environment.

One prominent MEA is the United Nations Framework Convention on Climate Change (UNFCCC), which sets the stage for global cooperation on climate change mitigation and adaptation measures. The Paris Agreement, a key outcome of the UNFCCC, seeks to limit global warming well below 2 degrees Celsius and pursue efforts to limit the temperature increase to 1.5 degrees Celsius above pre-industrial levels. It emphasizes the importance of reducing greenhouse gas emissions and enhancing resilience to climate change impacts.

Another significant MEA is the Convention on Biological Diversity (CBD), which aims to conserve biodiversity, ensure the sustainable use of its components, and promote equitable sharing of the benefits arising from the utilization of genetic resources. The CBD recognizes the role of trade in impacting biodiversity and calls for the integration of biodiversity considerations into trade-related policies and practices.

These international agreements provide a framework for countries to work together to address the environmental challenges associated with global trade.

However, their effectiveness depends on the commitment and actions of individual nations.

Trade and Environmental Policies

To promote environmental sustainability in the context of global trade, countries have implemented various trade and environmental policies. These policies aim to ensure that trade does not come at the expense of the environment and to create a level playing field for countries with different environmental standards.

One approach is the use of environmental regulations and standards. Countries can impose environmental requirements on imported goods, such as restrictions on the use of certain chemicals or the adoption of specific packaging materials. These measures aim to prevent the importation of products that do not meet the environmental standards set by the importing country.

Another approach is the implementation of market-based instruments, such as environmental taxes or tradable permits. These measures internalize the environmental costs associated with production and consumption, providing economic incentives for businesses and individuals to reduce pollution and resource consumption.

Additionally, eco-labeling and certification schemes have emerged to help consumers make informed choices by indicating the environmental credentials of products. These schemes verify that products have been produced in an environmentally responsible manner and meet specific sustainability criteria.

The challenge is to strike a balance between protecting the environment and avoiding unnecessary trade barriers. Environmental regulations and standards should be based on scientific evidence, transparent, non-discriminatory, and applied in a manner consistent with international law.

Promoting Sustainable Global Trade

While global trade poses environmental challenges, it also presents opportunities for promoting sustainability. Trade can contribute to sustainable development by enabling countries to access cleaner technologies, improve environmental management practices, and create economic opportunities for sustainable industries.

A key aspect of promoting sustainable global trade is the integration of environmental considerations into trade agreements. Provisions addressing environmental issues, such as the protection of endangered species, the conservation of natural resources, and the enforcement of environmental standards, can help ensure that trade contributes to environmental sustainability.

Capacity building and technical assistance programs play a vital role in supporting developing countries in implementing sustainable trade practices. These programs help countries develop their institutional capacity, improve environmental management systems, and comply with international environmental standards.

Moreover, fostering collaboration between governments, businesses, and civil society is essential. Multi-stakeholder partnerships can promote information sharing, best practices, and innovation in sustainable trade. Public-private partnerships can drive investments in green technologies and sustainable infrastructure, facilitating the transition to a low-carbon and resource-efficient economy.

Case Study: Sustainable Palm Oil Production

The production of palm oil is a relevant case study that highlights the complex relationship between global trade, environmental sustainability, and social justice. Palm oil is a versatile and highly demanded commodity used in various products, including food, cosmetics, and biofuels.

The expansion of palm oil plantations has resulted in deforestation, habitat destruction, and greenhouse gas emissions, primarily in Southeast Asian countries. This has raised concerns about biodiversity loss, climate change, and the violation of the rights of indigenous peoples and local communities.

To address these issues, the Roundtable on Sustainable Palm Oil (RSPO) was established. The RSPO is a certification scheme that aims to promote the production and use of sustainable palm oil. It sets criteria for environmental responsibility, social equity, and economic viability in the palm oil industry.

The RSPO certification ensures that palm oil is produced in compliance with specific sustainability standards, including the protection of high conservation value areas, the prohibition of burning, and the respect for the rights of workers and local communities. Products containing certified sustainable palm oil can carry the RSPO trademark, providing consumers with the choice to support sustainable palm oil production.

The case of sustainable palm oil production emphasizes the importance of multi-stakeholder initiatives and the role of consumers in driving demand for sustainable products. By choosing products with sustainable certifications, consumers can contribute to protecting the environment and promoting sustainable global trade.

Conclusion

The environmental challenges posed by global trade require concerted efforts from governments, businesses, civil society, and individuals. Balancing economic growth with environmental sustainability is essential for the well-being of current and future generations.

International environmental agreements provide a framework for global cooperation, while trade and environmental policies play a crucial role in promoting sustainable global trade. By integrating environmental considerations into trade agreements, implementing environmental regulations and standards, and fostering multi-stakeholder partnerships, we can strive towards a more sustainable and equitable world.

The case of sustainable palm oil production reminds us of the need to address the complex interplay between global trade, environmental sustainability, and social justice. By supporting initiatives such as certification schemes and making informed consumer choices, we can contribute to protecting the environment and promoting sustainable practices in global trade.

In the next section, we will delve into the ethical considerations related to the use of technology in legal practice and its impact on access to justice.

Ethical Leadership and Business Ethics

In this section, we will explore the concept of ethical leadership and its application to business ethics. Ethical leadership is a crucial aspect of maintaining integrity and promoting ethical behavior within an organization. We will discuss the principles and characteristics of ethical leadership, examine the role of leaders in shaping organizational culture, and explore the ethical challenges faced by leaders in the business environment.

Principles of Ethical Leadership

Ethical leadership involves the demonstration of moral values and principles in decision-making and behavior. Let's explore some key principles of ethical leadership:

1. Integrity: Ethical leaders act in accordance with their values and principles, consistently demonstrating honesty, transparency, and trustworthiness. They adhere to moral and ethical standards and lead by example.

2. Responsibility: Ethical leaders take responsibility for their actions and the impact they have on others and the organization. They recognize the consequences of their decisions and are willing to be held accountable.

3. Respect: Ethical leaders value and respect the dignity and rights of all individuals. They create an inclusive and diverse environment where everyone's voice is heard and respected.

4. Fairness: Ethical leaders treat all individuals fairly and impartially, ensuring that decisions and actions are based on objective criteria and not influenced by personal biases or preferences.

5. Empathy: Ethical leaders demonstrate empathy towards others, understanding their perspectives, and considering the impact of their decisions on their well-being. They are compassionate and strive to create an environment where everyone feels valued and supported.

6. Ethical Decision-Making: Ethical leaders employ a systematic approach to decision-making, considering the ethical implications and consequences of their choices. They involve stakeholders and seek diverse perspectives to ensure thorough and well-informed decisions.

Characteristics of Ethical Leaders

Ethical leadership requires a unique set of characteristics that inspire and motivate others to act ethically. Some key characteristics of ethical leaders include:

1. Vision: Ethical leaders have a clear vision of their organization's purpose and goals. They inspire others to work towards a shared vision, aligning their actions with the organization's ethical values.

2. Courage: Ethical leaders demonstrate courage in challenging unethical practices and making difficult decisions in the face of adversity. They are willing to take risks to uphold their ethical principles.

3. Transparency: Ethical leaders are open and transparent in their communication and decision-making. They provide clear explanations for their choices and engage in open dialogue with stakeholders.

4. Humility: Ethical leaders display humility and acknowledge their limitations. They are open to feedback and willing to learn from others. They prioritize the collective good over personal ego.

5. Strong Ethics Codes: Ethical leaders establish and enforce strong ethics codes within their organizations. They promote a culture of ethical behavior and ensure that employees are aware of and adhere to ethical standards.

Leadership and Organizational Culture

Organizational culture plays a significant role in shaping ethical behavior within an organization. Ethical leaders have the responsibility to create a culture where ethical behavior is valued and rewarded. Here are some ways ethical leaders can influence organizational culture:

1.   Setting the Tone: Ethical leaders set the tone for ethical behavior by consistently demonstrating ethical values in their actions and decisions. Their behavior serves as a benchmark for others to follow.

2.   Communication: Ethical leaders communicate their ethical expectations clearly and regularly to all stakeholders. They explain the importance of ethical behavior and provide guidance on how to navigate ethical challenges.

3.   Training and Development: Ethical leaders invest in training and development programs to cultivate ethical decision-making skills among employees. They provide opportunities for ethical discussions and encourage ethical reflection.

4.   Rewarding Ethical Behavior: Ethical leaders recognize and reward individuals who demonstrate ethical behavior and contribute to the organization's ethical culture. This aligns incentives with ethical conduct and reinforces the importance of ethical behavior.

5.   Addressing Unethical Behavior: Ethical leaders promptly address and address unethical behavior within the organization. They take appropriate measures to investigate and remedy ethical violations, ensuring a fair and transparent process.

Ethical Challenges for Leaders in the Business Environment

Leaders in the business environment face various ethical challenges that require careful consideration and decision-making. Some common ethical challenges include:

1. Balancing Stakeholder Interests: Ethical leaders must balance the interests of various stakeholders, including shareholders, employees, customers, and the community. They need to make decisions that consider the well-being of all stakeholders and avoid undue favoritism or exploitation.

2. Managing Conflicts of Interest: Ethical leaders must navigate conflicts of interest and ensure that personal or financial interests do not compromise ethical decision-making. They establish mechanisms to identify, disclose, and address conflicts of interest effectively.

3. Promoting Ethical Conduct in Supply Chains: Ethical leaders are responsible for promoting ethical behavior throughout the organization's supply chains. They need to ensure that suppliers and partners adhere to ethical standards and address unethical practices, such as child labor or environmental violations.

4. Dealing with Ethical Dilemmas: Ethical leaders often encounter complex ethical dilemmas that require balancing competing ethical principles. They need to apply ethical decision-making frameworks to guide their choices and ensure they align with the organization's values.

5. Navigating Legal and Ethical Boundaries: Ethical leaders need to navigate the intersection of legal requirements and ethical responsibilities. They should go beyond legal compliance and consider the broader ethical implications of their actions.

Case Study: The Volkswagen Emissions Scandal

The Volkswagen emissions scandal serves as a powerful example of ethical leadership failure in the business context. In 2015, it was revealed that Volkswagen had intentionally manipulated software in their diesel vehicles to cheat emissions tests. This scandal highlighted the ethical challenges faced by leaders in balancing business interests and ethical responsibilities.

The ethical failure in this case involved a lack of integrity, transparency, and accountability. Leaders at Volkswagen made a deliberate decision to deceive regulators and consumers, prioritizing short-term profits over ethical behavior. This unethical conduct not only had legal and financial consequences but also severely damaged the company's reputation and eroded public trust.

The scandal underscores the importance of ethical leadership in the business environment. Ethical leaders would have prioritized transparency, honesty, and accountability. They would have proactively addressed potential ethical issues and ensured that appropriate mechanisms were in place to prevent unethical practices.

Conclusion

Ethical leadership is essential for fostering an ethical organizational culture and promoting ethical behavior within the business environment. Ethical leaders adhere to principles such as integrity, responsibility, respect, and fairness. They shape organizational culture, navigate ethical challenges, and inspire others to act ethically. By embodying these principles and characteristics, ethical leaders contribute to a more sustainable and just business world.

Globalization, Social Justice, and Human Rights

In today's interconnected world, globalization has profoundly impacted various aspects of our lives, including social justice and human rights. Globalization refers to the increasing interconnectedness and interdependence of countries through the exchange of goods, services, information, and ideas. While globalization has brought numerous benefits, it has also given rise to several ethical challenges that need to be addressed in order to promote social justice and protect human rights.

Understanding Globalization

Globalization has reshaped the economic, political, and social landscape of nations, blurring the boundaries between countries and facilitating the flow of goods, capital, and people. It has led to the integration of economies, the creation of global markets, and the expansion of multinational corporations. Technological advancements, such as the internet and social media, have further accelerated the pace of globalization, enabling instant communication and global interconnectedness.

The Relationship between Globalization and Social Justice

Globalization has the potential to promote social justice by creating economic opportunities, reducing poverty, and improving living standards. However, it also poses significant challenges to achieving social justice. Economic globalization has resulted in economic inequalities, both within and between countries. Developed countries often benefit more from globalization, while developing countries may experience exploitation, resource depletion, and labor rights violations.

Furthermore, globalization has led to cultural homogenization and the erosion of traditional values and practices. Globalization has also created a digital divide, with marginalized communities having limited access to information and communication technologies.

Human Rights in the Era of Globalization

Globalization has both positive and negative impacts on human rights. On the one hand, it has facilitated the spread of democratic values, global norms, and human rights principles. It has also provided a platform for advocacy and activism to address human rights violations worldwide.

On the other hand, globalization has created challenges for the protection of human rights. Transnational corporations operating in developing countries often face allegations of human rights abuses, exploitation of workers, and environmental degradation. The global trade in goods, including illicit trade, can contribute to issues such as forced labor, child labor, human trafficking, and the violation of workers' rights.

Promoting Social Justice and Human Rights in a Globalized World

Addressing the ethical challenges arising from globalization requires a comprehensive approach that considers the principles of social justice and human rights. Governments, international organizations, civil society, and individuals all have a role to play in promoting social justice and protecting human rights in a globalized world. Here are some strategies and initiatives:

+ Strengthening international human rights frameworks: Governments should ratify and implement international human rights conventions, strengthen monitoring mechanisms, and hold states accountable for human rights violations.

+ Corporate social responsibility: Multinational corporations have a responsibility to respect human rights and adhere to ethical business practices throughout their global operations. This includes ensuring fair wages, safe working conditions, and environmental sustainability.

+ Fair trade and ethical consumption: Promoting fair trade practices and ethical consumption can provide economic opportunities to marginalized communities, protect workers' rights, and promote sustainable production and consumption.

+ Protecting labor rights: Governments and trade unions should work together to protect and promote labor rights, including freedom of association, collective bargaining, and fair wages.

+ Bridging the digital divide: Efforts should be made to ensure equitable access to information and communication technologies, bridging the digital divide and empowering marginalized communities.

+ Strengthening global governance: International organizations, such as the United Nations, should play a key role in coordinating efforts to address the ethical implications of globalization, promote social justice, and protect human rights.

Case Study: Sweatshops in the Global Garment Industry

One of the key ethical challenges in globalization is the issue of sweatshops in the global garment industry. Sweatshops are factories or workshops where workers, often in developing countries, face long working hours, low wages, poor working conditions, and limited labor rights.

The globalization of the garment industry has led to the relocation of production to countries with low labor costs, resulting in the exploitation of workers. Many multinational clothing brands outsource their production to factories in developing countries where labor laws are weakly enforced.

The ethical implications of sweatshops include the violation of workers' rights, poor wages that do not meet the basic needs of workers and their families, and unsafe working conditions that can lead to accidents and health issues. Sweatshops also perpetuate gender inequalities, as women make up a significant portion of the workforce in the garment industry.

Addressing sweatshop conditions requires a multi-stakeholder approach. Governments in both developed and developing countries need to enforce labor laws and promote decent work conditions. Clothing brands have a responsibility to ensure ethical sourcing and supply chain transparency, holding their suppliers accountable for fair labor practices. Consumers can play a role by making informed choices and supporting brands that prioritize ethical production.

Conclusion

Globalization presents both opportunities and challenges for social justice and human rights. While it has the potential to promote economic development and the spread of democratic values, it also exacerbates economic inequalities and poses risks to human rights. To address the ethical implications of globalization, it is crucial to adopt a holistic approach that integrates social justice principles and human rights considerations into policies, practices, and decision-making processes. By doing so, we can strive towards a globalized world that is fair, just, and respects the inherent dignity and rights of all individuals.

Globalization and Exploitation

Globalization has transformed the world in profound ways, connecting nations and cultures, and facilitating the exchange of goods, services, and ideas on a global scale. However, alongside the benefits of globalization, there are also significant ethical challenges, particularly in relation to exploitation. In this section, we will explore the ethical implications of globalization and how it can contribute to various forms of exploitation.

Understanding Globalization

Globalization refers to the increasing interconnectedness and interdependence of countries through the exchange of goods, services, information, and ideas. It is driven by advancements in technology, transportation, and communication, which have made it easier for individuals, companies, and governments to interact and conduct business across borders. Globalization has led to the growth of multinational corporations, the establishment of global supply chains, and the rise of international trade and investment.

Exploitation in Globalized Systems

One of the ethical concerns associated with globalization is the potential for exploitation. Globalized systems can create conditions that allow for the abuse and mistreatment of individuals, particularly those in vulnerable positions. Here are some examples of exploitation in the context of globalization:

1. **Labor Exploitation:** Globalization has led to the outsourcing of labor to countries with lower labor costs, where workers may be subjected to long working hours, low wages, unsafe working conditions, and inadequate labor protections. This can occur in industries such as manufacturing, agriculture, and services.

2. **Child Labor:** In many developing countries, globalization has perpetuated the cycle of child labor. Children are often forced to work in dangerous and exploitative conditions, depriving them of education, health, and a proper childhood.

3. **Human Trafficking:** Globalization has also contributed to the rise of human trafficking, a form of modern-day slavery. Criminal networks exploit vulnerable individuals for various purposes, including forced labor, sexual exploitation, and organ trafficking. The demand for cheap labor and commercial sex fuels this heinous practice.

4. **Environmental Exploitation:** Globalization has increased the demand for natural resources, leading to the exploitation and depletion of ecosystems. This can result in ecological damage, loss of biodiversity, and the displacement of indigenous communities who rely on these resources.

5. **Intellectual Property Exploitation:** With the global movement of ideas and information, issues of intellectual property rights arise. Developing countries often face challenges in protecting their traditional knowledge, cultural expressions, and indigenous technologies from appropriation, exploitation, and misappropriation by more powerful entities.

Causes and Contributors to Global Exploitation

Several factors contribute to exploitation in the globalized world. Understanding these causes is essential in addressing and mitigating the ethical challenges posed by globalization. Here are some key factors:

1. **Power Imbalances:** Globalization often perpetuates existing power imbalances between developed and developing nations. Developed countries and multinational corporations hold more economic and political power, enabling them to exploit the resources and labor of less powerful nations.

2. **Lack of Regulatory Oversight:** Weak or inadequate legal frameworks, lax enforcement, and corruption in some countries can create an environment where exploitation can thrive. Insufficient regulations and oversight fail to protect workers, consumers, and the environment from exploitation.

3. **Income Inequality:** Globalization has contributed to increasing income inequality within and between countries. The concentration of wealth in the hands of a few exacerbates exploitation by enabling the exploitation of vulnerable individuals who lack access to resources, education, and opportunities.

4. **Consumer Demand and Choices:** The demand for cheap goods and services by consumers in developed countries often drives exploitation. Consumers may unknowingly contribute to exploitation by purchasing products made under unethical conditions or by supporting companies that perpetuate exploitation in their supply chains.

5. **Lack of Awareness and Transparency:** Many instances of exploitation remain hidden or invisible from public view. Lack of transparency in global supply chains makes it challenging for consumers, organizations, and governments to identify and address instances of exploitation.

Addressing Global Exploitation

Tackling the ethical challenges posed by globalization and addressing global exploitation requires a multi-faceted approach involving multiple stakeholders. Here are some strategies and initiatives aimed at mitigating exploitation:

1. **Legislative and Regulatory Reforms:** Governments can enact and enforce robust labor laws, regulations, and human rights protections. Enhanced

legal frameworks and transparent enforcement mechanisms help prevent and address exploitation in various sectors.

2. **Corporate Social Responsibility**: Companies play a crucial role in addressing exploitation in their supply chains. Adopting responsible business practices, conducting due diligence, and ensuring fair and ethical treatment of workers can help mitigate exploitative practices.

3. **International Collaboration**: International organizations, governments, civil society groups, and businesses can collaborate to establish global standards and frameworks that promote ethical globalization. Initiatives such as the United Nations Global Compact and the International Labor Organization's Better Work program aim to improve working conditions and protect workers' rights globally.

4. **Consumer Awareness and Education**: Raising awareness among consumers about the ethical implications of their purchasing choices can drive demand for ethically produced goods and put pressure on companies to improve their practices. Education and advocacy campaigns can help consumers make informed choices and support fair and ethical trade.

5. **Supply Chain Traceability**: Enhancing supply chain transparency can help identify instances of exploitation and hold companies accountable for their practices. Technologies such as blockchain can facilitate traceability and provide consumers with information about the origins and conditions under which products are made.

6. **Capacity Building and Empowerment**: Supporting education, skills training, and economic empowerment in vulnerable communities can help break the cycle of exploitation. Investing in the development of local economies and empowering marginalized groups can reduce their vulnerability to exploitation.

Case Study: The Rana Plaza Factory Collapse

The Rana Plaza factory collapse in Bangladesh in 2013 serves as a tragic example of the ethical challenges in global supply chains. The collapse of the building, which housed several garment factories, resulted in the death of over 1,100 workers. This incident highlighted the exploitative working conditions and inadequate safety standards in the global garment industry. It prompted global outrage and a renewed focus on the need for improved labor rights and safety regulations in the industry.

The Rana Plaza disaster led to the formation of the Accord on Fire and Building Safety in Bangladesh, a legally binding agreement between global brands, trade unions, and NGOs. The Accord aimed to enhance worker safety in the garment industry by requiring signatory brands to conduct safety inspections of their supplier factories, make necessary repairs, and provide remediation assistance to affected workers. It serves as an example of collective action and collaboration to address exploitation in global supply chains.

Conclusion

Globalization has undoubtedly brought about significant benefits, but it also comes with ethical challenges, particularly in relation to exploitation. Addressing the ethical implications of globalization requires a comprehensive and collaborative approach involving governments, businesses, civil society organizations, and consumers.   By promoting fair labor practices, enhancing supply chain transparency, and empowering vulnerable communities, we can work towards a more just and ethical globalized world.

Conclusion

In conclusion, the field of legal studies is crucial in addressing the philosophical and ethical issues that arise within the legal profession.   By examining the moral foundations of law and justice, exploring ethical dilemmas in legal practice, and analyzing social justice and human rights, legal professionals can navigate the complexities of the legal system and promote justice in a more equitable and sustainable world.

Throughout this textbook, we have delved into various topics, including the interdisciplinary nature of legal studies, the relationship between philosophy and ethics, and ethical decision-making frameworks. We have examined the theories of law, legal rights and responsibilities, and ethical issues in the legal profession. Additionally, we have explored social justice and human rights, ethical concerns in criminal justice, and the ethical issues in the business and commerce sectors.

In this final section, we will summarize the key points discussed in this chapter and reflect on the importance of ethical considerations in the context of globalization and social justice. We will also explore the role of law in social change and reform, and how technology poses new ethical challenges for legal professionals.

First, we highlighted the significance of ethical considerations in the legal profession. Legal professionals have a vital role in upholding the principles of justice, fairness, and integrity. By adhering to professional codes of conduct and ethics, they can navigate the numerous ethical dilemmas that arise in legal practice and maintain the trust of their clients and the public.

We then examined the ethical challenges specific to the legal profession, including confidentiality and attorney-client privilege. We discussed the need for legal professionals to balance the duty of maintaining client confidences with other ethical obligations, such as preventing harm or promoting justice. We also acknowledged the complexities of managing conflicts of interest and the importance of transparency and accountability in maintaining ethical integrity.

Moving forward, we explored social justice and human rights, and their intersection with the legal system. We discussed various theories of social justice, such as egalitarianism, libertarianism, and communitarianism. We also analyzed the historical evolution of human rights and the challenges faced in their protection. Ensuring social justice requires addressing issues of poverty, inequality, gender equality, racial justice, LGBTQ+ rights, and environmental justice. Legal professionals play a crucial role in advocating for marginalized communities and ensuring equal access to justice.

Next, we delved into the ethical issues present in the criminal justice system. We examined the ethical principles guiding law enforcement, criminal prosecution, and the correctional system. We also delved into controversial topics, such as capital punishment, and explored the ethical implications of these practices. Additionally, we discussed the ethical challenges surrounding policing, including the use of force, racial profiling, and the need for accountability and transparency.

Furthermore, we explored the ethical issues that arise in the business and commerce sectors. Ethical considerations in corporate governance, marketing and advertising, and intellectual property rights were analyzed. We also examined the ethical challenges posed by globalization, including human rights in global supply chains, corruption and bribery, and environmental sustainability.

Lastly, we discussed the role of law in social change and reform. We examined how law can be a tool for social change, the impact of legal activism and public interest law, and the limitations and successes of using law for social justice. Additionally, we explored the role of law in promoting sustainable development and the ethical challenges posed by technological advancements, such as privacy and data protection, artificial intelligence, and cybersecurity.

As legal professionals, it is our responsibility to navigate these ethical dilemmas, promote justice, and shape a more equitable, just, and sustainable world. By critically analyzing the philosophical and ethical issues in legal studies, we can contribute to a legal system that upholds the principles of fairness, justice, and the common good.

We hope this textbook has provided you with a solid foundation to understand and navigate the complex ethical considerations in legal studies. It is our hope that you will carry the knowledge and ethical principles outlined in this textbook throughout your career, making informed decisions that promote justice and create positive societal change.

Remember, the field of legal studies is continuously evolving, and new ethical challenges will undoubtedly emerge. It is our duty as legal professionals to adapt to these changes, stay informed, and continually reflect on the ethical implications of our actions. Only by doing so can we contribute to a legal system that is truly just, equitable, and sustainable.

Thank you for embarking on this journey with us, and we wish you the best in your future endeavors in legal studies.

The Role of Law in Social Change and Reform

Law as a Tool for Social Change

Law and Social Movements

Introduction

Law plays a pivotal role in social movements, providing a framework within which individuals and groups can advocate for change and challenge existing power structures. Social movements aim to bring attention to specific issues, raise awareness, and mobilize communities to push for social, political, or cultural transformation. This section explores the dynamic relationship between law and social movements, examining how law can both shape and be shaped by these movements.

The Role of Law in Social Movements

1. Social Movements and Legal Activism: - Social movements often employ legal strategies and tactics to achieve their goals. This can include filing lawsuits, advocating for legislative changes, and challenging existing laws and policies. Legal activism involves using the legal system as a tool for social change and progress. - Examples of legal activism include the civil rights movement in the United States, which sought to end racial segregation and discrimination through litigation and advocacy, and the environmental movement, which relies on legal mechanisms to protect natural resources and combat climate change.

2. Impact Litigation: - Impact litigation refers to strategic legal actions aimed at achieving broader societal change. It involves bringing lawsuits that challenge discriminatory practices, unjust policies, or violations of human rights. Impact

litigation seeks to set legal precedents and influence future legal decisions.   -
Examples of impact litigation include the landmark case of Brown v. Board of
Education in the United States, which led to the desegregation of public schools,
and the Obergefell v. Hodges case, which legalized same-sex marriage nationwide.

3. Law as a Catalyst and Support for Social Change: - Law can act as a catalyst
for social change by providing a framework for addressing social injustices. Legal
reforms and changes in legislation can directly impact social movements and their
ability to achieve their goals. - Additionally, law can provide support and protection
for social movements. Constitutional rights such as freedom of speech, assembly,
and petition for redress are essential for facilitating social movements by ensuring
their ability to express dissent, mobilize supporters, and challenge the status quo.

Challenges and Limitations

1. Marginalization and Resistance: - Social movements often face resistance from
those in power who seek to maintain the status quo. Legal mechanisms can be
used to suppress or marginalize social movements, such as through restrictive laws,
surveillance, or violence. - While law can be a powerful tool for social change, it is
important to recognize that it is not always accessible, equitable, or just. Legal
systems can be biased, and marginalized communities may face additional barriers
when seeking justice.

2. Co-option and Dilution of Movement Goals: - Social movements that rely
extensively on legal strategies may face the risk of co-option, in which their goals
and demands are watered down or assimilated by the mainstream legal system. -
To maintain their integrity and effectiveness, social movements must navigate the
tension between working within existing legal frameworks and challenging them to
bring about more radical and transformative change.

Conclusion

Law and social movements are intricately connected, with law serving as both a
tool and a target for these movements. Social movements can shape laws and legal
practices, while law provides a framework for social change and protection for
activists. However, challenges and limitations exist, and social movements must
navigate the complexities and power dynamics inherent in legal systems. By
understanding the relationship between law and social movements, individuals can
better advocate for change and contribute to the pursuit of a more just and
equitable society.

Further Reading

- Charles R. Epp, Making Rights Real: Activists, Bureaucrats, and the Creation of the Legalistic State - Gerald N. Rosenberg, The Hollow Hope: Can Courts Bring About Social Change? - Philip Alston and Ryan Goodman (eds.), International Human Rights: Law, Policy, and Process - Douzinas, Costas. The End of Human Rights: Critical Legal Thought at the Turn of the Century

Legal Activism and Public Interest Law

Legal activism refers to the use of law as a tool for social change and the pursuit of a more equitable and just society. It involves the strategic and intentional use of litigation, advocacy, and policy work to challenge unjust laws, policies, and practices. Public interest law, on the other hand, focuses on representing individuals and groups who have limited resources and are unable to afford legal representation. It aims to advance the public interest and address systemic issues that affect marginalized communities.

Role of Legal Activism

Legal activism plays a crucial role in shaping the law and promoting social change. It empowers individuals and communities to challenge unjust systems and seek legal remedies for violations of their rights. By using the courts as a platform for advocating for change, legal activists can influence judicial decisions and shape legal interpretations that protect and advance human rights and social justice.

Moreover, legal activism goes beyond the courtroom. It includes grassroots organizing, community education, and policy advocacy to bring about broader social change. Legal activists often work in collaboration with grassroots organizations, community leaders, and advocacy groups to address systemic issues and ensure that marginalized voices are heard.

Strategic Litigation

Strategic litigation is a key aspect of legal activism. It involves strategically selecting cases that have the potential to have a significant impact on the law and society. These cases are often chosen for their ability to set legal precedents, challenge discriminatory practices, or address systemic issues.

Strategic litigation aims to achieve not only individual justice for the client but also broader social change. By strategically selecting cases, legal activists can bring attention to systemic issues, hold institutions accountable, and create legal precedents that protect the rights of marginalized communities.

An example of strategic litigation is the landmark case of Brown v. Board of Education in the United States. This case challenged racial segregation in schools and ultimately led to the desegregation of public schools nationwide. It was a pivotal moment in the civil rights movement and demonstrated the power of strategic litigation to challenge discriminatory practices and bring about systemic change.

Advocacy and Policy Work

In addition to litigation, legal activists engage in advocacy and policy work to address systemic issues and promote social justice. This involves lobbying lawmakers, drafting legislation, and advocating for policy changes that protect and advance human rights.

Legal activists often work in partnership with grassroots organizations and advocacy groups to amplify marginalized voices and influence policy decisions. Through their expertise in the law and legal frameworks, they can offer critical insights and recommendations for creating more equitable and just policies.

Advocacy and policy work can take various forms, including testifying before legislative bodies, participating in public consultations, and engaging in public awareness campaigns. By leveraging legal expertise and engaging in public discourse, legal activists can shape public opinion and influence policy decisions.

Challenges and Limitations

Despite its significant role in promoting social change, legal activism also faces challenges and limitations. One of the challenges is the resource constraints faced by legal activists and public interest law organizations. Limited funding and resources can hinder their ability to take on high-impact cases or engage in widespread advocacy efforts.

Additionally, legal activism often faces resistance from entrenched interests and powerful institutions. There may be efforts to undermine or discredit legal activists, making it difficult to achieve meaningful change. Furthermore, legal activism may be subject to criticism that it is undemocratic or too reliant on the judicial branch, bypassing legislative and political processes.

Moreover, legal activism is not a one-size-fits-all approach. Different contexts and issues require tailored strategies and approaches. Legal activists must be cognizant of the potential unintended consequences and limitations of their actions. They must navigate the complex dynamics between law, politics, and social change to ensure their efforts have a lasting and positive impact.

Despite these challenges, legal activism continues to play a vital role in advancing social justice. It serves as a powerful tool for challenging injustice, advocating for marginalized communities, and promoting a more equitable and just society.

Conclusion

Legal activism and public interest law are essential components of the pursuit of a more just and equitable society. By strategically using litigation, advocacy, and policy work, legal activists can challenge unjust systems and advocate for systemic change. They play a pivotal role in shaping the law, influencing policy decisions, and advancing human rights and social justice. While legal activism faces challenges and limitations, its impact in promoting social change cannot be overstated. Through its continued efforts, legal activism contributes to the creation of a more equitable and just world.

Impact Litigation and Strategic Litigation

Impact litigation and strategic litigation are two approaches within the legal profession that aim to create meaningful social change and reform. These approaches utilize the law as a tool to challenge existing legal frameworks and advocate for the rights and interests of marginalized individuals and communities. While they share a common goal, impact litigation and strategic litigation have distinct strategies and objectives. In this section, we will explore the principles, methods, and ethical considerations associated with these approaches.

Principles of Impact Litigation

Impact litigation is a legal strategy used to bring about large-scale change by challenging laws, policies, and practices that are perceived as unjust or discriminatory. It seeks to establish legal precedents that will have a lasting and far-reaching impact on society. The principles of impact litigation can be summarized as follows:

1. **Identifying systemic issues:** Impact litigation focuses on addressing systemic issues that affect a significant number of individuals or marginalized communities. By targeting laws or policies that perpetuate inequality or injustice, impact litigation aims to create broader social change.

2. **Strategic case selection:** When pursuing impact litigation, careful case selection is essential. Lawyers identify cases that have the potential to set legal

precedents, challenge existing norms, or change the interpretation of laws. These cases often involve unique or novel legal arguments that have the potential to create substantial social impact.

3. **Collaboration and partnerships**: Impact litigation requires collaboration between lawyers, activists, and organizations. Lawyers work closely with affected individuals or communities, human rights organizations, and advocacy groups to build strong cases, gather evidence, and mobilize support.

4. **Public awareness and education**: An important aspect of impact litigation is raising public awareness about the underlying social issues. Lawyers and organizations use media platforms, public campaigns, and educational initiatives to inform the public, challenge misconceptions, and build support for their cause.

5. **Long-term perspective**: Impact litigation is a long-term strategy that aims to bring about lasting change. Lawyers and organizations realize that the impact of their work extends beyond individual cases. They seek to create legal precedents that can be used in future cases and influence policy and legislative change.

Methods of Impact Litigation

Impact litigation employs various methods to challenge unjust laws, policies, or practices. Here are some common methods used in this approach:

1. **Constitutional challenges**: Impact litigators often challenge laws and policies that they view as unconstitutional. By arguing that a law or policy violates constitutional rights, impact litigators aim to secure legal rulings that can lead to broader systemic change.

2. **Class action lawsuits**: Class action lawsuits are a powerful tool used in impact litigation. They allow a group of individuals who have been similarly affected by an injustice or harm to bring a collective legal action. Class actions can aggregate resources, increase visibility, and address common issues faced by marginalized groups.

3. **Strategic litigation campaigns**: Impact litigation is often part of broader strategic campaigns aimed at addressing specific social issues. Lawyers and organizations strategically choose multiple cases to create a cumulative effect and bring about systemic change.

4. **Collaborative advocacy**: Impact litigators collaborate with other social justice advocates and organizations to build strong cases. These collaborations may involve sharing resources, expertise, and supporting each other's legal efforts.

5. **Litigation funding**: Impact litigation can be resource-intensive. Lawyers and organizations often rely on litigation funding from foundations, non-profit

organizations, or crowdfunding platforms to support their cases. These funding sources help level the playing field and enable marginalized groups to access justice.

Ethical Considerations

While impact litigation aims to create positive social change, it is essential to consider the ethical dilemmas and responsibilities associated with this approach. Some key ethical considerations include:

1. **Maintaining professional integrity**: Impact litigators must adhere to professional ethics and maintain the highest standards of integrity, honesty, and professionalism throughout the litigation process. This includes maintaining client confidentiality, avoiding conflicts of interest, and upholding the duty of loyalty to clients.

2. **Balancing legal and social objectives**: Impact litigators face the challenge of balancing their legal obligations and the broader social objectives of their cases. They must carefully navigate the tension between their duty to provide zealous advocacy for their clients and their commitment to achieving social justice outcomes.

3. **Representing marginalized clients**: Impact litigation often involves representing marginalized individuals or groups who have been historically marginalized or excluded from legal processes. Lawyers must be mindful of power imbalances, actively listen to their clients' needs, and ensure their voices are heard throughout the litigation process.

4. **Ensuring access to justice**: Impact litigation should aim to increase access to justice for marginalized individuals and communities. Lawyers should strive to remove barriers to justice, such as language barriers, financial constraints, or limited legal knowledge, and ensure that their clients have equal opportunities to participate in the legal process.

5. **Addressing unintended consequences**: Impact litigators should consider the potential unintended consequences of their legal challenges. They should anticipate and mitigate any negative impacts that their litigation may have on affected individuals, communities, or broader social systems.

Example Case: Brown v. Board of Education

A landmark example of impact litigation is the case of Brown v. Board of Education (1954) in the United States. In this case, the Supreme Court ruled that racial segregation in public schools was unconstitutional, overturning the "separate but equal" doctrine established in Plessy v. Ferguson (1896). The impact of this decision went beyond desegregating schools; it set a legal precedent that compelled the dismantling of racial segregation in various aspects of American society.

The case was strategically chosen to challenge racial segregation in education and was part of a broader civil rights movement. The lawyers argued that separate educational facilities for Black and white students violated the Fourteenth Amendment's Equal Protection Clause. By addressing segregation in schools, the lawyers aimed to challenge the broader systemic barriers faced by African Americans in the United States.

Through collaborative efforts, advocacy, and litigation expertise, impact litigators successfully challenged a deeply entrenched discriminatory practice. The Brown decision not only had a transformative effect on education but also contributed to broader civil rights advancements. It demonstrated the power of impact litigation in promoting social justice and societal change.

Resources for Impact Litigation

1. American Civil Liberties Union (ACLU) - The ACLU provides resources, training, and guidance for impact litigation across a wide range of social justice issues.

2. Public Interest Litigation (PIL) Network - The PIL Network is a global network of organizations and individuals working on public interest litigation. It provides resources and facilitates collaboration among impact litigators.

3. Impact Litigation Handbook - Various handbooks and guides on impact litigation are available, providing practical insights, strategies, and ethical considerations for impact litigators.

4. Judicial Impact Litigation Database - This database compiles significant impact litigation cases from around the world, allowing researchers and practitioners to examine successful strategies and outcomes.

Remember, impact litigation requires dedication, collaboration, and a deep commitment to social justice. By effectively utilizing this approach, lawyers can contribute to creating a more equitable and just society.

Exercise: Choose a social issue that you feel strongly about and identify potential legal strategies that could be used for impact litigation. Consider the principles, methods, and ethical considerations discussed in this section. How would you build a strong case to advocate for change? What organizations or individuals could you collaborate with? How would you raise public awareness about the issue?

Further Reading: - McCann, M. (2009). *Taking rights seriously: The role of lawyers in human rights work*. Human Rights Quarterly, 31(4), 1039-1058. - Sarat, A., & Scheingold, S. A. (2014). *Cause lawyering and the state in a global era*.

Stanford University Press. - Yamin, A. E. (2003). *Litigating health rights: Can courts bring more justice to health?* Harvard International Law Journal, 44(1), 289-324.

Law and Social Change: Successes and Limitations

Law plays a crucial role in driving social change and reform. It provides a framework for creating and implementing policies that aim to address societal issues and promote justice. In this section, we will explore the successes and limitations of using law as a tool for social change. We will also examine some of the key factors that can contribute to or hinder the effectiveness of legal interventions in promoting positive social transformations.

Successes of Law in Social Change

1. **Civil Rights Movement:** One of the most significant successes of law in social change is exemplified by the Civil Rights Movement in the United States. Legislation such as the Civil Rights Act of 1964 and the Voting Rights Act of 1965 played a pivotal role in dismantling racial segregation and discrimination, ensuring equal rights and opportunities for African Americans. These legal measures not only transformed societal attitudes but also paved the way for subsequent social justice movements.

2. **Marriage Equality:** The fight for marriage equality for same-sex couples serves as another notable example of the power of law to drive social change. Through legal challenges and landmark court decisions, many countries and regions around the world have recognized and legalized same-sex marriage. Such legal recognition has not only granted LGBTQ+ individuals the right to marry but has also contributed to an increased acceptance and normalization of diverse sexual orientations and gender identities.

3. **Environmental Protection:** Environmental issues, such as climate change and pollution, have become pressing concerns in recent years. Law has played a crucial role in addressing these challenges through the implementation of regulations and policies aimed at protecting the environment. The creation of environmental protection agencies, the establishment of emission standards, and the promotion of sustainable practices are some of the successes achieved through legal interventions.

Limitations of Law in Social Change

1. **Resistance and Backlash:** Despite the successes, law has its limitations in driving social change. Legal reforms often face resistance from individuals and groups who are resistant to change or who hold opposing ideological beliefs. For example, the struggle for reproductive rights and access to abortion has faced significant opposition, resulting in ongoing legal battles and limited progress in some regions. Resistance to change can hinder the effectiveness of legal measures in promoting social transformation.

2. **Slow Pace of Legal Processes:** Legal processes can be slow and cumbersome, especially when it comes to enacting social reforms. The complexities of drafting, debating, and passing legislation often result in lengthy delays. Additionally, legal challenges and appeals processes can further prolong the implementation of legal reforms. This slow pace can be frustrating for those advocating for social change and can hinder the timely resolution of pressing social issues.

3. **Inadequate Enforcement and Implementation:** Even when laws are enacted, their enforcement and implementation can pose significant challenges. In some cases, laws may exist on paper but lack adequate resources or political will for effective implementation. For example, laws designed to protect marginalized communities may be undermined by systemic biases within law enforcement agencies or insufficient funding for support services. This gap between legal existence and practical impact can limit the effectiveness of law as a mechanism for social change.

4. **Inherent Bias and Limitations:** Laws themselves can sometimes perpetuate or reinforce existing social inequalities and injustices. Legal frameworks may be rooted in historical biases or reflect the interests of powerful groups, leading to unequal treatment or inadequate protection for marginalized communities. Recognizing and addressing these inherent biases and limitations is crucial for ensuring that laws effectively drive social change.

Factors Influencing Successes and Limitations

1. **Public Awareness and Advocacy:** The level of public awareness and support for social issues can significantly impact the success of legal interventions. Mobilizing public opinion, organizing grassroots movements, and engaging in advocacy efforts can influence lawmakers, create momentum for change, and increase the likelihood of successful legal reforms.

2. **Judicial Activism:** The judiciary plays a crucial role in interpreting and enforcing laws. Judicial activism, where judges take an active role in shaping public

policy and addressing social issues, can lead to significant social change. When courts interpret laws in a progressive and inclusive manner, they can drive social transformation even in the absence of legislative action.

3. **Collaboration and Coalition-Building:** Collaborative efforts between various stakeholders, including policymakers, civil society organizations, and affected communities, can enhance the effectiveness of legal interventions. Building coalitions, sharing resources and expertise, and leveraging collective power can amplify the impact of legal actions and promote lasting social change.

4. **Societal Attitudes and Cultural Shifts:** The success of legal interventions in driving social change is closely tied to broader societal attitudes and cultural shifts. Legal reforms are more likely to succeed when they align with evolving social norms and values. Efforts to change attitudes and perceptions through education, media, and public discourse can create a fertile ground for the success of legal interventions.

In conclusion, law can be a powerful tool for social change, but it also has its limitations. The successes achieved through legal interventions demonstrate the potential impact of laws in promoting justice and advancing societal values. However, resistance, slow legal processes, inadequate enforcement, and inherent biases can hinder the effectiveness of legal reforms. By understanding these factors and working collaboratively, stakeholders can navigate these limitations and strive towards a more equitable and just society.

Future Directions in Law and Social Change

The field of law and social change is constantly evolving, driven by societal shifts, technological advancements, and emerging global challenges. As we look to the future, several key directions will shape the way law and social change intersect and influence each other.

Interdisciplinary Collaboration

One important future direction is the increasing emphasis on interdisciplinary collaboration in addressing complex social issues. Recognizing that legal problems are often intertwined with other societal challenges, such as poverty, inequality, and environmental degradation, legal practitioners and scholars are now working more closely with professionals from diverse fields such as social work, economics, public health, and environmental science.

This collaboration allows for a more comprehensive understanding of the root causes of social problems and enables the development of holistic solutions. For example, in tackling environmental issues, lawyers can partner with scientists to develop evidence-based policies, while also working with community organizers to empower marginalized groups affected by environmental injustices.

Technology and Innovation

The rapid advancement of technology brings new opportunities and challenges to the legal field. Future directions in law and social change will be marked by the integration of technology and innovation. For instance, the use of artificial intelligence and machine learning algorithms can enhance legal research, document analysis, and contract drafting, increasing efficiency and accessibility.

However, the ethical implications of these technologies must also be carefully considered. Issues such as data privacy, algorithmic biases, and the digital divide need to be addressed to ensure that the benefits of technology are shared equitably and do not perpetuate existing social inequalities.

Access to Justice

Ensuring access to justice for all individuals, regardless of their socioeconomic status or other marginalized identities, is a critical future direction in law and social change. Many people face significant barriers in accessing legal services and navigating the legal system, leading to inequalities in the administration of justice.

To address this, innovative approaches such as online dispute resolution, legal aid clinics, and pro bono initiatives are being developed to provide affordable and accessible legal services. Additionally, community-based organizations and grassroots movements are working towards empowering marginalized communities and amplifying their voices in legal decision-making processes.

Advocacy and Activism

Looking ahead, the role of advocacy and activism will continue to be a driving force in law and social change. Grassroots movements and social justice organizations play a crucial role in mobilizing communities, raising awareness, and advocating for policy changes.

Social media platforms and digital technologies provide new avenues for activism and organizing, allowing individuals to connect globally and amplify their voices. Future directions in law and social change will involve harnessing the power of technology and social media to drive systemic and transformative change.

Global and Comparative Perspectives

As our world becomes increasingly interconnected, future directions in law and social change will also involve a greater emphasis on global and comparative perspectives. The challenges we face, such as climate change, migration, and human rights violations, require international collaboration and cross-cultural understanding.

International legal frameworks and institutions play a crucial role in addressing these global challenges. Lawyers and scholars will need to navigate diverse legal systems, cultural norms, and political landscapes to promote social justice on a global scale.

Education and Empowerment

The future of law and social change also lies in education and empowerment. It is essential to equip future legal professionals with the knowledge and skills necessary to navigate complex ethical dilemmas, work collaboratively with diverse stakeholders, and advocate for social justice.

Law schools and educational institutions will need to adapt their curricula to incorporate interdisciplinary perspectives, critical thinking, and practical training in areas such as negotiation, mediation, and dispute resolution.

Additionally, community outreach programs, public legal education initiatives, and pro bono work can empower individuals and communities to understand their legal rights and navigate the legal system effectively.

Conclusion

The future directions in law and social change provide us with an optimistic outlook, despite the challenges we face. By embracing interdisciplinary collaboration, leveraging technology for innovation, ensuring access to justice, empowering advocacy and activism, adopting global and comparative perspectives, and investing in education and empowerment, we can work towards a more equitable, just, and sustainable world. It is through these collective efforts that we can navigate moral dilemmas, promote justice, and shape a better future for all.

Law and Social Justice Movements

Law and social justice are deeply intertwined, as the law plays a vital role in addressing social inequalities and promoting a more equitable society. Social justice movements advocate for equal rights, fair treatment, and access to opportunities for marginalized groups. In this section, we will explore the relationship between law and social justice movements, the impact of legal activism, and the role of the legal system in advancing social change.

Understanding Social Justice Movements

Social justice movements are collective efforts by individuals and groups to address disparities and promote equal rights and opportunities in society. These movements aim to challenge systemic discrimination, inequality, and oppression based on factors such as race, gender, socioeconomic status, sexual orientation, and disability.

The goals of social justice movements can vary, but often include promoting economic justice, ending racial discrimination, fighting for gender equality, advocating for LGBTQ+ rights, and combating environmental injustices. These movements are driven by the desire to create a more inclusive and just society, where every individual has the opportunity to thrive and live a dignified life.

Legal Activism and Social Change

Legal activism is a powerful tool used by social justice movements to effect change and challenge unjust laws and practices. Legal activists work within the legal system to advocate for the rights of marginalized communities, raise awareness about social inequalities, and challenge discriminatory policies through litigation, advocacy, and grassroots organizing.

Through strategic litigation, legal activists strategically choose cases that have the potential to establish legal precedents or challenge existing laws. By bringing these cases to court, they seek to change legal interpretations and reshape legal frameworks to better align with principles of social justice.

Legal activism can also involve lobbying for legislative reforms, drafting and proposing new laws, and mobilizing public support for social justice causes. By engaging with lawmakers and policymakers, legal activists influence the creation and implementation of laws that promote equality and justice.

The Role of the Legal System

The legal system plays a crucial role in advancing social justice movements. It provides a framework for addressing grievances, resolving conflicts, and shaping society. However, the legal system is not immune to biases and can often perpetuate social inequalities.

To ensure that the legal system promotes social justice, it is important to consider the following:

+ **Legal Representation:** Access to quality legal representation is essential for individuals and communities fighting for social justice. However, marginalized groups often face barriers such as financial constraints and lack of representation. Efforts should be made to provide equal access to legal representation, particularly for marginalized communities.

+ **Equal Protection under the Law:** The principle of equal protection under the law requires that all individuals are entitled to the same legal rights and protections. Social justice movements work to ensure that the legal system treats all individuals fairly and without discrimination.

+ **Addressing Systemic Discrimination:** Social justice movements aim to challenge and dismantle systemic discrimination within the legal system. This includes biases in law enforcement practices, sentencing disparities, and unequal access to justice.

+ **Law Reform:** Social justice movements often advocate for legal reforms to address systemic inequalities. This may involve changes to existing laws, the creation of new laws, or the implementation of policies that promote social justice.

+ **Collaboration between Movements and the Legal System:** Collaboration between social justice movements and the legal system is essential for meaningful change. Movements can provide valuable insights into the lived experiences of marginalized communities, while the legal system can offer avenues for legal recourse and protection.

Examples of Social Justice Movements

There have been numerous social justice movements throughout history that have shaped the legal landscape and brought about significant social change. Here are a few examples:

1. **Civil Rights Movement (1950s-1960s):** The Civil Rights Movement in the United States fought against racial segregation and discrimination. Legal activism and grassroots organizing led to landmark civil rights legislation, such as the Civil Rights Act of 1964 and the Voting Rights Act of 1965.

2. **Feminist Movement (1960s-present):** The feminist movement advocates for gender equality and women's rights. Legal victories have been achieved in areas such as reproductive rights, workplace discrimination, and sexual harassment. The movement continues to address intersectional inequalities faced by women of color, LGBTQ+ individuals, and other marginalized groups.

3. **Marriage Equality Movement (2000s-present):** The movement for marriage equality sought to secure the legal recognition of same-sex marriage. Through litigation, advocacy, and public awareness campaigns, the movement led to significant legal victories, including the landmark Supreme Court ruling in Obergefell v. Hodges (2015) which legalized same-sex marriage in the United States.

4. **Black Lives Matter Movement (2013-present):** The Black Lives Matter movement emerged in response to police violence and systemic racism against Black individuals. The movement has brought attention to issues of racial profiling, police brutality, and the need for criminal justice reform. Legal activism has focused on advocating for policy changes and accountability within law enforcement agencies.

Challenges and Future Directions

While social justice movements have achieved significant progress, there remain persistent challenges in their pursuit of equality and justice. Some of these challenges include:

+ **Backlash and Resistance:** Social justice movements often face backlash and resistance from those who benefit from existing power structures. This can manifest in the form of opposition to legal reforms, attempts to undermine the credibility of movements, or violence against activists.

+ **Intersectionality and Inclusivity:** Social justice movements must recognize and address the intersecting forms of oppression faced by individuals who belong to multiple marginalized groups. Ensuring inclusivity and centering the voices of all affected communities is crucial for creating lasting change.

+ **Legal Limitations:** The legal system has constraints that can hinder the pursuit of social justice. These limitations may include conservative judicial interpretations, legal loopholes, and barriers to legal recourse. Movements need to navigate these limitations and find innovative ways to challenge existing legal norms.

+ **Sustaining Momentum:** Sustaining the momentum and energy of social justice movements over time can be challenging. Movements must find ways to engage and mobilize communities, maintain public support, and continue advocating for change even after initial successes.

To address these challenges and shape a more just society, social justice movements must continue to evolve and adapt. This includes leveraging legal strategies, fostering intersectional collaborations, and mobilizing public support through grassroots efforts and awareness campaigns.

Resources for Further Exploration

+ Books:

    – "The New Jim Crow: Mass Incarceration in the Age of Colorblindness" by Michelle Alexander

    – "Feminism is for Everybody: Passionate Politics" by bell hooks

    – "The Queer Art of Failure" by Jack Halberstam

    – "When They Call You a Terrorist: A Black Lives Matter Memoir" by Patrisse Khan-Cullors and asha bandele

+ Documentaries/Films:

    – "13th" (2016, directed by Ava DuVernay)

    – "RBG" (2018, directed by Betsy West and Julie Cohen)

    – "I Am Not Your Negro" (2016, directed by Raoul Peck)

    – "Crip Camp: A Disability Revolution" (2020, directed by James LeBrecht and Nicole Newnham)

+ Organizations:

    – American Civil Liberties Union (ACLU)

    – NAACP Legal Defense and Educational Fund

    – Human Rights Campaign

    – National Organization for Women (NOW)

    – Amnesty International

    – Environmental Justice Foundation

Conclusion

Law and social justice movements are intricately connected, with the law serving as a critical tool for promoting equality and addressing systemic injustices. Legal activism plays a vital role in challenging discriminatory laws and practices, shaping legal frameworks, and advancing social change. By understanding the role of the legal system in social justice movements and working towards inclusive and sustainable solutions, we can strive towards a more equitable and just society for all.

Law and Policy Advocacy

Law and policy advocacy play a crucial role in shaping the legal landscape and promoting social change. Advocacy involves the active and strategic pursuit of specific legal and policy objectives, often conducted by individuals, organizations, or groups seeking to influence decision-makers and bring about desired outcomes. This section explores the importance of law and policy advocacy, the strategies and techniques used, and the ethical considerations involved in this process.

The Importance of Law and Policy Advocacy

Law and policy advocacy serve as powerful tools for advancing social justice, promoting human rights, and addressing systemic inequalities. Advocacy can bring about meaningful change by influencing legislative actions, public opinion, and judicial decisions. It enables individuals and organizations to actively participate in the democratic process and hold decision-makers accountable for their actions.

By engaging in law and policy advocacy, individuals and organizations can raise awareness about important legal and social issues, propose and shape legislation, contribute to public policy debates, and influence the interpretation and application of laws. Advocacy efforts can lead to the establishment of new laws, the reform of existing laws, and the creation of policies that promote equality, justice, and the protection of individual rights.

Strategies and Techniques

Effective law and policy advocacy requires careful planning, strategic thinking, and the use of various techniques to influence decision-making processes. Some common strategies and techniques include:

1. **Research and Analysis:** Advocates conduct thorough research and analysis of legal and policy issues to understand the current landscape, identify gaps, and develop evidence-based arguments to support their positions.

2. **Coalition Building:** Advocates form alliances and build partnerships with like-minded individuals, organizations, and communities to amplify their voices, share resources, and increase their collective influence.

3. **Education and Awareness Campaigns:** Advocates develop educational materials, organize workshops, and conduct public awareness campaigns to inform the public about specific legal and policy issues, raise awareness, and foster support for their cause.

4. **Lobbying:** Advocates engage in direct communication and negotiations with policymakers, legislators, and government officials to express their concerns, provide expert advice, and influence decision-making processes.

5. **Litigation and Legal Challenges:** Advocates use the court system to challenge unjust laws, advocate for legal interpretations that align with their objectives, and seek legal remedies for those affected by unjust policies.

6. **Media and Public Relations:** Advocates leverage media platforms, social media, and public events to shape public opinion, generate media coverage, and increase public pressure on decision-makers.

7. **Policy and Legislative Drafting:** Advocates work alongside policymakers and legislators to draft new legislation or propose amendments to existing laws, aiming to address specific legal and policy issues.

8. **Community Engagement and Grassroots Mobilization:** Advocates empower affected communities, facilitate their participation in decision-making processes, and mobilize grassroots movements to effect change from the ground up.

Ethical Considerations

While engaging in law and policy advocacy, it is essential to uphold ethical standards to maintain integrity, credibility, and respect for the rule of law. Advocates must consider the following ethical considerations:

1. **Transparency and Accountability:** Advocates should be transparent about their objectives, funding sources, and potential conflicts of interest. They should be accountable to their constituents and adhere to ethical guidelines and legal regulations.

2. **Accuracy and Truthfulness:** Advocates must ensure the accuracy and truthfulness of the information they present to decision-makers, the public, and the media. Misrepresentation or manipulation of facts undermines the credibility of their cause.

3. **Respect for Diversity and Inclusion:** Advocates should promote diversity, inclusivity, and equal representation in their advocacy efforts. They should avoid promoting discriminatory or exclusionary policies that harm marginalized communities.

4. **Respect for Legal Processes:** While advocating for legal and policy change, advocates should respect the existing legal processes and institutions. They should seek change through lawful means and work within the framework of the democratic system.

5. **Confidentiality and Privacy:** Advocates should respect the confidentiality and privacy of individuals involved in their advocacy efforts, particularly when dealing with sensitive information or personal stories.

6. **Conflict Resolution and Compromise:** Advocates should be open to dialogue, negotiation, and compromise when engaging with opposing viewpoints. Constructive engagement can lead to meaningful change and broader coalition building.

Case Study: Campaign for Marriage Equality

A prominent example of law and policy advocacy is the campaign for marriage equality. Advocates for marriage equality utilized a range of strategies to advocate for legal recognition of same-sex marriage. They conducted research, engaged in public education campaigns, organized grassroots movements, and litigated cases challenging the constitutionality of laws prohibiting same-sex marriage.

Through their strategic advocacy efforts, including media campaigns, public demonstrations, and lobbying efforts, marriage equality advocates successfully shifted public opinion and influenced legal and policy changes. Their advocacy efforts were aided by legal arguments based on principles of equality, dignity, and fundamental human rights.

The campaign for marriage equality serves as a groundbreaking example of how law and policy advocacy can lead to social change and the recognition of previously marginalized rights.

Conclusion

Law and policy advocacy are essential tools for social change and reform. They enable individuals and organizations to shape laws, influence policy decisions, and promote social justice. Effective advocacy involves strategic planning, coalition building, and the use of various techniques to influence decision-makers and public opinion. It is crucial for advocates to uphold ethical standards, ensuring transparency, accountability, and respect for legal processes. Through thoughtful and strategic advocacy efforts, meaningful change can be achieved, leading to a fairer, more just, and equitable society.

Conclusion

In this section, we have explored the role of law in social change and reform. We have seen how law can be a powerful tool for promoting social justice and sustainable development. Through legal activism, public interest law, and impact litigation, individuals and organizations can challenge unjust laws and bring about meaningful change in society.

One of the key aspects discussed in this section is the relationship between law and social movements. We have seen that social movements often rely on legal strategies to advance their causes and bring about social change. Legal activism, which involves using legal means to challenge social injustices, plays a crucial role in advocating for marginalized communities and addressing systemic issues.

Furthermore, we have examined the concept of law as a tool for sustainable development. As the world faces pressing environmental challenges, such as climate change and biodiversity loss, the role of law becomes even more important. International legal frameworks for sustainable development provide a basis for countries to work together in addressing these global issues. Environmental regulation, as a part of sustainable development, aims to balance economic growth with environmental protection.

We have also delved into the ethical implications of technological advancements. As technology continues to advance at a rapid pace, issues such as privacy, data protection, and artificial intelligence pose complex ethical dilemmas. The regulation and governance of technology become crucial in ensuring that it is used ethically and for the benefit of society.

It is important to note that while the law can be a powerful force for social change, it also has its limitations. Legislation and policy alone may not be sufficient to bring about lasting change, as social attitudes and behaviors also play a role.

However, by combining legal strategies with grassroots activism and public advocacy, we can create a more equitable and just society.

In conclusion, the study of philosophical and ethical issues in legal studies is vital for navigating moral dilemmas, promoting justice, and shaping a more equitable, just, and sustainable world. Understanding the relationship between law, ethics, and social change provides a foundation for addressing the pressing issues of our time. As future legal professionals, it is our responsibility to approach legal practice with ethical integrity and a commitment to social justice. By doing so, we can contribute to a more inclusive and sustainable society for all.

Law, Policy, and Sustainable Development

Understanding Sustainable Development

Sustainable development is an important concept that integrates environmental, social, and economic considerations to ensure the well-being of present and future generations. It is a holistic approach that recognizes the interconnectedness of various systems and aims to balance economic growth with environmental protection and social equity.

Background

The concept of sustainable development emerged in the late 20th century as a response to the growing recognition of the negative impacts of industrialization and economic development on the environment and society. It gained international prominence through the publication of the Brundtland Report in 1987, which defined sustainable development as "development that meets the needs of the present without compromising the ability of future generations to meet their own needs."

Principles of Sustainable Development

Sustainable development is guided by several key principles that provide a framework for decision-making and action. These principles include:

+ **Inter-generational equity:** This principle emphasizes the importance of considering the needs and interests of future generations in decision-making processes. It recognizes that current actions and choices can have long-term impacts on the well-being of future generations and aims to ensure their ability to meet their own needs.

- **Intra-generational equity:** In addition to inter-generational equity, sustainable development also emphasizes the need for fairness and justice within the current generation. This principle calls for the equitable distribution of resources and opportunities, ensuring that all individuals have access to a decent standard of living and are not disproportionately burdened by the negative consequences of development.

- **Environmental stewardship:** Sustainable development recognizes the fundamental importance of protecting and preserving the natural environment. It promotes the sustainable use of natural resources, the conservation of biodiversity, and the mitigation of pollution and climate change impacts.

- **Integration and interdependence:** Sustainable development encourages the integration of environmental, social, and economic considerations in decision-making processes. It recognizes the interdependencies between these different aspects of development and aims to achieve a balance that promotes long-term sustainability.

- **Precautionary approach:** The precautionary approach is based on the idea that in the face of uncertainty and potential risks, it is better to take precautionary measures to prevent harm. This principle calls for decision-makers to anticipate and consider potential negative impacts and to take action to avoid or minimize them, even in the absence of scientific certainty.

Goals of Sustainable Development

The goals of sustainable development are centered around achieving a balance between economic growth, environmental protection, and social equity. These goals are often articulated through the framework of the Sustainable Development Goals (SDGs) adopted by the United Nations in 2015. The SDGs provide a set of 17 interconnected goals that aim to address the most pressing social, economic, and environmental challenges facing the world today.

Some of the key goals of sustainable development include:

1. **Eradicating poverty:** Sustainable development seeks to alleviate poverty and improve the well-being of all individuals, particularly those in developing countries. It aims to ensure access to basic necessities such as food, water, healthcare, and education, while also addressing the root causes of poverty.

2. **Promoting sustainable economic growth**: Sustainable development aims to foster economic growth that is environmentally sustainable and socially inclusive. It seeks to decouple economic growth from environmental degradation by promoting resource efficiency, clean technologies, and sustainable consumption and production patterns.

3. **Ensuring environmental sustainability**: Sustainable development recognizes the importance of protecting the natural environment and addressing climate change and other environmental challenges. It aims to promote the sustainable use of resources, reduce pollution and waste, conserve biodiversity, and mitigate the impacts of climate change.

4. **Promoting social inclusion and equity**: Sustainable development seeks to ensure that all individuals have equal opportunities and access to resources and services. It aims to eliminate discrimination and inequality based on gender, race, ethnicity, age, disability, and other factors, and to promote social inclusion and cohesion.

5. **Building sustainable and resilient infrastructure**: Sustainable development emphasizes the importance of building infrastructure that is sustainable, resilient, and inclusive. It calls for the development of affordable, reliable, and sustainable energy, transportation, and communication systems, as well as the promotion of sustainable urbanization and the protection of cultural and natural heritage.

Challenges and Solutions

While the concept of sustainable development has gained widespread recognition, there are several challenges to its effective implementation. These challenges include:

+ **Lack of political will**: Sustainable development requires strong political commitment and leadership to prioritize long-term sustainability over short-term economic interests. However, in many cases, short-term economic considerations, political conflicts, and vested interests hinder progress towards sustainable development goals.

+ **Resource constraints**: Achieving sustainable development requires the wise and efficient use of resources. However, the increasing global population and consumption patterns are putting significant pressure on natural resources. Finding innovative solutions to resource scarcity and promoting resource efficiency are critical for sustainable development.

+ **Inequality and social exclusion:** Sustainable development cannot be achieved without addressing the deep-rooted inequalities and social exclusion that exist in society. In many parts of the world, marginalized groups, including women, indigenous peoples, and the poor, face barriers to accessing resources and opportunities. Promoting social inclusion and equity is vital for sustainable development.

+ **Climate change and environmental degradation:** Climate change and environmental degradation pose significant challenges to sustainable development. Rising temperatures, extreme weather events, deforestation, and loss of biodiversity threaten ecosystems and livelihoods. Mitigating and adapting to climate change and promoting sustainable environmental practices are essential for sustainable development.

Addressing these challenges requires a multi-faceted approach that involves the collaboration of various stakeholders, including governments, civil society organizations, businesses, and individuals. It requires the integration of sustainability considerations into policy-making processes, the development of innovative technologies and practices, and the promotion of education and awareness about sustainable development.

Examples and Real-World Applications

Sustainable development principles and goals are being applied in various sectors and contexts around the world. Here are some examples of real-world applications of sustainable development:

+ **Renewable energy:** The transition from fossil fuels to renewable energy sources, such as solar and wind power, is a key component of sustainable development. Many countries are investing in renewable energy infrastructure to reduce greenhouse gas emissions and promote clean energy technologies.

+ **Circular economy:** The concept of a circular economy aims to minimize waste and maximize resource efficiency. It promotes the reuse, recycling, and repurposing of materials and products, reducing the reliance on virgin resources and minimizing environmental impacts.

+ **Sustainable agriculture:** Sustainable agricultural practices prioritize environmental stewardship, biodiversity conservation, and the well-being of farmers and rural communities. These practices include organic farming, agroforestry, crop rotation, and the use of natural fertilizers, reducing the reliance on synthetic chemicals and promoting sustainable food production.

+ **Smart cities:** Smart city initiatives integrate technology and data to improve the overall sustainability and livability of urban areas. They focus on optimizing energy and resource use, enhancing mobility and transportation systems, and promoting citizen engagement and well-being.

Resources and Further Reading

To delve deeper into the understanding of sustainable development, the following resources and readings are recommended:

1. United Nations Development Programme (UNDP). (2020). *Sustainable Development Goals.* Retrieved from `https://www.undp.org/sustainable-development-goals`

2. World Commission on Environment and Development. (1987). *Our Common Future (The Brundtland Report).* Retrieved from `https://sustainabledevelopment.un.org/content/documents/5987our-common-future.pdf`

3. Sachs, J. D. (2015). *The Age of Sustainable Development.* Columbia University Press.

Exercises

Here are some exercises to reinforce your understanding of sustainable development:

1. Conduct research on a sustainable development project or initiative in your local area or country. Describe the goals, challenges, and outcomes of the project.

2. Identify a pressing environmental or social challenge and propose a sustainable development solution that addresses the issue. Explain how your solution integrates economic, environmental, and social elements.

3. Analyze the sustainability practices of a business or organization of your choice. Assess their strengths and weaknesses in terms of environmental management, social responsibility, and economic performance. Recommend improvements based on sustainable development principles.

Remember, sustainable development is not a static concept. It continues to evolve as new challenges and opportunities emerge. By understanding the principles and goals of sustainable development, we can contribute to shaping a more equitable, just, and sustainable world for present and future generations.

International Legal Frameworks for Sustainable Development

Sustainable development is a multidimensional concept that encompasses social, economic, and environmental concerns. It aims to meet the needs of the present without compromising the ability of future generations to meet their own needs. Achieving sustainable development requires the integration of environmental protection, social justice, and economic growth.

To address the global nature of sustainability issues, international legal frameworks have been developed to guide countries in their efforts to promote sustainable development. These frameworks provide a common set of principles, goals, and standards that countries can use to develop their own policies and laws. In this section, we will explore some of the key international legal frameworks for sustainable development and their implications.

The United Nations Framework Convention on Climate Change (UNFCCC)

The UNFCCC is an international treaty that aims to stabilize greenhouse gas concentrations in the atmosphere to prevent dangerous anthropogenic interference with the climate system. It sets out the framework for countries to cooperate on reducing greenhouse gas emissions and adapting to the impacts of climate change.

The UNFCCC establishes the principle of common but differentiated responsibilities, recognizing that developed countries should take the lead in mitigating climate change and assisting developing countries in their efforts. It also establishes the principle of intergenerational equity, recognizing the rights and interests of future generations.

Under the UNFCCC, countries are required to submit national communications detailing their greenhouse gas emissions, vulnerability to climate change, and measures taken to address climate change. The treaty also establishes a financial mechanism to support developing countries in their efforts to mitigate and adapt to climate change.

The Sustainable Development Goals (SDGs)

The SDGs, also known as the Global Goals, are a set of 17 interconnected goals adopted by all United Nations Member States in 2015. They provide a blueprint for achieving a better and more sustainable future for all by 2030. The SDGs cover a wide range of issues, including poverty eradication, education, gender equality, clean water and sanitation, affordable and clean energy, sustainable cities and communities, responsible consumption and production, climate action, and biodiversity conservation.

The SDGs emphasize the importance of integrated and holistic approaches to sustainable development. They call for the integration of social, economic, and environmental policies and the involvement of all stakeholders, including governments, civil society, the private sector, and the scientific community.

To monitor progress towards the SDGs, countries are encouraged to develop their own national indicators and reporting mechanisms. Regular reviews at the global and national levels help identify challenges and opportunities and guide policy responses.

The Convention on Biological Diversity (CBD)

The CBD is an international treaty that aims to conserve biodiversity, ensure its sustainable use, and promote the fair and equitable sharing of benefits derived from genetic resources. It recognizes the intrinsic value of biodiversity and the critical role it plays in sustaining ecosystems, livelihoods, and human well-being.

The CBD establishes three main objectives: the conservation of biodiversity, the sustainable use of its components, and the fair and equitable sharing of benefits arising from the use of genetic resources. It requires countries to develop national strategies and action plans for biodiversity conservation and sustainable use.

The CBD also promotes the integration of biodiversity concerns into sectors such as agriculture, forestry, fisheries, and tourism. It encourages the use of traditional knowledge and the involvement of indigenous and local communities in biodiversity conservation and management.

The Paris Agreement

The Paris Agreement is an international treaty adopted under the UNFCCC that aims to strengthen the global response to climate change. It sets out a long-term goal of keeping the increase in global average temperature well below 2 degrees Celsius above pre-industrial levels and to pursue efforts to limit the temperature increase to 1.5 degrees Celsius.

The Paris Agreement establishes a framework for countries to submit and regularly update their nationally determined contributions (NDCs) outlining their efforts to mitigate greenhouse gas emissions and adapt to the impacts of climate change. It also establishes a transparency framework to enhance the clarity and comparability of countries' efforts.

The Paris Agreement recognizes the importance of supporting developing countries in their climate change efforts, including through financial resources, technology transfer, and capacity-building. It also emphasizes the role of non-state actors, such as cities, businesses, and civil society, in contributing to climate action.

The World Trade Organization (WTO)

The WTO is an international organization that regulates international trade and promotes economic development. While not exclusively focused on sustainable development, the WTO has provisions that address environmental and social concerns.

The WTO allows countries to take measures to protect the environment, human, animal, or plant life or health, and to support sustainable development. It recognizes the right of countries to adopt trade measures necessary to achieve legitimate policy objectives, such as the conservation of natural resources or the protection of public health.

However, trade and sustainable development can sometimes be in tension. The challenge is to strike a balance between promoting trade liberalization and ensuring that trade rules do not undermine social and environmental objectives.

In conclusion, international legal frameworks play a crucial role in promoting sustainable development by providing a common framework for action and cooperation. These frameworks address a wide range of issues, including climate change, biodiversity conservation, poverty eradication, and trade. By adhering to these frameworks and implementing national policies and laws consistent with their objectives, countries can contribute to a more sustainable and equitable future for all.

Role of Law in Promoting Sustainable Development

Sustainable development is a critical global objective that aims to balance economic growth, social progress, and environmental protection. It recognizes the interconnectedness between economic, social, and environmental factors, and seeks to ensure that present and future generations can meet their needs without compromising the ability of future generations to meet their own needs. The role of law in promoting sustainable development is fundamental, as it provides the legal framework for implementing and enforcing policies and practices that promote sustainability.

1. Importance of Legal Frameworks

Law plays a crucial role in promoting sustainable development by providing the necessary legal frameworks for setting and implementing policies, regulations, and standards.   These frameworks guide decision-making processes, ensure accountability, and provide a basis for evaluating and addressing environmental and social challenges. Without a legal framework, sustainable development goals would lack the necessary tools for effective implementation and enforcement.

2. Environmental Law

Environmental law is a key component of the legal framework for promoting sustainable development.   It encompasses a wide range of legal principles, regulations, and instruments designed to protect the environment and promote sustainability. Environmental laws address issues such as pollution control, waste management, biodiversity conservation, natural resource management, and climate change mitigation and adaptation.

3. Sustainable Development Goals and Legal Implementation

The United Nations Sustainable Development Goals (SDGs) provide a global blueprint for sustainable development, with 17 goals and numerous targets to be achieved by 2030.   Law plays a vital role in the implementation of these goals, as it sets the legal basis for the adoption of policies, strategies, and programs aimed at achieving the SDGs. It also provides mechanisms for monitoring progress, ensuring accountability, and addressing legal barriers to sustainability.

4. Integration of Sustainability into Legal Systems

Promoting sustainable development requires the integration of sustainability principles into legal systems at all levels, including international, regional, national, and local.   This involves harmonizing laws, regulations, and policies to ensure consistency and coherence in the pursuit of sustainability objectives.   It also requires the development of legal frameworks that incentivize and encourage sustainable practices in various sectors, such as energy, agriculture, transportation, and construction.

5. Access to Justice and Environmental Rights

Access to justice is a fundamental principle of sustainable development.   It ensures that individuals and communities have the right to seek legal remedies and challenge decisions that violate their environmental rights. Environmental rights include the right to a clean and healthy environment, the right to participate in decision-making processes, and the right to information and access to environmental justice.   Legal systems need to provide mechanisms for effective access to justice, including affordable and accessible legal procedures, legal aid, and public interest litigation.

6. International Cooperation and Legal Mechanisms

Sustainable development is a global challenge that requires international cooperation and coordination. International law provides mechanisms for addressing transboundary environmental issues, promoting cooperation on sustainable development goals, and ensuring compliance with international environmental agreements. It also provides a platform for sharing best practices, capacity-building, and technology transfer to support developing countries in their pursuit of sustainable development.

7. Challenges and Future Directions

Despite the progress made in integrating sustainability into legal systems, several challenges remain. These include the lack of enforcement mechanisms, limited capacity for implementation, conflicting legal frameworks, and inadequate resources. Addressing these challenges requires a multi-sectoral approach, involving collaboration between governments, civil society, academia, and the private sector. It also requires the development of innovative legal solutions, such as market-based incentives, public-private partnerships, and alternative dispute resolution mechanisms.

In conclusion, the role of law in promoting sustainable development is pivotal. It provides the legal framework for setting and implementing policies, regulations, and standards that promote sustainability. By integrating sustainability principles into legal systems, ensuring access to justice, and fostering international cooperation, law plays a central role in shaping a more equitable, just, and sustainable world.

Environmental Regulation and Sustainability

In this section, we will explore the crucial role of environmental regulation in promoting sustainability. Environmental regulation refers to the laws and policies that aim to protect and preserve the natural environment, while sustainability focuses on meeting the current needs of society without compromising the ability of future generations to meet their needs. Together, these concepts provide a framework for effectively managing resources, minimizing environmental impact, and achieving long-term ecological balance.

Importance of Environmental Regulation

Effective environmental regulation is essential for several reasons. First, it helps prevent environmental degradation and the depletion of natural resources. By setting standards and guidelines for pollution control, resource extraction, and waste management, regulations ensure that human activities are conducted in a sustainable manner.

Second, environmental regulation protects public health and well-being. Many environmental pollutants, such as toxic chemicals and air pollutants, have harmful effects on human health. Regulations establish limits on the emission of hazardous substances and promote the use of cleaner technologies, reducing the risk of adverse health impacts.

Third, environmental regulation promotes ecological integrity and biodiversity conservation. Through measures such as protected areas, endangered species protection, and habitat restoration, regulations safeguard ecosystems and their biodiversity. This is crucial for maintaining ecosystem services, such as air and water purification, pollination, and climate regulation, which are essential for human well-being.

Principles of Environmental Regulation

To achieve sustainability, environmental regulations are guided by several principles. These principles provide a framework for effective decision-making and policy implementation. Some key principles include:

+ **Precautionary Principle:** This principle states that if an action or policy has the potential to cause significant harm to the environment, even in the absence of scientific certainty, preventative measures should be taken. It emphasizes the importance of anticipating and addressing potential environmental risks before they materialize.

+ **Polluter Pays Principle:** According to this principle, those who pollute or cause environmental damage should bear the cost of remediation and cleanup. It encourages the internalization of environmental costs and provides an economic incentive for businesses and individuals to adopt cleaner and more sustainable practices.

+ **Integrated Approach:** Environmental regulation should take an integrated approach, considering the interconnectedness of ecosystems, social systems, and the economy. It recognizes that environmental issues cannot be effectively addressed in isolation and require a holistic perspective that balances ecological, social, and economic aspects.

+ **Public Participation:** In order to ensure transparency and accountability, environmental regulation should involve public participation. This includes seeking public input in decision-making processes, providing access to information, and fostering collaboration between government, businesses, communities, and other stakeholders.

+ **Sustainable Development:** Environmental regulation should align with the principles of sustainable development, which seek to meet the needs of the present generation without compromising the ability of future generations to meet their own needs. It promotes long-term thinking, resource conservation, and the integration of environmental, social, and economic considerations.

Key Areas of Environmental Regulation

Environmental regulation spans across various sectors and addresses a wide range of issues. Some key areas of environmental regulation include:

+ **Air Quality:** Regulations controlling emissions from industrial processes, vehicles, and other sources aim to improve air quality and reduce the impact of pollutants on human health and the environment. These regulations may include emissions standards, monitoring requirements, and pollution control technologies.

+ **Water Management:** Regulations governing water resources and quality target the protection and conservation of freshwater ecosystems and the provision of clean drinking water. They may encompass measures such as water pollution control, watershed management, water use permits, and water conservation strategies.

+ **Waste Management:** Regulations related to waste management focus on reducing the production and disposal of waste, promoting recycling and reuse, and ensuring the safe handling and treatment of hazardous materials. These regulations may cover waste disposal standards, recycling initiatives, waste reduction targets, and the management of hazardous waste.

+ **Land Use and Conservation:** Regulations concerning land use and conservation aim to safeguard natural habitats, prevent habitat fragmentation, and promote sustainable land management practices. They may involve zoning regulations, protected areas designation, land restoration requirements, and sustainable agriculture practices.

+ **Energy Efficiency:** Regulations targeting energy efficiency seek to reduce energy consumption, promote the use of renewable energy sources, and decrease greenhouse gas emissions. These regulations may include building energy codes, appliance efficiency standards, incentives for energy conservation, and the integration of renewable energy into the electricity grid.

Challenges and Solutions

While environmental regulation plays a crucial role in promoting sustainability, it also faces several challenges. Some of these challenges include:

+ **Complexity:** Environmental issues often involve complex scientific, technical, and socioeconomic considerations. Designing effective regulations that consider these complexities can be challenging.

+ **Enforcement:** Ensuring compliance with environmental regulations can be difficult, particularly in cases of illegal activities, weak enforcement capacity, or limited resources. Adequate enforcement mechanisms and penalties are necessary to deter non-compliance.

+ **Conflicting Interests:** Environmental regulations may encounter resistance from industries, businesses, or other stakeholders whose interests conflict with sustainable environmental practices. Balancing these conflicting interests requires careful negotiation and collaboration.

+ **Global Challenges:** Environmental issues, such as climate change and biodiversity loss, require international cooperation and coordinated action. Harmonizing environmental regulations across different jurisdictions and addressing transboundary concerns can be complex.

To address these challenges, innovative approaches and solutions are being explored. These include:

+ **Technology and Innovation:** Advancements in technology can enhance the effectiveness of environmental regulation. For example, remote sensing, data analytics, and blockchain technology can improve monitoring, enforcement, and transparency in environmental compliance.

+ **Market-Based Instruments:** Market-based instruments, such as carbon pricing and emissions trading schemes, provide economic incentives for businesses to reduce their environmental impact. These mechanisms harness market forces to drive sustainable behavior and achieve environmental goals.

+ **Collaborative Governance:** Collaborative governance models involve stakeholders, including government, businesses, communities, and NGOs, in the decision-making process. Such models foster dialogue, build trust, and promote collective action toward sustainable environmental outcomes.

+ **Education and Awareness:** Increasing public awareness and environmental literacy can foster a culture of sustainability and support compliance with environmental regulations. Education initiatives and public outreach campaigns are essential for building a more environmentally conscious society.

Conclusion

Environmental regulation is a critical component of sustainability efforts, aiming to protect the environment, promote public health, and conserve natural resources. By incorporating key principles and addressing various environmental issues, regulations play a fundamental role in shaping a more sustainable future. However, they also face challenges that require innovative solutions and coordinated action. Through effective regulation, collaboration, and public engagement, we can create a more environmentally resilient and sustainable world for current and future generations.

Challenges and Opportunities in Implementing Sustainable Development Goals

Implementing Sustainable Development Goals (SDGs) is a complex task that requires addressing various challenges and opportunities. SDGs aim to promote sustainable development by addressing social, economic, and environmental issues. In this section, we will explore some of the key challenges and opportunities associated with the implementation of SDGs.

Challenges

1. **Lack of Awareness and Understanding:** One of the major challenges in implementing SDGs is the lack of awareness and understanding among stakeholders. Many individuals, communities, and even government entities may not fully grasp the significance and implications of the SDGs. This can hinder the effective implementation of initiatives and policies related to sustainable development.

2. **Lack of Political Will and Commitment:** Another challenge is the lack of political will and commitment to prioritize and allocate resources for SDG implementation. Political agendas and short-term priorities may overshadow long-term sustainability goals. It is important to engage political leaders and stakeholders at various levels to ensure that sustainable development remains a priority.

3. **Insufficient Financial Resources:** Implementing SDGs requires significant financial resources. Developing countries, in particular, may face challenges in mobilizing the necessary funds to support sustainable development initiatives. Inadequate financial resources can limit the capacity to invest in infrastructure, renewable energy, education, healthcare, and other sectors crucial for sustainable development.

4. **Inequality and Social Injustice:** Achieving sustainable development goals requires addressing inequality and social injustice. This includes reducing poverty, improving access to education and healthcare, and promoting gender equality. However, existing social and economic disparities pose challenges in implementing interventions that can effectively uplift marginalized communities.

5. **Lack of Institutional Capacity:** Implementation of SDGs requires strong institutional capacity at various levels. However, many countries may lack the necessary institutional frameworks, policies, and regulatory mechanisms to support sustainable development initiatives. Strengthening institutional capacity is crucial for effective implementation.

Opportunities

1. **Innovation and Technological Advancements:** Technological advancements can provide solutions to many sustainability challenges. Renewable energy technologies, sustainable agriculture practices, and eco-friendly manufacturing processes offer opportunities for achieving SDGs. Encouraging innovation and fostering technological advancements can help in overcoming sustainability challenges.

2. **Collaboration and Partnerships:** Implementing SDGs requires collaboration and partnerships among different stakeholders, including governments, civil society organizations, businesses, and academia. Collaborative efforts can lead to shared knowledge, expertise, and resources, enhancing the overall effectiveness of sustainable development initiatives.

3. **Education and Awareness:** Promoting education and awareness about sustainable development is vital for its successful implementation. By educating individuals and communities about the importance of sustainable practices, we can

foster behavioral changes and promote sustainable lifestyles. Educational institutions play a crucial role in equipping future generations with the knowledge and skills needed to address sustainability challenges.

4. **Policy Integration and Coherence:** Integrating sustainable development principles into policy frameworks and decision-making processes is essential. Governments can align their policies across sectors to ensure coherence and promote sustainability. This includes incorporating sustainable development considerations into economic planning, urban development, environmental regulations, and social welfare programs.

5. **Data and Monitoring Systems:** Developing robust data collection and monitoring systems is crucial for tracking progress towards SDGs. Accurate and up-to-date data helps in identifying gaps, evaluating the impact of interventions, and making evidence-based policy decisions. Investing in data infrastructure and capacity-building is essential for effective implementation.

6. **International Cooperation and Support:** Global partnerships and international cooperation are essential for the successful implementation of SDGs. Developed countries can provide financial and technical support to developing countries, fostering capacity-building and knowledge exchange. International frameworks and agreements, such as the Paris Agreement on climate change, create opportunities for collective action towards sustainable development.

In conclusion, implementing Sustainable Development Goals involves addressing a range of challenges while embracing various opportunities. Overcoming barriers such as lack of awareness, political will, and financial resources requires collaborative efforts, innovation, and strong institutional frameworks. By seizing opportunities like technological advancements, education, and policy coherence, we can make significant progress towards achieving sustainable development and creating a more equitable and just world for all.

Law, Sustainable Development, and Climate Change

In recent years, the issue of climate change has gained significant attention worldwide. It is now widely recognized that human activities are contributing to global warming, leading to adverse effects on the environment and posing serious threats to the sustainability of our planet. In response to this pressing issue, there is a growing need for laws and regulations that promote sustainable development and address the challenges posed by climate change.

Understanding Sustainable Development

Sustainable development refers to the concept of meeting the needs of the present generation without compromising the ability of future generations to meet their own needs. It requires a balanced approach that takes into account economic, social, and environmental considerations. The goal of sustainable development is to achieve a harmonious relationship between human activities and the natural environment to ensure the well-being of current and future generations.

International Legal Frameworks for Sustainable Development

The international community has recognized the importance of sustainable development and has developed several legal frameworks to address environmental issues, including climate change. The United Nations Framework Convention on Climate Change (UNFCCC) is one of the key international agreements aimed at combating climate change. It sets out the overall framework for intergovernmental efforts to tackle climate change and promotes the stabilization of greenhouse gas concentrations in the atmosphere.

Another important international legal instrument is the Paris Agreement, adopted under the UNFCCC in 2015. The Paris Agreement aims to limit global warming to well below 2 degrees Celsius above pre-industrial levels and to pursue efforts to limit the temperature increase to 1.5 degrees Celsius. It also establishes mechanisms for countries to enhance their mitigation and adaptation efforts and provides a framework for international cooperation on climate change.

Role of Law in Promoting Sustainable Development

Law plays a crucial role in promoting sustainable development and addressing the challenges of climate change. It provides a legal framework for the implementation of sustainable development principles and the regulation of activities that contribute to climate change. Here are some key ways in which law promotes sustainable development and addresses climate change:

1. **Mitigation:** Laws and regulations set targets and standards for reducing greenhouse gas emissions and promote the use of renewable energy sources. They may require the adoption of energy-efficient technologies, the establishment of emissions trading schemes, and the implementation of policies to promote energy conservation.

2. **Adaptation:** Laws can facilitate measures to adapt to the impacts of climate change. They may regulate land-use planning, require the consideration of climate

change in infrastructure development, and establish mechanisms for the protection of vulnerable communities and ecosystems.

3. **International Cooperation:** International environmental law provides a framework for countries to cooperate and coordinate their efforts in addressing climate change. It establishes mechanisms for climate finance, technology transfer, and capacity-building, enabling developing countries to enhance their resilience and adapt to the impacts of climate change.

4. **Compliance and Enforcement:** Laws and regulations establish mechanisms for monitoring and enforcing compliance with environmental standards. They may introduce penalties for non-compliance and require the reporting of emissions and the implementation of environmental impact assessments.

Environmental Regulation and Sustainability

To promote sustainable development and address climate change, environmental regulation plays a critical role. Environmental regulation refers to the set of laws and regulations that govern human activities and their impacts on the environment. It aims to prevent or minimize environmental harm, promote the sustainable use of natural resources, and ensure the protection of ecosystems and biodiversity.

Effective environmental regulation requires a comprehensive approach that takes into account the complex interrelationships between human activities and the environment. It should incorporate principles such as the precautionary principle, which advocates for precautionary measures to be taken in the face of scientific uncertainty, and the polluter pays principle, which holds polluters responsible for the costs of pollution and environmental damage.

Challenges and Opportunities in Implementing Sustainable Development Goals

While there has been significant progress in addressing climate change and promoting sustainable development, several challenges still need to be overcome. These challenges include:

1. **Political Will:** The implementation of sustainable development goals requires strong political will and commitment from governments and other stakeholders. It may require making difficult policy choices and overcoming resistance from vested interests.

2. **Financing:** Adequate financing is crucial for the implementation of sustainable development projects and initiatives. Mobilizing financial resources, especially for developing countries, remains a major challenge.

3. Technology Transfer: Access to and transfer of environmentally sound technologies are essential for developing countries to adopt sustainable practices. However, there are barriers to technology transfer, including intellectual property rights and lack of capacity.

4. Awareness and Education: Raising awareness and educating the public about the importance of sustainable development and climate change is essential. It requires efforts to promote environmental literacy and foster a sense of responsibility among individuals and communities.

Despite these challenges, there are also significant opportunities for promoting sustainable development and addressing climate change. Advances in technology, such as renewable energy and sustainable agriculture practices, offer innovative solutions. International cooperation and collaboration can leverage resources and expertise to support sustainable development efforts. Public-private partnerships can also play a vital role in driving change and mobilizing resources.

Conclusion

Law plays a critical role in promoting sustainable development and addressing the challenges of climate change. By establishing legal frameworks and regulations, it provides guidance and incentives for individuals, businesses, and governments to adopt sustainable practices and reduce their impact on the environment. However, the implementation of sustainable development goals requires collective action and collaboration at the international, national, and local levels. By working together, we can create a more sustainable and resilient future for generations to come.

Law, Sustainable Development, and Poverty

Law plays a crucial role in promoting sustainable development and addressing poverty. Sustainable development aims to meet the needs of the present generation without compromising the ability of future generations to meet their own needs. Poverty, on the other hand, is a complex and multidimensional issue characterized by lack of basic necessities, low income, and limited access to resources and opportunities. In this section, we will explore how law can contribute to sustainable development by addressing poverty and promoting social justice.

Understanding Poverty

Before delving into the relationship between law, sustainable development, and poverty, let us first understand the concept of poverty. Poverty is not just the absence of monetary resources; it encompasses a lack of access to education, healthcare, clean water, and sanitation, among other essential elements of a dignified life. Poverty is often interlinked with social inequality and discrimination, intensifying the hardships faced by marginalized communities.

The Role of Law in Poverty Alleviation

Law plays a pivotal role in poverty alleviation by establishing the legal framework necessary to address the root causes and consequences of poverty. It provides a foundation for social protection, access to justice, and the promotion of human rights. Here are some ways in which law can contribute to poverty reduction:

1. **Social Welfare Programs and Policies:** Legal frameworks can be used to develop and implement social welfare programs that provide targeted assistance to individuals and communities living in poverty. These programs may include cash transfers, food subsidies, housing assistance, and healthcare initiatives. Laws can also support policies that promote inclusive economic growth and reduce income inequality.

2. **Labor and Employment Laws:** Fair labor laws can help protect the rights of workers, ensuring they receive just wages, safe working conditions, and access to social security benefits. Laws that promote decent work and regulate informal employment can uplift individuals out of poverty by providing stable income and improving job prospects.

3. **Land and Property Rights:** Secure land tenure and property rights are crucial for poverty reduction. Laws that recognize and protect the rights of marginalized communities to access and control land can empower them economically and provide a foundation for sustainable livelihoods.

4. **Access to Justice:** Ensuring access to justice for all is essential in combating poverty. Legal aid programs, pro bono services, and effective dispute resolution mechanisms can help individuals living in poverty seek redress and protect their rights. Laws can also address barriers to justice such as high legal costs and complex legal procedures.

Sustainable Development Goals (SDGs)

The United Nations' Sustainable Development Goals (SDGs) are a set of 17 interconnected goals aimed at addressing poverty, inequality, and environmental sustainability by 2030. The goals provide a blueprint for action and call for the active involvement of governments, civil society, and the private sector. Some of the SDGs directly related to poverty and sustainable development include:

1. **Goal 1: No Poverty:** End poverty in all its forms everywhere.

2. **Goal 2: Zero Hunger:** End hunger, achieve food security, and improve nutrition and sustainable agriculture.

3. **Goal 5: Gender Equality:** Achieve gender equality and empower all women and girls.

4. **Goal 8: Decent Work and Economic Growth:** Promote sustained, inclusive, and sustainable economic growth, full and productive employment, and decent work for all.

5. **Goal 10: Reduced Inequalities:** Reduce inequality within and among countries.

6. **Goal 16: Peace, Justice, and Strong Institutions:** Promote peaceful and inclusive societies for sustainable development, provide access to justice for all, and build effective, accountable, and inclusive institutions at all levels.

Challenges and Limitations

Despite the potential of law to contribute to sustainable development and poverty reduction, there are several challenges and limitations that need to be addressed. These include:

1. **Implementation Gap:** Laws alone are insufficient; effective implementation and enforcement are crucial. Inadequate resources, corruption, and weak institutional capacity can hinder the translation of legal frameworks into meaningful action.

2. **Lack of Awareness and Access:** Many individuals living in poverty may not be aware of their rights or the legal remedies available to them. Limited access to legal services and information further exacerbates the justice gap.

3. **Conflicting Legal Frameworks:** In some cases, existing laws and regulations may perpetuate inequalities and contribute to poverty. Harmonizing legal frameworks to ensure consistency with sustainable development principles can be a complex task.

4. **Environmental Degradation:** Environmental degradation, including climate change, can disproportionately affect communities living in poverty. Legal frameworks need to integrate environmental considerations to promote sustainable practices and protect vulnerable populations.

Case Study: Microfinance and Legal Empowerment

Microfinance is an example of a legal tool that has been used to address poverty and promote sustainable development. Microfinance involves providing small loans, financial services, and entrepreneurship training to individuals and small businesses that do not have access to traditional banking services. By combining financial assistance with legal empowerment initiatives such as legal education, microfinance programs aim to uplift individuals out of poverty, improve economic opportunities, and promote social inclusion.

A key aspect of microfinance is the use of contracts and legal agreements to ensure borrower accountability and repayment. By formalizing transactions and providing legal recourse in case of default or disputes, microfinance programs create a conducive environment for economic growth and poverty reduction. However, it is important to ensure that such programs avoid predatory lending practices and prioritize the welfare of borrowers.

Conclusion

Law plays a crucial role in the pursuit of sustainable development and poverty alleviation. By establishing legal frameworks that promote social protection, access to justice, and human rights, law can provide the necessary tools to address the root causes and consequences of poverty. However, challenges such as implementation gaps, lack of awareness, and conflicting legal frameworks need to be addressed for law to effectively contribute to sustainable development. Through innovative approaches such as microfinance and legal empowerment, there is potential for transformative change in the lives of individuals living in poverty. Thus, the intersection of law, sustainable development, and poverty offers a promising avenue for creating a more equitable and just world.

Conclusion

In this section, we explored the role of law in promoting social change and sustainable development. We discussed the importance of law as a tool for driving social progress and examined its impact on various aspects of society, including social justice, human rights, and environmental sustainability. Additionally, we delved into the intersection of law and technology, exploring the ethical challenges brought about by technological advancements.

Overall, we have learned that law plays a crucial role in shaping a more equitable and just society. Through legal frameworks and regulations, we can address societal issues, protect individual rights, and promote fairness and equality. By understanding the principles of law and its relationship with social change, we can effectively advocate for justice and bring about meaningful reform.

One of the key areas where law can drive social change is through legal activism and public interest law. Lawyers and legal professionals have the power to challenge existing laws and advocate for the rights of marginalized groups. Impact litigation, strategic litigation, and policy advocacy have proven to be effective tools for bringing about significant social change. By addressing systemic issues through the legal system, we can lay the foundation for a more just and inclusive society.

Sustainable development is another critical area where law plays a pivotal role. We explored the various international legal frameworks that promote sustainable development and discussed the role of environmental regulation in ensuring the long-term well-being of our planet. By implementing and enforcing laws that prioritize sustainability, we can mitigate the adverse effects of climate change, protect natural resources, and achieve a balance between economic development and environmental conservation.

Furthermore, we investigated the ethical implications of technological advancements. In the digital age, privacy and data protection have become pressing concerns. The use of artificial intelligence and automation in legal practice raises questions about accountability and the potential for bias. Cybersecurity issues and the regulation of technology further highlight the need for ethical considerations in this rapidly evolving landscape. By understanding the ethical dilemmas brought about by technological innovations, legal professionals can navigate these challenges and ensure that technology is used responsibly and in the service of justice.

To further our understanding of the topics covered in this section, it is essential to engage in critical thinking and reflection. Students can explore real-world case studies, analyze the impact of specific laws and policies, and engage in discussions about the ethical dimensions of legal practice. By examining current events and staying informed about emerging legal and ethical issues, students can develop the skills and knowledge necessary to navigate the complex intersection of law, social change, and sustainable development.

In conclusion, the study of law and its ethical dimensions is crucial for addressing societal challenges and promoting justice, equality, and sustainability. By applying the principles and concepts discussed in this section, we can actively contribute to a more equitable and just world. Through legal activism, sustainable development, and responsible technological innovation, we can shape the future in a way that aligns with our shared values and aspirations. The opportunities for transformative change are within our reach, and it is through our collective efforts that we can create a more inclusive, equitable, and sustainable future for all.

Technology and Legal Challenges

Ethical Implications of Technological Advancements

Technology has become an integral part of our daily lives, transforming the way we work, communicate, and interact with the world. While technological advancements bring numerous benefits and opportunities, they also raise important ethical considerations that must be addressed. In this section, we will explore the ethical implications of technological advancements and discuss key principles and frameworks that can guide us in navigating these challenges.

Understanding the Impact of Technology

Before delving into the ethical implications, it is essential to understand the profound impact that technology has on society. Technological advancements, such as artificial intelligence, automation, and the Internet of Things, have revolutionized various industries, including healthcare, education, finance, and transportation. These technologies have the potential to enhance efficiency, improve productivity, and drive economic growth. However, they also introduce novel ethical dilemmas that require careful consideration.

Ethics in Technology Development and Deployment

One of the key ethical challenges in technology lies in its development and deployment. Technologists and engineers have a responsibility to ensure that technology is designed and used in a manner that aligns with ethical principles and values. This includes considering issues such as privacy, security, fairness, accountability, and transparency.

For example, in the development of artificial intelligence systems, it is crucial to address biases in data and algorithms that can perpetuate discrimination and prejudice. Moreover, there is an ongoing debate surrounding the ethical use of facial recognition technology, as it raises concerns about privacy invasion and potential misuse. It is imperative that technologists engage in ethical thinking and decision-making throughout the development lifecycle to mitigate these risks and promote responsible technology.

Data Privacy and Security

The collection, storage, and use of personal data are central to many technological advancements. With the increasing digitization of our lives, concerns about data privacy and security have come to the forefront. It is crucial to establish robust ethical frameworks and legal regulations to safeguard individuals' privacy rights and protect against data breaches and cyber-attacks.

Organizations and individuals must be transparent about the data they collect, how it is used, and obtain explicit consent from users. Additionally, implementing secure data storage practices and encryption methods can help mitigate the risks associated with data breaches and unauthorized access. Technological advancements should prioritize the protection of personal information while enabling individuals to have control over their data.

Automation and Job Displacement

One of the ethical dilemmas posed by technological advancements is the impact on employment. Automation and artificial intelligence have the potential to replace human labor in various industries, leading to job displacement and economic inequalities. The ethical question here lies in how we ensure a just transition for workers in the face of technological disruption.

Addressing this issue requires proactive measures such as reskilling and upskilling programs, as well as providing support for affected workers to transition into new roles or industries. Furthermore, there is a need for policies and regulations that promote fair distribution of benefits derived from technology and prevent the exacerbation of social and economic inequalities.

Ethics in AI and Algorithmic Decision-Making

Artificial intelligence and algorithmic decision-making pose unique ethical challenges. The use of AI systems in areas such as healthcare, criminal justice, and finance raises concerns about bias, fairness, and accountability. Algorithms may unintentionally discriminate against certain individuals or groups, perpetuating systemic biases present in the data used to train them.

To address these challenges, it is important to develop transparent AI systems that can be audited and explainable. Additionally, diversity and inclusivity in the teams developing AI technologies can help mitigate biases and ensure a more ethical and fair approach to decision-making. Ethical guidelines and regulations specific to AI and algorithmic systems can provide a framework for responsible development and use.

Digital Divide and Access to Technology

Another ethical consideration in technological advancements is the digital divide, referring to the unequal access to and use of technology in different communities. As technology becomes increasingly essential for communication, education, and participation in the digital economy, those without access are at a disadvantage. Bridging the digital divide is crucial for promoting social justice and ensuring equal opportunities for all.

Efforts should be made to provide affordable access to technology, especially in disadvantaged communities. Additionally, digital literacy programs can empower individuals with the knowledge and skills necessary to participate fully in the digital world. Public-private partnerships and government initiatives play a vital role in addressing the digital divide and promoting equal access to technology.

Emerging Ethical Challenges

As technology continues to evolve rapidly, new ethical challenges will undoubtedly arise. Some of the emerging ethical considerations include the ethical implications of emerging technologies like blockchain, virtual reality, and autonomous vehicles. It is crucial to stay vigilant, engage in ongoing ethical discussions, and adapt ethical frameworks accordingly to tackle these emerging challenges.

Conclusion

Technological advancements bring great potential for improving our lives, but they also introduce ethical complexities that must be navigated carefully. It is essential to prioritize ethical principles and values in technology development, deployment, and decision-making. By addressing the ethical implications of technological advancements, we can ensure a more equitable, just, and sustainable world for all.

Privacy and Data Protection in the Digital Age

In the digital age, the protection of privacy and personal data has become a pressing issue. With the widespread use of technology and the internet, individuals are increasingly vulnerable to privacy breaches and data misuse. This section explores the ethical and legal considerations surrounding privacy and data protection, as well as the challenges and strategies for safeguarding personal information in the digital landscape.

Understanding Privacy and Data Protection

Privacy refers to an individual's right to control access to their personal information. It encompasses the ability to keep certain information confidential and maintain autonomy over one's personal life. Data protection, on the other hand, focuses on safeguarding personal data from unauthorized access, use, or disclosure.

The digital age has introduced new dimensions of privacy and data protection concerns. Online activities, such as social media and e-commerce, generate vast amounts of personal data, including sensitive information like financial details and health records. This data can be collected, stored, analyzed, and shared by various entities, raising concerns about individuals' privacy and the potential for misuse.

Ethical Considerations in Privacy and Data Protection

Privacy and data protection have significant ethical implications. Respecting individuals' privacy rights is crucial for promoting autonomy, trust, and human dignity. Ethical considerations in this context include:

1. **Informed Consent:** Individuals should have knowledge and control over how their data is collected and used. Obtaining informed consent ensures that individuals have the autonomy to make informed decisions about sharing their personal information.

2. **Transparency and Accountability:** Organizations must be transparent about their data collection practices and accountable for any misuse or breaches. They should implement robust security measures and promptly notify individuals in the event of a breach.

3. **Minimization and Purpose Limitation:** Data collection should be minimized, and personal information should only be collected for specific, legitimate purposes. Data controllers should avoid data hoarding and refrain from using personal information beyond what is necessary.

4. **Proportionality and Necessity:** Organizations should ensure that data collection and processing activities are proportional to their intended purposes. Unjustified mass surveillance and indiscriminate data collection should be avoided.

Legal Frameworks for Privacy and Data Protection

Various laws and regulations have been enacted to protect privacy and personal data in the digital age. These frameworks aim to balance the legitimate interests of organizations with the rights and freedoms of individuals. Key legal principles include:

1. **General Data Protection Regulation (GDPR):** The GDPR, implemented in the European Union, sets forth comprehensive data protection rules. It applies to organizations that handle the personal data of EU citizens, regardless of their location. The GDPR emphasizes individual rights, such as the right to access, rectify, and erase personal data, as well as the right to be informed about data processing activities.

2. **California Consumer Privacy Act (CCPA):** Enacted in California, the CCPA grants consumers the right to know what personal information is being collected, sold, or disclosed by businesses. It also gives consumers the right to opt-out of the sale of their personal data, with penalties for non-compliance.

3. **Personal Information Protection and Electronic Documents Act (PIPEDA):** PIPEDA is a Canadian law that governs the collection, use, and disclosure of personal information by organizations in the private sector. It requires organizations to obtain consent for data collection, protect personal information, and provide individuals with access to their data.

Challenges in Privacy and Data Protection

Privacy and data protection face numerous challenges in the digital age. Some of the key challenges include:

1. **Data Breaches:** Data breaches occur when unauthorized individuals gain access to sensitive personal information. Cybercriminals exploit vulnerabilities in digital systems, putting individuals' privacy at risk.

2. **Data Mining and Profiling:** Companies collect vast amounts of data and use advanced analytics to create detailed profiles of individuals. This data mining and profiling raise concerns about individual privacy, as it enables targeted advertising and potential discrimination.

3. **Cross-Border Data Flows:** In a globalized world, personal data often moves across borders. Differences in privacy laws and enforcement pose challenges in ensuring consistent privacy protection for individuals.

4. **Emerging Technologies:** Emerging technologies, such as artificial intelligence and the Internet of Things, introduce new privacy and data protection risks. Smart devices and algorithms may collect and process personal information without individuals' awareness or explicit consent.

Strategies for Privacy and Data Protection

Protecting privacy and personal data requires a multi-faceted approach that involves individuals, organizations, and policymakers. Here are some strategies for safeguarding privacy in the digital age:

1. **Individual Empowerment:** Individuals should educate themselves about privacy risks, understand privacy policies, and use privacy-enhancing tools such as encryption and virtual private networks (VPNs).

2. **Data Minimization:** Organizations should adopt data minimization practices, only collecting personal information that is necessary for their services. This reduces the risk of data breaches and limits potential harm if a breach occurs.

3. **Data Security Measures:** Organizations should implement robust security measures to protect personal data from unauthorized access. This includes measures such as encryption, regular security audits, and employee training on data protection.

4. **Privacy by Design:** Privacy considerations should be integrated into the design and development of digital products and services. Privacy by design principles promote proactive privacy protection throughout the entire lifecycle of a product or service.

5. **International Cooperation:** Governments and organizations should collaborate to establish harmonized privacy standards and frameworks that enable consistent privacy protection across borders.

Conclusion

In an increasingly digital world, privacy and data protection are vital for maintaining individual autonomy and trust. Ethical considerations and legal frameworks play a significant role in shaping privacy policies and safeguarding personal data. However, challenges such as data breaches and emerging technologies require ongoing efforts to ensure effective privacy protection. By adopting strategies for privacy and data protection, individuals, organizations, and policymakers can work together to create a more privacy-conscious digital age.

Additional Resources:

- Solove, D. J. (2011). *Understanding privacy*. Harvard University Press.

- Cavoukian, A., & Tapscott, D. (2017). *Who knows: Safeguarding your privacy in a networked age*. Random House Canada.

- European Data Protection Board. (2020). *Guidelines on the concepts of controller and processor in the GDPR*.

- Office of the Privacy Commissioner of Canada. (2021). *Privacy toolkit*.

Artificial Intelligence and Automation in Legal Practice

Artificial Intelligence (AI) has revolutionized various industries, including the legal sector. With advancements in technology and machine learning algorithms, AI systems are becoming increasingly capable of performing legal tasks that were previously done by humans. In this section, we will explore the use of AI and automation in legal practice, its benefits, challenges, and ethical considerations.

Understanding Artificial Intelligence in Legal Practice

AI refers to the development of computer systems that can perform tasks that typically require human intelligence, such as perception, reasoning, learning, and decision-making. In the context of legal practice, AI technologies, such as natural language processing, machine learning, and data analytics, are utilized to assist lawyers and legal professionals in their work.

Benefits of AI and Automation in Legal Practice

AI and automation offer several benefits in the legal field:

1. **Efficiency and Cost Savings:** AI technologies can automate repetitive and time-consuming tasks, such as contract review, legal research, and document analysis. This leads to increased efficiency, reduced workload, and cost savings for law firms and clients.

2. **Improved Accuracy and Quality**: AI systems can analyze vast amounts of legal data and precedents, ensuring accurate and reliable results. This reduces the risk of human error and improves the quality of legal work.

3. **Enhanced Legal Research**: AI-powered legal research tools can quickly and comprehensively analyze legal documents, statutes, and case laws. This enables lawyers to access relevant information more efficiently and make well-informed decisions.

4. **Predictive Analytics**: AI algorithms can analyze historical legal data to predict case outcomes, assess risks, and provide insights into legal strategies. This assists lawyers in making informed decisions and providing better advice to clients.

5. **24/7 Accessibility**: AI-based chatbots and virtual assistants can provide legal information and guidance to individuals at any time. This enhances access to justice by making legal resources more readily available.

Challenges and Ethical Considerations

While AI and automation offer significant benefits, their implementation in legal practice also raises several challenges and ethical considerations:

1. **Job Displacement**: The automation of certain legal tasks may lead to job displacement for some legal professionals. It is important to consider the impact on the legal workforce and develop strategies to retrain and adapt to the changing landscape.

2. **Bias and Fairness**: AI systems are trained on existing legal data, which may contain biases. If not appropriately addressed, AI algorithms can perpetuate and amplify bias in decision-making. Steps must be taken to ensure fairness, transparency, and accountability in AI systems.

3. **Data Privacy and Security**: The use of AI in legal practice involves the processing and storage of sensitive personal and legal information. It is crucial to have robust data privacy and security measures in place to protect client confidentiality and comply with legal obligations.

4. **Ethical Use of AI**: Legal professionals must adhere to ethical guidelines and standards when utilizing AI technologies. They need to ensure that AI systems are used for the benefit of clients and the public, without compromising professional integrity and legal ethics.

5. **Limitations and Reliability**: AI systems are not devoid of limitations. They may struggle with complex legal reasoning, context interpretation, and ethical judgment. Legal professionals need to understand the limitations of these systems and exercise caution in relying solely on AI-generated outcomes.

Case Study: AI in Legal Research

To illustrate the practical application of AI in legal practice, let's consider a case study on the use of AI in legal research.

Scenario: A law firm wants to streamline its legal research process, which is currently time-consuming and resource-intensive. They decide to implement an AI-powered legal research tool to enhance efficiency and accuracy.

Solution: The law firm integrates an AI platform that utilizes natural language processing and machine learning algorithms. The tool scans and analyzes vast amounts of legal documents, statutes, and case laws, extracting relevant information and providing comprehensive search results.

Benefits: The AI-powered legal research tool significantly reduces the time and effort required for legal research. Lawyers can quickly access relevant precedents, statutes, and case laws, enabling them to provide timely and accurate advice to clients. The tool's machine learning capabilities continuously improve search accuracy, further enhancing the quality of legal research.

Ethical Considerations: While the AI tool offers numerous benefits, lawyers must exercise caution in relying solely on its results. They need to review and verify the extracted information to ensure accuracy and relevance. Lawyers should also consider the potential biases in the underlying legal data and assess the tool's fairness and transparency in its decision-making processes.

Resources and Further Reading

To delve deeper into the topic of AI and automation in legal practice, the following resources and references are recommended:

1. Susskind, R., & Susskind, D. (2018). The Future of the Professions: How Technology Will Transform the Work of Human Experts.

2. Dabbagh, L., & Dabbagh, N. (2020). Artificial Intelligence for Lawyers: How AI is Revolutionizing Legal Services.

3. Richard, S. J. (2019). The Promise and Peril of Artificial Intelligence in Legal Practice. Stanford Technology Law Review, 22(2), 329-394.

These resources provide valuable insights into the current trends, challenges, and ethical considerations surrounding AI and automation in legal practice.

Exercises

To consolidate your understanding of AI and automation in legal practice, consider the following exercises:

1. Research and analyze a real-world case where AI was used in legal practice. Discuss the benefits, challenges, and ethical considerations of its implementation.

2. Identify one potential ethical concern related to the use of AI in legal practice and propose strategies to address it.

3. Compare and contrast the benefits of AI in legal research with its limitations. How can legal professionals maximize the advantages of AI technology while mitigating its drawbacks?

4. Reflect on the impact of AI and automation on the future of the legal profession. Discuss potential ethical and societal implications.

These exercises will enhance your critical thinking and facilitate a deeper understanding of the complexities surrounding AI in the legal field.

Conclusion

AI and automation have the potential to revolutionize legal practice, improving efficiency, accuracy, and access to justice. However, their implementation also raises ethical considerations, such as biases, data privacy, and limitations. Legal professionals must navigate these challenges while harnessing the benefits of AI to provide quality legal services in a rapidly evolving technological landscape. By embracing responsible and ethical AI practices, the legal profession can leverage technology to promote justice and enhance the rule of law in society.

Cybersecurity and Ethical Issues

In today's digital age, cybersecurity has become a critical concern for individuals, organizations, and governments. With the increasing reliance on technology and interconnected systems, the protection of sensitive information and the prevention of unauthorized access have become paramount. However, the pursuit of cybersecurity also raises ethical questions and dilemmas that need to be addressed.

Understanding Cybersecurity

Cybersecurity refers to the practice of protecting computer systems, networks, and data from digital attacks, unauthorized access, and damage. It encompasses various measures and technologies aimed at safeguarding information and ensuring the confidentiality, integrity, and availability of digital assets. Cybersecurity involves the use of encryption, firewalls, intrusion detection systems, and other tools to detect, prevent, and respond to cyber threats.

Ethical Issues in Cybersecurity

The field of cybersecurity brings forth several ethical concerns that need to be considered. These issues arise due to the complex and ever-evolving nature of technology and the potential implications of cybersecurity measures on individual privacy, societal values, and human rights. Let's explore some of the key ethical issues in cybersecurity:

Privacy and Surveillance Protecting individual privacy is of utmost importance in the context of cybersecurity. While the implementation of cybersecurity measures may help safeguard data and systems, it can also lead to increased surveillance and intrusion into personal lives. Balancing the need for security with individual privacy rights is a crucial ethical challenge in the field.

For example, the collection and analysis of user data by tech companies and government agencies raise concerns about the extent of surveillance and the potential misuse of personal information. Striking a balance between cybersecurity and individual privacy requires robust legal frameworks, transparent policies, and informed consent from individuals.

Cyber Warfare The rise of cyber warfare has introduced new ethical dilemmas. Nations engage in cyber attacks for various reasons, including espionage, economic advantage, and military superiority. However, these attacks can have severe consequences, both for the targeted nation and innocent civilians.

One ethical issue in cyber warfare is the attribution problem, which involves correctly identifying the responsible party for a cyber attack. This attribution challenge often leads to difficulty in assigning responsibility and taking appropriate countermeasures. Another concern is the potential escalation of cyber conflicts into physical conflicts, leading to significant human suffering.

Cybercrime and Law Enforcement Dealing with cybercrime poses unique ethical challenges for law enforcement agencies. While efforts to apprehend cybercriminals and protect victims are essential, the methods and techniques used can potentially infringe upon individual rights and civil liberties.

One ethical issue is the tension between the need for law enforcement to access encrypted data and the right to privacy. Governments have sought to mandate backdoors in encryption systems, raising concerns about the weakening of security and potential abuse of such measures by malicious actors.

Cybersecurity Workforce Ethics   As the demand for cybersecurity professionals increases, ethical considerations within the workforce become crucial. Professionals in this field often have access to sensitive information and hold great power in protecting digital assets. Ethical behavior is essential to maintain trust and ensure responsible use of this power.

One ethical concern is the potential conflict of interest that cybersecurity professionals may face. The temptation to exploit vulnerabilities for personal gain or engage in unauthorized activities can undermine the trust placed in them. Upholding professional standards, maintaining ethical codes of conduct, and promoting a culture of integrity are necessary to address these concerns.

Addressing Ethical Issues in Cybersecurity

To navigate the ethical challenges in cybersecurity, a multidimensional approach incorporating legal, technical, and ethical frameworks is necessary. Here are some strategies to address these issues:

Ethical Training and Education   Promoting ethical awareness and providing comprehensive training to cybersecurity professionals and students is crucial. Education should focus on the ethical implications of cybersecurity practices, privacy rights, responsible disclosure of vulnerabilities, and the importance of upholding moral standards in the field.

Privacy by Design   Integrating privacy considerations into the design and development of technology systems can help address privacy concerns proactively. Privacy-enhancing technologies, such as encryption and anonymization, should be prioritized to protect individuals' personal information.

Transparency and Accountability   Promoting transparency and accountability in cybersecurity practices is essential to earn public trust. Organizations and governments should adopt transparent policies regarding data collection, sharing, and use. They should also be accountable for any misuse or breaches of personal information.

International Cooperation   Given the global nature of cybersecurity threats, international collaboration is crucial. Governments, organizations, and experts need to work together to establish common standards, norms, and regulations to address ethical issues effectively. International agreements on cyber warfare, data protection, and privacy can help foster a more secure and ethical cyberspace.

Case Study: Ethical Dilemma in Vulnerability Disclosure

A common ethical dilemma faced by cybersecurity professionals is determining when and how to disclose vulnerabilities discovered in software or systems. On one hand, responsible disclosure can prevent potential exploitation and prompt timely fixes. On the other hand, disclosing vulnerabilities publicly without the consent of the affected organizations may expose users to risks.

For example, consider a cybersecurity researcher who discovers a critical vulnerability in a widely used software application. The researcher faces the ethical dilemma of balancing the public interest in knowing about the vulnerability with the potential harm that could result from disclosing it before a patch is available.

To address this dilemma, many ethical frameworks advocate for responsible disclosure practices. This typically involves notifying the affected organization privately, allowing them a reasonable amount of time to develop and deploy a patch, and coordinating public disclosure to ensure user safety.

By following responsible disclosure practices, cybersecurity professionals can navigate the ethical challenges associated with vulnerability disclosure and work towards enhancing the overall cybersecurity posture of software and systems.

Conclusion

Cybersecurity presents a myriad of ethical issues that need to be carefully addressed to protect individuals, organizations, and society at large. Striking the right balance between security, privacy, and individual rights requires a holistic approach involving legal frameworks, technical solutions, and ethical considerations. By embracing transparency, accountability, and responsible practices, we can shape a more secure and ethically sound cyberspace for the future.

Regulation and Governance of Technology

Technological advancements have undoubtedly revolutionized our society, from the way we communicate and access information to the way we conduct business and interact with the world. However, along with these advancements come ethical and legal challenges that need to be addressed. In this section, we will explore the regulation and governance of technology, examining the principles and frameworks that guide these processes.

The Need for Regulation

As technology continues to evolve at a rapid pace, it is essential to have regulations in place to ensure the responsible and ethical use of these advancements. Regulation helps protect individuals and society as a whole from potential harm that may arise from the misuse of technology. It also provides a framework for establishing standards, ensuring compliance, and resolving conflicts that may arise.

Ethical Considerations

When it comes to technology, ethical considerations play a crucial role in determining the boundaries and limits of its use. Ethical frameworks such as utilitarianism, deontology, and virtue ethics provide guidance on moral decision-making in the context of technology. For instance, utilitarianism emphasizes maximizing overall societal well-being, while deontology focuses on the adherence to moral principles and obligations. Virtue ethics, on the other hand, emphasizes the development of virtuous character traits in individuals.

In the context of technology, ethical considerations include issues such as privacy, data protection, fairness, transparency, accountability, and social justice. These considerations help shape regulations by setting the standards for responsible technological practices.

Legal Frameworks

To effectively govern and regulate technology, legal frameworks must be established. These frameworks encompass laws, rules, and guidelines that dictate how technology should be developed, used, and managed. Key legal areas for technology regulation include intellectual property rights, privacy laws, antitrust laws, contract laws, and liability laws.

Intellectual property rights protect the rights of creators and innovators by granting them exclusive rights to their inventions or creations. Patents, copyrights, and trademarks are primary forms of intellectual property protection. These laws are crucial in promoting innovation and preventing unauthorized use or exploitation of intellectual property.

Privacy laws govern the collection, use, and storage of personal information. They ensure that individuals have control over their personal data, limiting access by unauthorized parties and promoting transparency in how data is handled.

Antitrust laws aim to prevent monopolistic practices and promote fair competition in the market. In the context of technology, these laws help regulate dominant technology companies and prevent them from engaging in anti-competitive behaviors that could harm consumers or hinder innovation.

Contract laws establish legal agreements between parties involved in technology-related transactions. These laws ensure that parties fulfill their obligations and provide remedies in case of contract breaches.

Liability laws determine who is held responsible for any damages or harm caused by technology. These laws help allocate accountability and provide legal recourse for individuals or entities affected by technology-related incidents.

Challenges in Regulating Technology

Regulating technology poses several challenges due to its dynamic and ever-changing nature. One significant challenge is keeping up with rapid technological advancements. Technological innovation often outpaces the development of regulations, leaving gaps in legal frameworks. Regulators need to adopt agile approaches to grasp emerging technologies' potential risks and implications adequately.

Another challenge is the global nature of technology. Technology operates across national boundaries, making it challenging to enforce regulations uniformly. International cooperation and harmonization of laws are essential to address these challenges effectively.

Furthermore, regulating technology requires comprehensive knowledge and expertise in both technology and legal domains. Bridging the gap between these two fields can be challenging, as legal professionals may lack technical expertise, and technology professionals may have limited knowledge of legal frameworks.

Emerging Issues in Technology Regulation

Technology continues to disrupt and shape various sectors, leading to emerging issues that require careful regulation. Some of these issues include:

+ **Artificial Intelligence (AI) and Algorithmic Bias:** As AI becomes more prevalent in decision-making processes, the issue of algorithmic bias arises. AI systems can unintentionally perpetuate discriminatory practices if not properly regulated. Ensuring fairness, transparency, and accountability in AI algorithms is a critical regulatory challenge.

+ **Cybersecurity:** With increasing connectivity, cybersecurity becomes a pressing concern. Regulations must be in place to protect individuals, organizations, and critical infrastructure from cyber threats. Balancing security measures with individual privacy rights is a delicate challenge faced by regulators.

+ **Digital Rights and Freedom of Expression:** Regulating technology needs to strike a balance between preserving individuals' digital rights and safeguarding public interests. Freedom of expression online, data protection, and access to information are critical aspects that need to be addressed in technology regulation.

+ **Emerging Technologies:** The advent of new technologies such as blockchain, Internet of Things (IoT), and autonomous vehicles presents unique regulatory challenges. Establishing clear rules and standards for these technologies is crucial to mitigate potential risks.

Regulatory Strategies and Approaches

Regulating technology requires adopting various strategies and approaches tailored to the specific challenges posed by different technologies. Some common regulatory strategies include:

+ **Prescriptive Regulation:** This approach involves setting specific rules and requirements that technology developers and users must follow. It provides clear guidelines and standards, but it may struggle to keep up with technological advancements.

+ **Principles-based Regulation:** This approach focuses on establishing broad principles and outcomes that technology developers and users should strive to achieve. It allows flexibility and encourages innovation but may lack clarity or specificity.

+ **Self-regulation:** Self-regulation empowers technology developers and industry stakeholders to set their own standards and guidelines voluntarily. However, self-regulation requires trust and may not be sufficient in addressing broader social and ethical concerns.

+ **Collaborative Regulation:** This approach involves partnerships and collaboration between regulators, industry stakeholders, and civil society organizations. It allows for comprehensive perspectives and collective decision-making but may face challenges in consensus-building and balancing competing interests.

To effectively regulate technology, a combination of these approaches may be necessary, depending on the specific context and technology involved.

Conclusion

Regulation and governance of technology play a vital role in ensuring responsible and ethical use of technological advancements. Ethical considerations, legal frameworks, and regulatory strategies shape the boundaries and standards governing technology. As technology continues to evolve, addressing emerging issues and keeping pace with advancements pose ongoing challenges in technology regulation. However, by fostering collaboration, adopting diverse regulatory approaches, and maintaining a strong ethical foundation, we can navigate the complex landscape of technology and promote its positive impact on society.

Technology, Ethics, and Access to Justice

In today's rapidly advancing technological landscape, the intersection of technology, ethics, and access to justice presents a myriad of complex issues for legal professionals and society as a whole. The impact of technology on the legal system has been both transformative and disruptive, providing new opportunities for efficiency and accessibility, while also raising ethical concerns and challenges. In this section, we will explore the ethical implications of technology in the context of access to justice and discuss the ways in which technology can be harnessed to promote equal access to legal services.

The Role of Technology in Access to Justice

Access to justice, a fundamental principle of the legal system, ensures that all individuals have the ability to seek and obtain legal remedies. However, numerous barriers often hinder individuals from accessing legal services, such as cost, geographical location, and limited availability of legal professionals. Technology has the potential to address many of these barriers and level the playing field, thereby increasing access to justice for marginalized and underserved populations.

One of the most significant contributions of technology to access to justice is the ability to provide legal information and resources online. Legal websites, online databases, and virtual libraries offer users the opportunity to access legal materials, research legal issues, and understand their rights and obligations without the need for expensive legal assistance. For example, websites like LegalZoom and Rocket Lawyer provide affordable online legal services, enabling individuals to draft legal documents and obtain legal advice at a fraction of the cost of traditional legal representation.

Furthermore, technology has facilitated the emergence of online dispute resolution mechanisms, such as mediation and arbitration platforms, which offer accessible and cost-effective alternatives to traditional court-based litigation. These platforms employ video conferencing, electronic filing, and case management systems to streamline the dispute resolution process and make it more accessible to individuals who may face geographical barriers or financial constraints.

Ethical Considerations in Technology and Access to Justice

While technology has the potential to enhance access to justice, ethical considerations must be carefully navigated to ensure that the benefits are maximized and potential harms are mitigated. One of the key ethical considerations is the digital divide, which refers to the disparity in access to technology and digital resources among different socio-economic groups. If technology is not inclusively and equitably deployed, it can exacerbate existing inequalities and further marginalize vulnerable populations. Legal professionals and policymakers must work to bridge the digital divide through initiatives such as enhancing digital literacy programs and providing affordable access to technology in underserved communities.

Another ethical consideration is the privacy and security of individuals accessing legal services online. With the proliferation of online legal platforms and databases, the collection and storage of personal and sensitive information raise concerns about data breaches, confidentiality, and informed consent. Legal professionals have an ethical obligation to ensure the security and privacy of client information and must stay informed about the evolving legal and ethical frameworks governing technology use in the legal profession.

Regulatory Challenges and Solutions

The rapid advancement of technology has outpaced the development of legal and ethical frameworks to govern its use in the legal profession. As a result, regulatory challenges have arisen, requiring legal professionals, policymakers, and technologists to collaborate and adapt existing laws and ethical guidelines to account for technological innovations.

One significant regulatory challenge is ensuring that online legal services adhere to the same ethical standards as traditional legal services. While platforms like LegalZoom have made legal services more accessible, they have also been criticized for the lack of personalized legal advice and the potential for legal errors. Regulators must strike a balance between allowing innovation and ensuring consumer protection by imposing appropriate regulations and oversight on online legal service providers.

Additionally, the use of artificial intelligence (AI) and machine learning algorithms in the legal profession raises ethical concerns related to transparency, bias, and accountability. AI-powered systems can assist in legal research, document review, and drafting, enhancing efficiency and reducing costs. However, biases present in AI algorithms, which can perpetuate societal biases, must be ethically addressed to avoid unjust outcomes. Legal professionals have an ethical duty to critically evaluate and monitor the decisions made by AI systems, ensuring they align with legal and ethical standards and promoting the transparency and explainability of AI-powered processes.

Promoting Ethical Technology and Access to Justice

To promote ethical technology and access to justice, legal professionals and policymakers can take several proactive measures. Firstly, continuing legal education programs should emphasize the ethical implications of technology in the legal profession, ensuring that legal professionals are equipped with the knowledge and skills to navigate the evolving technological landscape responsibly.

Secondly, collaboration between legal professionals and technologists is crucial in developing ethical standards and guidelines for the use of technology in the legal system. By involving diverse stakeholders, such as legal scholars, technology experts, and representatives of marginalized communities, policymakers can create comprehensive and inclusive frameworks that address the ethical concerns and promote equal access to justice.

Moreover, legal professionals can leverage technology to enhance their pro bono work, reaching underserved populations and expanding access to justice. Online legal clinics, virtual legal aid centers, and mobile applications can provide free legal assistance, legal information, and referral services to individuals who may not otherwise have access to legal resources.

Case Study: Legal Chatbots

Legal chatbots are a prime example of how technology can be used to improve access to justice. A legal chatbot is a computer program that uses artificial intelligence and natural language processing to interact with users and provide legal information and guidance. These chatbots can assist users with various legal issues, such as generating legal documents, providing legal advice, and guiding individuals through legal processes.

For example, DoNotPay, an AI-powered chatbot, has helped individuals contest parking tickets, navigate small claims court, and access government benefits. The chatbot employs a simple, user-friendly interface, guiding users through a series of questions to determine their legal issue and providing appropriate resources and information based on their responses.

While legal chatbots have the potential to democratize access to legal information and empower individuals to navigate the legal system independently, ethical considerations must be addressed. The accuracy and quality of legal information provided by chatbots, the duty to ensure informed consent, and the risk of relying solely on automated systems are all ethical challenges that legal professionals must grapple with.

Conclusion

Technology has the power to revolutionize access to justice by overcoming barriers and providing innovative solutions. However, ethical considerations must underpin the development and deployment of technology in the legal profession. By bridging the digital divide, ensuring privacy and security, and addressing regulatory challenges, legal professionals can utilize technology ethically, promoting equal access to justice and a more just and sustainable world.

Technology and Social Justice

In today's rapidly evolving world, technology plays a significant role in shaping our society and influencing various aspects of our lives. From communication to education, transportation to healthcare, technology has transformed how we interact with the world around us. However, with every advancement, there may also be ethical and social implications that need to be considered. In this section, we will explore the intersection of technology and social justice, examining the potential benefits, challenges, and ethical considerations associated with the use of technology in promoting social justice.

The Role of Technology in Social Justice

Technology has the potential to be a powerful tool for promoting social justice. It can increase access to information, empower marginalized communities, and facilitate the mobilization and coordination of social movements. For instance, social media platforms have played a crucial role in raising awareness of social justice issues and connecting individuals who share a common cause. Online petitions and crowdfunding campaigns have mobilized resources and support for disadvantaged groups, enabling them to advocate for their rights.

Furthermore, technology can enhance transparency and accountability. For example, video recording devices, such as smartphones and body cameras, have provided indisputable evidence in cases of police misconduct, promoting accountability and demanding justice. Similarly, open data initiatives and online platforms that track government spending increase transparency and enable citizens to hold public institutions accountable for their actions.

Digital Divide and Access to Technology

One of the key challenges in utilizing technology for social justice is the existence of the digital divide. The digital divide refers to the gap between those who have access to and can effectively use technology and those who do not. This divide can exacerbate existing social inequalities, as marginalized communities are often disproportionally affected by limited access to technology and the internet.

To address this issue, initiatives are being implemented to bridge the digital divide and increase access to technology for underserved communities. Governments and non-profit organizations are working together to provide affordable internet access, computer literacy training, and technology resources to ensure equal opportunities for all. Additionally, efforts are being made to promote digital inclusivity by designing user-friendly technology interfaces and considering the needs and preferences of diverse user groups.

Ethical Considerations in Technology and Social Justice

As technology continues to advance, it is important to address the ethical considerations that arise in its application for social justice. One of the primary concerns is privacy and data protection. The collection, storage, and use of personal data can be exploited for various purposes, including surveillance, targeted advertising, and social profiling. Safeguarding individuals' privacy rights and ensuring the responsible handling of data is crucial to protect vulnerable communities from potential harm.

Another consideration is the potential for bias and discrimination in technology. Algorithms and artificial intelligence systems can perpetuate existing social injustices if they are trained on biased data or are not designed with fairness in mind. For example, automated decision-making systems used in criminal justice or hiring processes may disproportionately harm marginalized communities if biases are not detected and addressed.

To mitigate these ethical concerns, it is essential to adopt ethical frameworks and guidelines for technology development and deployment. Transparency in algorithmic decision-making, ensuring diverse representation in technology development teams, and conducting regular audits to identify and rectify biases are some ways to promote fairness and social justice in technology.

Examples of Technology and Social Justice

To better understand the potential impact of technology in promoting social justice, let's consider a few real-world examples:

1. **Access to Education:** Online learning platforms and educational apps can provide individuals from disadvantaged backgrounds with access to quality education and resources. By breaking down traditional barriers to education, technology can empower individuals to acquire new skills, improve their job prospects, and escape the cycle of poverty.

2. **Environmental Justice:** Technology can be used to monitor and address environmental issues that disproportionately affect marginalized communities. For instance, wearable air quality sensors can provide real-time data on pollution levels, enabling individuals to take precautions and advocate for policy changes to improve air quality in their communities.

3. **Digital Activism:** Social media platforms and online petitions have become powerful tools for raising awareness and mobilizing support for social justice causes. Hashtags like #BlackLivesMatter and #MeToo have amplified marginalized voices, shining a light on systemic injustices and demanding change.

By understanding the potential benefits and challenges of technology in promoting social justice and addressing ethical considerations, we can harness its power to create a more equitable and just society.

Conclusion

Technology has the potential to be a catalyst for social change and justice. By increasing access, promoting transparency, and facilitating activism, technology can empower marginalized communities and mobilize support for social justice causes. However, it is crucial to address the digital divide, prioritize privacy and data protection, and mitigate biases and discrimination in technology. By adopting ethical frameworks, promoting inclusivity, and considering the impact of technology on social justice, we can harness its power to create a more equitable and sustainable future.

Conclusion

In this section, we have explored the ethical challenges and considerations arising from the intersection of technology and the legal field. We have examined the ethical implications of technological advancements and their impact on various aspects of the legal profession. From privacy and data protection to artificial intelligence and automation, we have delved into the ethical considerations that lawyers and legal practitioners need to address in the digital age.

One of the key ethical concerns in the digital age is privacy and data protection. As technology advances, so do the capabilities for collecting, storing, and analyzing vast amounts of personal data. This raises important questions about the ethical use of data, the need for informed consent, and the protection of individuals' privacy rights. Legal professionals must navigate the complex landscape of privacy laws and regulations to ensure that technology is used ethically and in compliance with the law.

Artificial intelligence (AI) and automation have also become increasingly prevalent in the legal field. While these technologies offer numerous benefits, such as increased efficiency and accuracy, they also raise ethical concerns. The use of AI and automation in legal practice can lead to the displacement of certain jobs, the potential for biased algorithms, and the erosion of human judgment and decision-making. Legal professionals must critically assess the risks and benefits of using such technologies and ensure that they are implemented ethically and responsibly.

Cybersecurity is another area of ethical concern in the digital age. With the growing reliance on technology, the risk of cyber threats and data breaches has significantly increased. Legal professionals have a duty to protect the sensitive information entrusted to them and must implement robust cybersecurity measures to safeguard client confidentiality and uphold ethical obligations. Additionally, legal professionals must also consider the ethical implications of hacking, surveillance, and other practices that violate privacy and undermine the integrity of the legal system.

Regulation and governance of technology present significant challenges. As technology advances at a rapid pace, laws and regulations struggle to keep up. Legal professionals must advocate for the development of regulatory frameworks that address the ethical and societal implications of technology. They play a crucial role in shaping policies and regulations that promote fairness, transparency, and accountability in the use of technology.

Access to justice is a fundamental principle of the legal system, and technology has the potential to bridge the gap between legal services and those in need. However, ethical considerations must be made to ensure that technology does not perpetuate existing barriers or create new ones. Legal professionals must strive to make legal technology inclusive, affordable, and user-friendly, allowing individuals from all backgrounds to access legal information, resources, and services.

In conclusion, technology presents both opportunities and challenges for the legal profession. Ethical considerations are paramount in harnessing the benefits of technology while mitigating its risks. Legal professionals must stay informed about technological advancements, critically assess their ethical implications, and apply ethical principles to guide their decision-making. By doing so, they can navigate the digital age with integrity, ensuring that technology is used to promote justice, equity, and the rule of law.

9 781779 619143